ABANDONED NYC

WILL ELLIS

Schiffer Publishing Ltd
4880 Lower Valley Road • Atglen, PA 19310

Other Schiffer Books on Related Subjects:
Abandoned: America's Vanishing Landscape, $50.00
978-0-7643-4660-6
Urban Atrophy, $39.99
978-0-7643-3738-3
The World of Urban Decay, $34.99
978-0-7643-4569-2

Library of Congress Control Number: 2014951675

Designed by Brenda McCallum
Cover Designed by Justin Watkinson
Type set in Helvetica Condensed/ Futura
ISBN: 978-0-7643-4761-0
Printed in China

Published by Schiffer Publishing, Ltd.
4880 Lower Valley Road
Atglen, PA 19310
Phone: (610) 593-1777; Fax: (610) 593-2002
E-mail: Info@schifferbooks.com

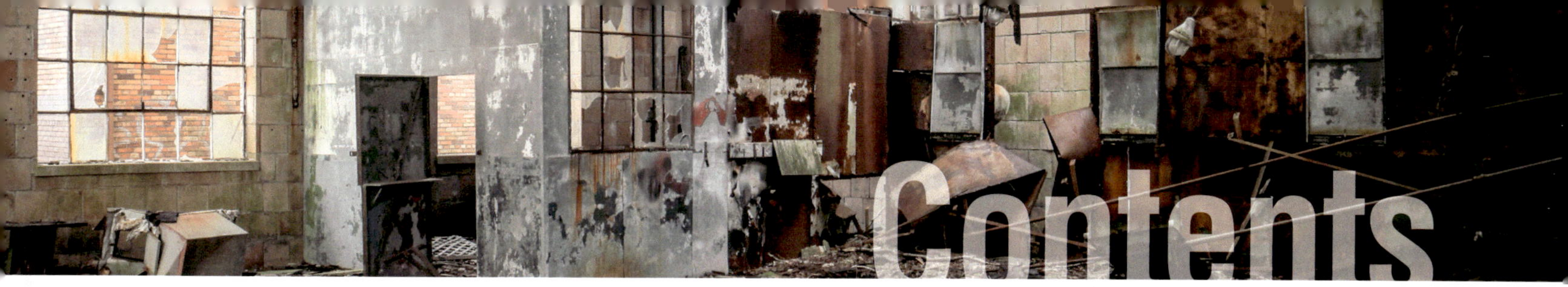

Contents

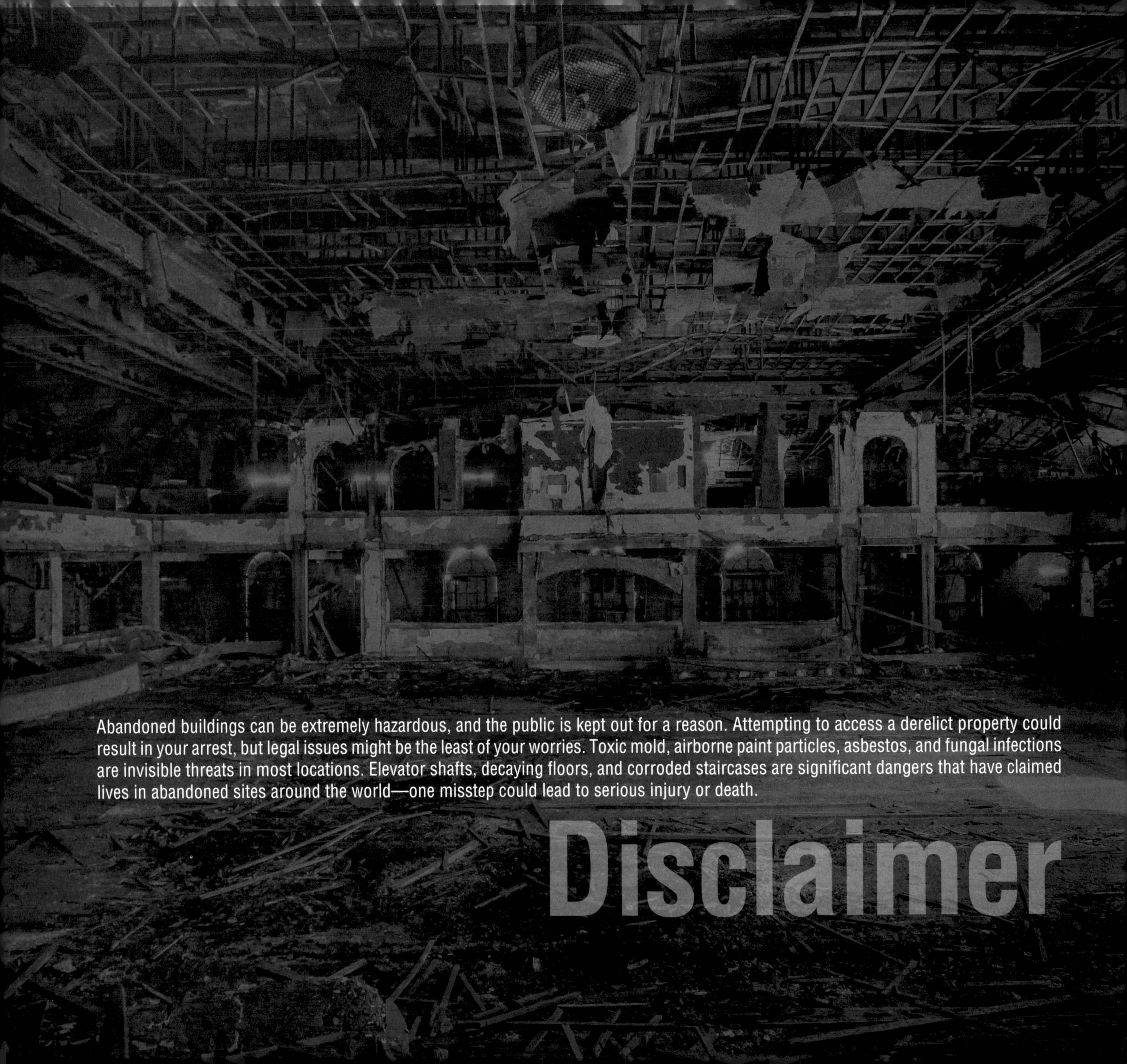

Abandoned buildings can be extremely hazardous, and the public is kept out for a reason. Attempting to access a derelict property could result in your arrest, but legal issues might be the least of your worries. Toxic mold, airborne paint particles, asbestos, and fungal infections are invisible threats in most locations. Elevator shafts, decaying floors, and corroded staircases are significant dangers that have claimed lives in abandoned sites around the world—one misstep could lead to serious injury or death.

Disclaimer

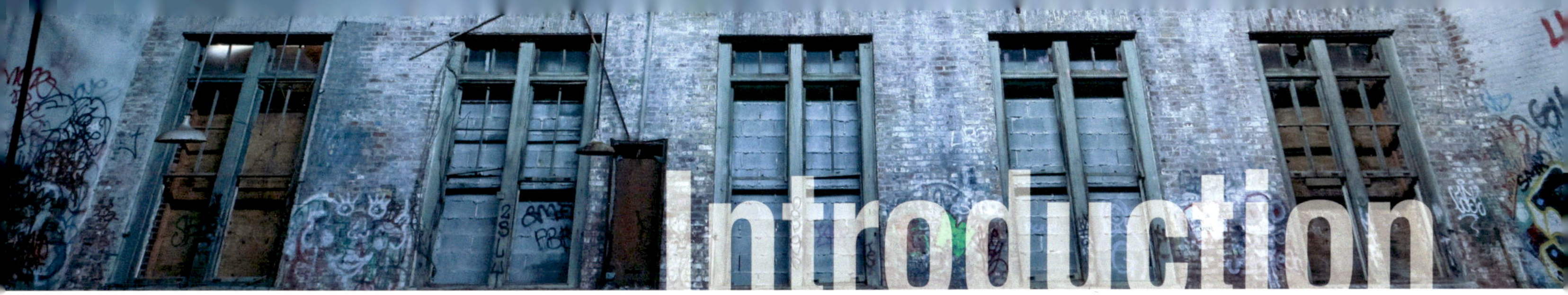

Introduction

Far from the teeming avenues of Midtown, New York still claims a few quiet places. In between and underneath the streets we know, the spaces we leave behind are some of the only pockets of the city that exist outside our control. Through decades of neglect, an abandoned building becomes a kind of wilderness. Floors, walls, and ceilings unhinge; fences buckle. New York City opens its doors and airs its secrets.

In the five boroughs, these places are altered as much by man as they are by the elements. Most abandoned buildings show signs of human habitation, but more often they're hangouts for teenagers, canvases for graffiti artists, and destinations for the curious. The old, empty house on the hill has always been inviting, for some—read any good English ghost story and you'll recognize the theme. Today, the same instinct has given rise to a worldwide community of urban explorers, and for many the hobby goes beyond an appreciation for the beauty of decay. As monuments to outdated systems, attitudes, and technology, abandoned buildings have an uncanny ability to shed light on periods of our history, including some we'd rather forget.

On the once-rural outskirts of the city center, urban legends hang like a fog over the ruins of New York's old institutions. Massive, vilified, and difficult to repurpose, most of these facilities have been left to rot, becoming landscapes of regret and subjects of morbid fascination. Meanwhile, empty factories and crumbling piers have become barometers for change on the Brooklyn waterfront. All of the industrial sites featured in this book have been slated for redevelopment, poised to enter a new life as artists' studios, convention centers, and luxury condominiums.

Flanking the harbor, you'll find traces of New York's rich military legacy—defense structures that quietly served the city for over a century, in some cases, but were never called to action. Today, most of the city's ex-military sites languish as underfunded public parks, where overgrown batteries, barracks, and officer's quarters are falling to rack and ruin. Often, the city's abandoned places don't fit into a unified narrative, but every building has a story, and the same goes for our tunnels, waterways, and railroads. When a place is left behind, the city spills into it—squatters settle, landfills breach the surface, graffiti fills the void.

In uncovering the history of New York's forgotten places, I'm most indebted to the archives of the *New York Times,* which make up an unparalleled record of the last 150 years of New York City history. The *Brooklyn Eagle,* the *Staten Island Advance,* and the *Queens Courier* have helped fill in the gaps for their respective boroughs. In cases where buildings have been designated historic or architectural landmarks, reports from the New York City Landmarks Preservation Commission have proven another invaluable resource.

With this collection of images, I hope you'll experience some of the same moments of inspiration and reflection that I had while photographing these spaces—hours passed in peace, quiet, and connection to the city I call home. My dreams and nightmares often take me back to the haunting classrooms of P.S. 186 or the surreal fourth floor of Building 25. Inside these remnants of New York City's past, I've felt shaken, humbled, but never alone, standing in the company of all those who've gone before.

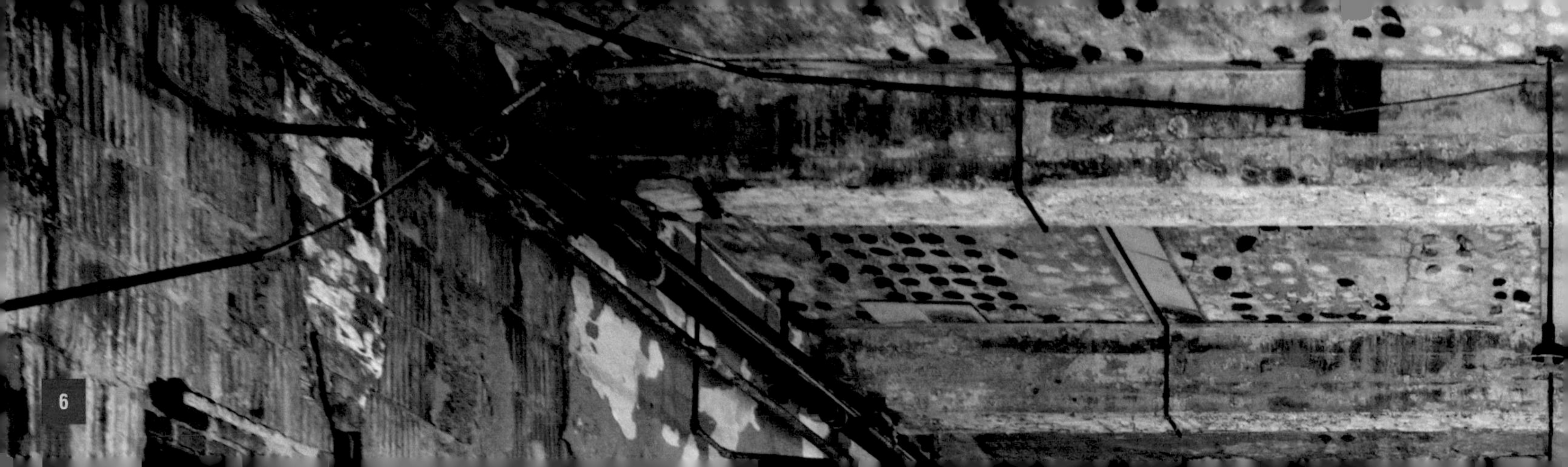

The New York City Farm Colony

Letchworth Village

North Brother Island

Hospitals and Institutions

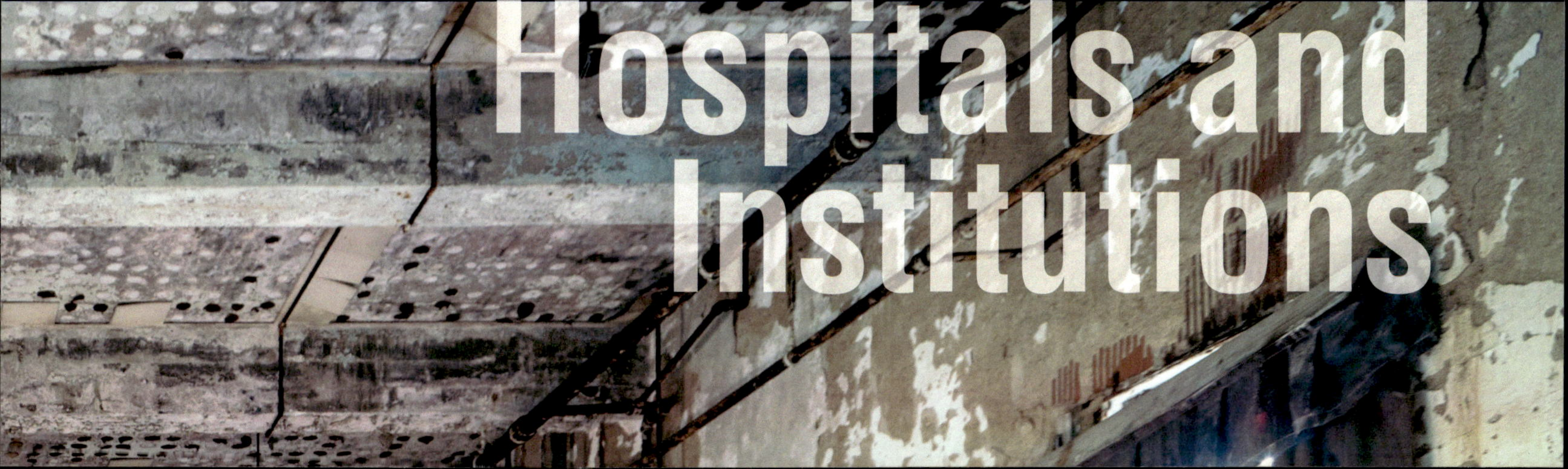

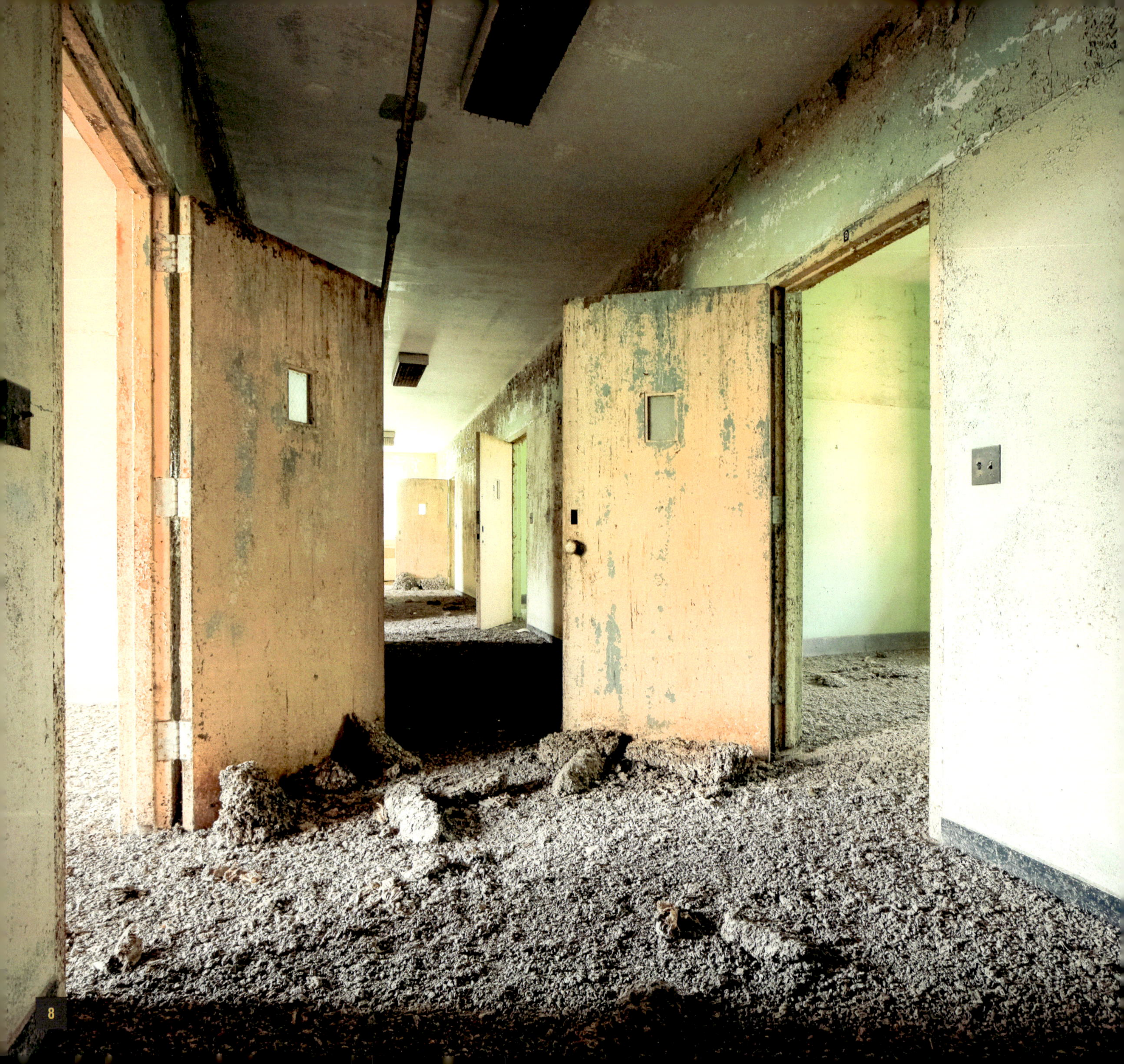

Creedmoor State Hospital's Building 25

Queens Village, Queens

In Queens Village, mere inches of brick and mortar separate the world we know from one of the strangest places in the city. Tucked away in the sprawling Creedmoor Psychiatric Center, beneath an unassuming façade, Building 25 has undergone something of a transformation over its 40 years of neglect. Once a haven for the city's cast-out mentally ill, the long-abandoned ward is inhabited by an equally misunderstood breed of New Yorker today, and you won't believe what they've done with the fourth floor.

Creedmoor was founded in 1912 as the Farm Colony of Brooklyn State Hospital, one of hundreds of similar psychiatric centers established at the turn of the 20th century to house and rehabilitate those who were ill equipped to function on their own. As the century progressed, asylums across the country became overrun with patients, and many institutions became desperately understaffed and dangerously underfunded. Circumstances at some psychiatric wards grew dire—patient abuse and neglect was not uncommon.

The Creedmoor campus was plagued with scandal during this period, beginning in the 1940s with an outbreak of dysentery that resulted from unsanitary living conditions in the wards. During the worst times, a single attendant might be left in charge of 100 patients. Conditions had spiraled completely out of control by 1974, when the state ordered an inquiry into an outbreak of crime at the institution. Within 20 months, three rapes, 22 assaults, 52 fires, 130 burglaries, six instances of suicide, a shooting, a riot, and an attempted murder were reported, prompting an investigation into all downstate mental hospitals. As late as 1984, the violent ward of Creedmoor Psychiatric Center made headlines after the death of a patient, who had been struck in the throat by a staff member while restrained in a straitjacket.

The development of antipsychotic medications and new standards of treatment for the mentally ill ushered in a trend toward deinstitutionalization in the late 20th century. A series of dramatic budget cuts and dwindling patient populations led to the closing of asylums across the United States and a marked decline at Creedmoor. The hospital still operates today, housing only a few hundred patients and providing outpatient services. Many of the buildings have been sold off to new tenants. Others, like Building 25, lie fallow.

opposite The unusual interior of Building 25's fourth floor.

This building without a name was an active ward until some time in the 1970s, and retains many mementos from its days as a residence and treatment center for the mentally ill. With peeling paint, dusty furniture, and dark corridors, the lower floors are typical of a long-abandoned building. But upstairs, the effect of time has taken a grotesque turn.

For four decades, generations of pigeons have defecated on the fourth floor of Building 25, far removed from their dim-witted dealings with the human world, assembling a monument all their own. Pigeon poop accumulates in grey mounds under popular roosts, with the tallest columns reaching several feet in height. Like the myriad formations of a cavern, Building 25's guano stalagmites are a work in progress—pigeons roost at every turn, punctuating an otherworldly soundscape of low, rumbling coos with violent outbursts of flight.

Two levels down and a world away from the top floor, a kitchen is filled with years' worth of garbage intersected by narrow pathways. Loosely organized objects litter every surface—toiletries, clothing, hundreds of dead D batteries. Some of the belongings look like they haven't been touched in decades, but others confirm that the place is still inhabited by someone.

On my last visit, I found him snoozing peacefully in a light-filled dayroom, surrounded by a series of patient murals. Declining to introduce myself, I passed once more through the dark, decaying halls of Building 25, leaving its charms, horrors, and mysteries for the birds.

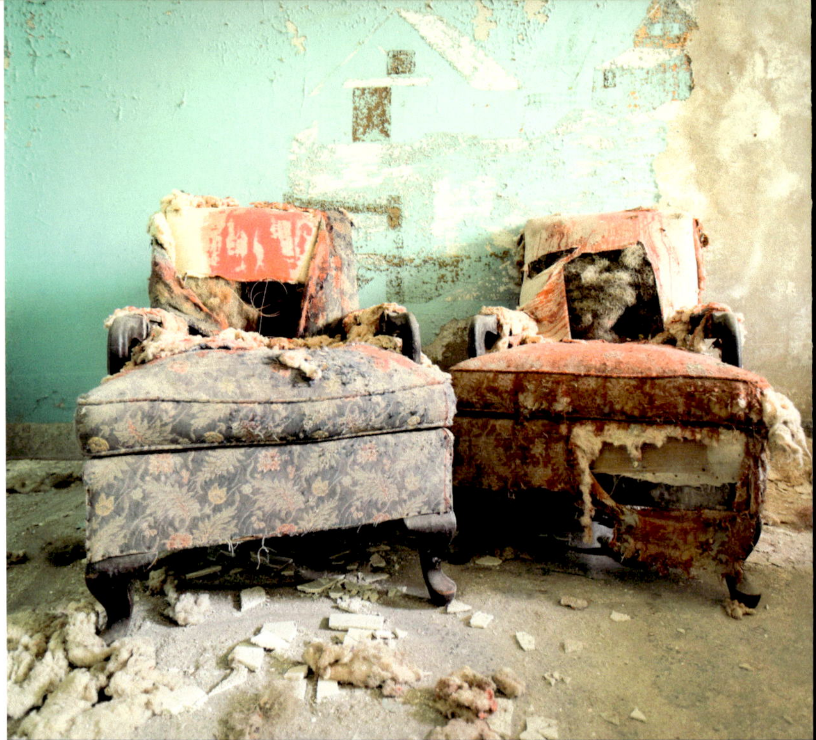

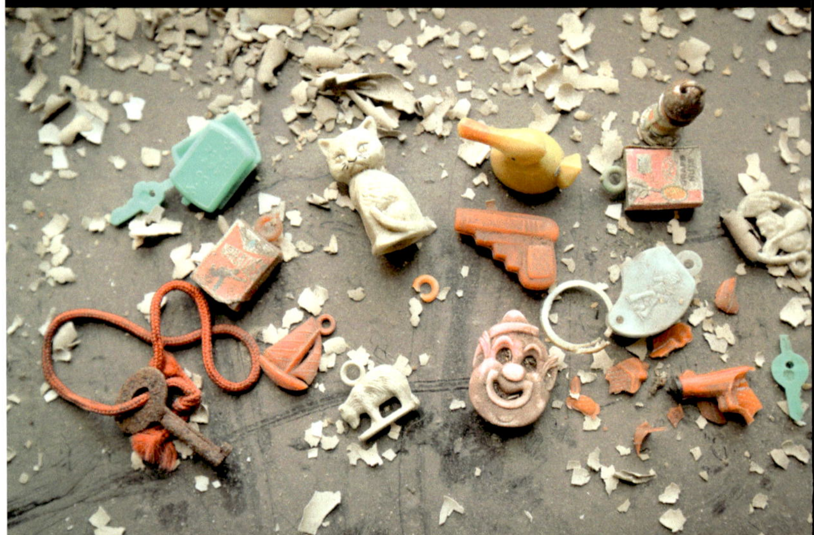

top These chairs are popular subjects for urban explorers; one went as far as dousing them in fake blood.

bottom A tiny toy collection arranged on a windowsill.

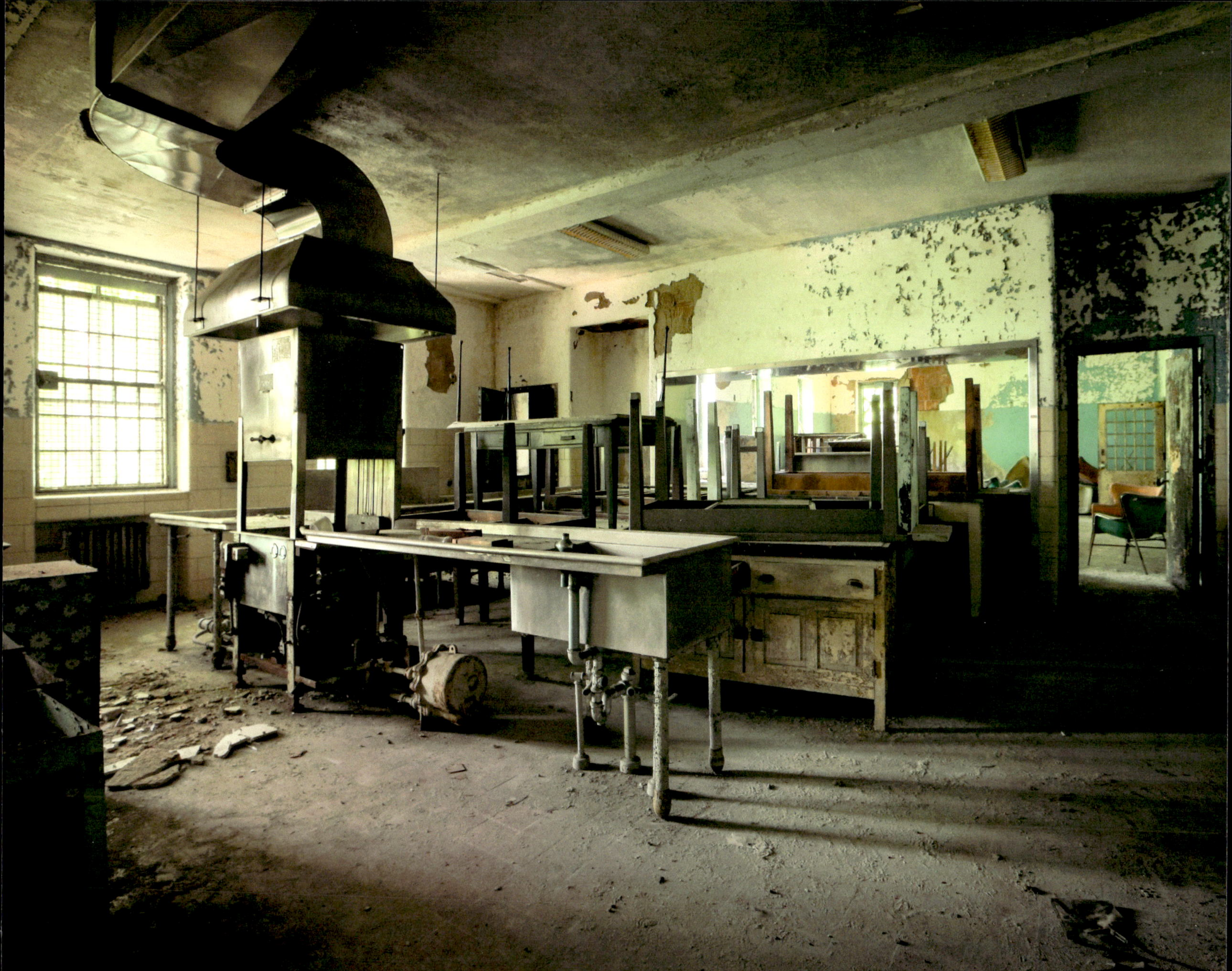

above Tables, chairs, and kitchen appliances remain in the cafeteria.

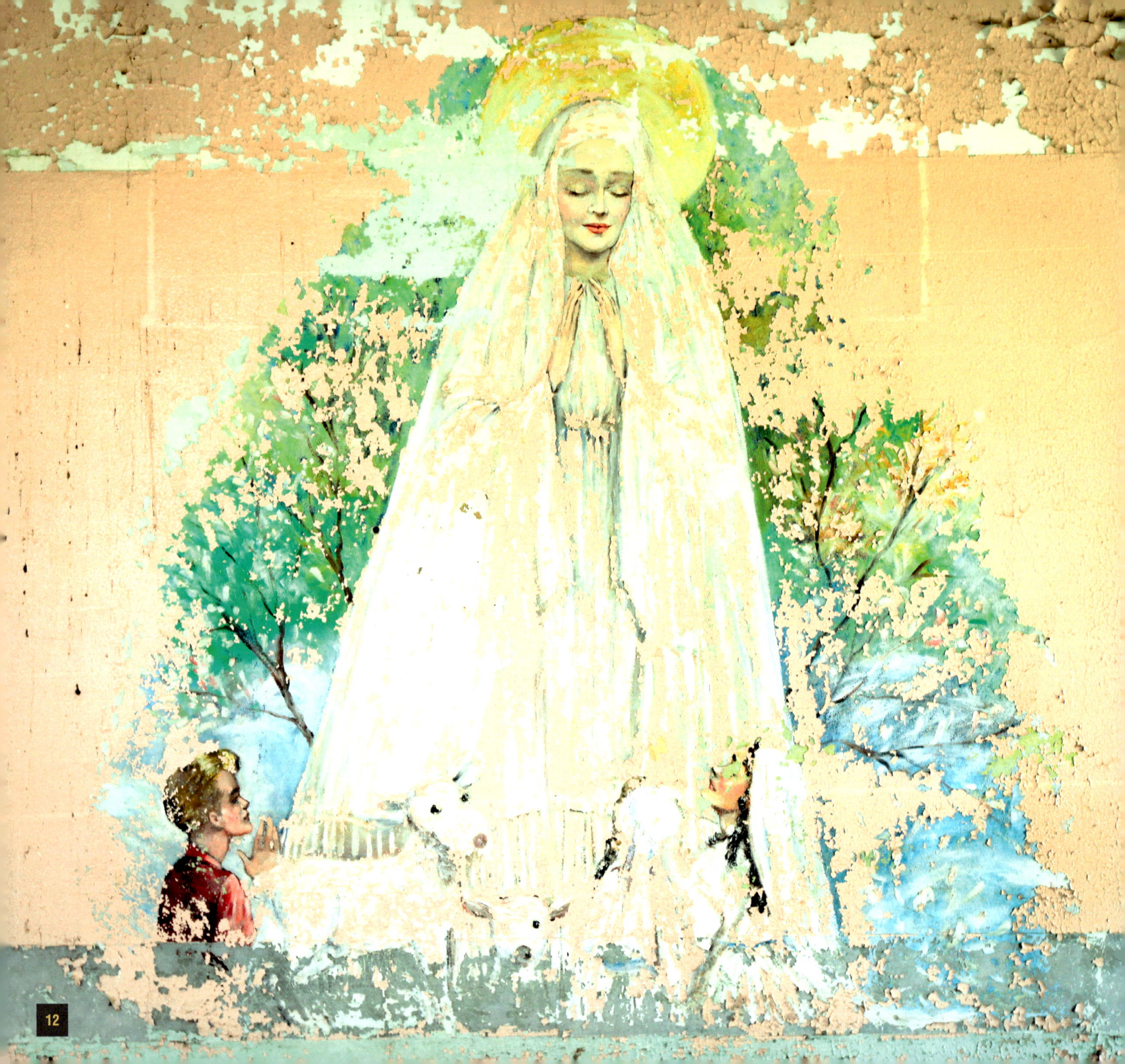

12

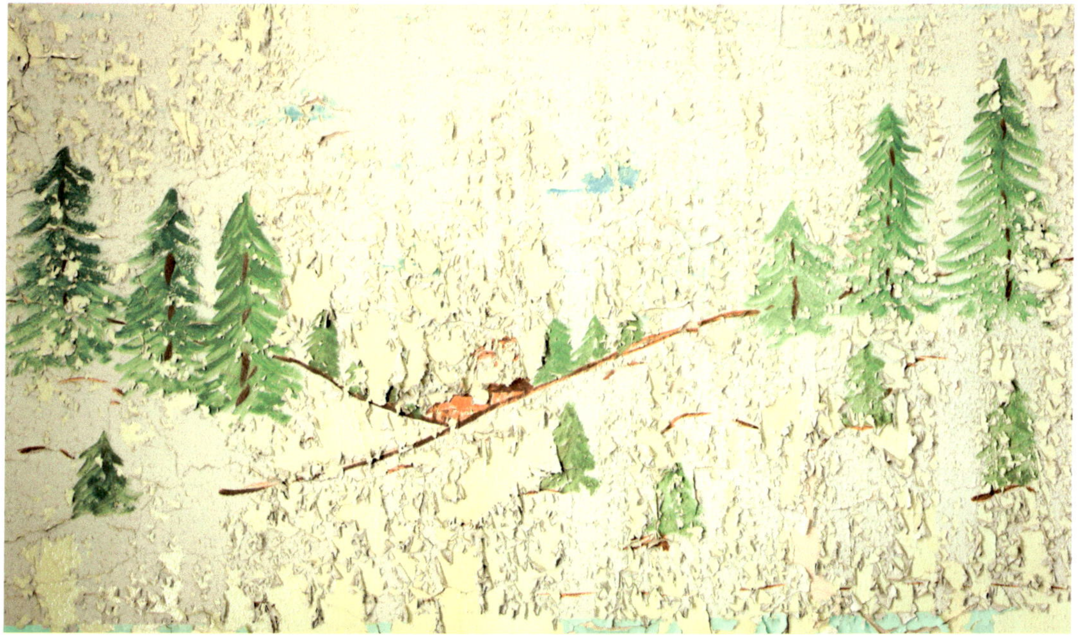

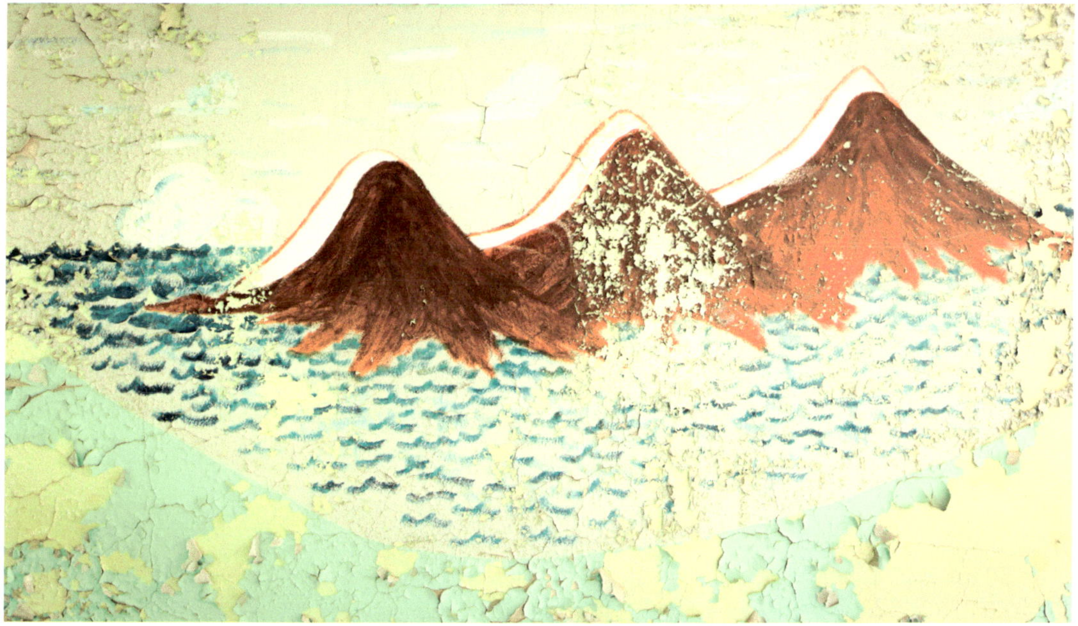

opposite Once painted over, an image of Our Lady of Fatima is coming to light again as time peels back the layers.

top Images of the natural world are common subjects in patient murals — residents rarely had an opportunity to leave the confines of the institution.

bottom The mounds in this image bear a striking resemblance to the current condition of the fourth floor.

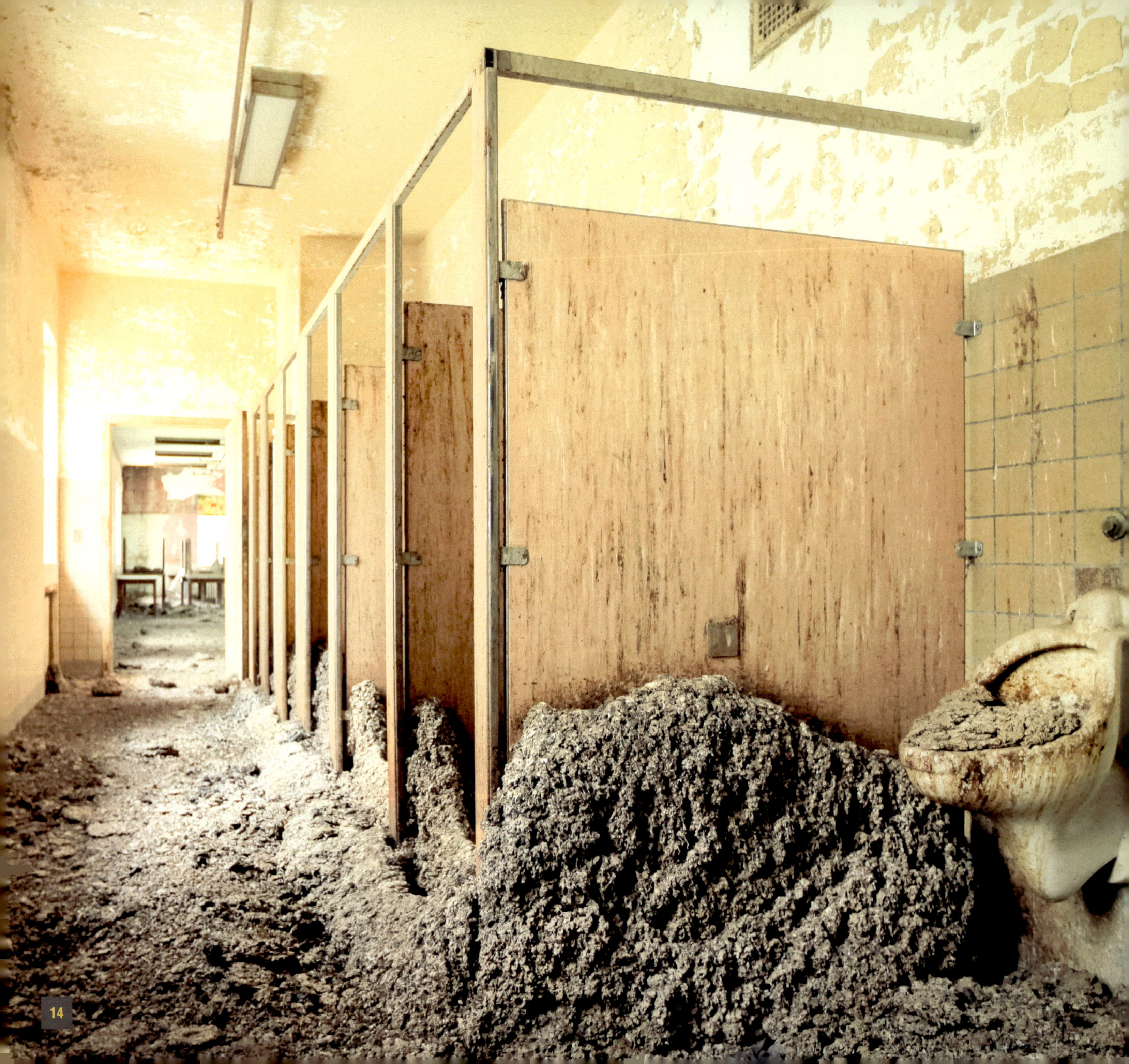

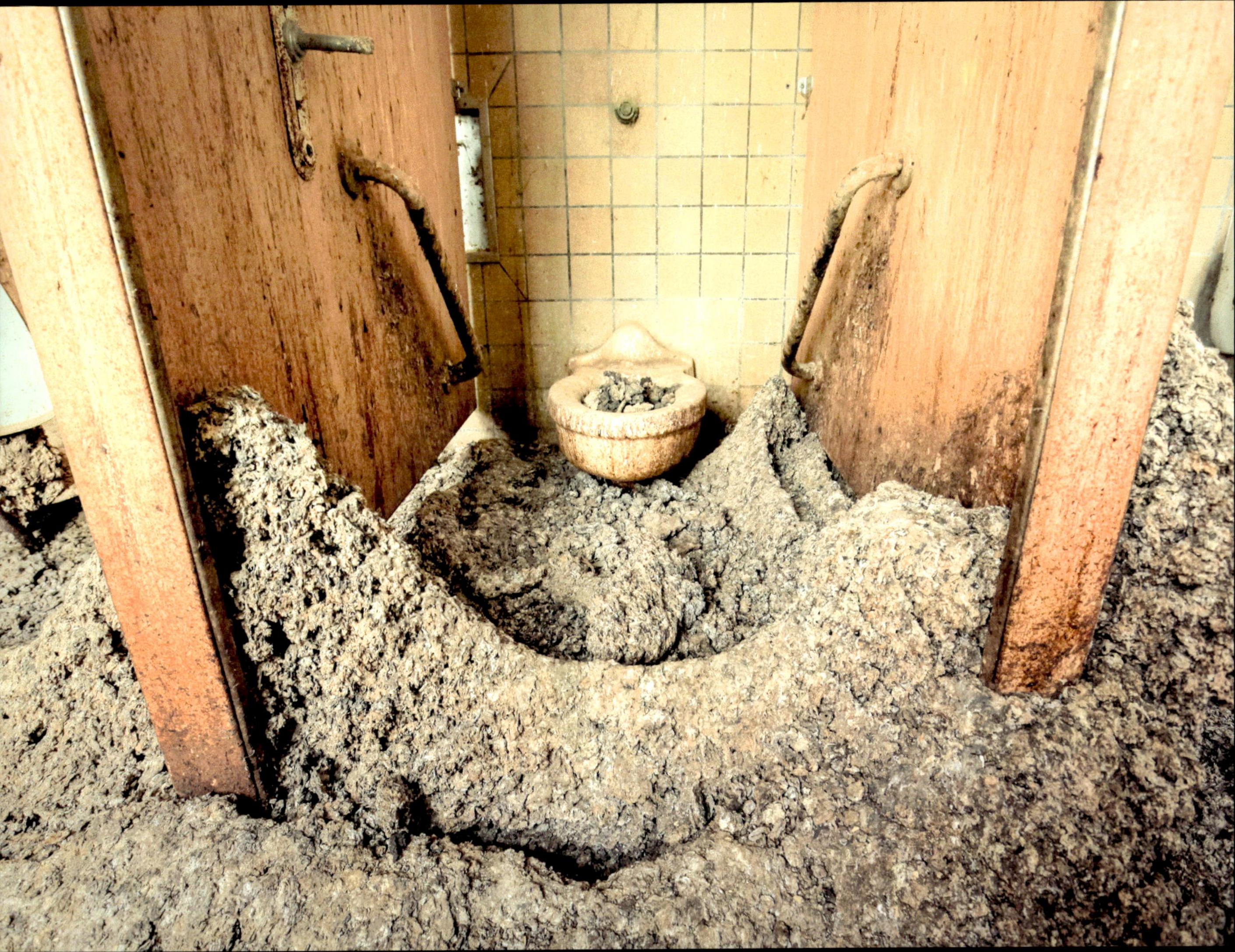

opposite A bathroom held the largest amount of fecal matter. Droppings pile up under popular roosts.

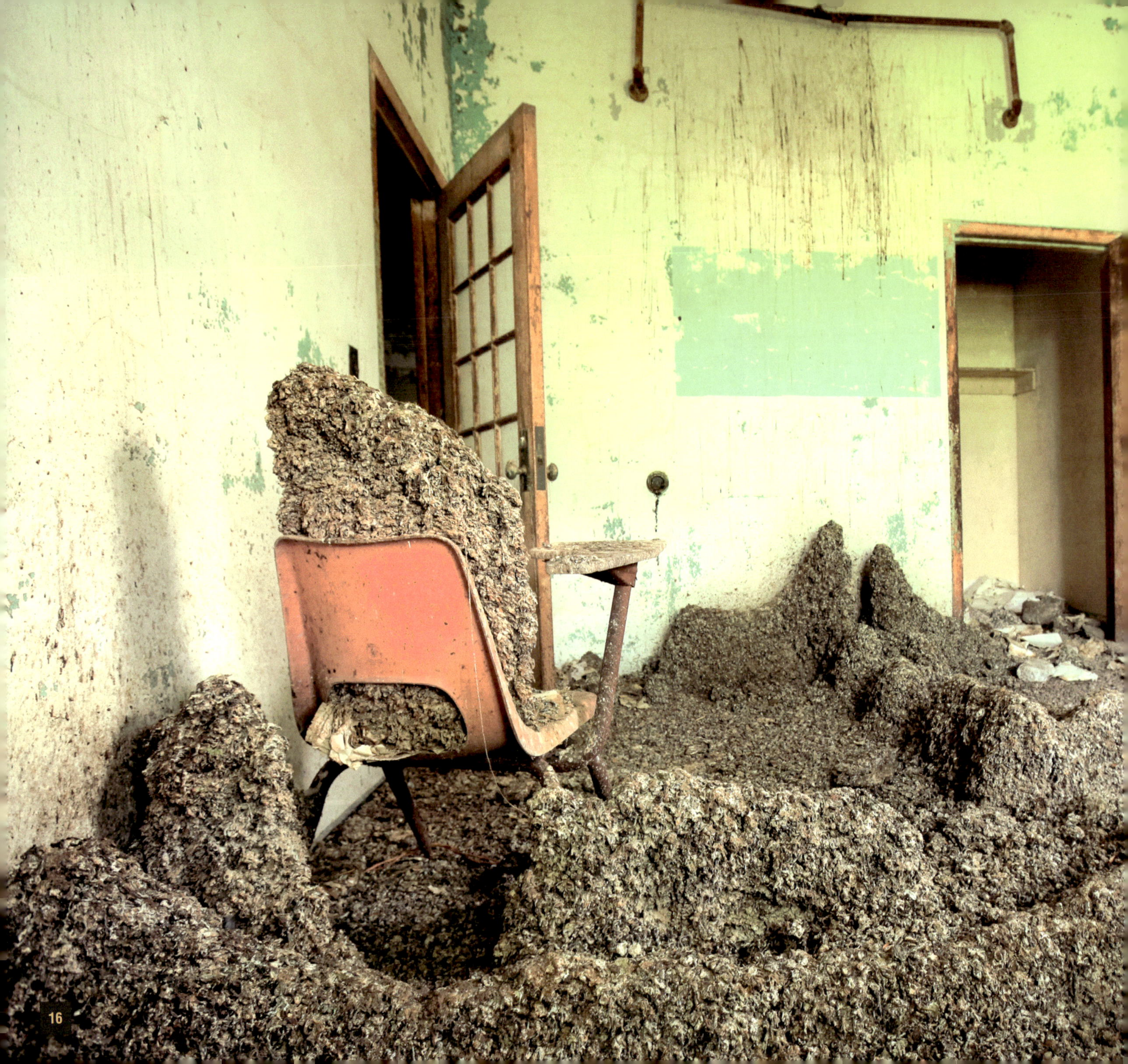

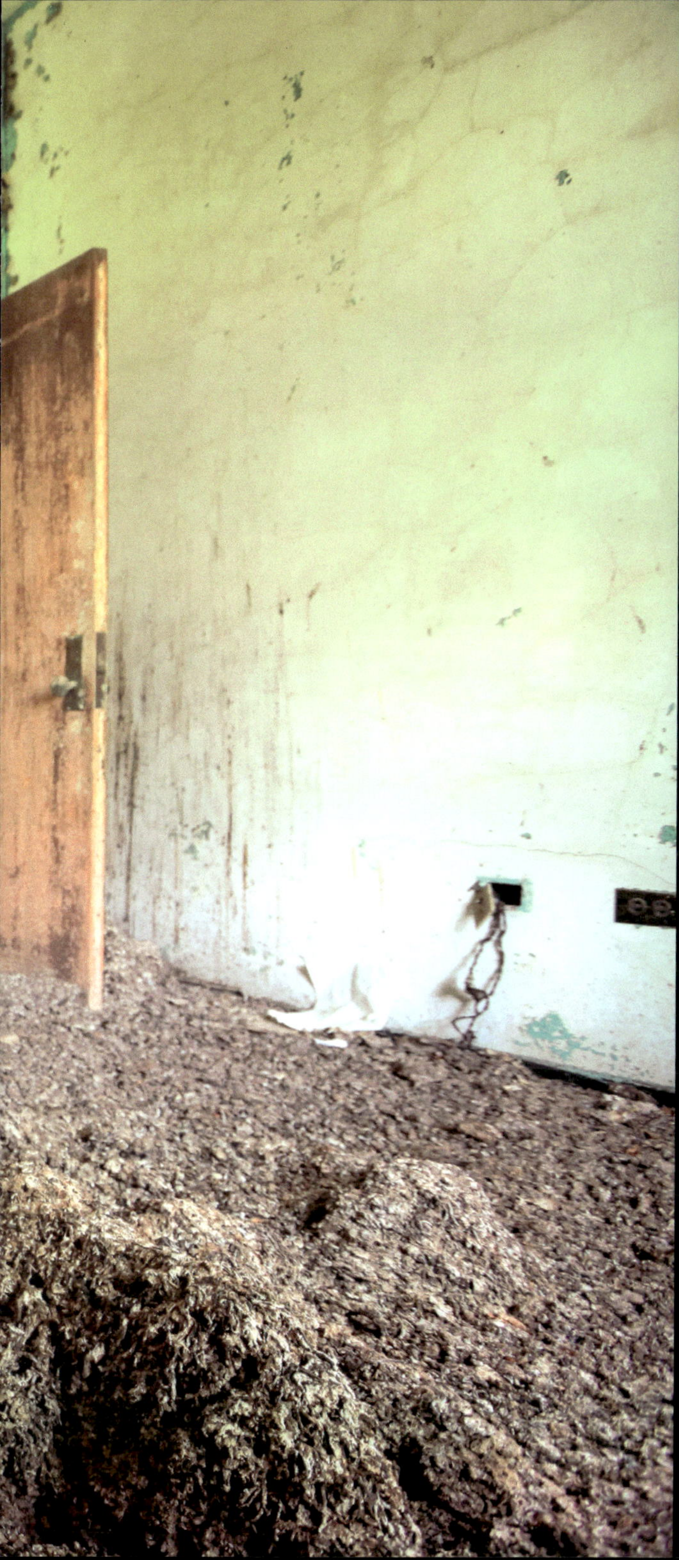

Formations accrue under the pipes of a sprinkler system. Pigeon carcasses litter the surface, hinting at an even larger number entombed within.

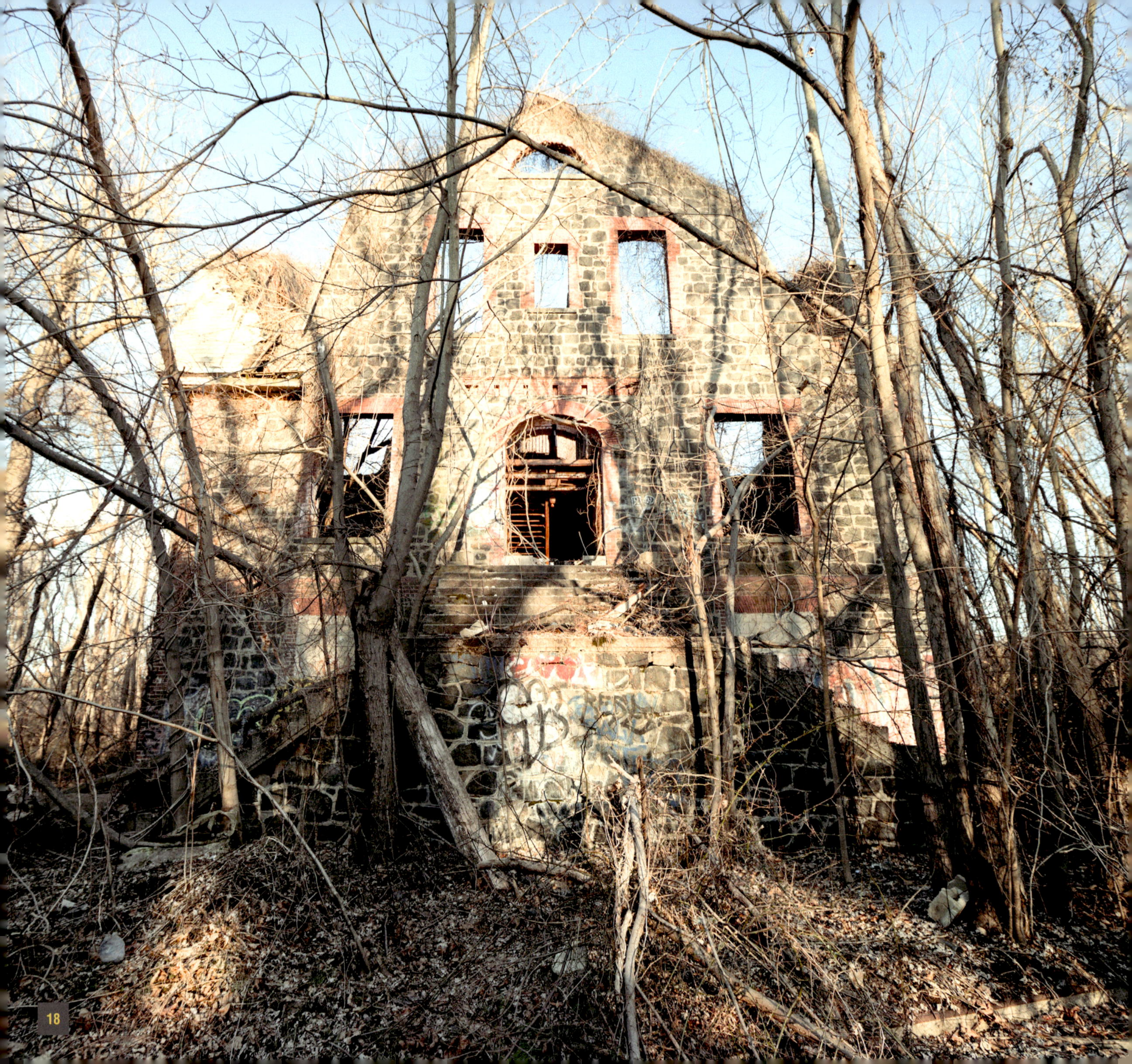

The New York City Farm Colony

Staten Island Greenbelt

At the center of Staten Island lies a city-owned amalgam of parks, scout camps, and overgrown lots collectively known as the Greenbelt. It's an area known for its natural beauty, its murders, and its ruins. On the southern rim, off Brielle Avenue, there are not one, but two historic hospitals crumbling to oblivion. The grounds of Seaview Hospital and the New York City Farm Colony may be the most forgotten quarter of the "forgotten borough," with over two dozen derelict buildings scattered through 300 acres of wooded land.

In the Farm Colony, the distinctive gambrel roofs of the oldest structures hearken back to a period long before their hundred-year history. Modeled in the Dutch Colonial Style, the dormitories were designed to evoke the ease of rural living, avoiding an institutional aesthetic to reflect changing attitudes toward the treatment of the poor. This was the era of the farm colonies, when able-bodied inmates were expected to work the land in exchange for their room and board.

By the late 1890s, Staten Island was incorporated as a borough of New York City, and the Richmond County Poor Farm was renamed the New York City Farm Colony. At one point, 200 residents could grow enough vegetables to feed 3,000, but as the population aged, the institution faced a perplexing problem. As early as 1910, 75% of the residents were over 50, with a quarter over 70, and the majority were unfit for manual labor. By 1925, work was no longer mandatory, but a reward system was put in place for voluntary farming and maintenance jobs. Over the next 50 years, increased prosperity nationwide and the introduction of social security depleted the population, and the property was abandoned in 1975.

Through four decades of abandonment, the grounds of the institution have never been open to the public, but that hasn't stopped them from becoming a shared space. If you grew up on Staten Island, chances are you've heard of the Farm Colony, and it's likely you've been there. Teenagers swarm the buildings after dark, intent on getting loose and getting scared.

opposite The Farm Colony only comes out in the winter.

Legends of an axe-wielding killer called Cropsey have circulated through campfires of the Staten Island Greenbelt for generations, but the area hosted a series of real-life tragedies in the second half of the 20th century. Sinister abuses at the nearby Willowbrook School for the Developmentally Disabled cast a pall over the area following a 1972 exposé by a young Geraldo Rivera. A former orderly at the facility is thought to be responsible for a series of child murders that shocked the borough in the 1970s and '80s. In 1987, the body of one of his alleged victims was found buried in a shallow grave not far from the abandoned Willowbrook campus, where he was rumored to be living. The hospital was renovated and incorporated into the College of Staten Island in the 1990s, and the Farm Colony seems to have taken its place in the collective imagination as the destination most associated with these tragic events.

Though the property was designated a historic district in 1985, next to nothing has been done to protect the structures. The city has been trying to drum up interest in the site over the last decade, shortlisting the Farm Colony as a possible location for a new police academy and later a school of engineering. City council member James Oddo, who called the Farm Colony the "bane of his existence," made another appeal in 2012 for expressions of interest. This resulted in a new plan to transform the area into a senior living facility called the "Landmark Colony." Six of the buildings will be preserved, but at least five of the oldest structures face demolition. In their final days, the ruins of the Farm Colony remain an unauthorized playground for the young and adventurous—a place to harbor our fears—and face them.

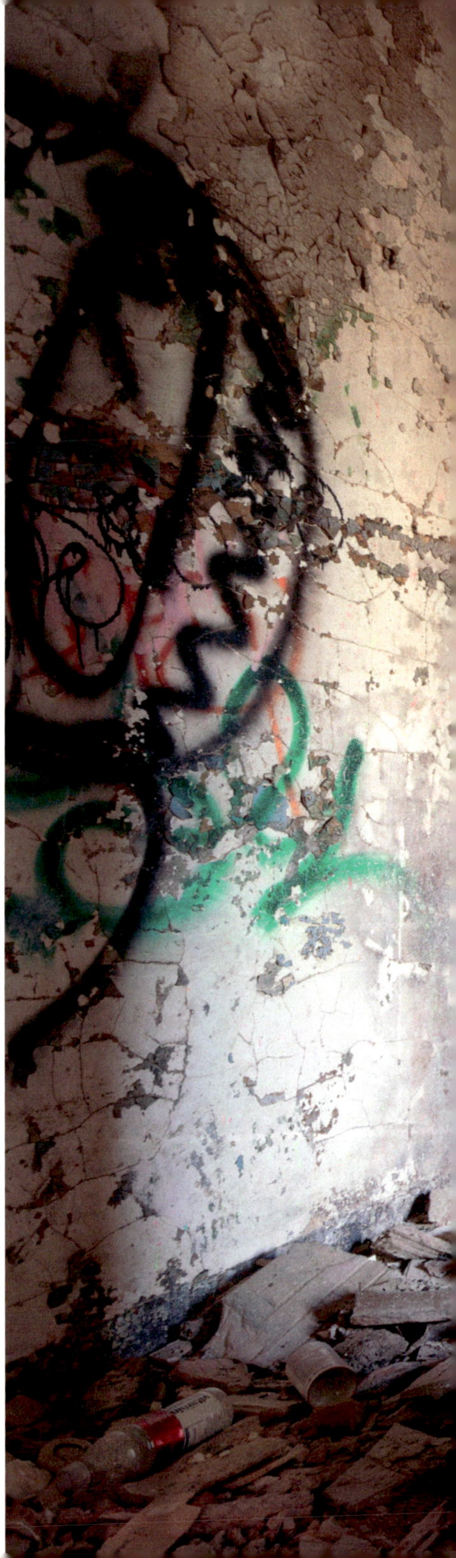

The dining hall is covered with juvenile graffiti.

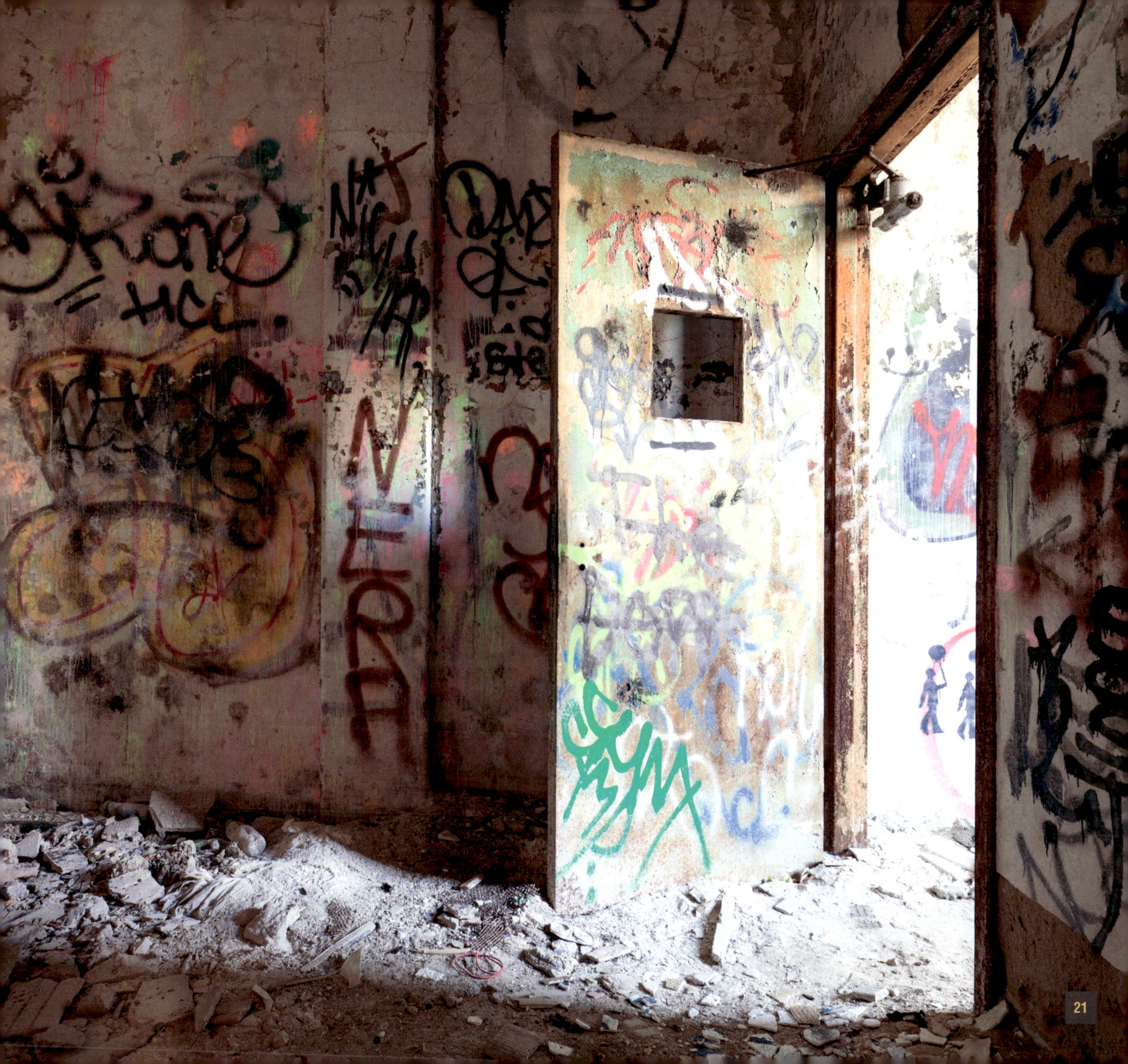

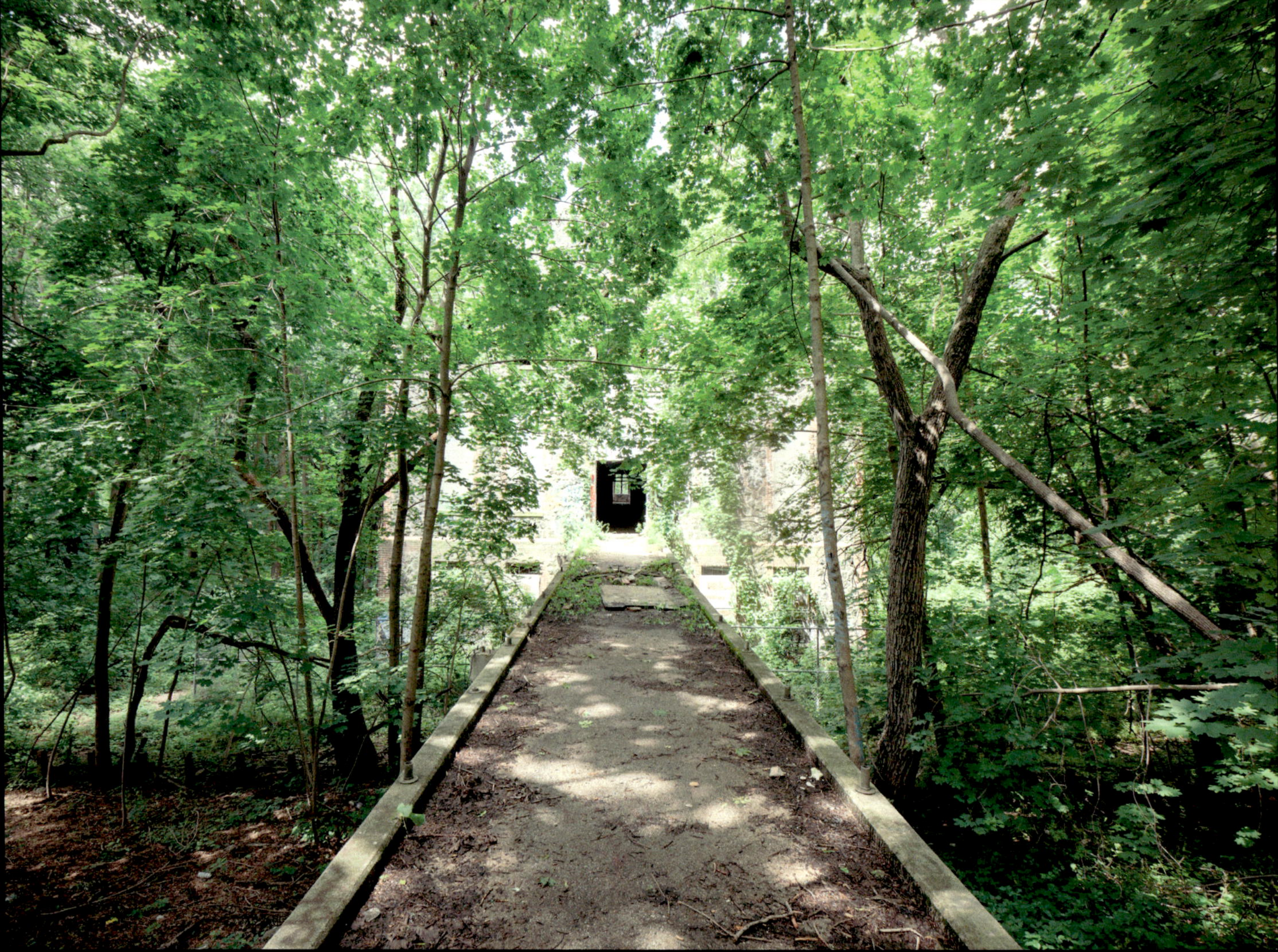

From May to November, thick greenery conceals
the ruins of the institution.

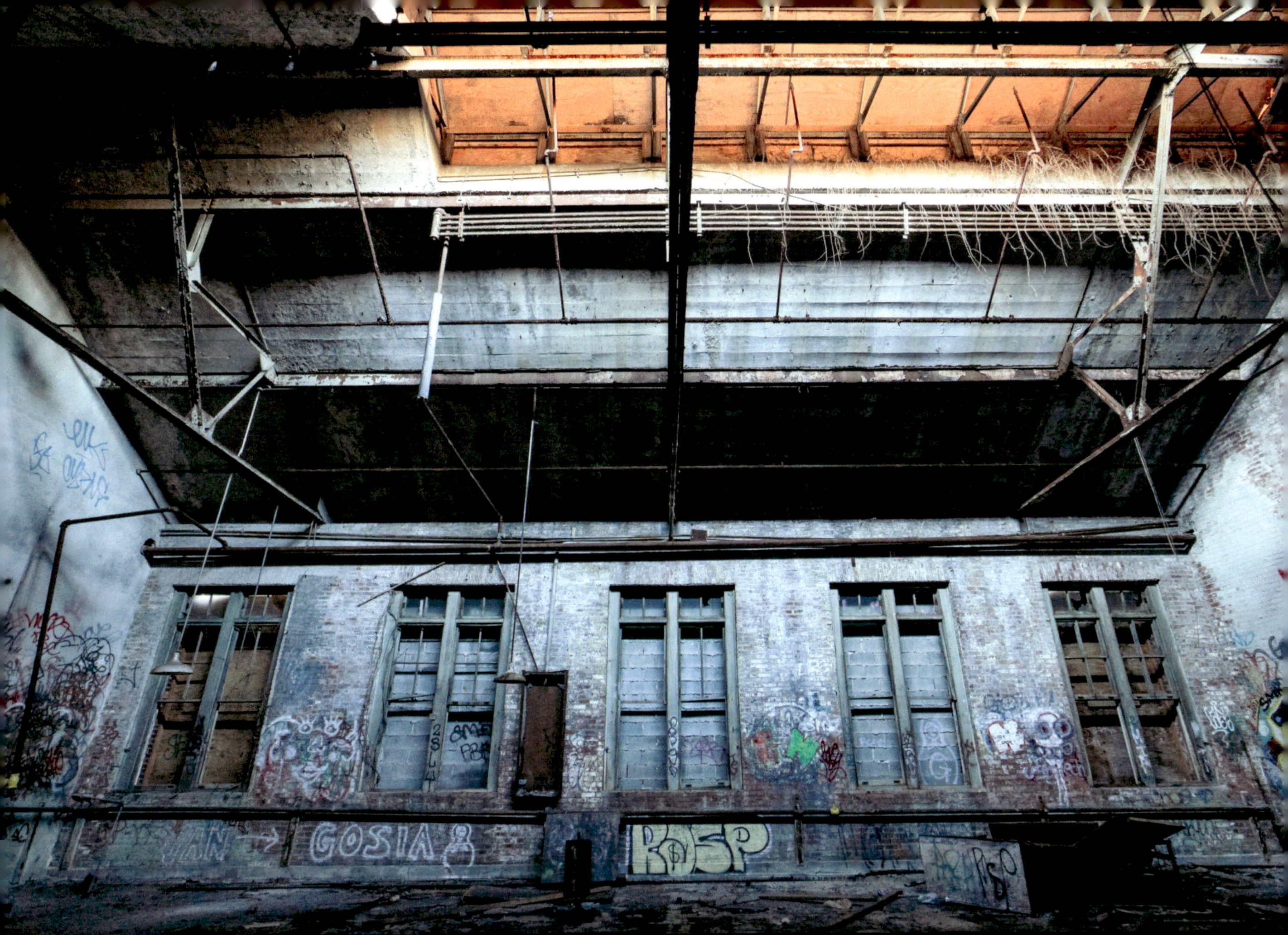

The laundry and industrial building once
housed shops for printing, carpentry, and broom making.

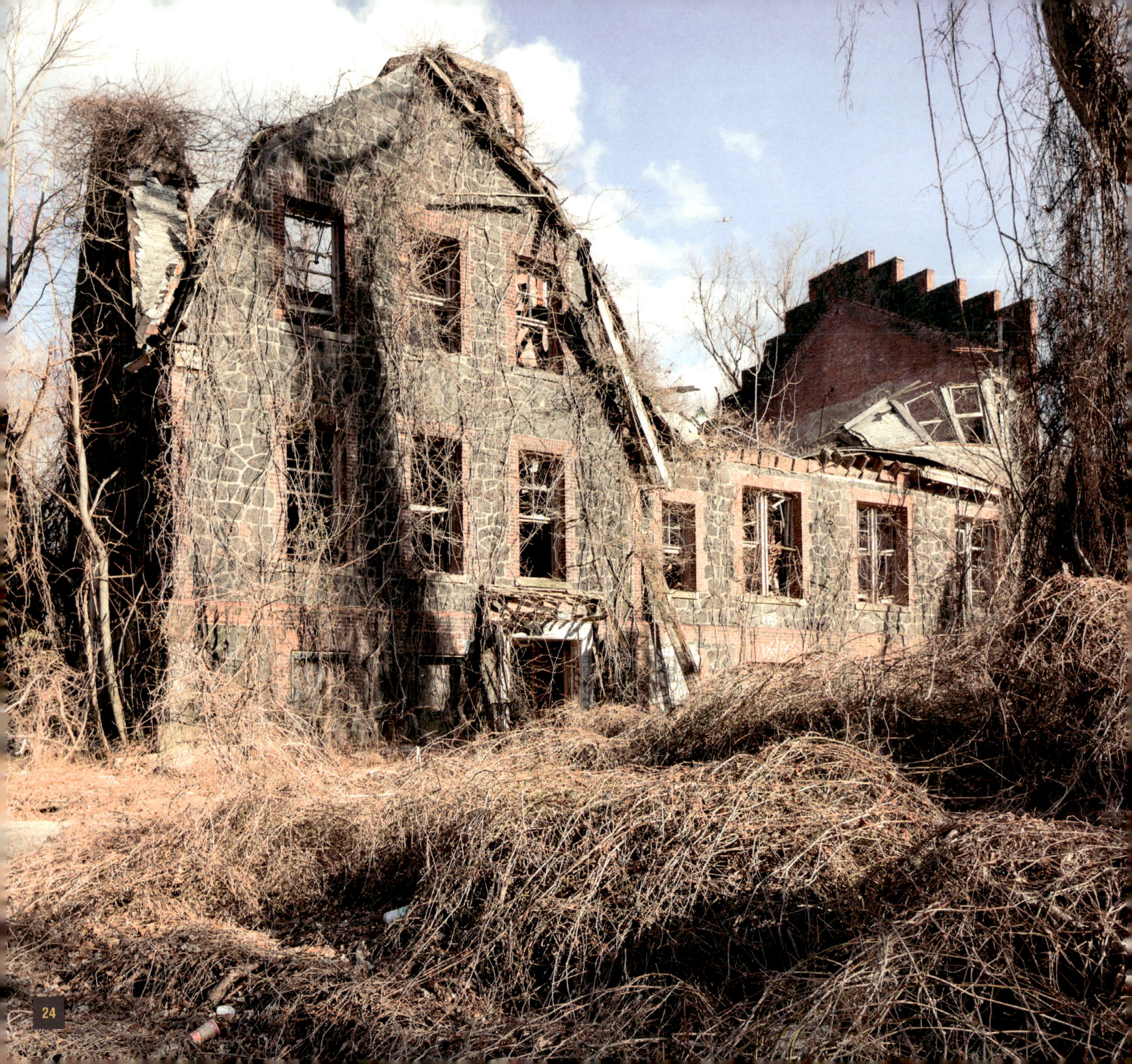

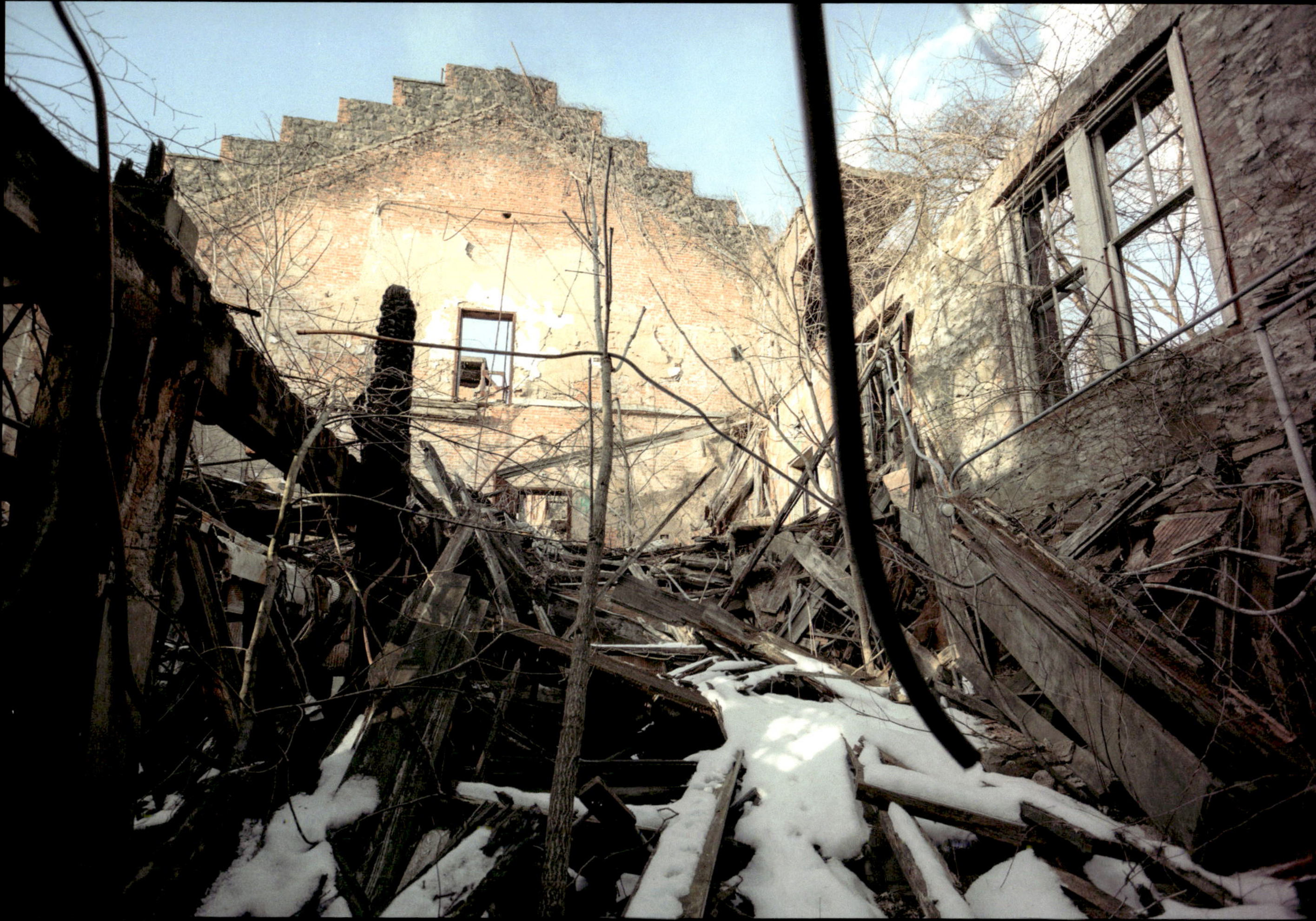

opposite The oldest dormitories were built to replace the charmless farmhouses of the Richmond County Poor Farm, which had operated on the spot since 1829.

above Though the Farm Colony is designated as a historic district, many of its structures are in a state of progressive decay.

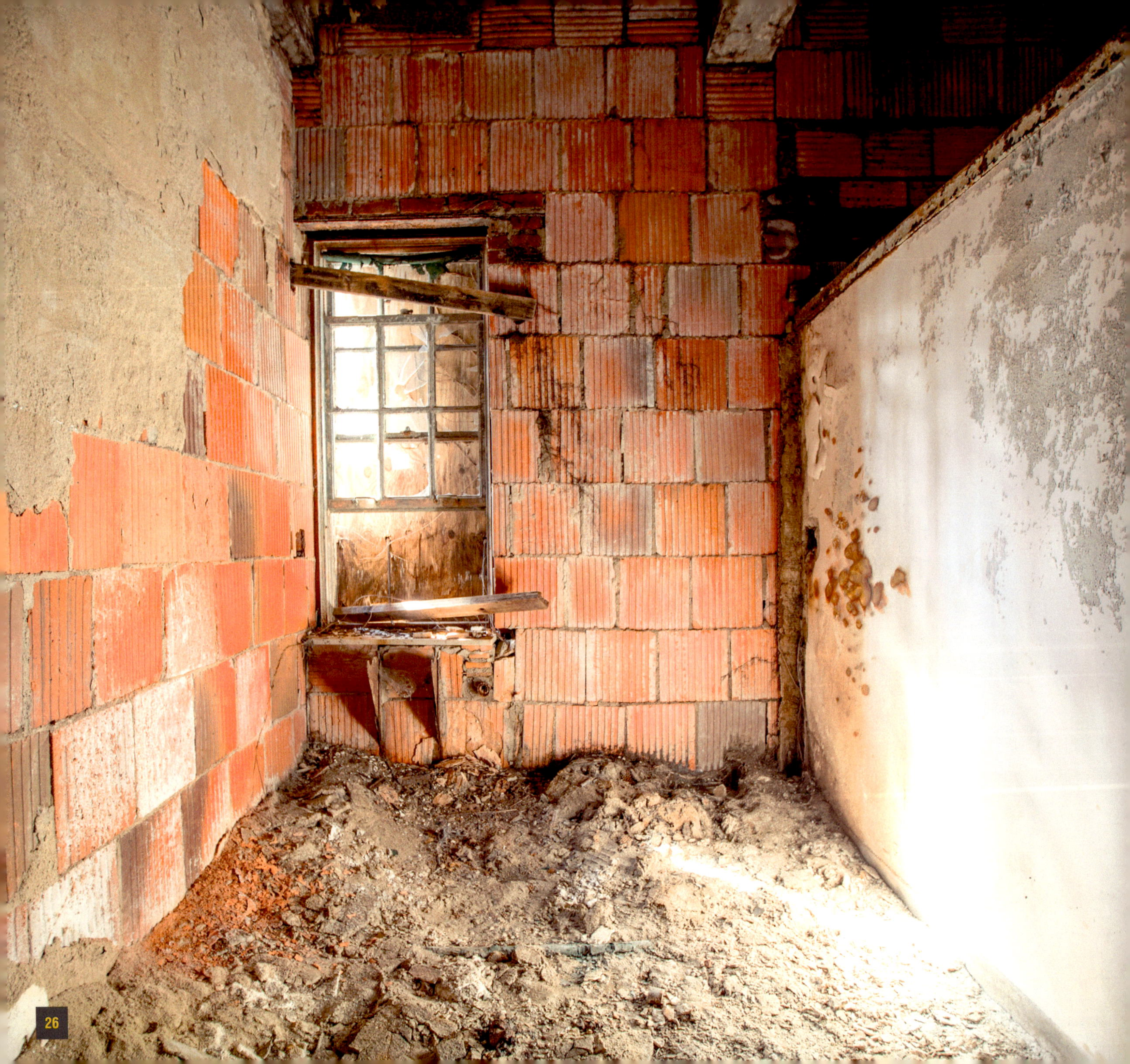

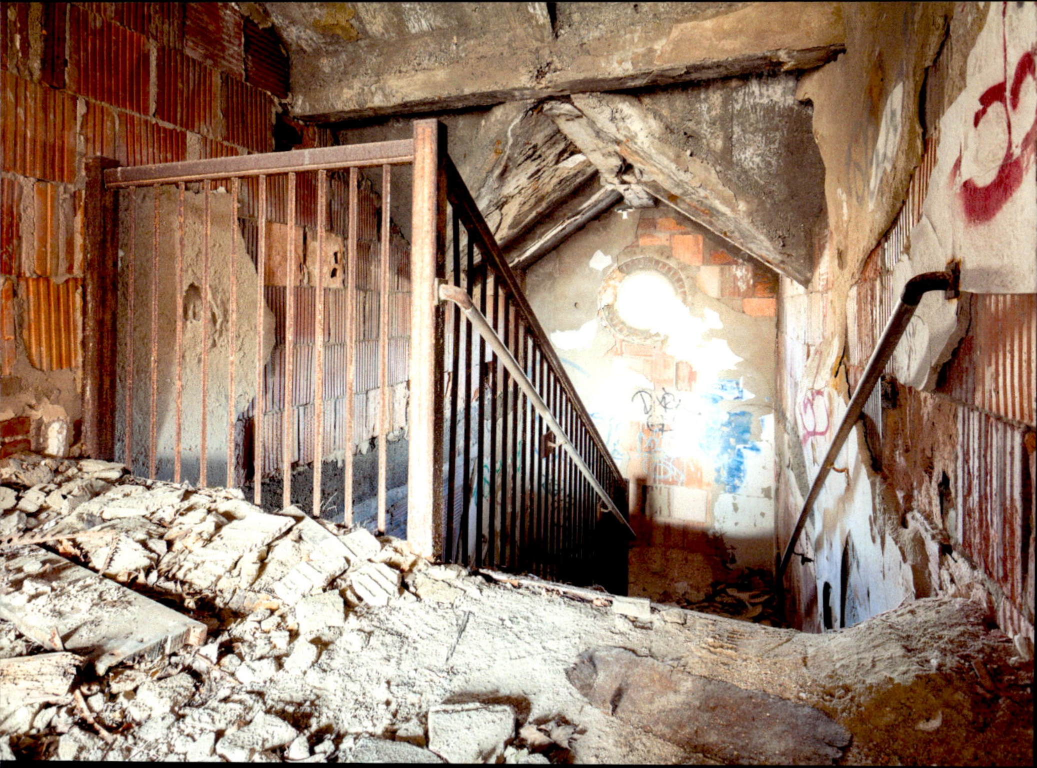

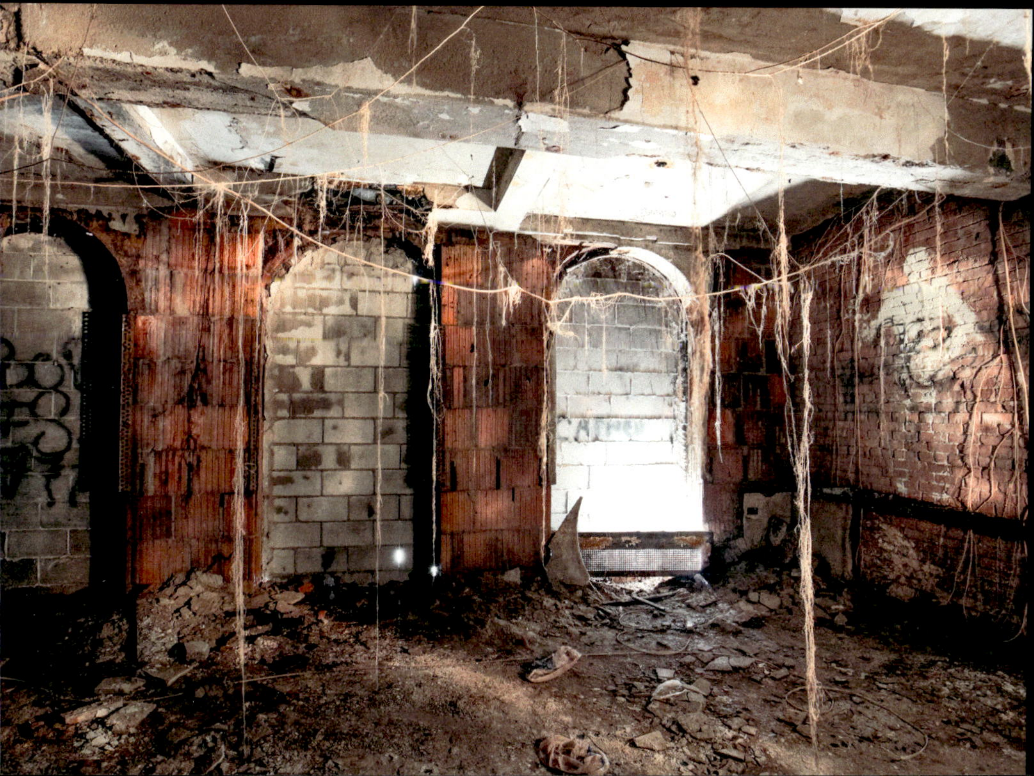

opposite The newer concrete dormitories have fared better, though generations of vandalism have eviscerated the interiors.

above Plaster dust accrues in drifts, exposing a patchwork of masonry.

below Featherweight vines dangle from the darkest chambers like an alien weed.

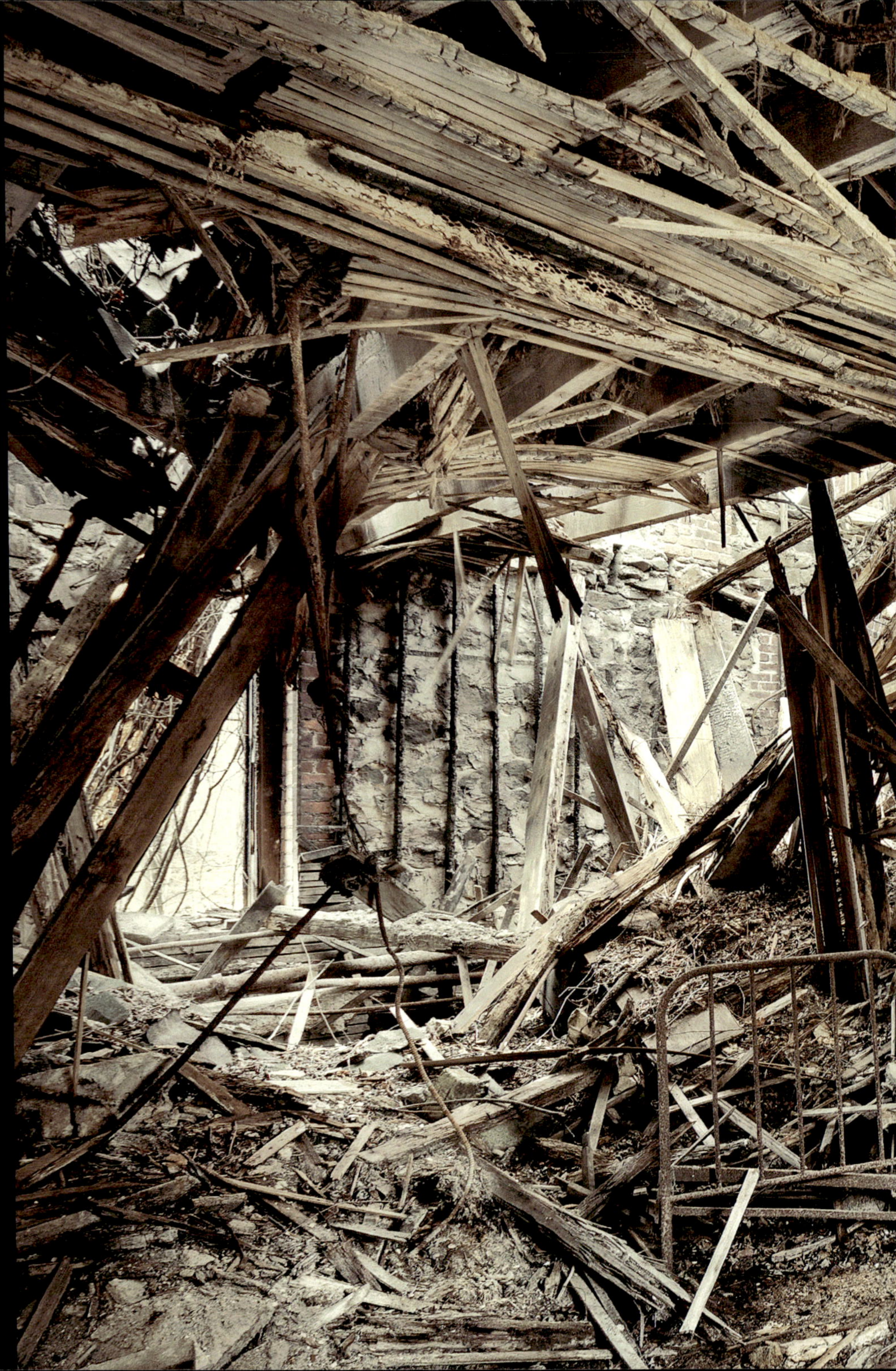

The only room left intact in this residence hall was a wreck of splintered beams and nail-studded boards. It had collapsed by my next visit.

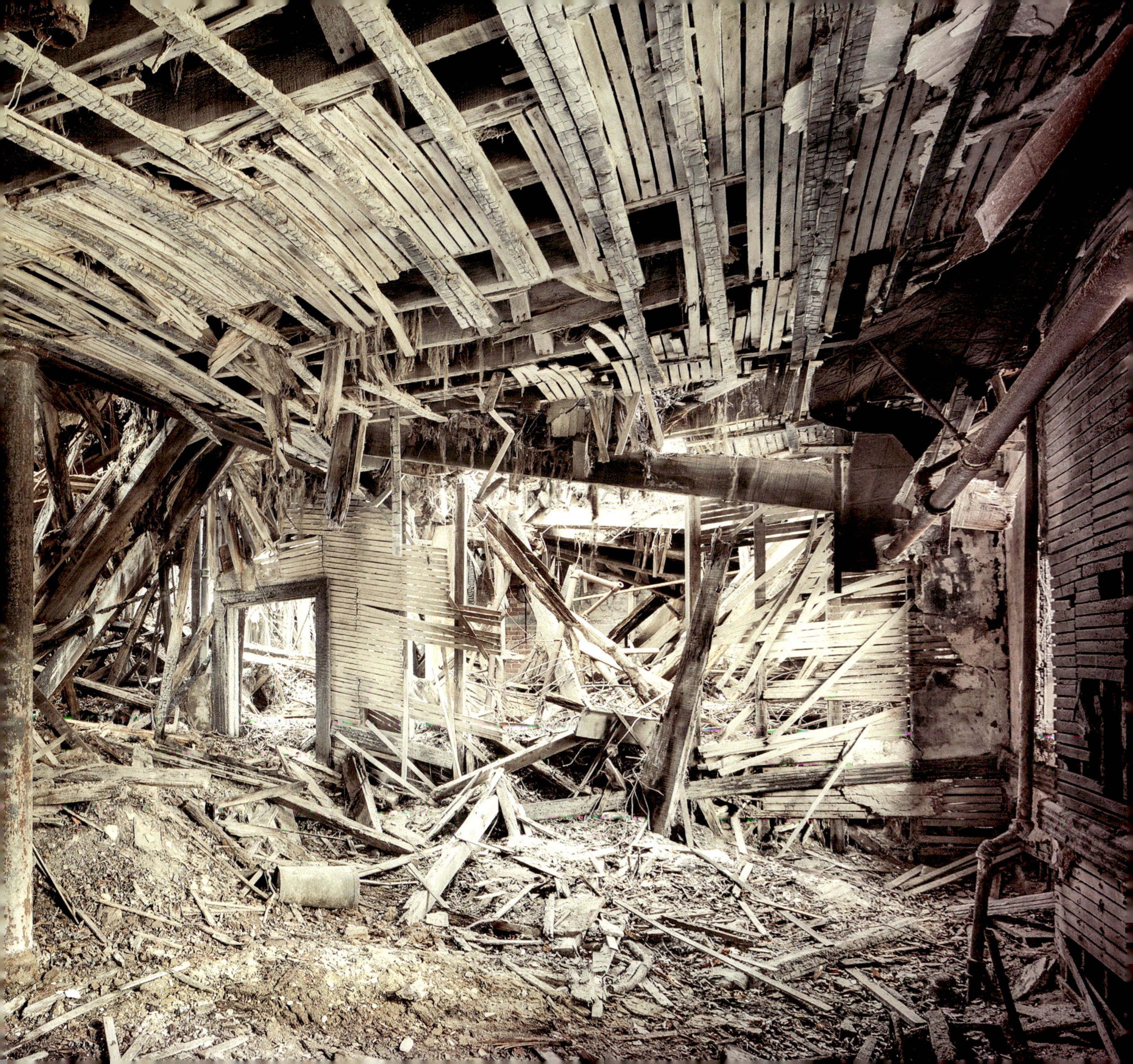

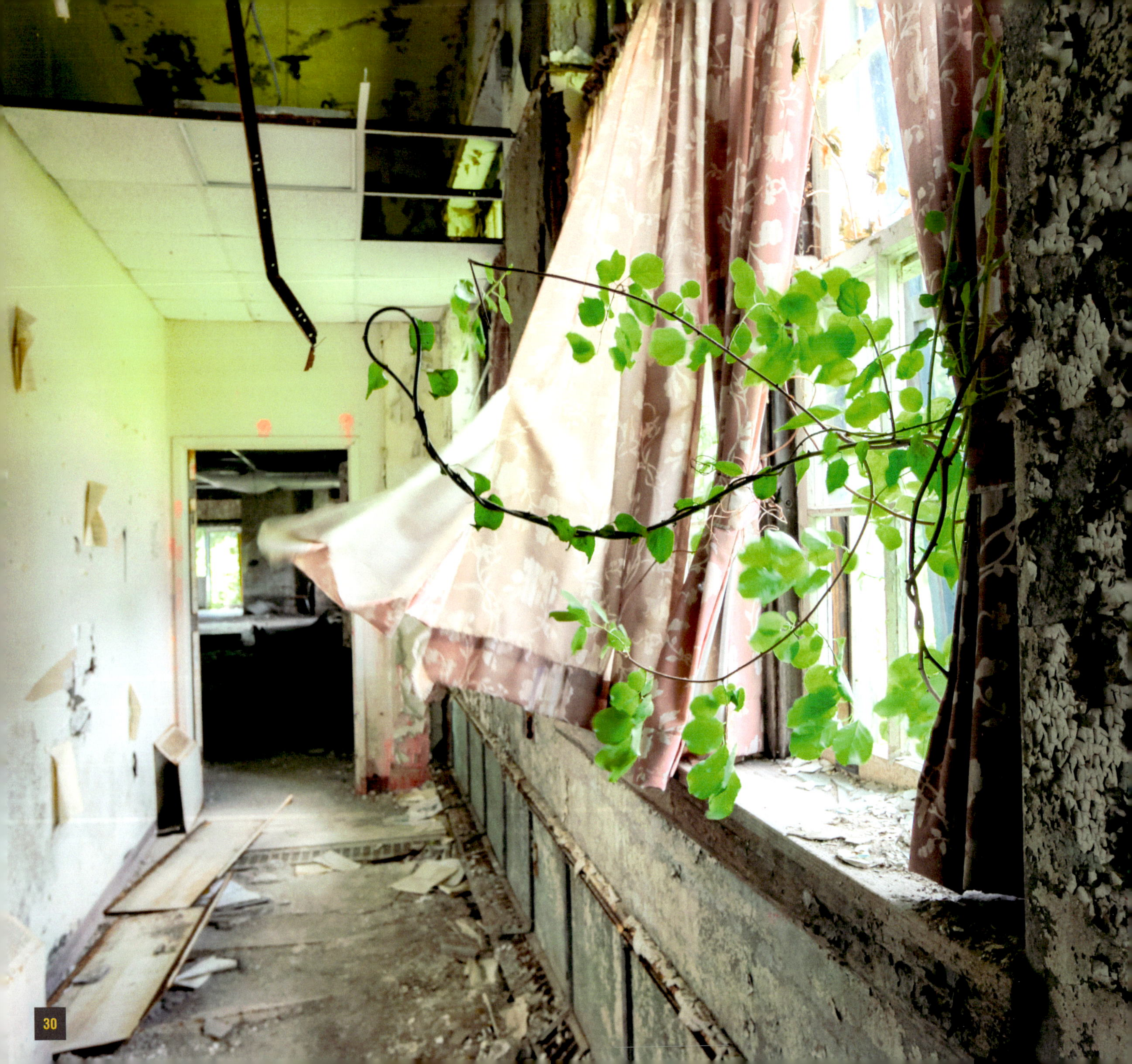

Letchworth Village

Thiells, NY

Letchworth Village rests on a placid corner of rural Thiells, a hamlet west of Haverstraw set amid the gentle hills and vales of the surrounding Ramapo Mountains. Just a short stretch of farmhouses separates this former home for the mentally disabled from the wilderness of Harriman State Park, and nature has been quick to reclaim the grounds, shrouding an unpleasant memory in a thick green veil. Abandonment becomes this "village of secrets," intended from its inception to be unseen, forgotten, and silent as the tomb.

By the end of 1911, the first phase of construction was completed on this 2,362-acre "state institution for the segregation of the epileptic and feeble-minded." With architecture modeled after Monticello, Letchworth Village was lauded as a model institution for the treatment of the developmentally disabled and a humane alternative to high-rise asylums.

The picturesque community was founded on several guiding principles that were revolutionary at the time. The grounds were divided by the Minisceongo Creek, which delineated areas for the two sexes. Separate living and training facilities for children, adults, and the infirm were not to exceed two stories or house more than 70 residents. Until the 1960s, the able-bodied labored on communal farms, raising enough food and livestock to feed the entire population. Other tenets of the Letchworth plan were sinister by today's standards. Unable to give or deny consent, many children became unwitting test subjects—in 1950, the institution gained notoriety as the site of one of the first human trials of a still-experimental polio vaccine.

The well-intentioned plans for Letchworth Village didn't hold up in practice, and by 1942 the population had swelled to twice its intended occupancy. From there, the severely underfunded facility fell into a lengthy decline. Many of the residents, whose condition necessitated ample time and attention for feeding, became seriously ill or malnourished as a result of overcrowding. At one point, over 500 patients slept on mattresses in hallways and dayrooms of the facility, meagerly attended by a completely overwhelmed staff tasked with the impossible.

opposite A breeze stirs a faded curtain in the west wing of Letchworth Village hospital. Through 16 years of abandonment, the grounds have become a subject of local legend.

Having discontinued the use of the majority of its buildings and relocated most of its charges into group homes, the institution closed down in 1996 as old methods of segregating the developmentally disabled were replaced with more inclusive practices. The state has made efforts to sell the property, with mixed results. Several buildings on the northern part of the institution have been reused for commercial purposes, and a middle school makes use of nine buildings of the former girls' group. The rest of the neglected campus retains a kind of elegiac beauty, making it a popular spot for small-town dog walkers and amateur photographers. But by night, another group of visitors descends on the grounds.

For the young and curious, a moonlit pilgrimage to a haunted location promises a brush with the unknown and an affirmation of courage—"legend tripping" is a ritual that's become commonplace at Letchworth Village. The most popular hangouts are marked with pervasive graffiti, which often alludes to the institution's horrific past or warns of its vengeful spirits. Every year, more buildings fall victim to fires stemming from these visits. Perhaps without realizing it, these young people are scouring away a shameful memory, absolving a collective guilt with paintballs, matchbooks, and pentagrams.

In a little-known and easy-to-miss cemetery about a mile from the facility, amends are being made more constructively. Off Call Hollow Road, a new sign marks the "Old Letchworth Village Cemetery." Down a seldom-traveled path, an unusual crop of T-shaped markers appears on a dappled clearing; they are graves, but they bear no names. Here, in the presence of so many human lives devalued, displaced, and forgotten, the sorrow of Letchworth Village is keenly felt.

As part of a movement taking place across the country, state agencies and advocates recently funded the installation of a permanent plaque inscribed with the names of these silent dead, and a fitting epitaph: "Those Who Shall Not Be Forgotten."

Letchworth Village isn't a house of horrors, but it has become a thing of the past and a symbol of our failings. Now, its ruins are vanishing—any moment, they'll crumble to dust, dirt, and ash. Soon, only soot-black foundations, half-remembered histories, and 900 numbered graves—poignant reminders of an all-too-recent injustice—will remain.

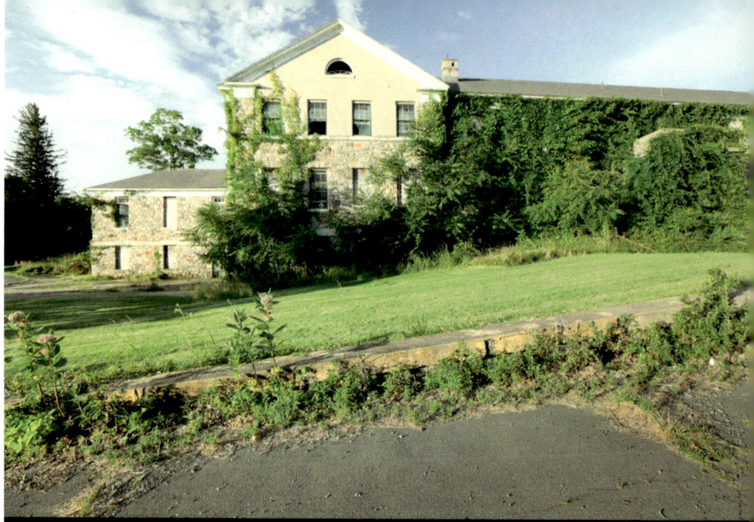

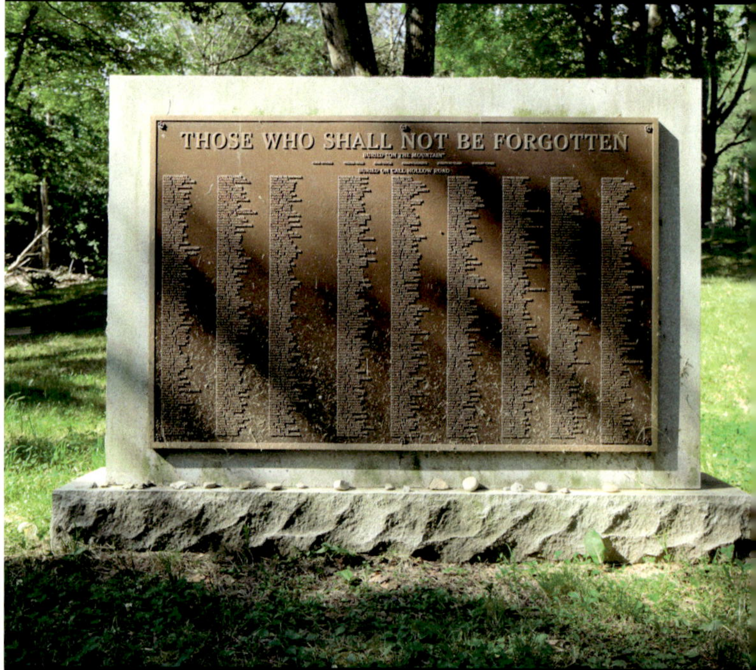

top The hospital is the most visited building at Letchworth Village; it's also known as a supernatural hotspot.

bottom A new memorial in the Old Letchworth Village Cemetery.

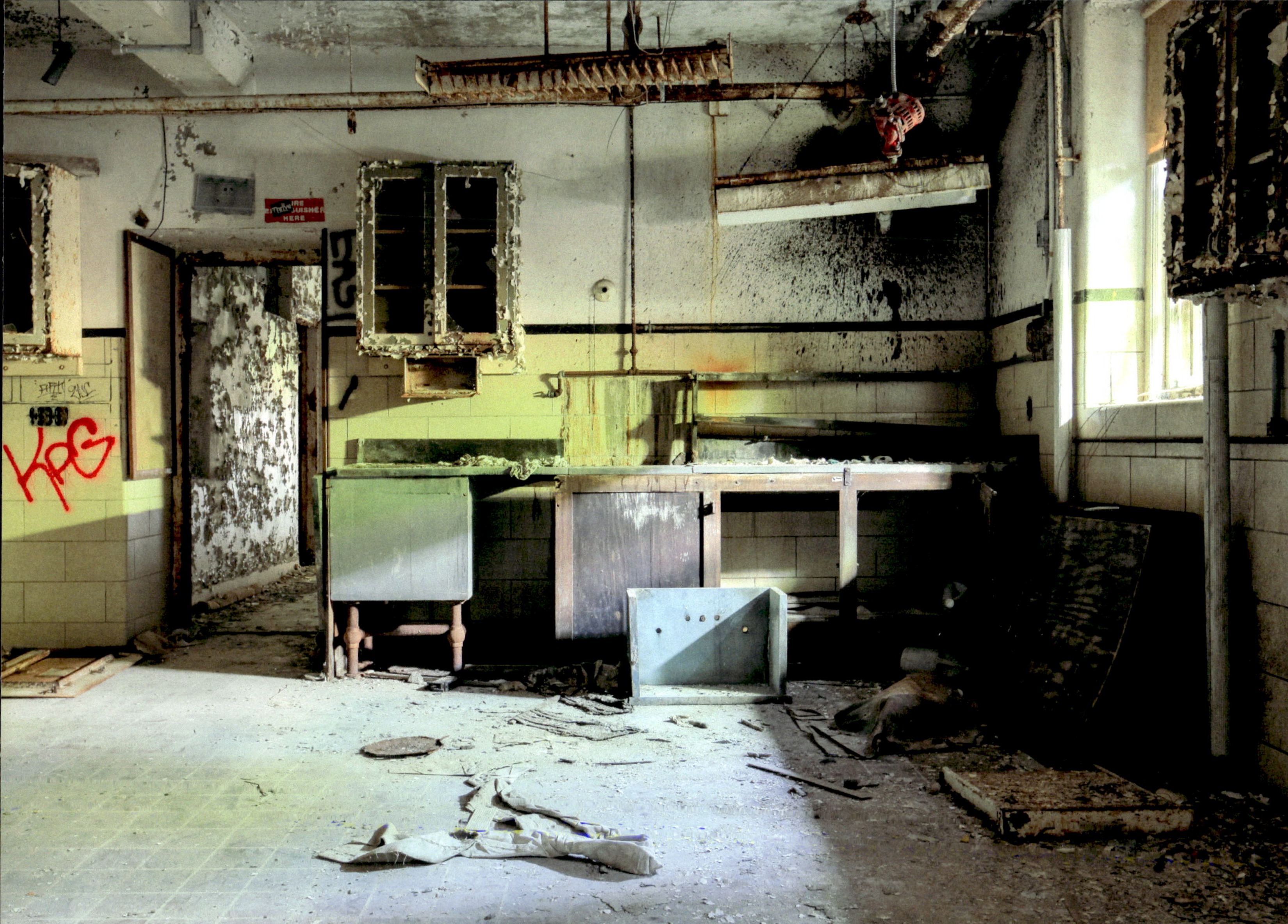

above Brain specimens were supposedly kept in jars in this laboratory after being removed from deceased residents.

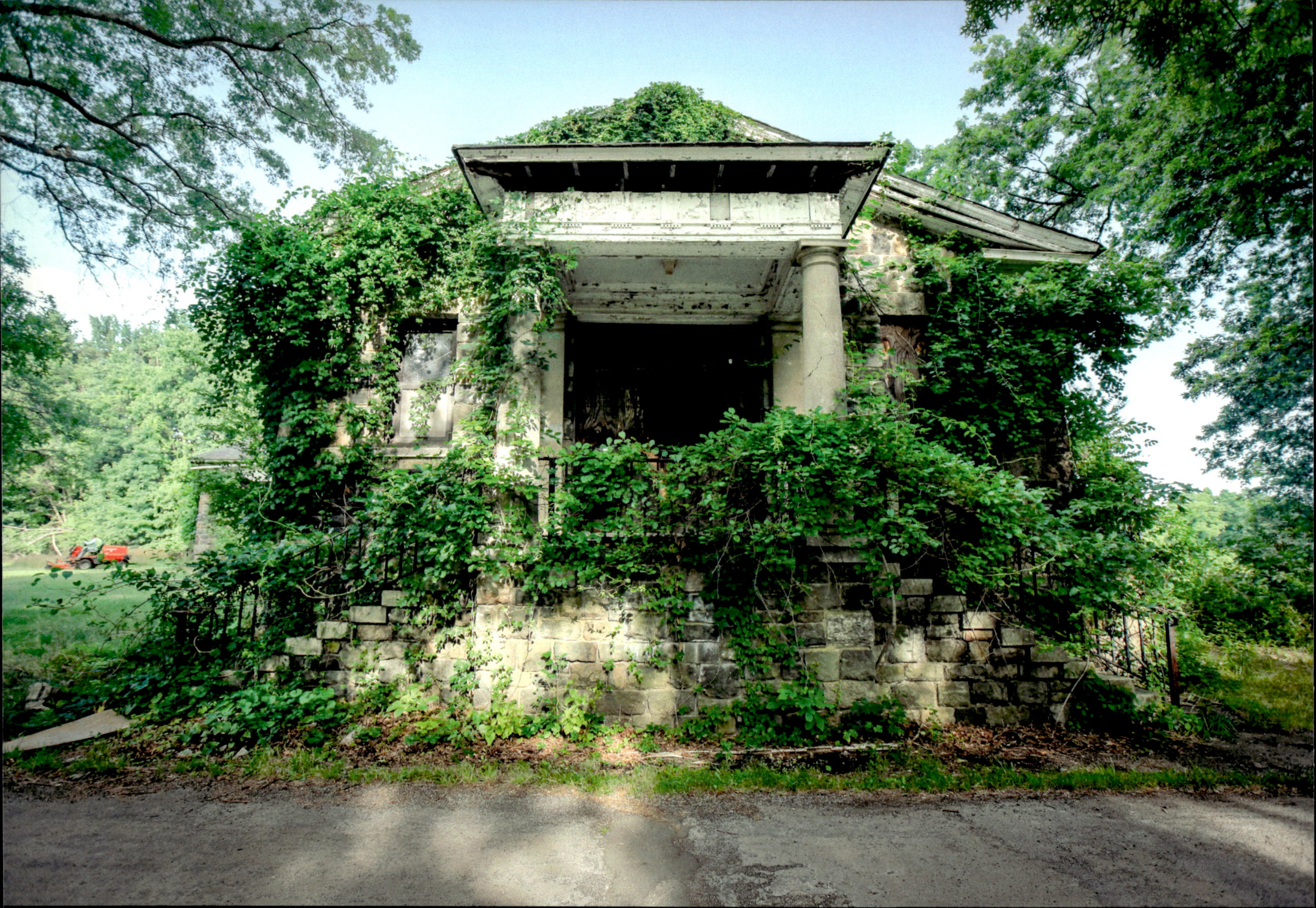

above An overgrown dormitory in the boy's ward.

Each group included six to eight small residence halls with central

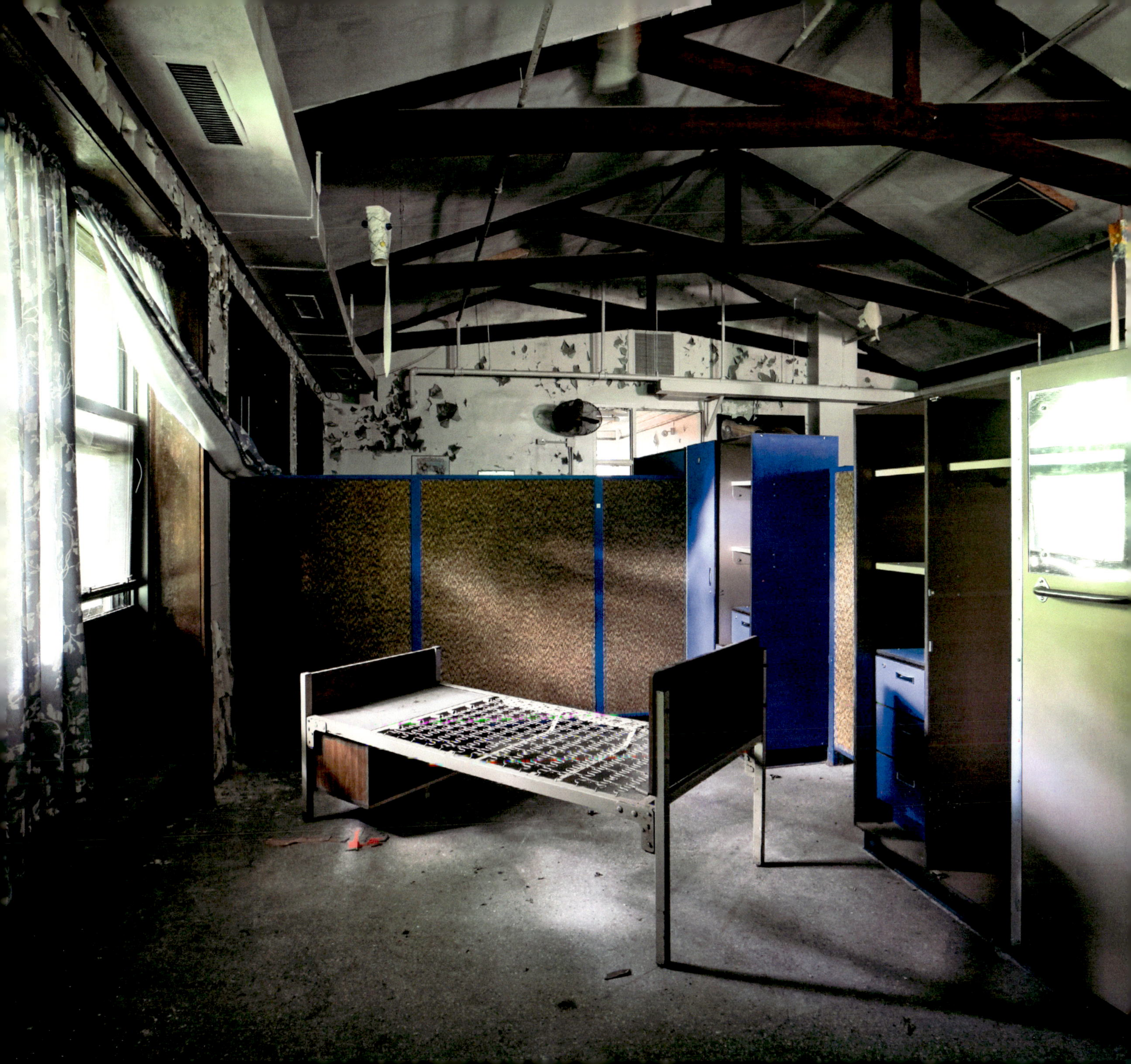

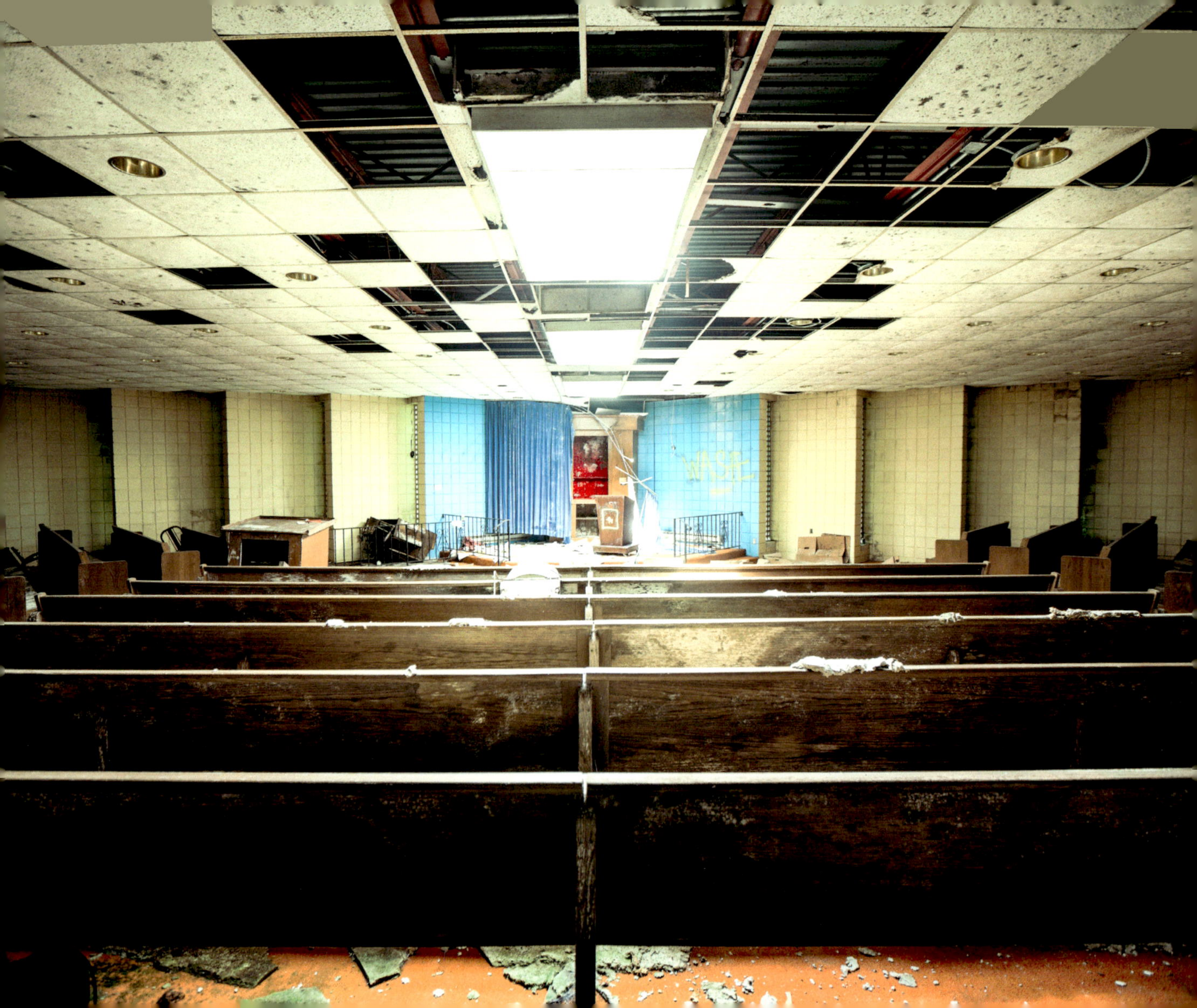

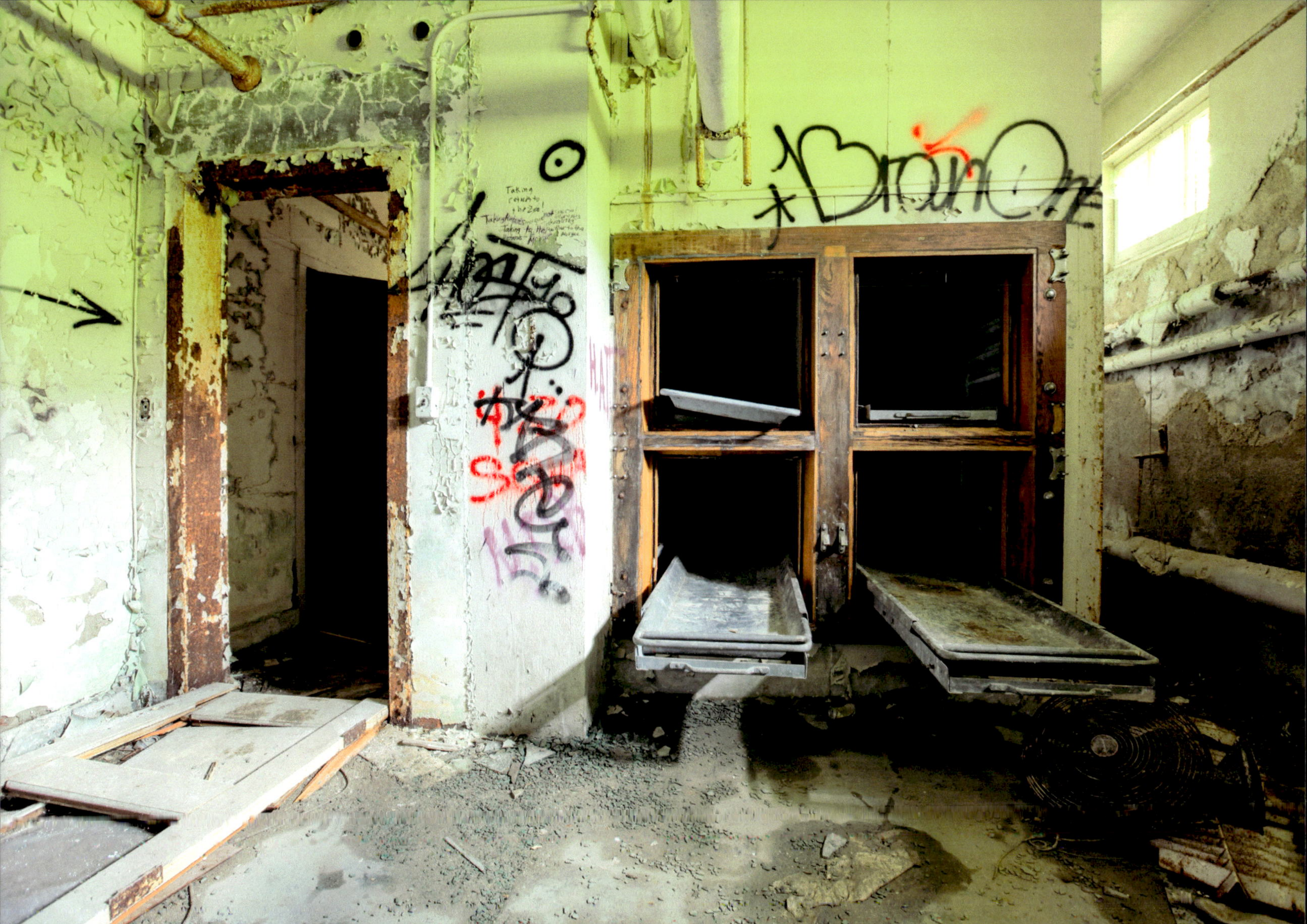

opposite A small synagogue catered to the residents' religious needs. The property also includes a larger chapel.

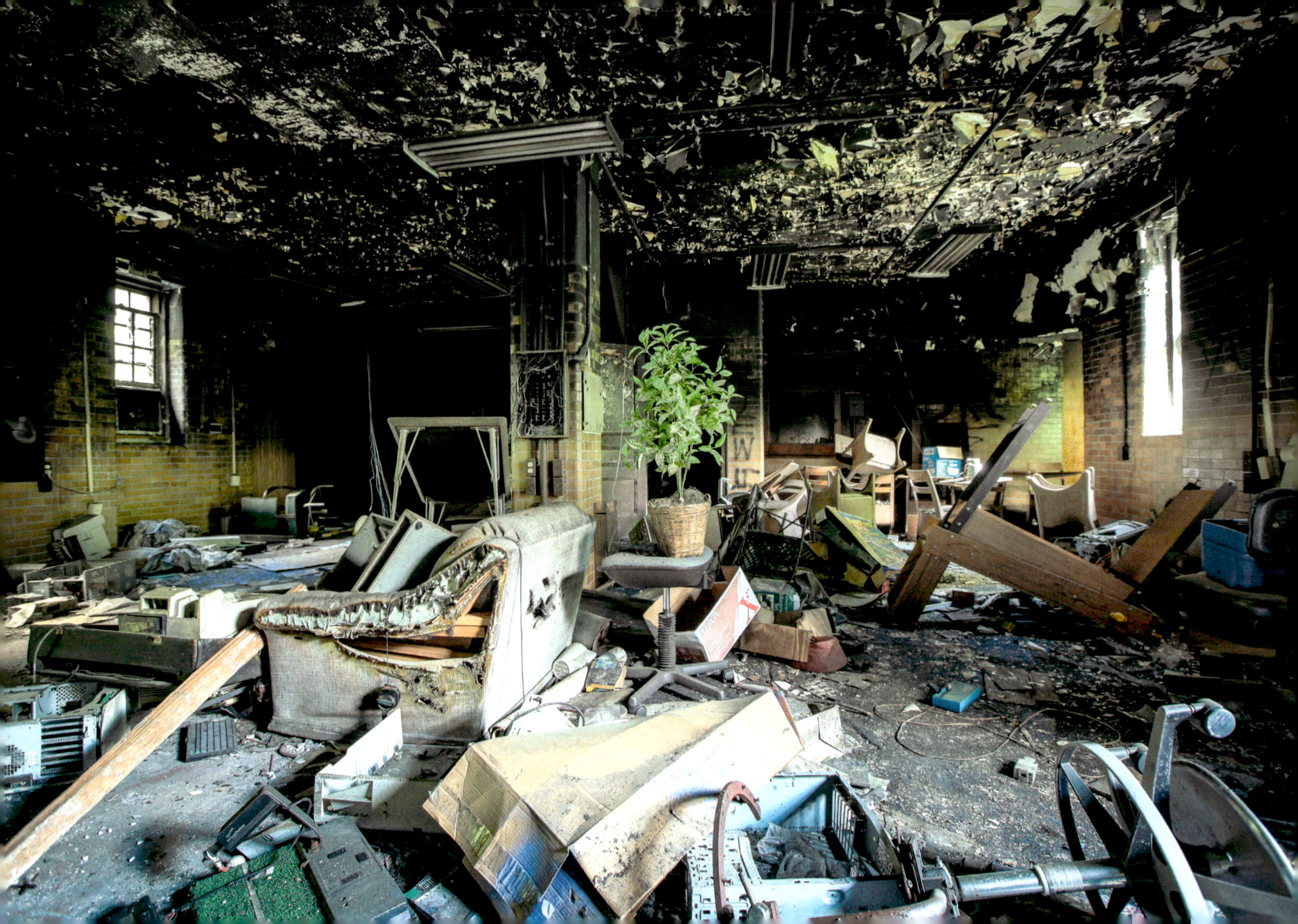

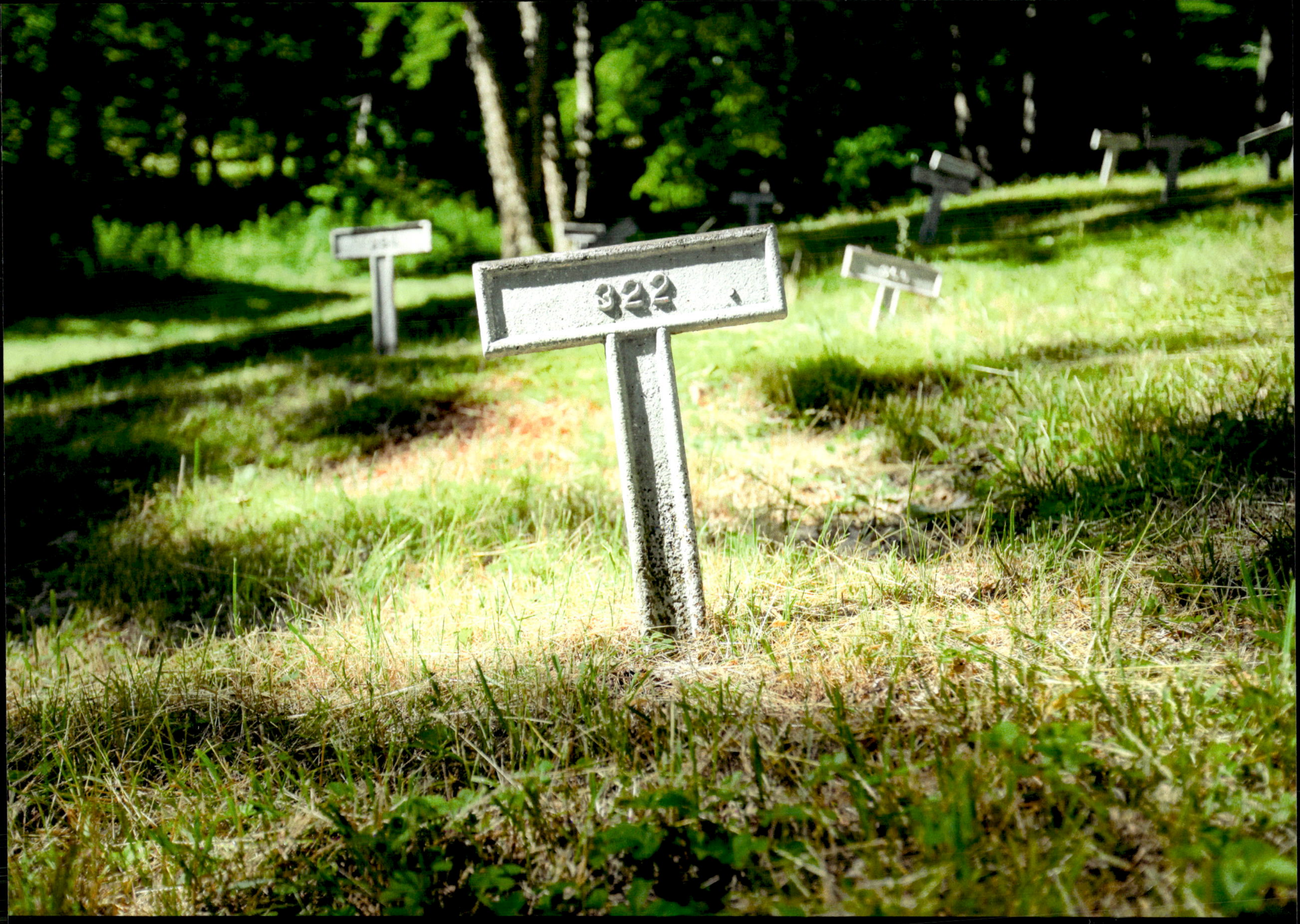

Many family secrets are buried among the
900 deceased in the Old Letchworth Village Cemetery.

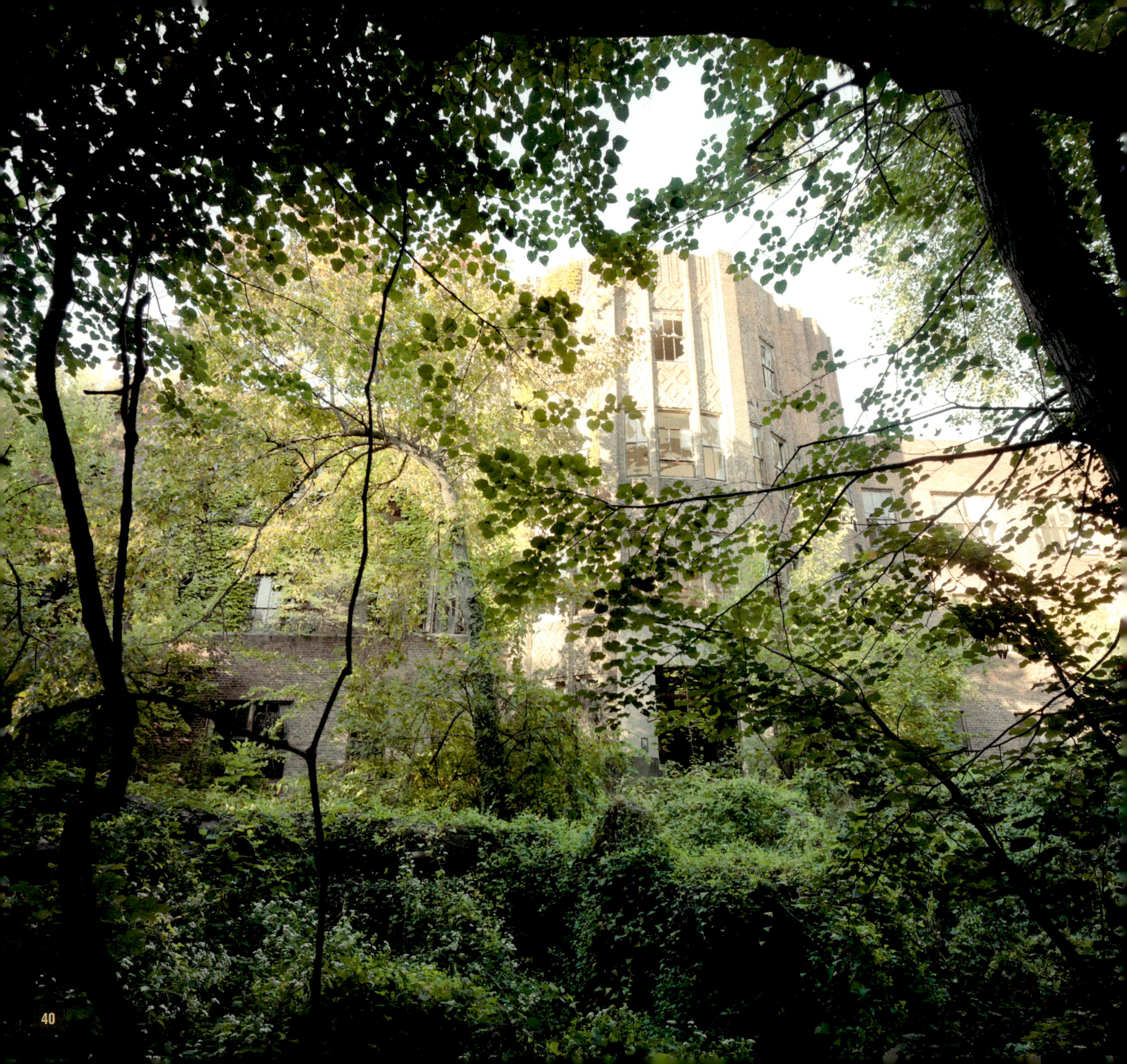

North Brother Island

Bronx, NY

opposite Riverside Hospital's Art Deco tuberculosis pavilion emerges from the wilds of North Brother Island.

On Thanksgiving Day of 1985, a homeless man took a drug-fueled dip in the East River and found himself stranded on a deserted island. He spent a week attempting to flag down passing vessels before he was finally spotted—starving, frostbitten, and completely alone—just a stone's throw from the Rikers Island jail complex. The hapless gentleman had washed up on the shore of North Brother Island, one of New York City's least accessible places, and perhaps its most mysterious. As the site of Riverside Hospital, the island once served as the city institution for quarantinable diseases, a function well suited to its complete isolation.

In the late 19th century, New York City's health department took an aggressive stance against the spread of contagious diseases, the most dreaded of which were smallpox and typhoid. As soon as a case was reported, a health inspector was dispatched to remove the sick individual and deliver them to Riverside Hospital, where they would be kept in isolation until they had either fully recovered or succumbed to their illness. Outbreaks often occurred along racial lines, erupting in the tenements among immigrant populations, who quickly grew to fear the island. Though some patients claimed they were treated with kindness and consideration at Riverside, others described a pesthouse of "filth, neglect, horrors without name." Upon inspection, the Health Commissioner found that the latter description was borne out, and appropriated $500,000 to update the hospital's dilapidated facilities.

On June 15, 1904, North Brother Island became the site of the worst maritime disaster in New York City history when the *General Slocum* capsized off its shores. The passenger ship had departed at 9:30 that morning carrying a church group on an annual picnic excursion, but by 10:00, the cheerful scene descended into chaos when a fire erupted on a lower deck and began to spread with terrifying speed. Fire hoses proved worthless when the crew attempted to respond. Doomed passengers watched life preservers sink like lead or crumble in their hands. It was later revealed that the ship's safety equipment hadn't been maintained in 13 years, which amounted to criminal negligence on behalf of the *Slocum's* captain. Over 1,000 had perished by the time the ship ran aground on North Brother Island. Nearly all were women and children.

The annals of Riverside Hospital are filled with anonymous tragedies, but one resident made international headlines as the infamous "Typhoid Mary," the Irish immigrant identified as the first asymptomatic carrier of typhoid fever in the United States. Mary Mallon was often described as a "human culture tube" by her physicians, having spread more than 50 cases of typhoid fever over the course of her career as a cook. Though outbreaks occurred in almost every household where she was employed, she never accepted responsibility and was known to violently resist authorities. After spending three years in isolation on North Brother Island, Mary was released in 1907 on the condition that she never seek employment as a cook again. She stayed out of the public eye until 1915, when health inspectors learned she was working in the kitchen of a maternity hospital under an assumed name. She spent the rest of her days in a private cottage on the south side of North Brother Island, where she reportedly adopted a philosophic attitude toward her unfortunate lot in life.

With the development of preventive medicine and the near-elimination of diseases like smallpox and cholera, Riverside was almost exclusively used as a tuberculosis hospital by the 1930s. A modernized tuberculosis pavilion was constructed in the 1940s, but the hospital closed before the new building could be used for its intended purpose. After the Second World War, the structure provided housing to returning veterans attending city colleges, though its location proved problematic. Students often missed classes when morning fog prevented the ferry from running.

By the 1950s, teenage narcotics addiction was becoming a serious problem in New York City, and Riverside Hospital was chosen as the site of an experimental treatment facility for adolescent addicts. Less than a year after Riverside was reopened, serious doubts were raised about the effectiveness of the program. Staff found it impossible to deal with the severe withdrawal symptoms and emotional problems of the population, and surveys found that 90% of those admitted relapsed soon after they were discharged. The failed experiment was abandoned in 1964 amid rumors of bribery, corruption, and sexual abuse between patients and staff.

This left the city-owned island without a concrete future, though prisons, parks, and casinos were proposed throughout the '70s and '80s. While government officials disputed these plans, the sparsely planted hospital campus was transforming into a bona fide wilderness. Today, opportunistic ivy floods the old lawns and races up the corners of the dormitories. Elsewhere, invasive kudzu holds at least an acre of land in its leafy grip. In 1995, the Parks department set its sights on the island, recognizing its importance as a bastion of plant life and a vital breeding ground for migratory birds. In 2001, the island assumed its noble role as a wildlife sanctuary. Today, North Brother Island reminds us that as much as we think we have a handle on things, nature is never far behind. Just give it time.

opposite Black cherry, American elm, and Norway maple rise from the ruins after 50 years of abandonment.

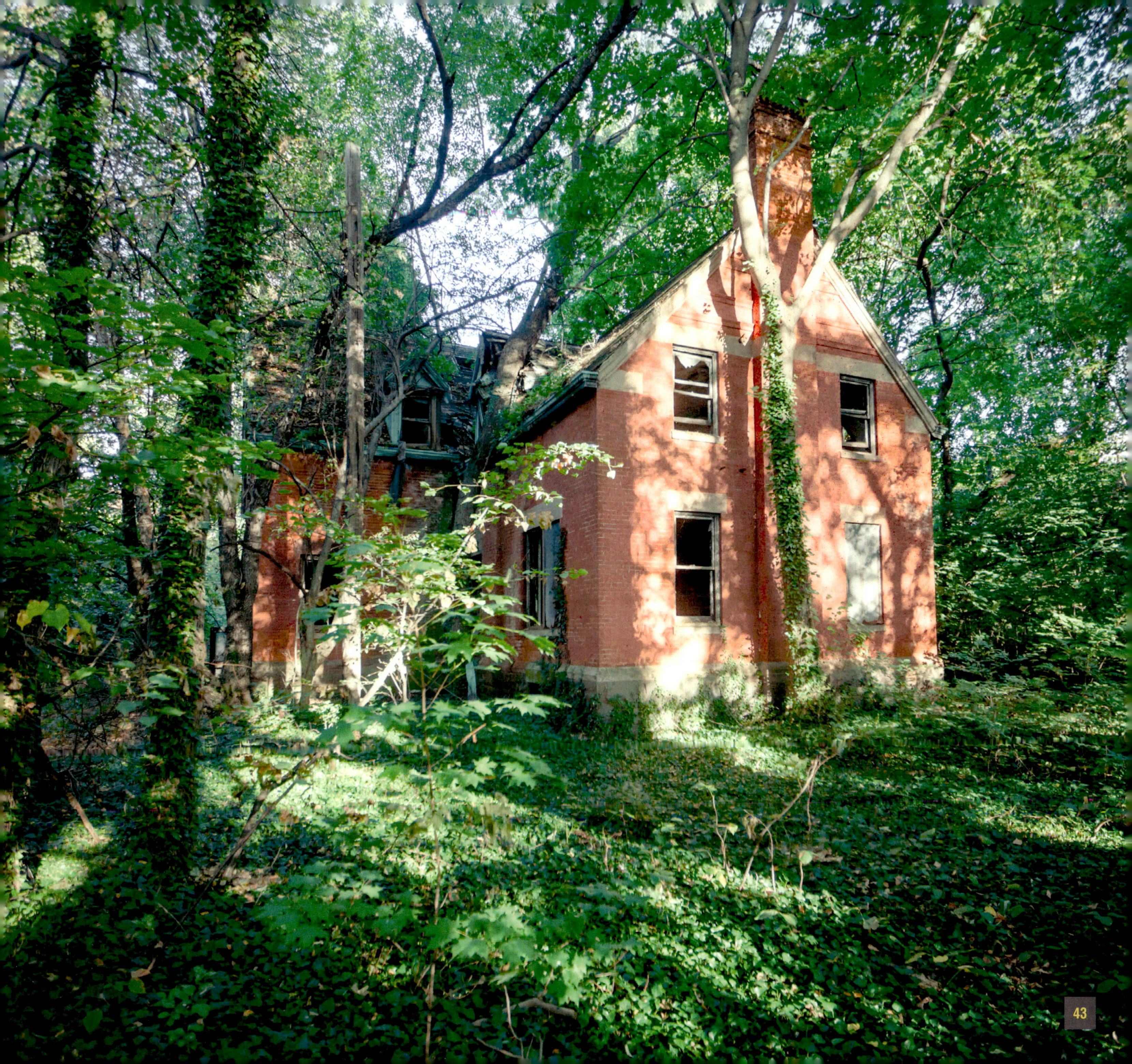

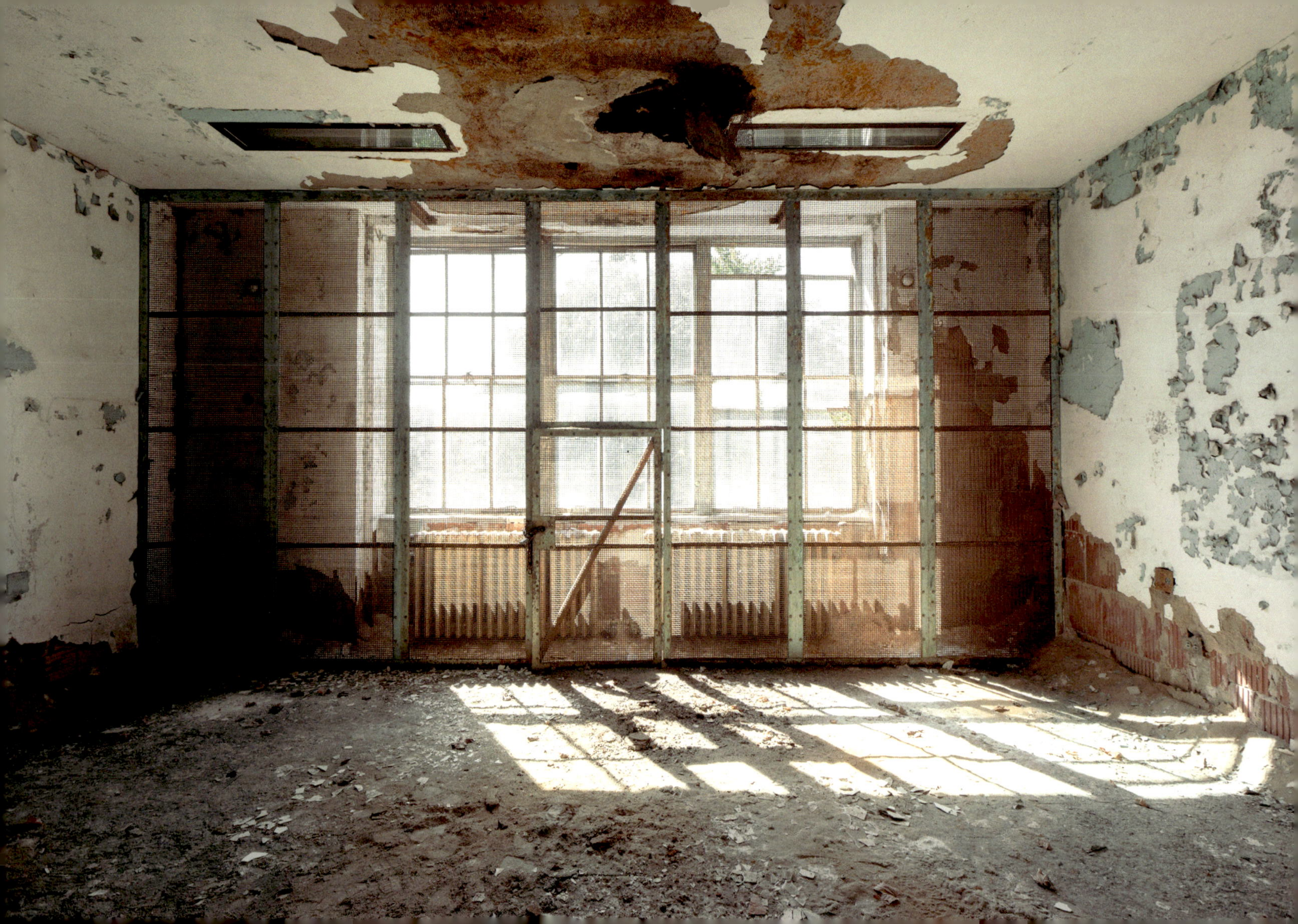

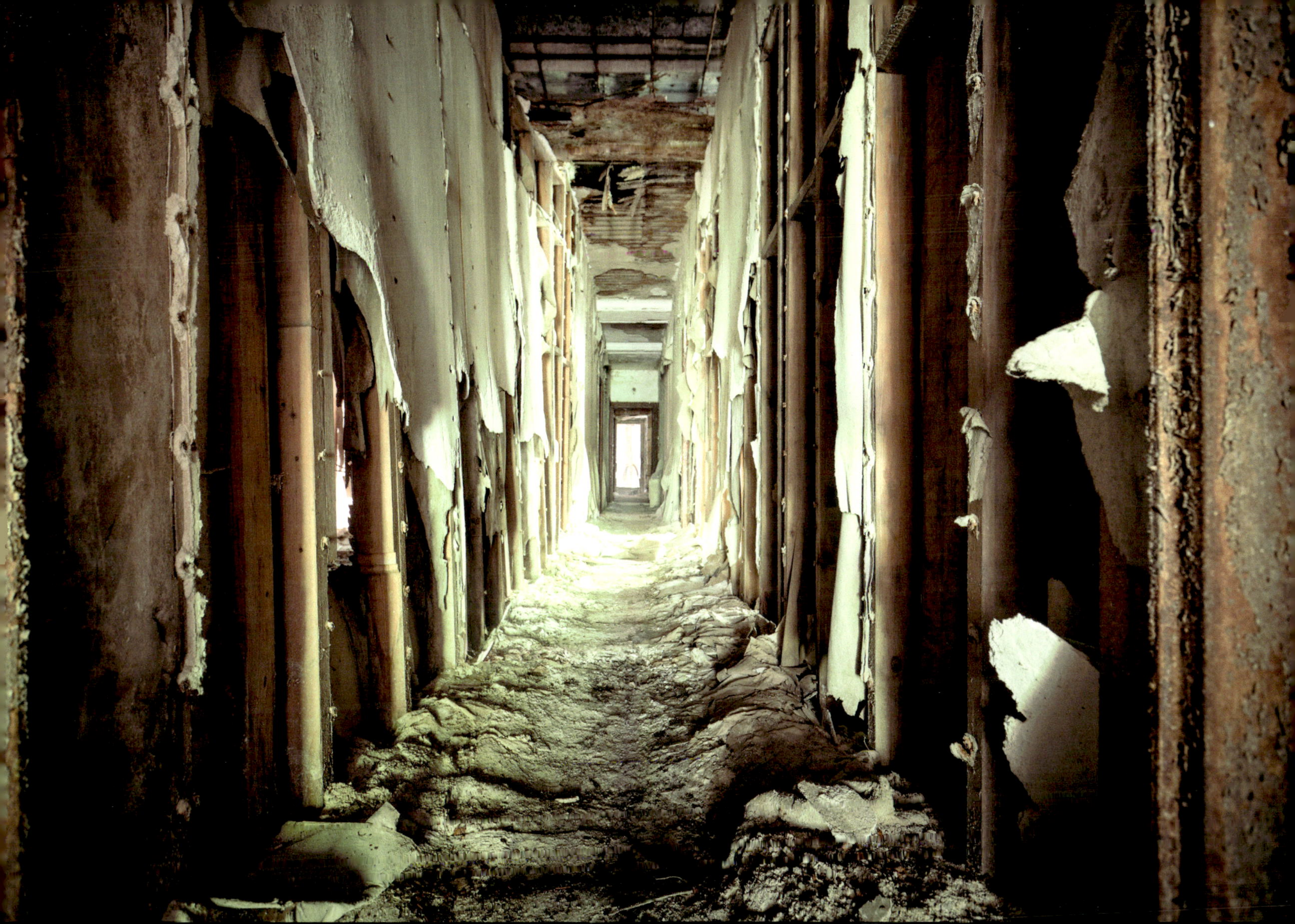

Many of the older structures are splitting at the seams, but there's little hope or interest in preserving them.

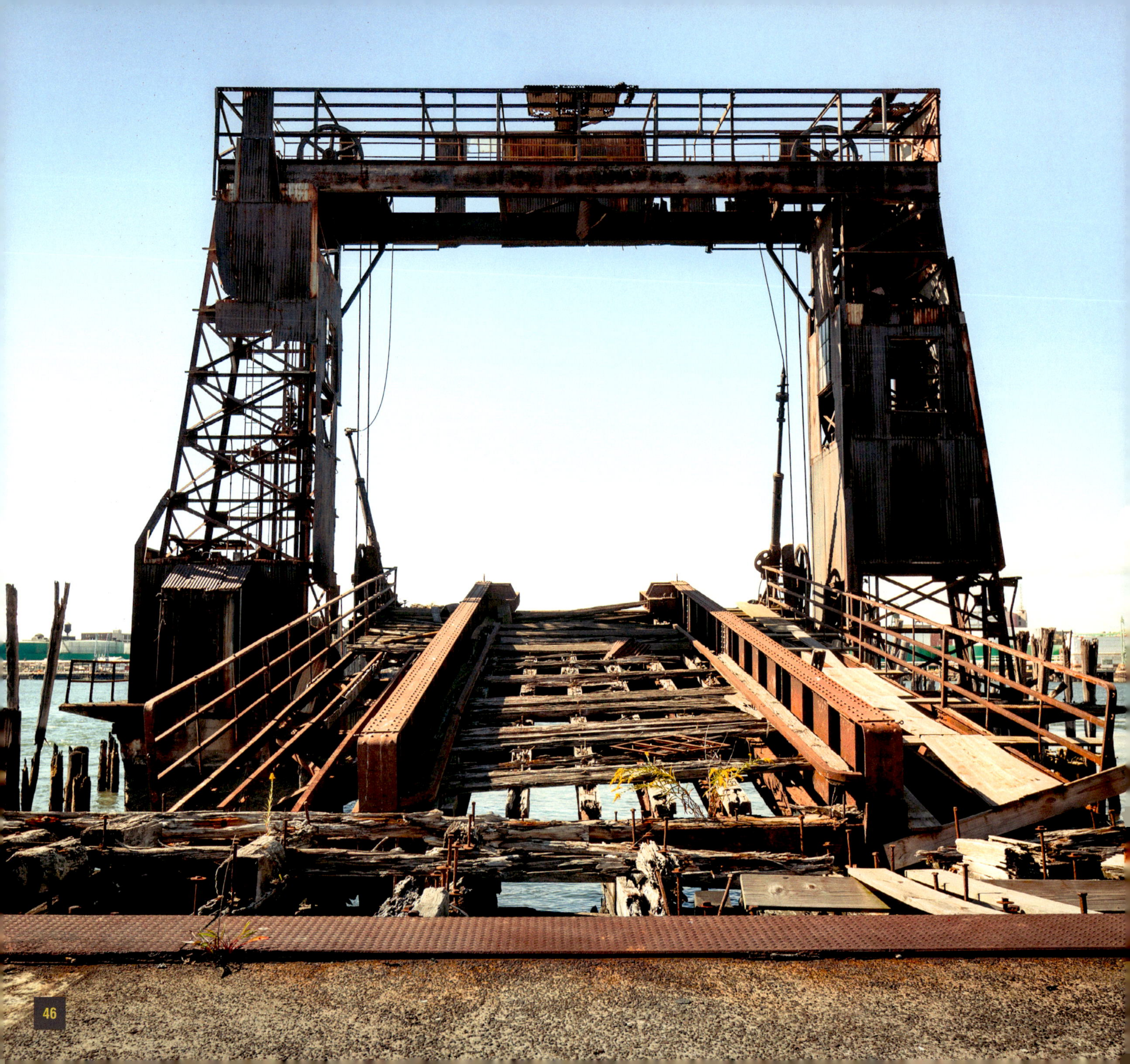

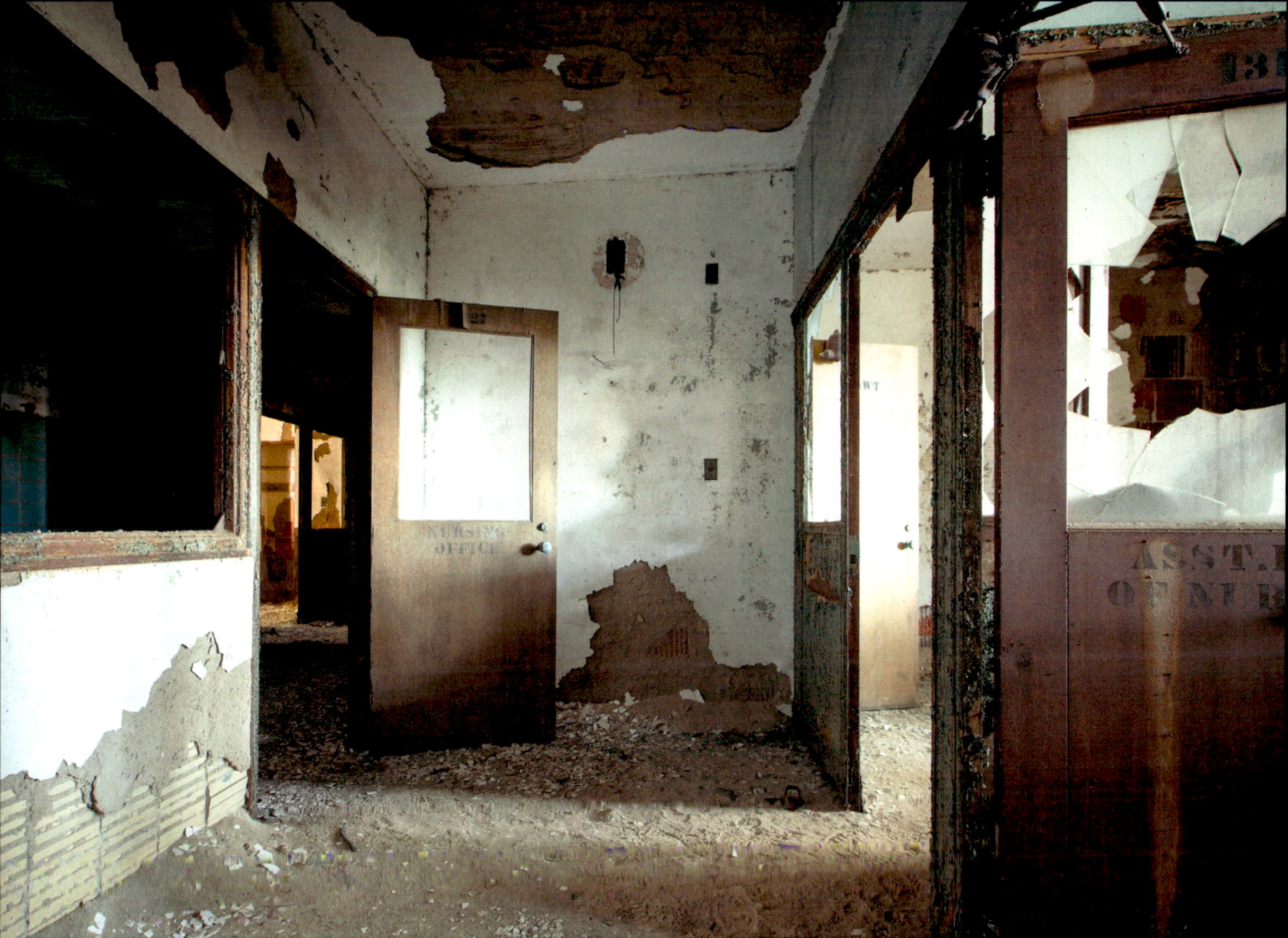

opposite During the winter months, patients were exposed to chilling blasts while being transported to this ferry landing on the west side of the island.

above Glass fixtures on the ground floor of the tuberculosis pavilion have been knocked out by vandals over the years.

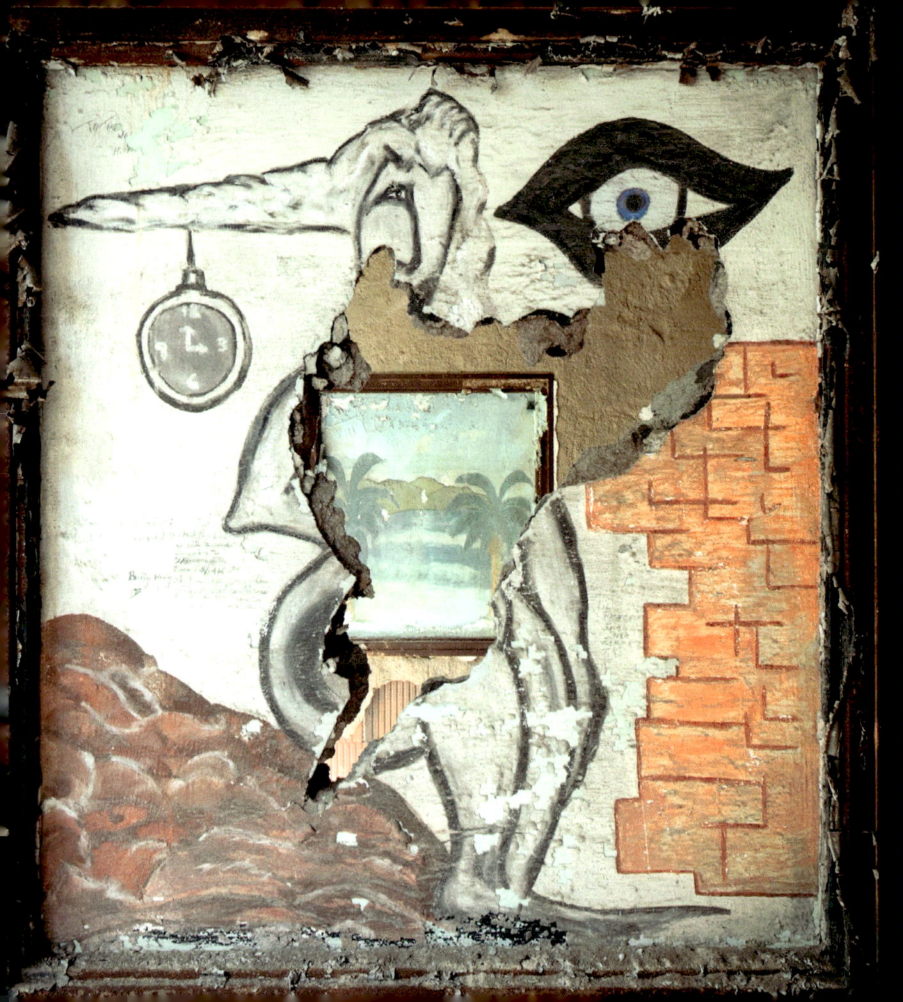

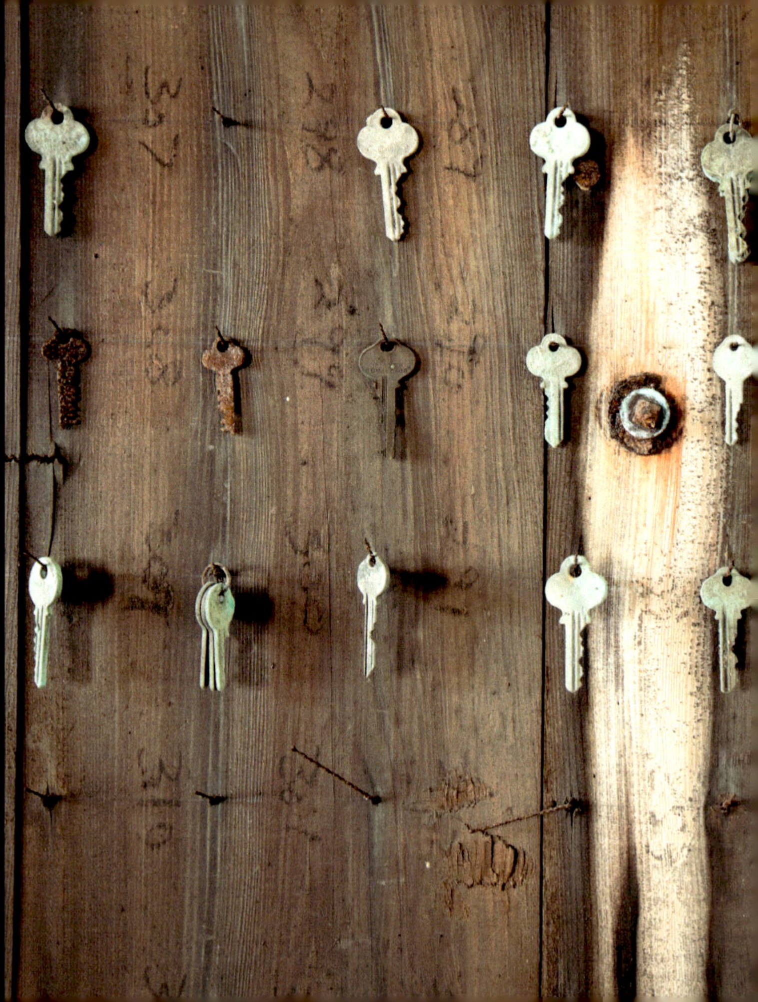

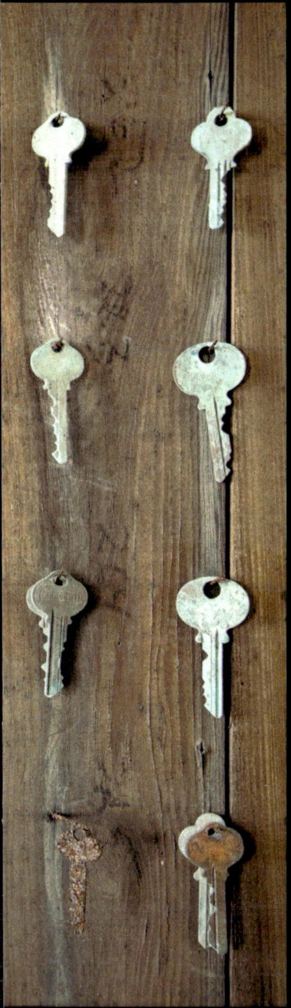
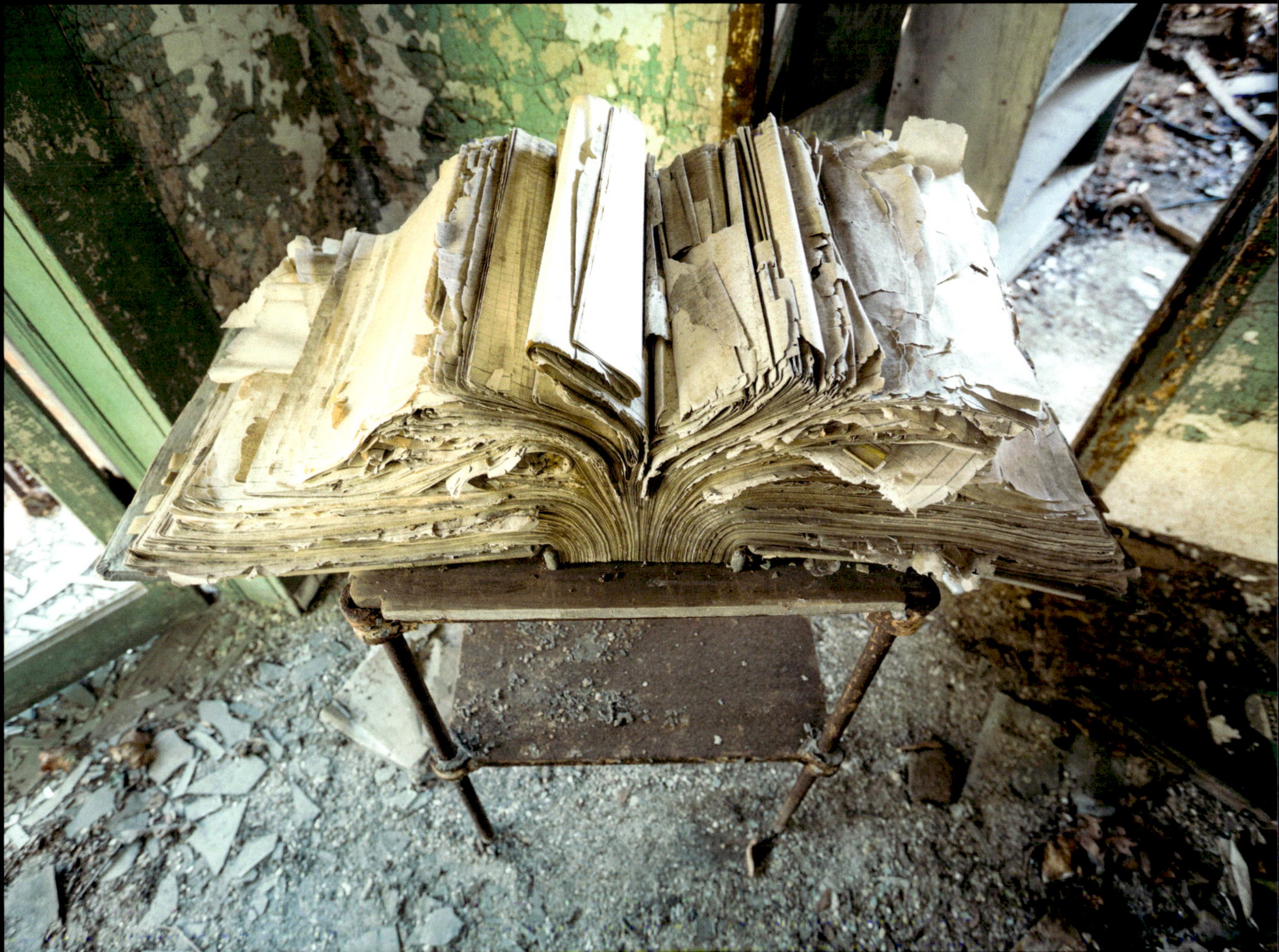

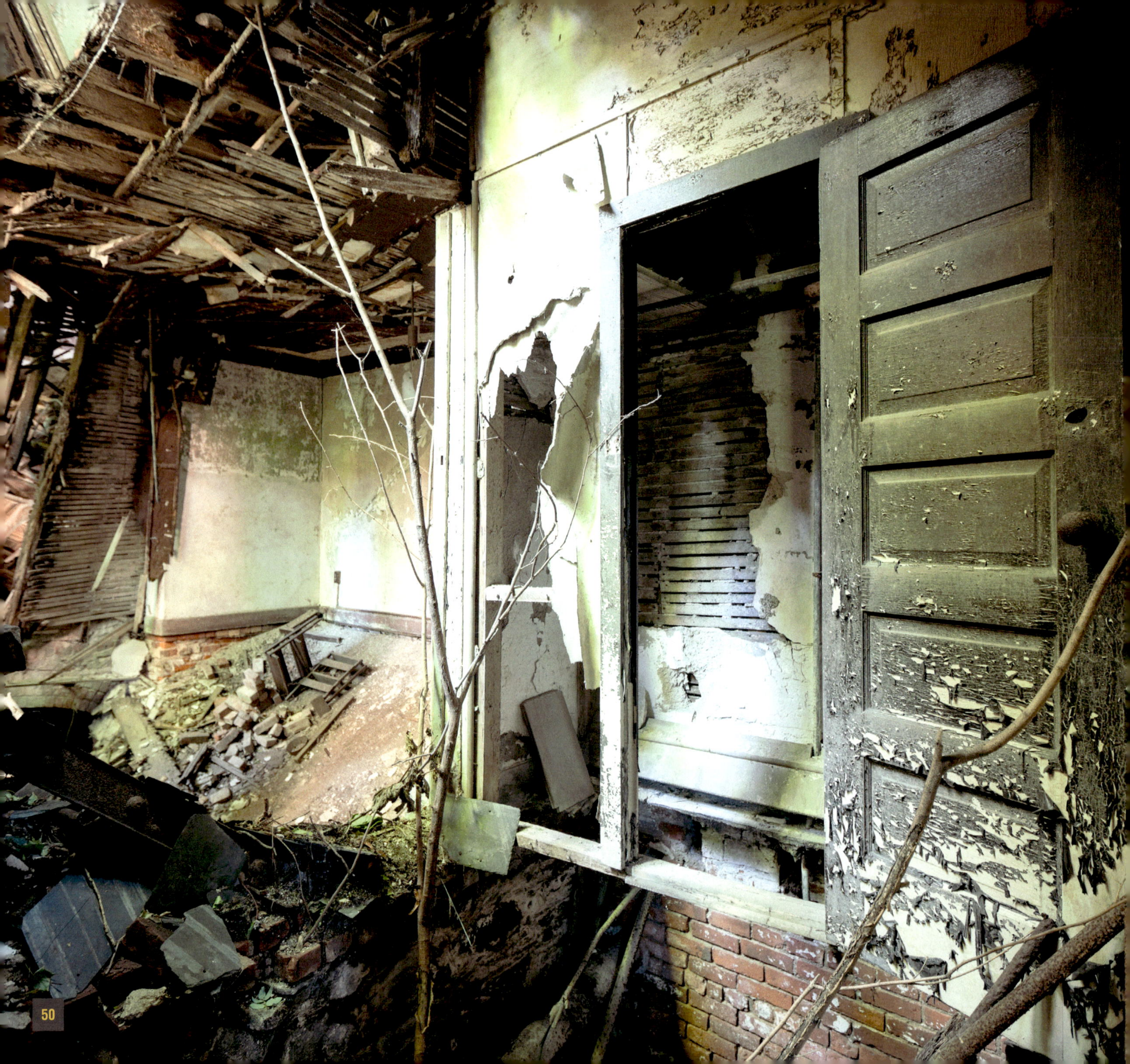

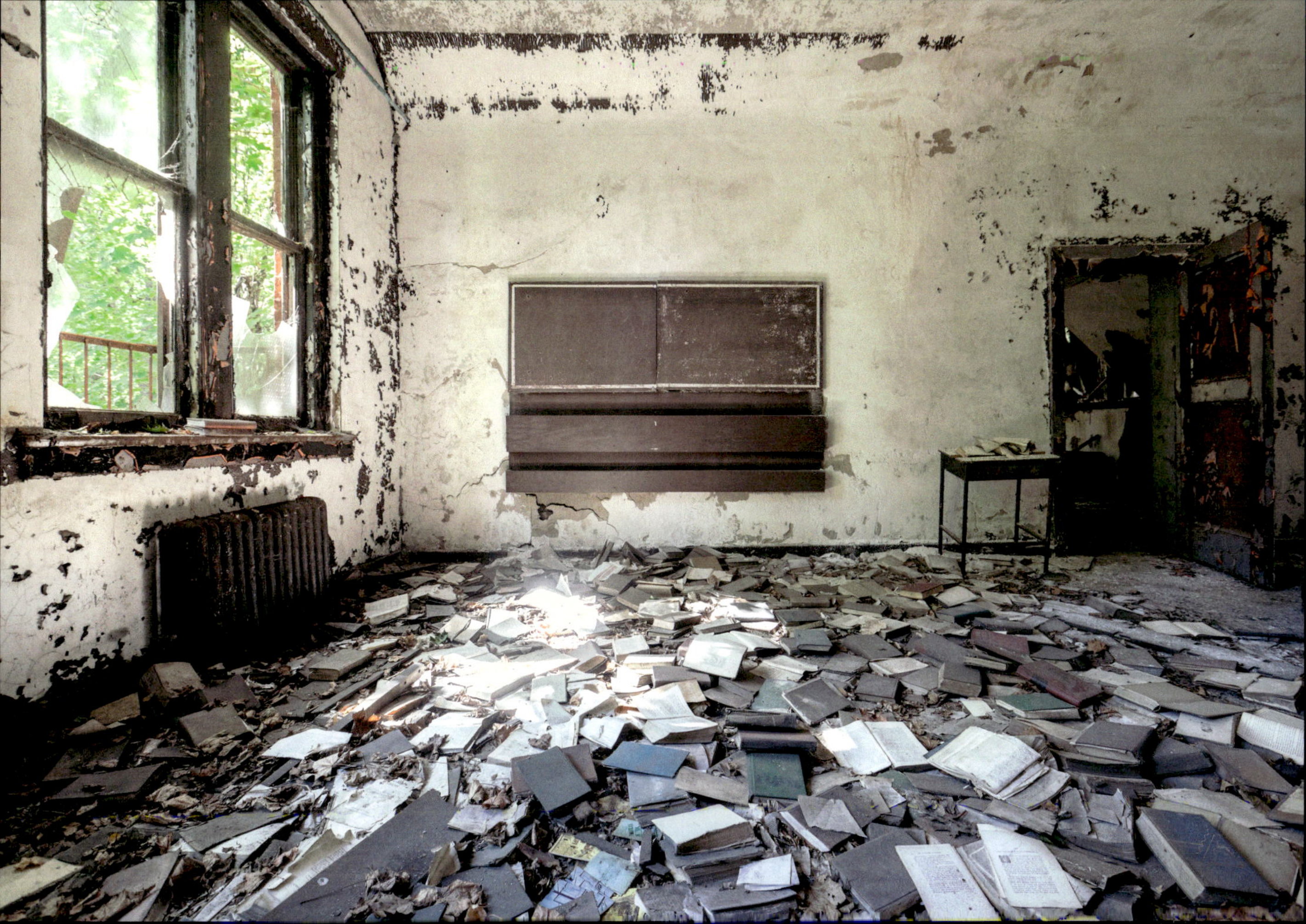

opposite In the collapsed central section of a doctor's cottage saplings take root in a room without floors.

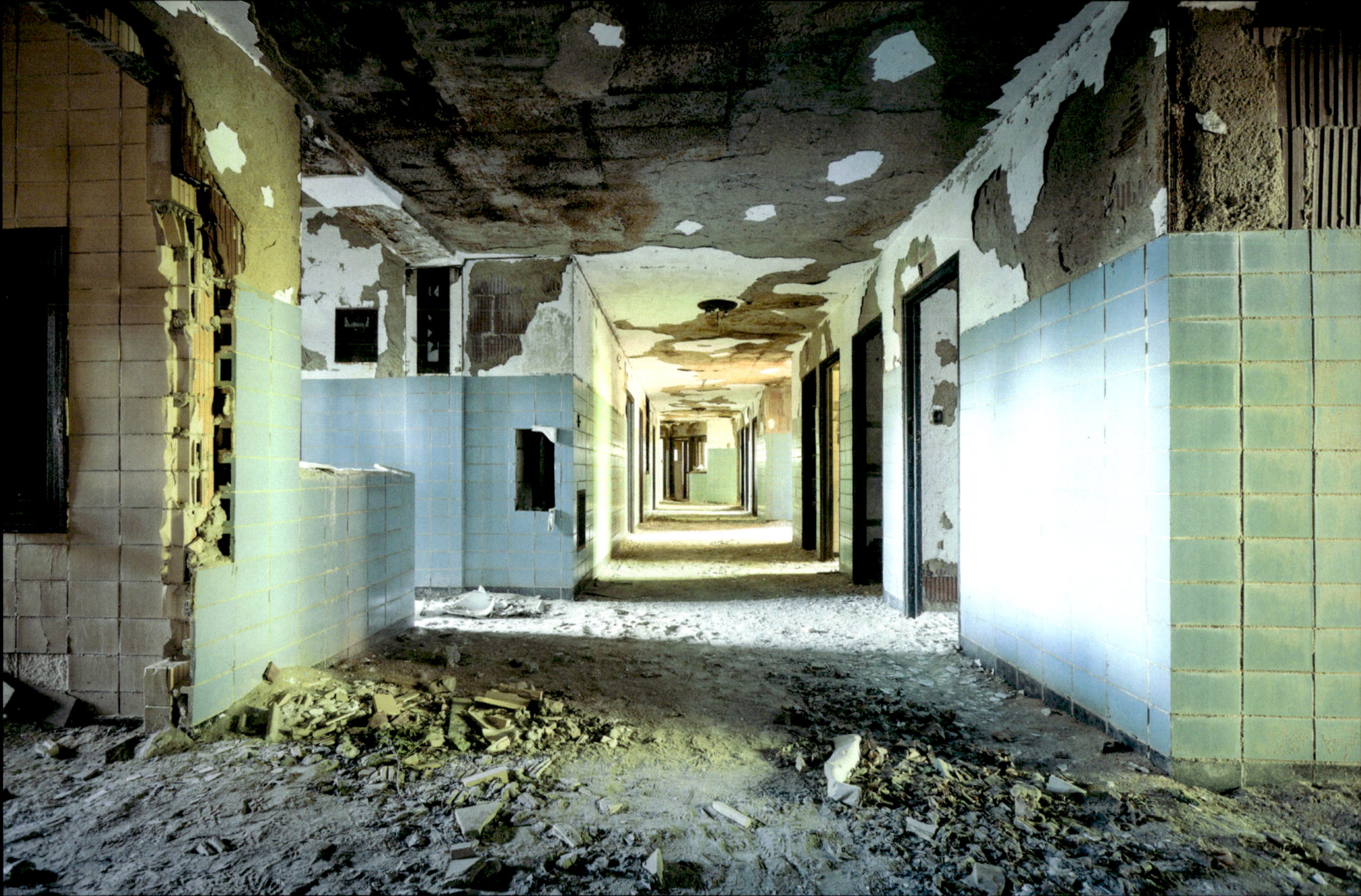

above Interiors exhibit a striking lack of graffiti, though much of the island was vandalized in the 1970s.

opposite An attractive spiral staircase leans precariously in the nurses' residence.

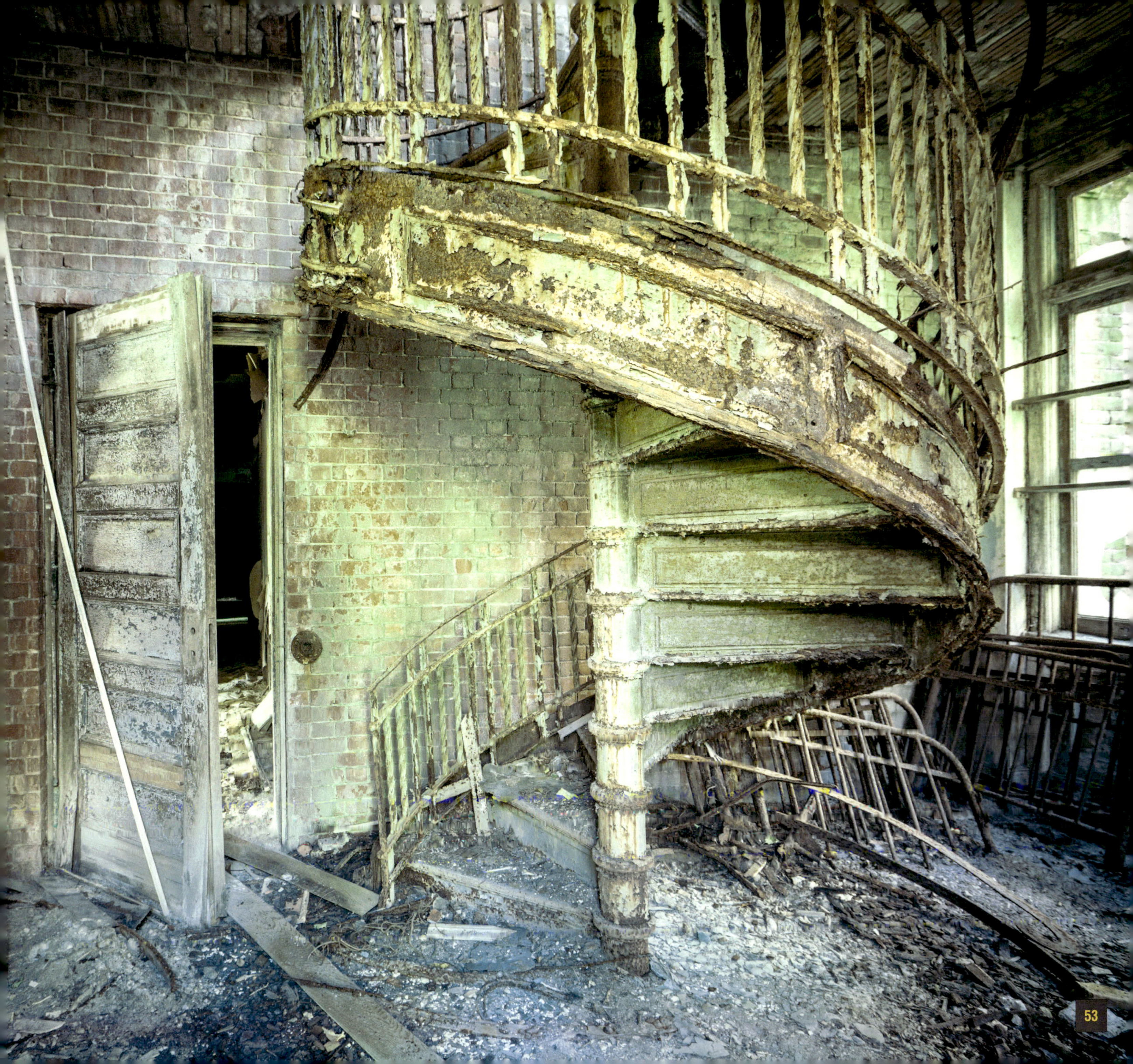

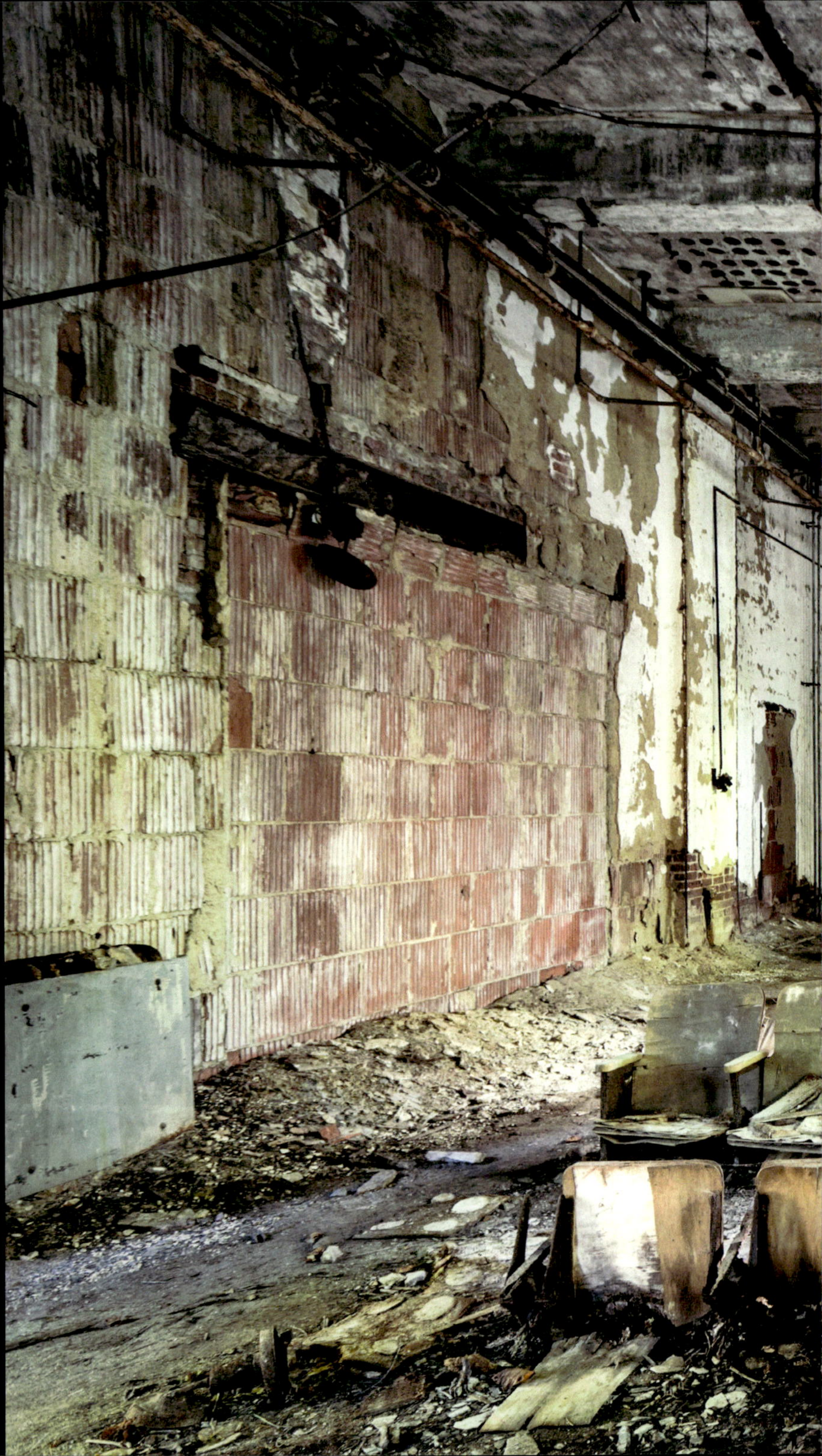

Jewel tones reflected from the outdoors illuminate a moldering auditorium.

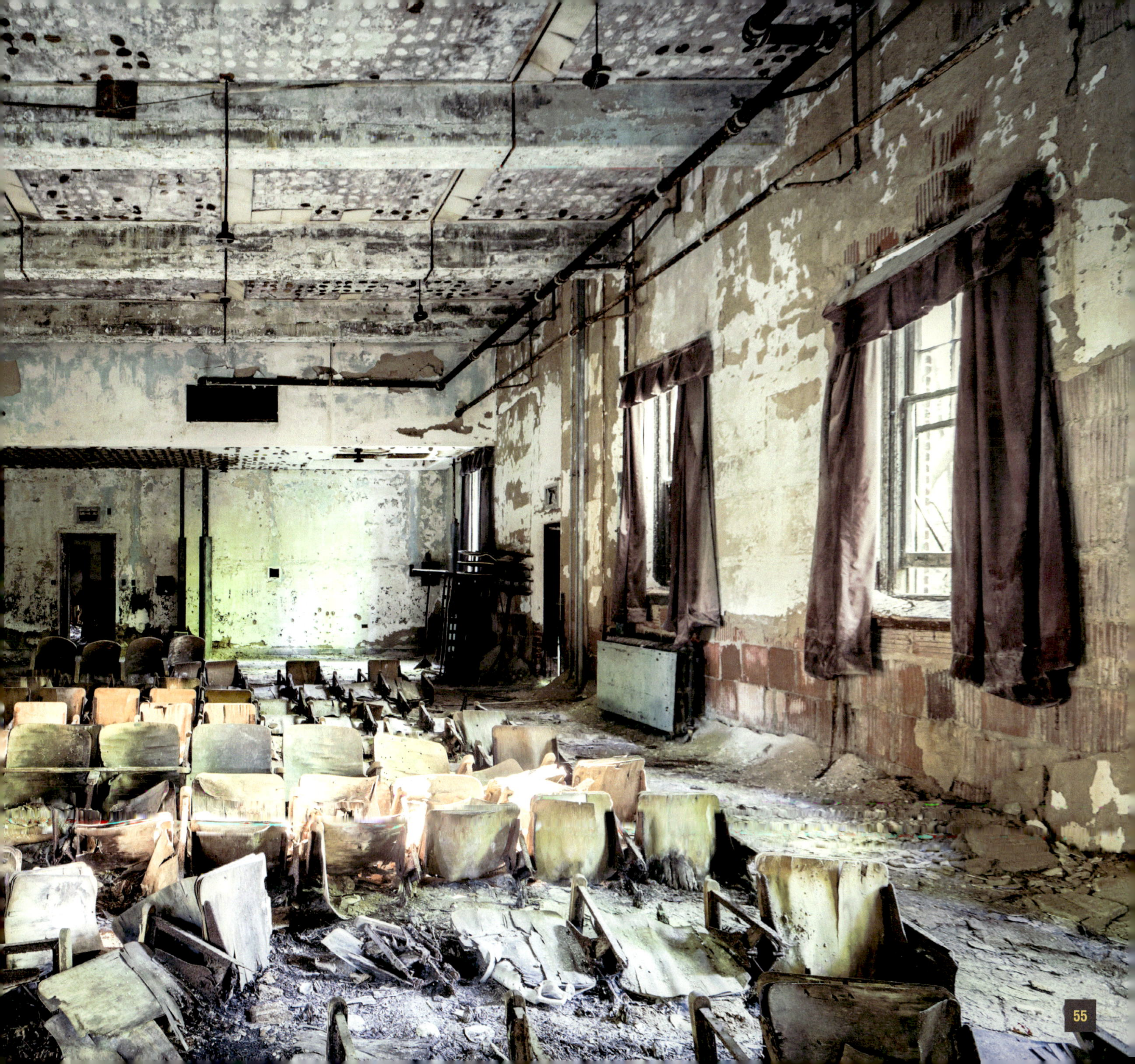

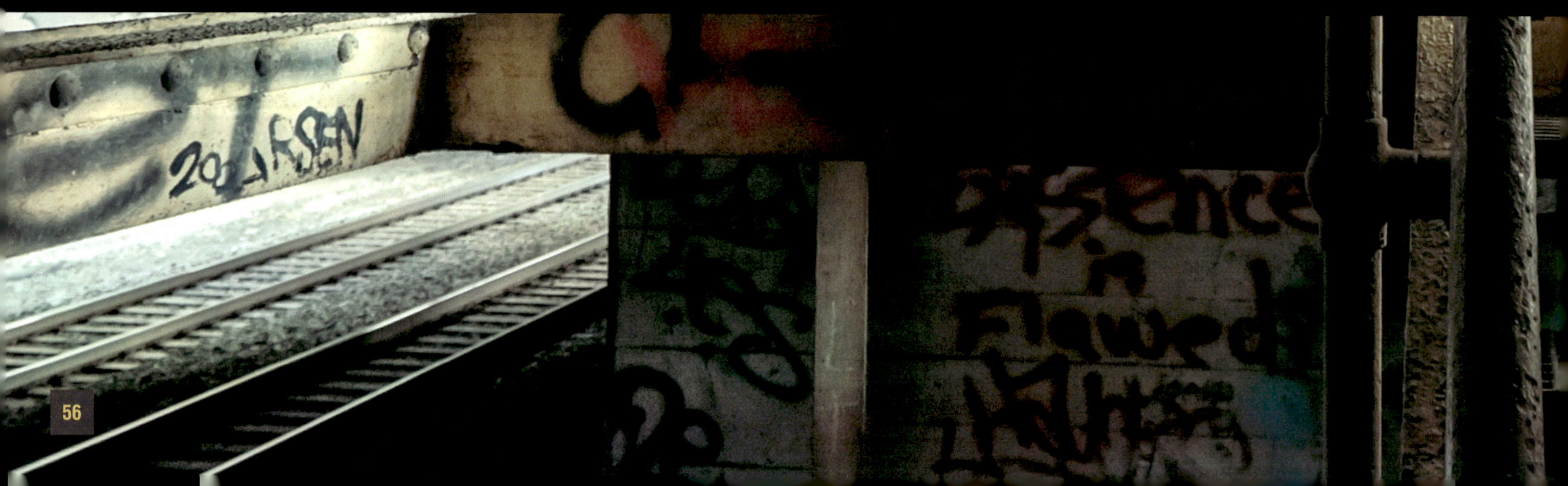

Railroads and Waterfronts

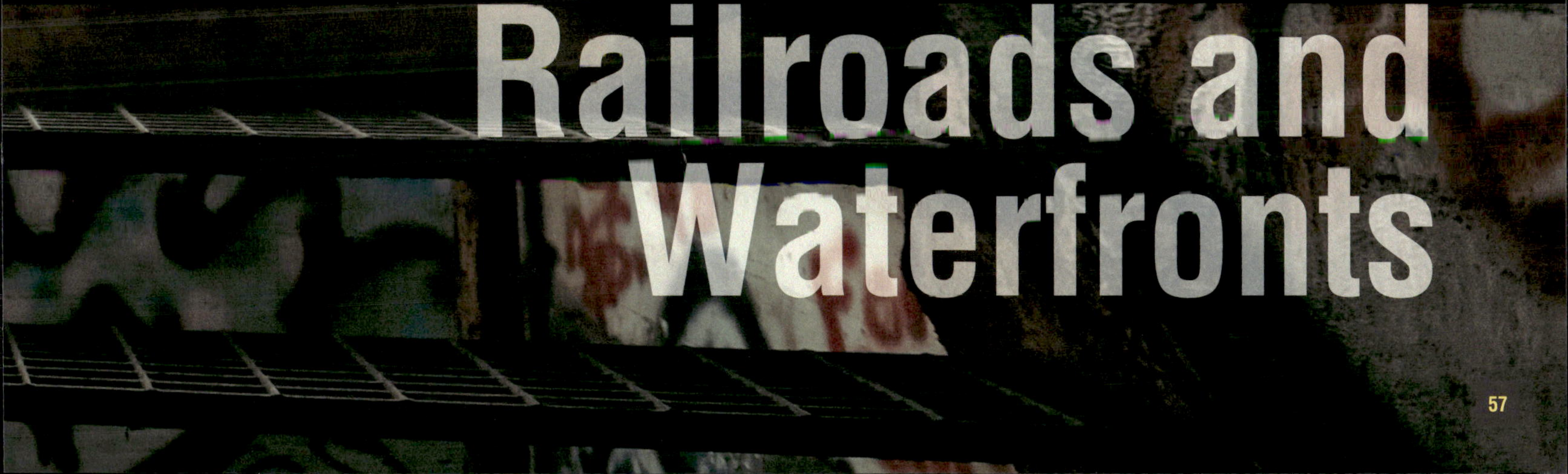

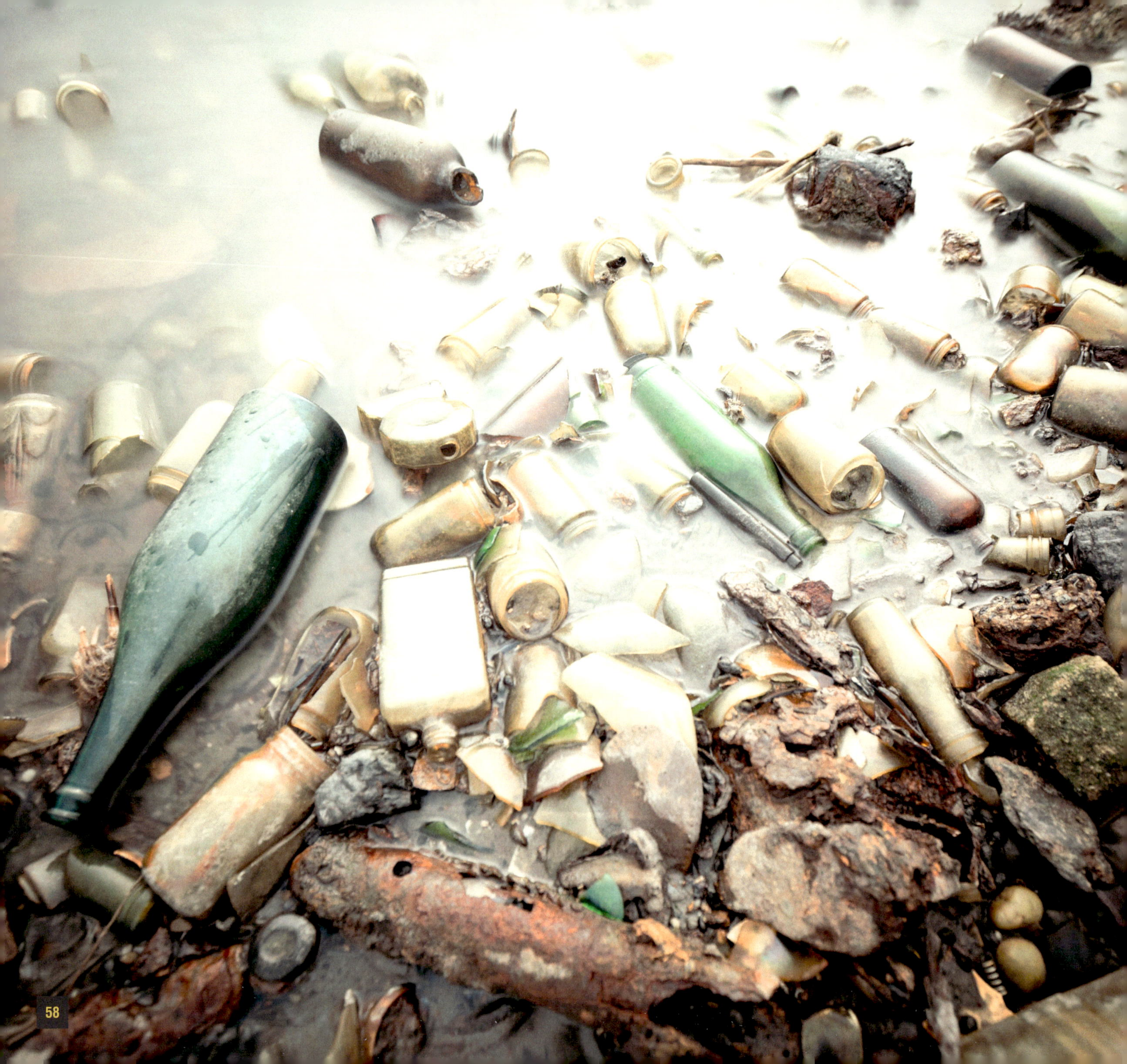

Dead Horse Bay

Southeast Brooklyn

On an isolated landmass that was once called Barren Island, there's a small notch of shoreline with a ghastly name and a ghoulish history. It's difficult to conceive of a more sickening enterprise than the industries that thrived at Dead Horse Bay, which once served New York City as the final destination for its equine dead.

Beginning in the 1850s, when carriages ruled the roadways, deceased horses were harvested from the city streets and delivered to gargantuan rendering plants on the shores of Dead Horse Bay, where they were boiled, masticated, and steamed into various products, including glue. By 1895, new facilities were constructed that were capable of processing all of New York City's garbage, replacing the tried and true method of dumping the trash into the city's waterways. Waste material was put through a lengthy industrial process that converted the refuse to saleable fertilizers and oils used in soap making, of all things.

During the late 1800s, the island was home to about 500 Polish and Italian immigrants, all of whom were supported by the factories at Dead Horse Bay. Families lived in close quarters under miserable conditions, with little to connect them to the outside world. Born and raised on the island, most workers passed on their livelihood to future generations. In 1897, the population was beleaguered by an outbreak of diphtheria, which doctors at the time blamed not on the residents' working conditions but their ignorance of the "rules of health."

If you were living in south Brooklyn at the turn of the 20th century, you might not know how to get to Barren Island, but you certainly knew how it smelled. When the wind was right, the charnel stench of putrefied animal carcasses and liquid garbage could travel six to ten miles, causing hotel patrons in nearby Manhattan Beach to evacuate and property values to plummet. On the state and local levels, concerned citizens tried in vain to abolish the factories, but no one at the time expressed concern for the workers themselves.

A series of disasters in the early 20th century marked the beginning of the end for Barren Island's industrial boom. In 1905, workers were convinced that the island was collapsing into the bowels of the earth when a full acre of land sank into the Jamaica Bay. The event was attributed to submarine quicksand, but many who fought against the factories saw it as an act of divine providence. The following year, two of the largest plants burned to the ground in a blaze that covered 16 acres. In 1909, the island was infested with upwards of 1,000 wild hogs, prompting a hunting party of police officers to raid the island. The night ended with what had to have been a legendary barbecue.

opposite At low tide, century-old garbage covers the shores of Dead Horse Bay, which is known by some locals as "Bottle Beach."

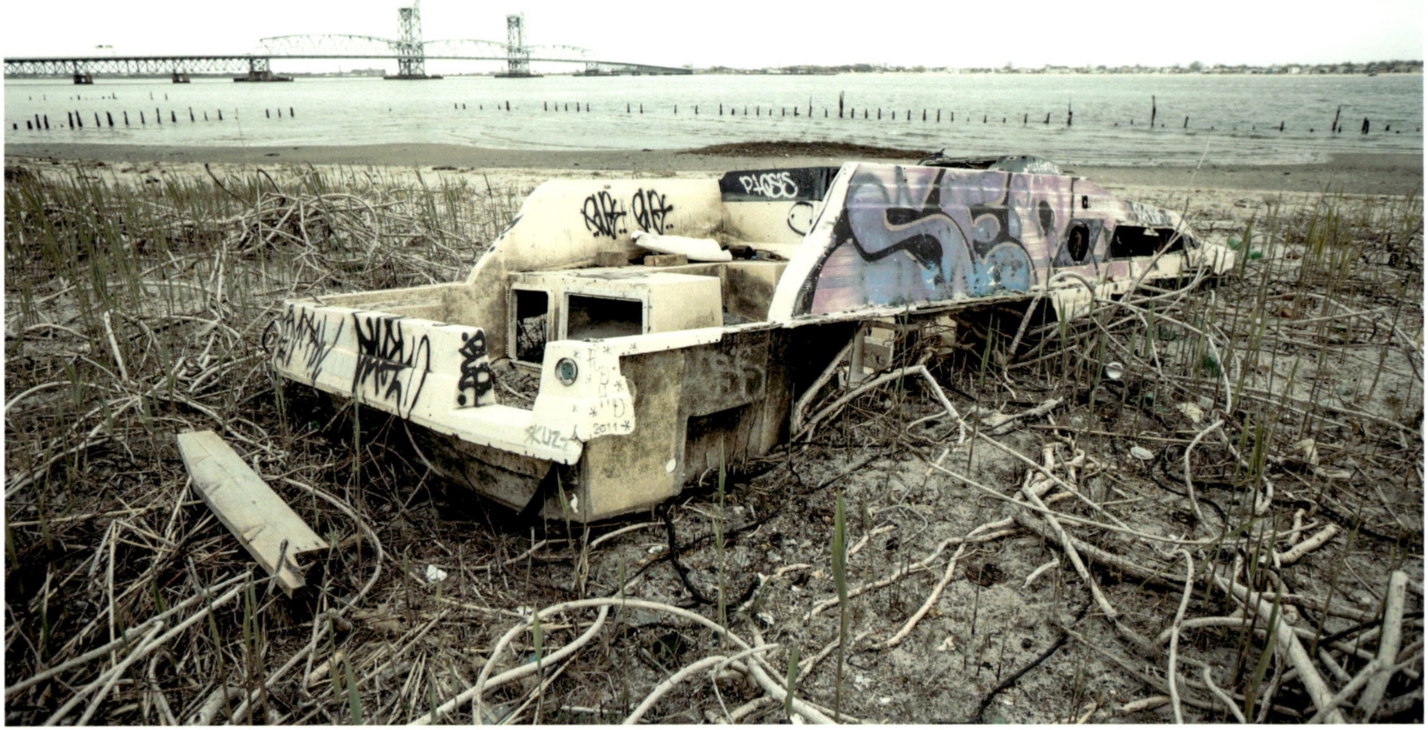

With the rise of the automobile, dead horses became a dying industry, and the factories at Dead Horse Bay began shutting down. In 1926, Barren Island was connected to the mainland with landfill as part of the Flatbush Avenue Extension, and later filled in for the construction of New York's first municipal airport (see Floyd Bennett Field, page 85). For so many years, garbage had been the lifeblood of the island; now it was literally composed of it.

Over the next 70 years, erosion has caused the man-made beach at Dead Horse Bay to dissipate, exposing a broken landfill cap. With each successive tide, more garbage is sifted out of the shoreline, offering a fascinating look at what New Yorkers were throwing away in the 1920s. Most sunny days, you'll see half a dozen people on the beach, filling plastic bags with sandy discoveries. Without knowing it, the beachcombers at Dead Horse Bay are enacting a tradition, endowing useless objects with fabricated value on a stretch of shoreline that seems predestined for the purpose. What is the strange alchemy at work at Dead Horse Bay?

Several years after the last rendering plant shuttered, many of the factory workers and their families stayed behind in a shantytown on the edge of the Jamaica Bay. When the last of these residents were evicted in 1939, a *Times* reporter observed an intriguing detail—over several generations of garbage picking, the families had built up a trove of prized possessions. Living in squalor, without running water or plumbing, they furnished their shacks with silver, set their tables with fine china, and decked their wives with jewels. They must have felt right at home in this landscape of contradictions.

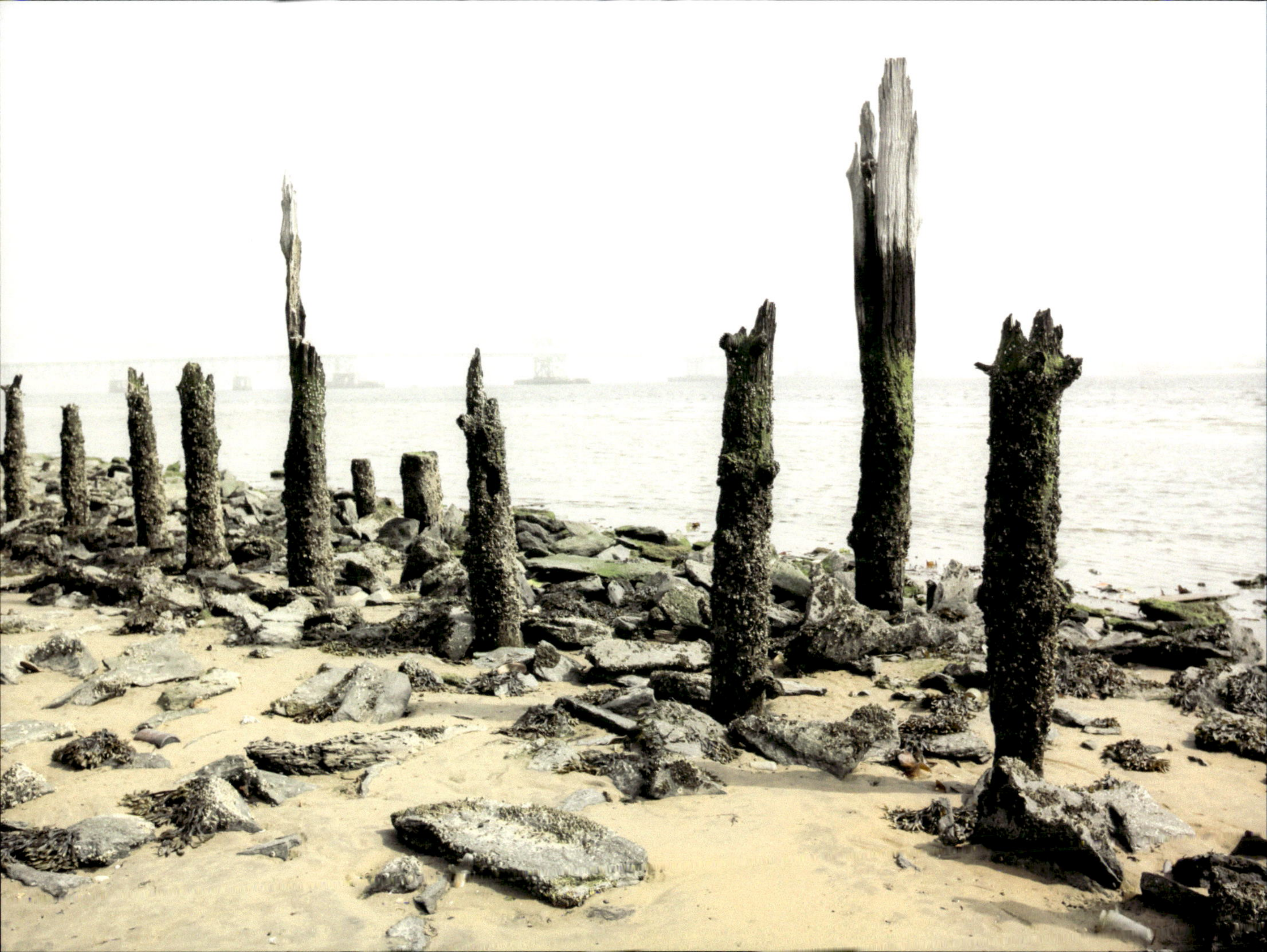

opposite A population of abandoned watercraft is constantly shuffled by storms.

above Nothing remains of the factories that once lined the shore, but there are plenty of artifacts to go around

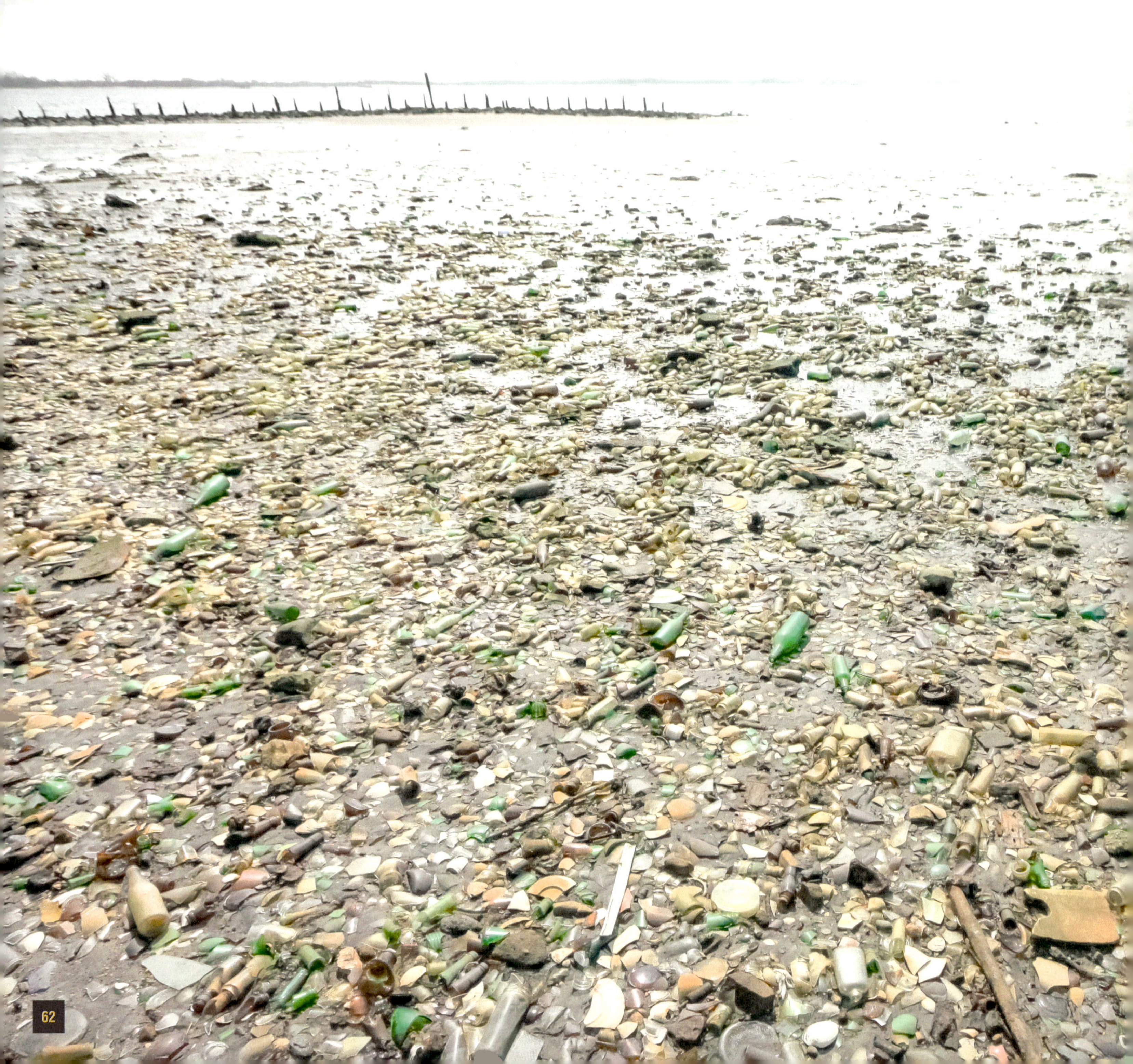

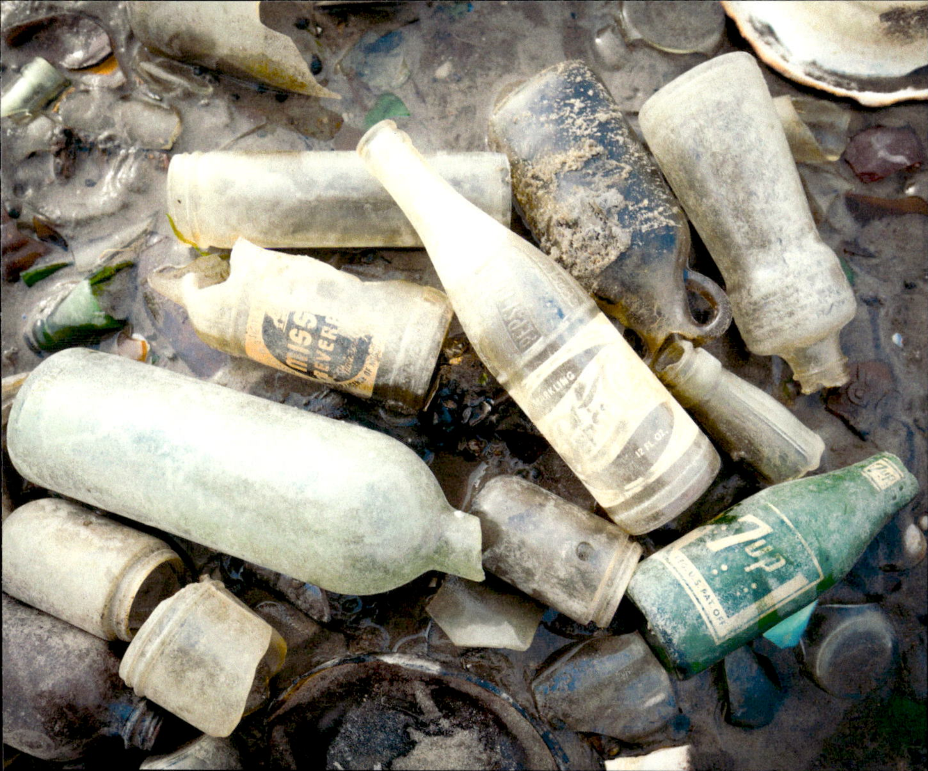

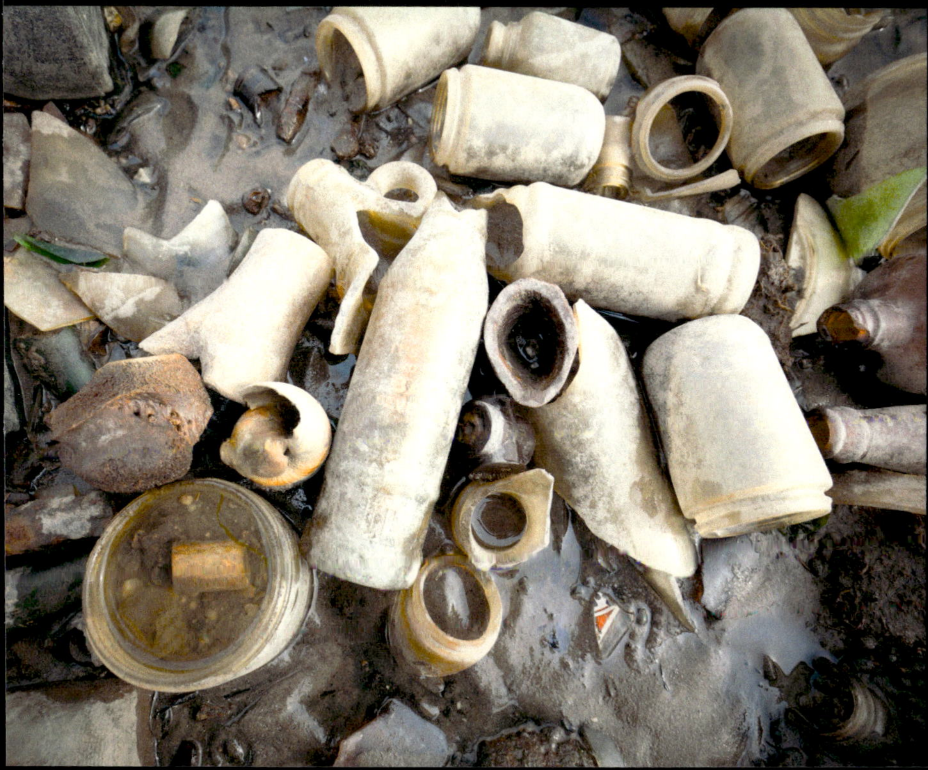

opposite Finds from Dead Horse Bay are scattered on mantles and windowsills across New York City.

top Vintage graphics for familiar brands can be found on many of the artifacts.

bottom Some of the garbage could date back over 150 years—you're guaranteed to spot a few segments of horse bone from the area's industrial age.

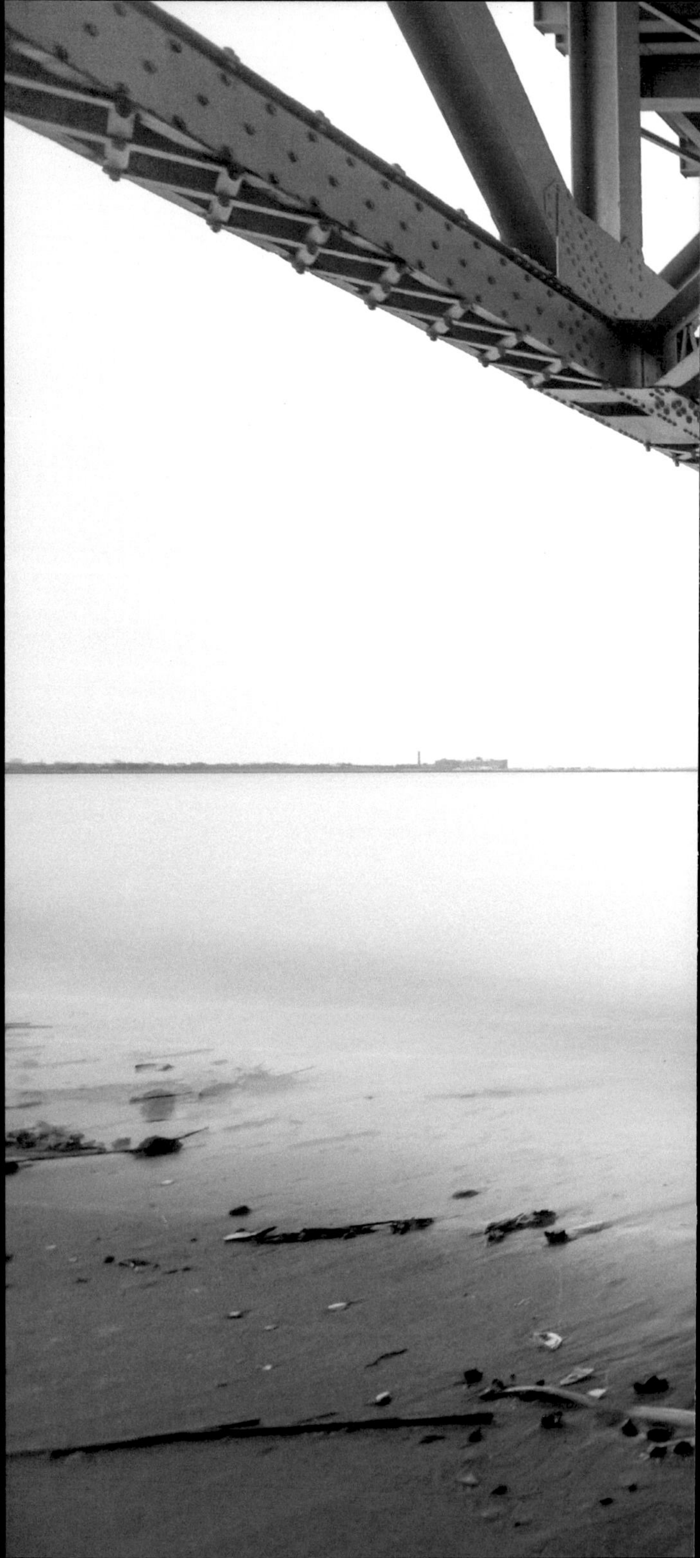

Beneath the Marine Parkway Bridge, a dead skate rots on a desolate shoreline.

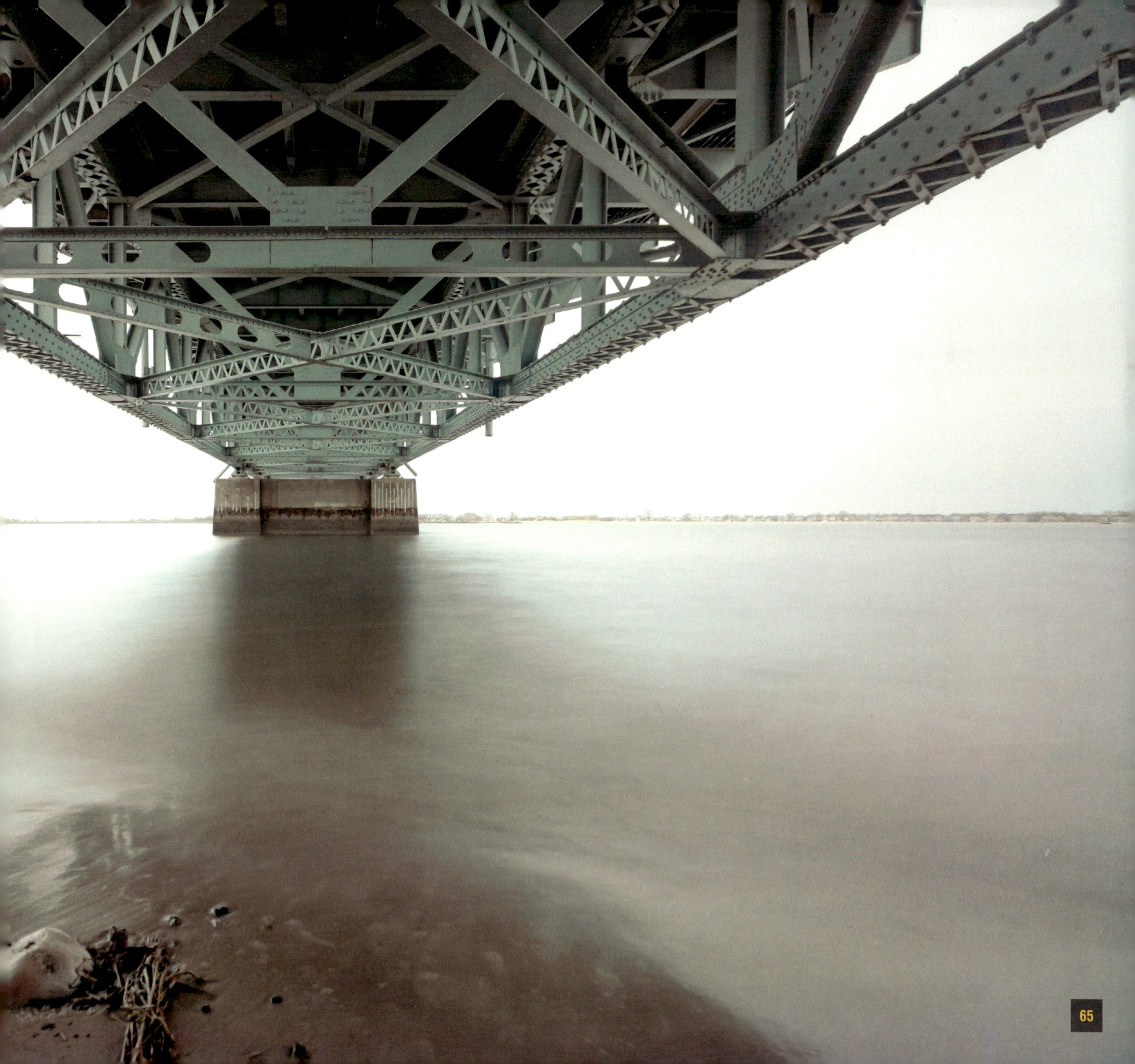

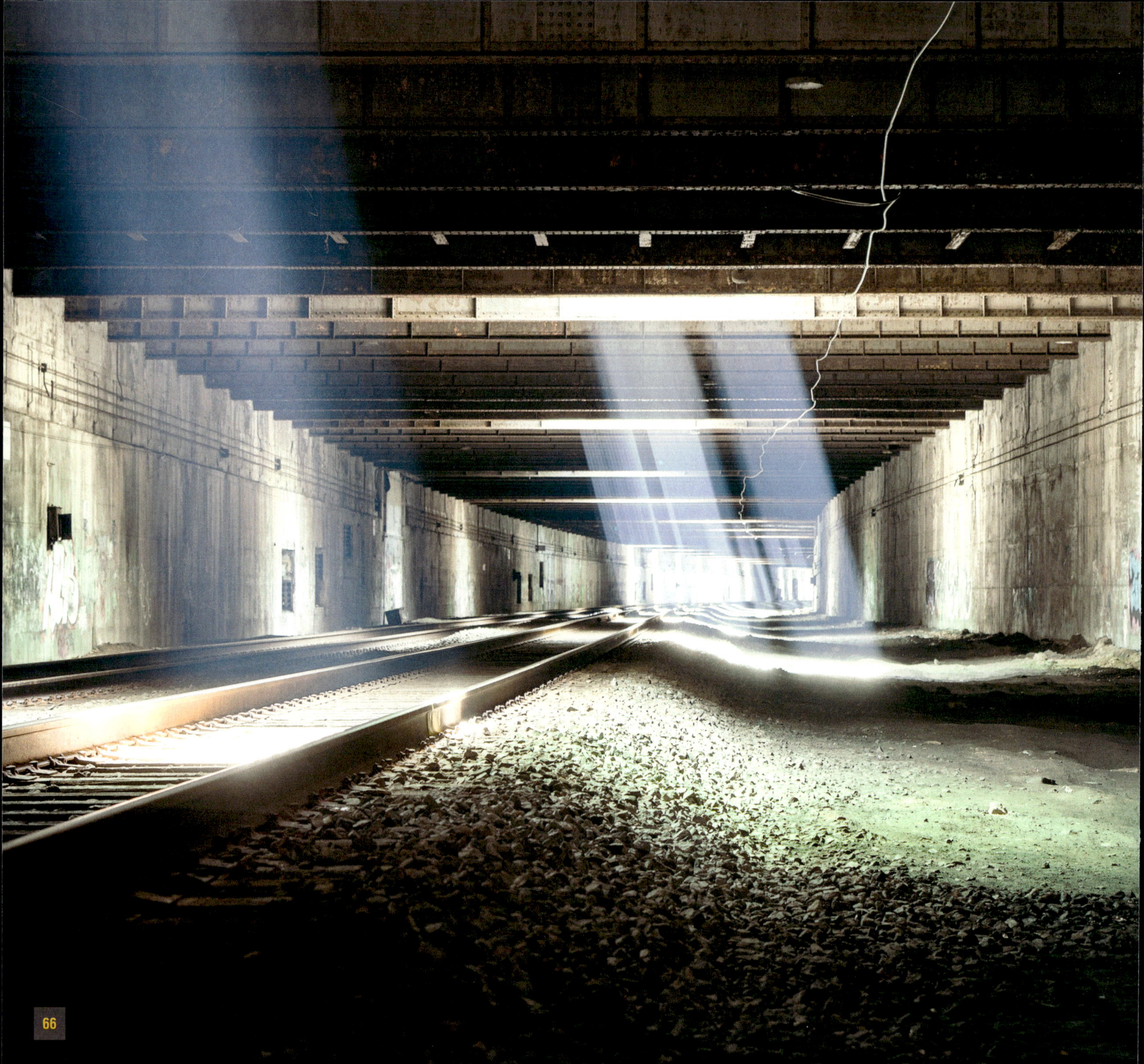

The Freedom Tunnel

Upper West Side, Manhattan

Even in New York's most isolated spaces, you're walking in the footsteps of multitudes. Skimming two and a half miles of Upper West Side shoreline under Riverside Park, the Freedom Tunnel remains the most well-known, well-traveled, and well-documented section of the city's "off-limits" subterranean transit system. Trains stick right on schedule, tracks are clear of litter, rats don't run, but something's amiss in the tunnel today. Where have the mole people gone?

The West Side Line has been inhabited for decades, as late as 2011, but there's no trace of the colony today. If history repeats itself, the situation might not be permanent—shantytowns have prospered and fallen on this spot since the mid-19th century. During the Great Depression, an unsightly Riverside Park was crowded by a vast Hooverville, but in 1934, legendary city planner Robert Moses set out to change all that, inadvertently creating one of the most enduring havens for New York City's homeless.

Moses's Westside Improvement Project aimed to transform the park from a hazardous wasteland to the "finest waterfront pleasure ground in the world." It also put an end to grisly conditions along "Death Avenue," a street-level railroad line that claimed the lives of dozens of pedestrians in the early 1900s. By sinking track along 11th Avenue and covering the West Side Line that ran through Riverside Park, street-level crossings were eliminated and the Freedom Tunnel was born.

Not long after the tunnel's completion, the advent of trucking led to the track's abandonment. By the mid-'70s, homeless people living in Riverside Park discovered the area and word began to spread. Through the '80s, a community of hundreds of squatters resided in the tunnels, constructing elaborate bunkers from scrap metal, plywood, and cinderblocks, with salvaged furniture, electrical hookups, and even pens for cats and dogs. For so many, this way of life was a welcome alternative to living in shelters, which were well-known breeding grounds for disease and hotbeds of assault and theft.

opposite The "mole people" may sound like the stuff of urban legend, but their story is far from false.

For a quarter of a century, the mole people were simply left alone, but by 1990, Amtrak® began laying fresh track to reactivate the line. In the years to come, residents would have to contend with eighty-mile-per-hour trains, threats of eviction, and the meddling of reporters and documentarians that sought to improve or exploit their situation. Amtrak attempted to lure the squatters away with government programs and subsidized housing, but resorted to forcibly removing them with the help of the NYPD in 1996.

Walking the right-of-way today, you'll notice the place is surprisingly clean, with no indication of the vast community that once existed here, but lining the walls are pieces of a separate, though intertwined, history. As an epicenter of New York street culture, the Freedom Tunnel has attracted some of the most well-respected graffiti artists over the years, most notably Chris Pape, whose nickname, "Freedom," earned the tunnel its name.

Pape was one of the most active and accomplished New York graffiti artists of the '80s and '90s, and he's best known for his large-scale murals in the Amtrak tunnels. By recreating works of art like Goya's *Third of May* and Michaelangelo's *David,* he was elevating graffiti as an art form and as a means of expression. His work was never intended to last forever, but for almost three decades, visitors to the tunnel respected the Freedom murals. In 2009, Amtrak began painting over some of the largest pieces, angering an entire community of artists and enthusiasts who lionized Chris Pape for his contributions to graffiti culture.

New barriers and enhanced security were positioned at the entrances to the tunnel, but authorities are facing an uphill battle. The walls of the tunnel are already being reclaimed as a new generation picks up where the last left off. The Upper West Side may have lost its grit, but the spirit of the Freedom Tunnel is alive and well.

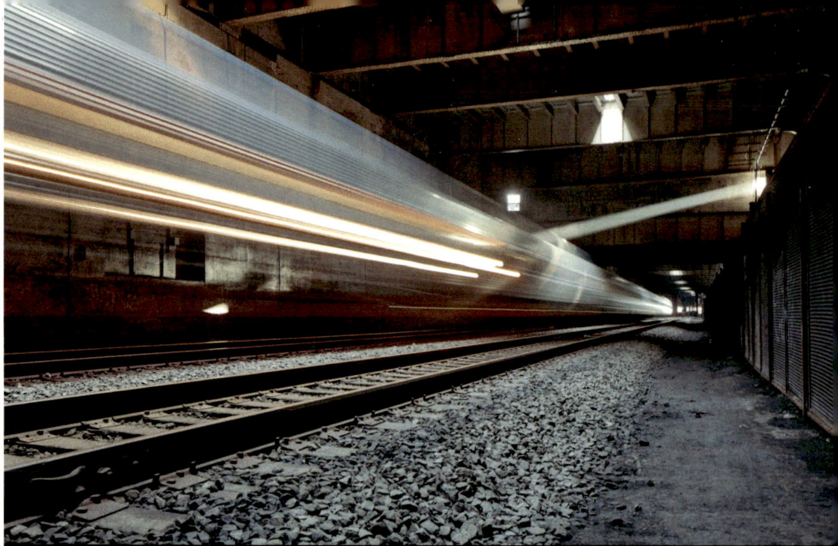

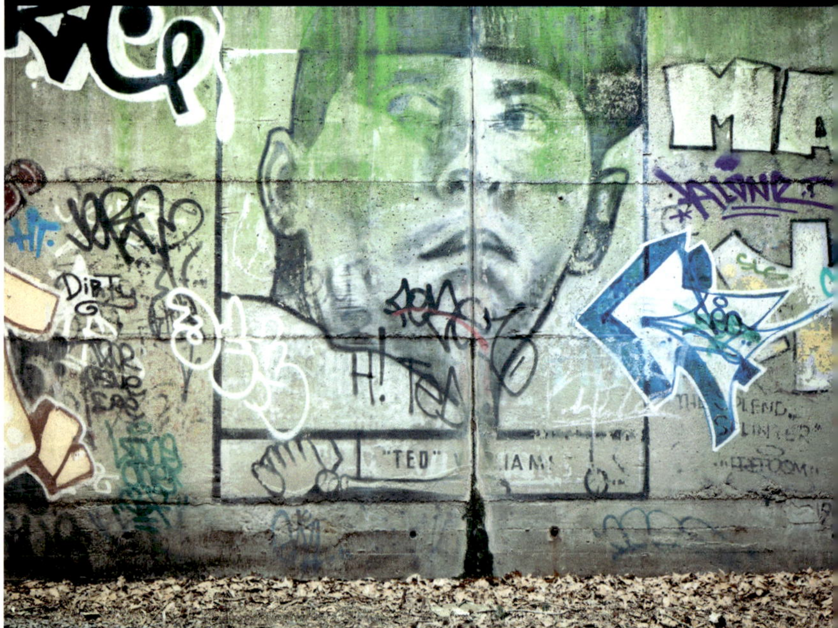

top An Amtrak® train briefly interrupts the silence of the track.

bottom The seclusion of the tunnel allowed street artists to work for long hours without being bothered by authorities.

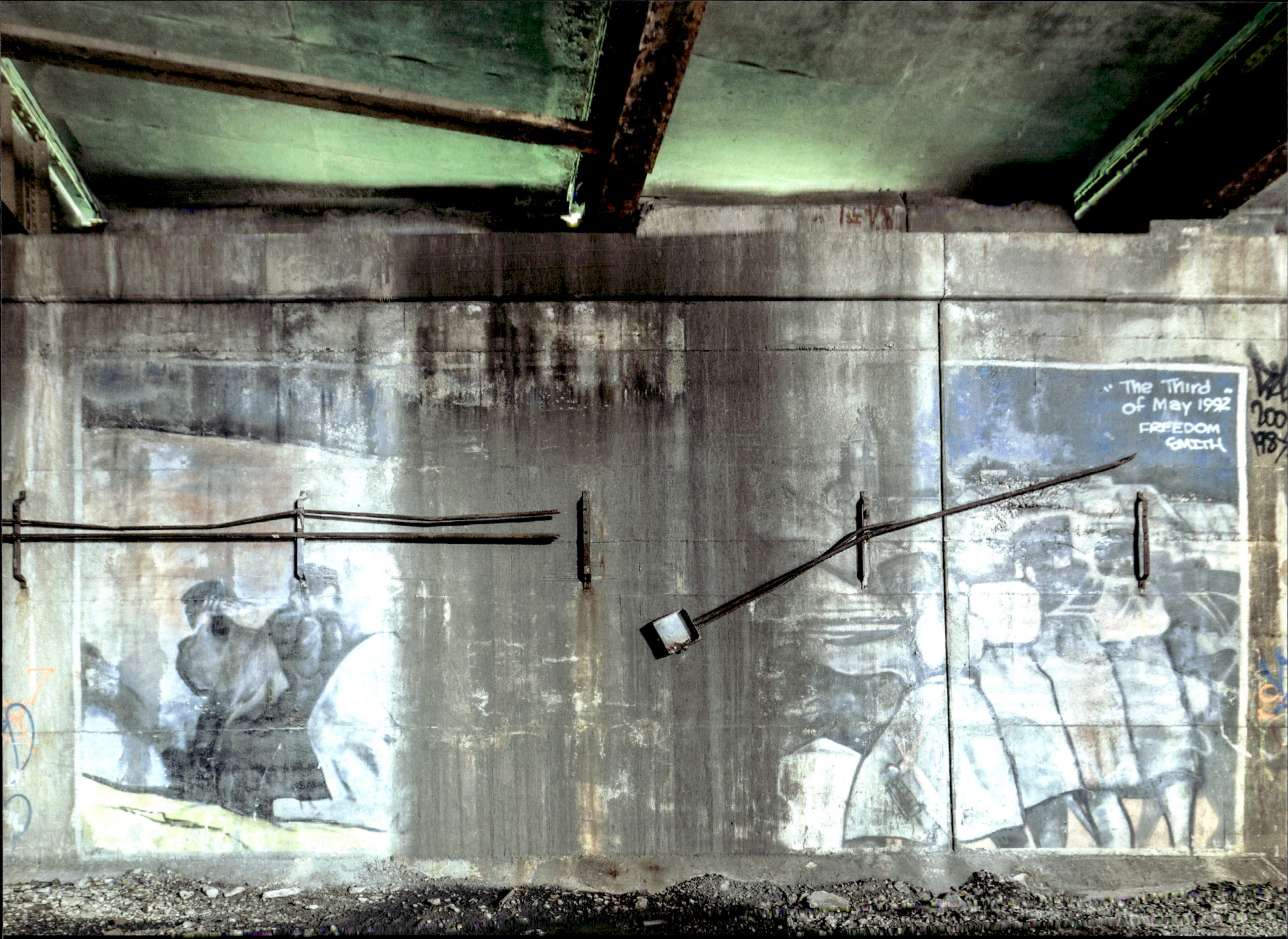

above When the mole people were evicted in 1992, Chris Pape commented on their plight with one of his

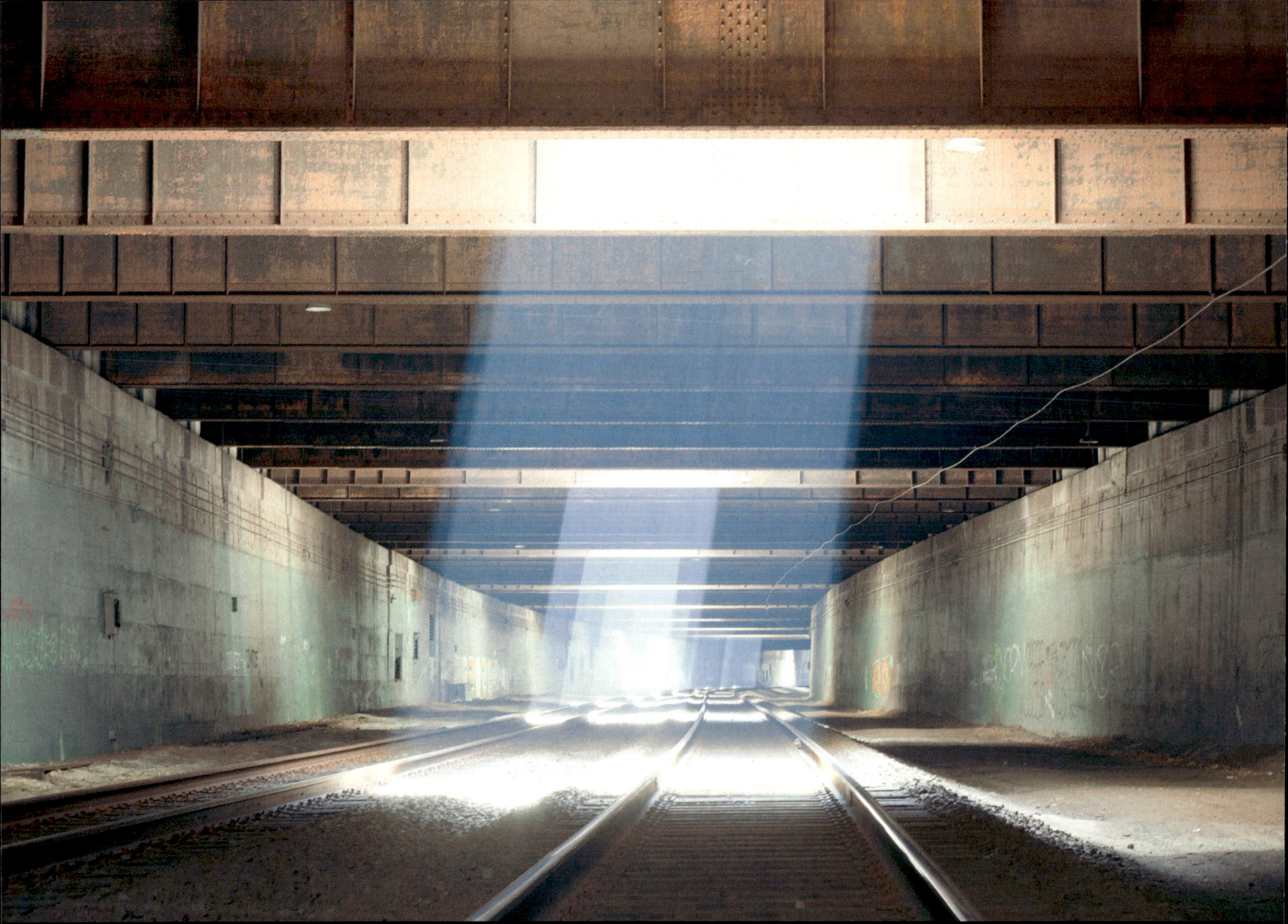

above Over a mile in, the monotony of the tunnel seems like something out of a dream, with identical views ahead and behind, as far as the eye can see.

opposite An opening leads to a fenced-in enclosure in Riverside Park.

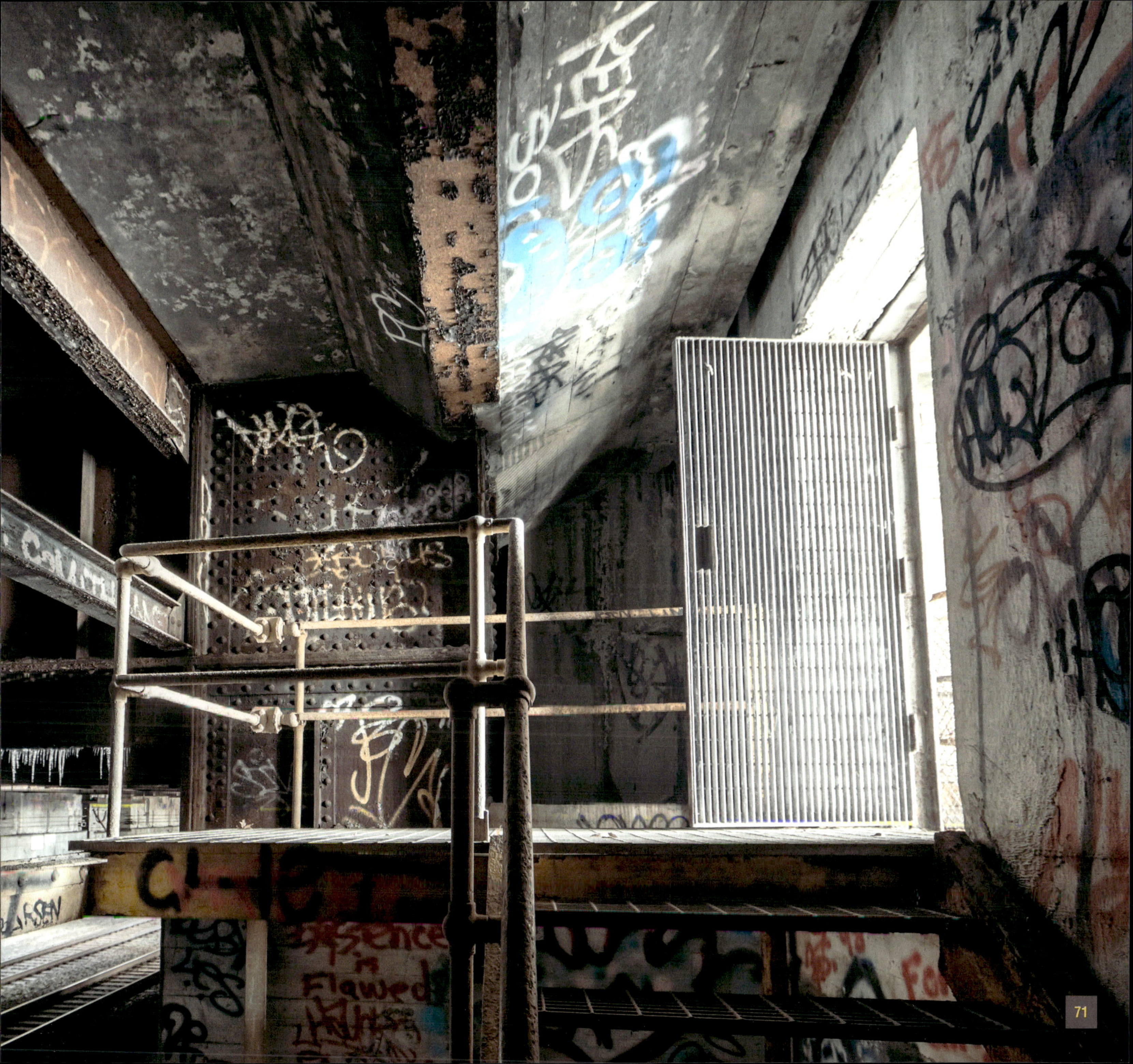

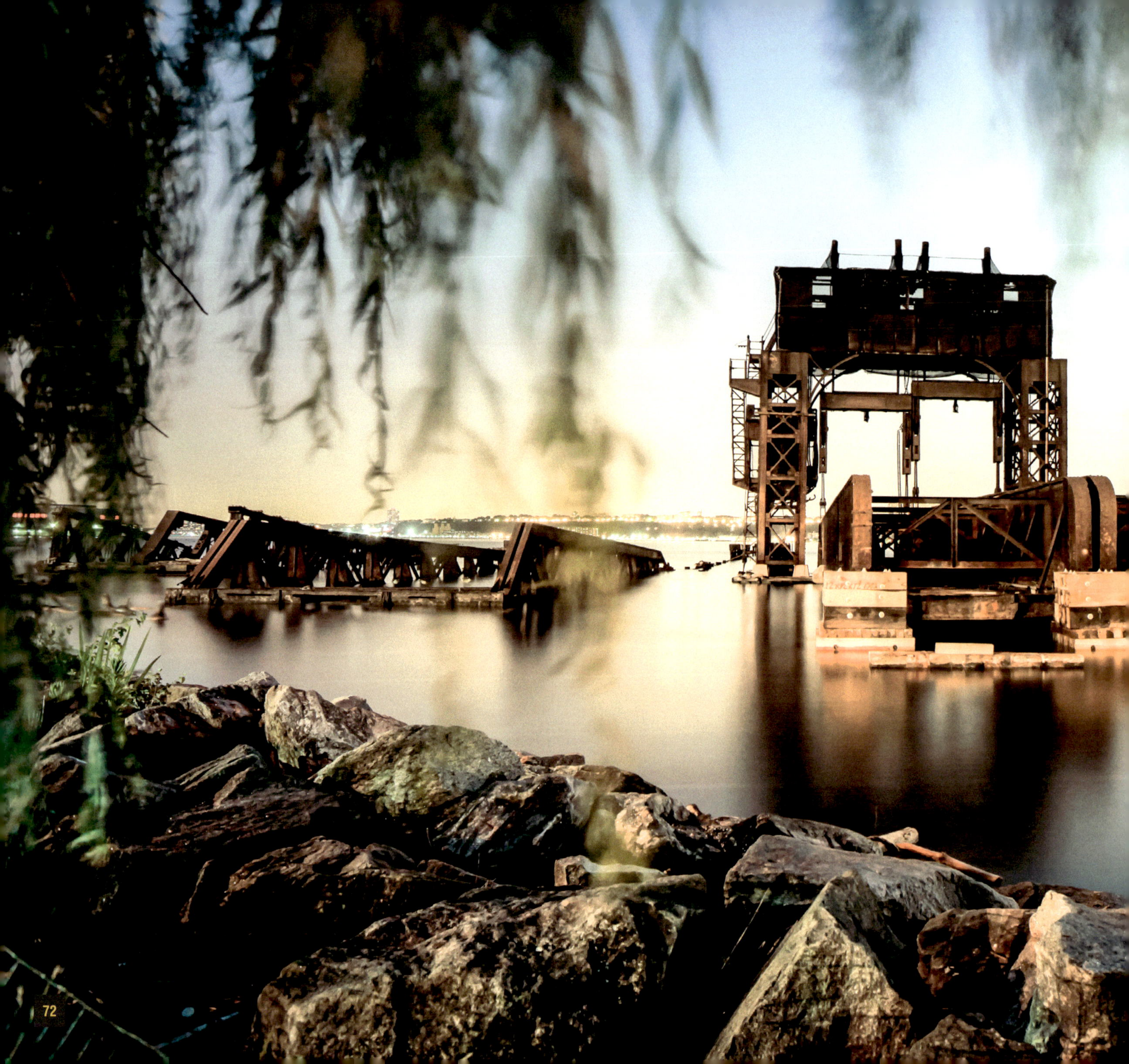

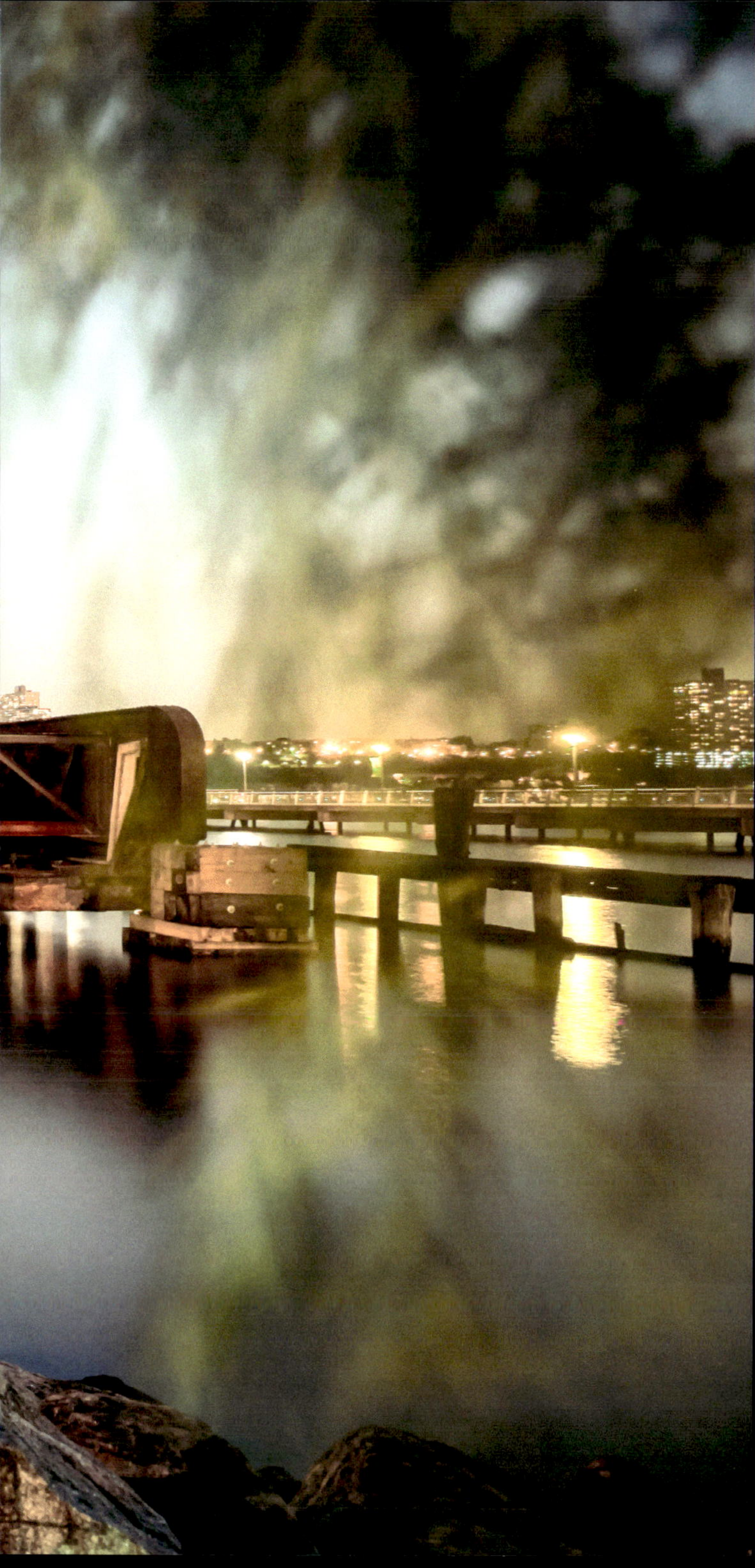

The 69th St. Transfer Bridge once carried freight from the Hudson River to the West Side Line. It was listed on the National Register of Historic Places in 2003.

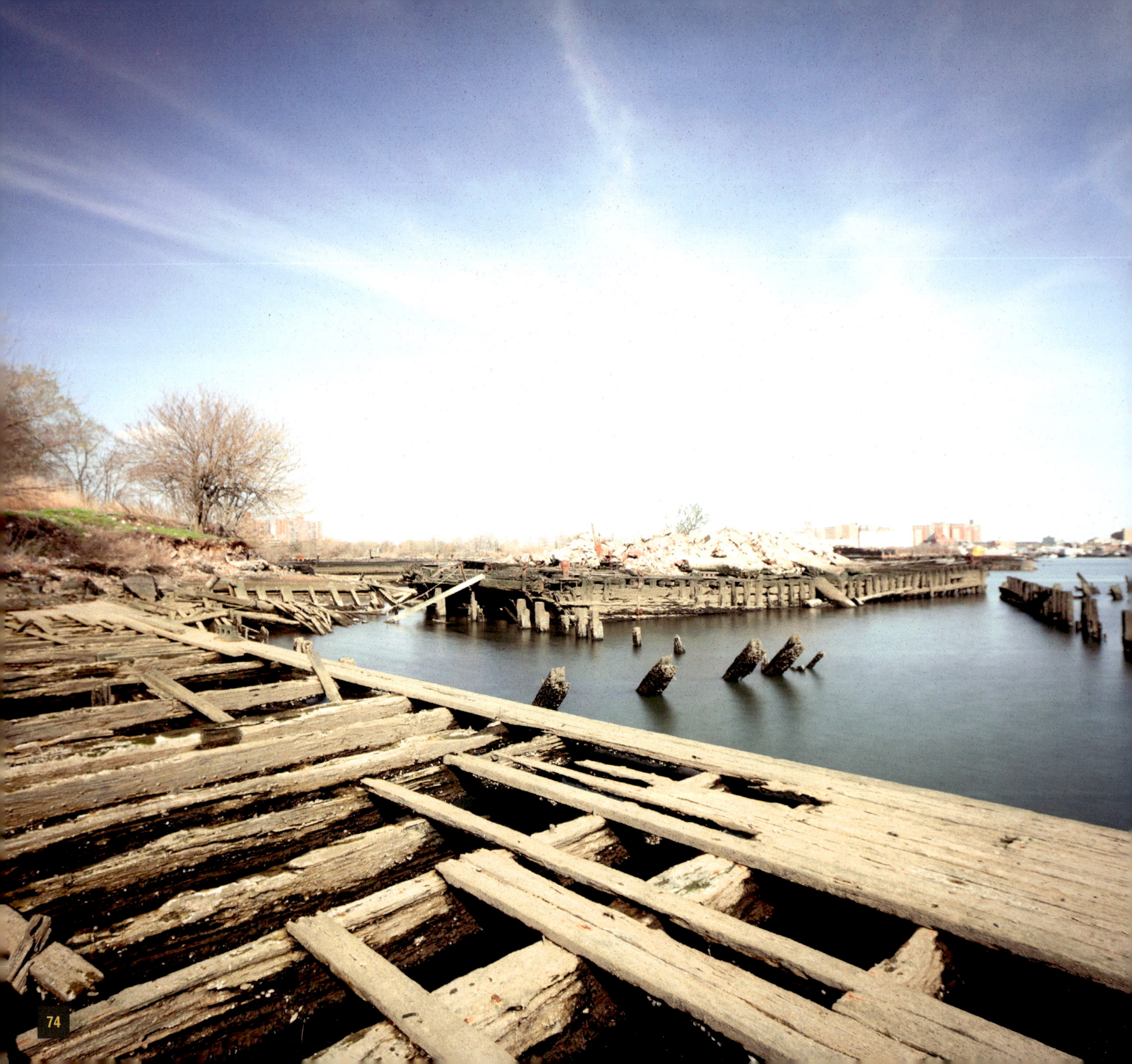

Coney Island Creek

Gravesend, Brooklyn

Coney Island Creek commences in a shallow, wedge-shaped bay, tapering into a narrow strait and turning twice at right angles before meeting an abrupt end at Shell Road and the Belt Parkway. Like its meandering course, the history of this narrow Brooklyn waterway is full of sudden turns and unexpected endings. Over the centuries, the creek has been lengthened for commerce, filled in for development, and put through the worst environmental abuses.

In the late 18th century, Thomas Stillwell established the Gravesend Ship Canal by connecting the creek to the Sheepshead Bay, thereby creating a true "Coney Island." Though the area was best known at the time for its diverse population of rabbits, the new canal was projected to transform Coney Hook into a bustling commercial harbor. The region never flourished as a shipping hub, and by 1929 the modification was filled in for the construction of Robert Moses's Bay Parkway.

Throughout the 20th century, the creek was notorious for its foul-smelling water (to this day, its floor is largely composed of what our ancestors flushed down the toilet). In the '20s and '30s, locals consistently fought for its improvement to no avail. By the time Coney Island's entertainment district had tanked in the '60s and '70s, the creek was considered a cesspool. Conditions have improved in recent years, but decades of illegal dumping have left a permanent mark on the landscape.

Over the years, the mud of Coney Island Creek has built up an impressive collection of nautical curiosities, including the skeletal remains of dozens of abandoned ships and one homemade submarine. The latter is attributed to a local shipyard worker named Jerry Bianco, who set out to uncover the spoils of an ocean liner in 1970. Tragically, the watercraft he called the *Quester* tipped over and reeled into the creek bed shortly after its launch, where it remains to this day. In chasing a legend, he inadvertently created one.

As the sun slips behind the embankment, the yellow conning tower of the Bianco Submarine catches its last light, glowing red in the deepening blue as shadows settle over the ghost ships of Coney Island Creek. The calling of night birds seems to set the stage for the supernatural, especially if you've done your research—bodies have been turning up in the creek since the late 1800s with unsettling regularity.

opposite No one knows for sure when the boats started appearing in Coney Island Creek.

Over the years, these waters have claimed the lives of frolicking children, ill-fated divers, the victims of countless car accidents, untold murders, and at least one suicide. In 1992, the remains of two of serial killer Joel Rifkin's victims were found inside a 40-gallon steel drum. The most mysterious death associated with the creek is of Calvert Vaux, one of the visionary landscape architects behind Central Park and the unlikely namesake of the desolate public park that borders Coney Island Creek. One foggy November morning, Vaux went for a walk while visiting his son in Gravesend and never came back. His body was found hours later floating in the Sheepshead Bay. The death has never been explained.

Though some claim the creek is haunted, its eeriest presence may come in the form of a bright orange box. At nightfall, a massive Home Depot® throws its fluorescent glow over a tiny residential block at Cropsey Avenue and Belt Parkway. These two dozen houses are all that remain of White Sands, a lost community of dead-end streets and blue-collar pride named for the pristine soil that lined the shores of the creek in distant memory. In 1999, 41 homes were demolished to make way for the home improvement megastore. But back in the day, White Sands was closely tied to the creek on its southern border. The local football team was called "the Creek," neighborhood kids made playgrounds of the abandoned boats, and Jerry Bianco and his submarine were born there.

Today, Calvert Vaux Park is typically deserted, with the exception of a few bird watchers. The silence is often interrupted by a ruckus of honking and feathers as enormous flocks of geese pass by overhead. When the dust settles, you might catch a glimpse of a loner bird foraging among the ruins, like the slow and mysterious heron or the blue egret. Coney Island Creek—the failed canal, the open sewer, the dumping ground—is reawakening as a habitat, reprising a role it's played for thousands of years, long before the Home Depot, before Thomas Stillwell, before man, when its shores were covered with white sands.

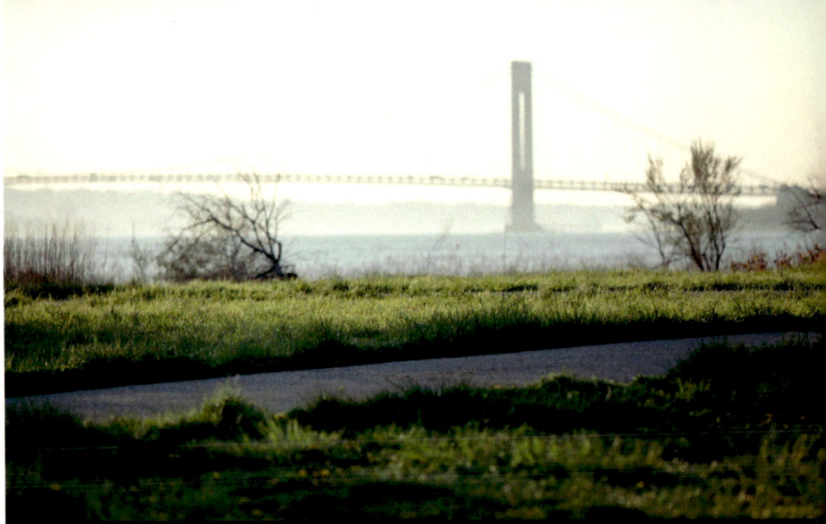

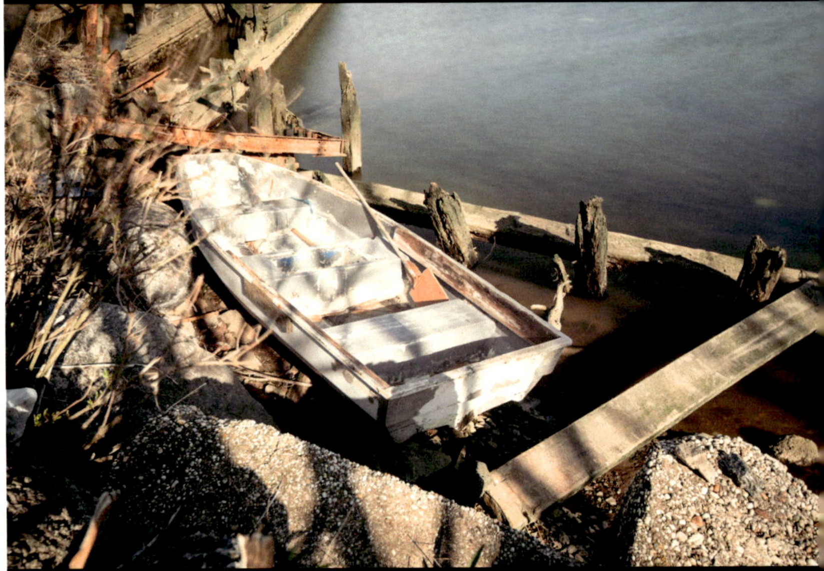

top The hazy outline of the Verrazano Bridge hovers over Calvert Vaux Park.

bottom A few of the boats were recent additions, but most date back several decades.

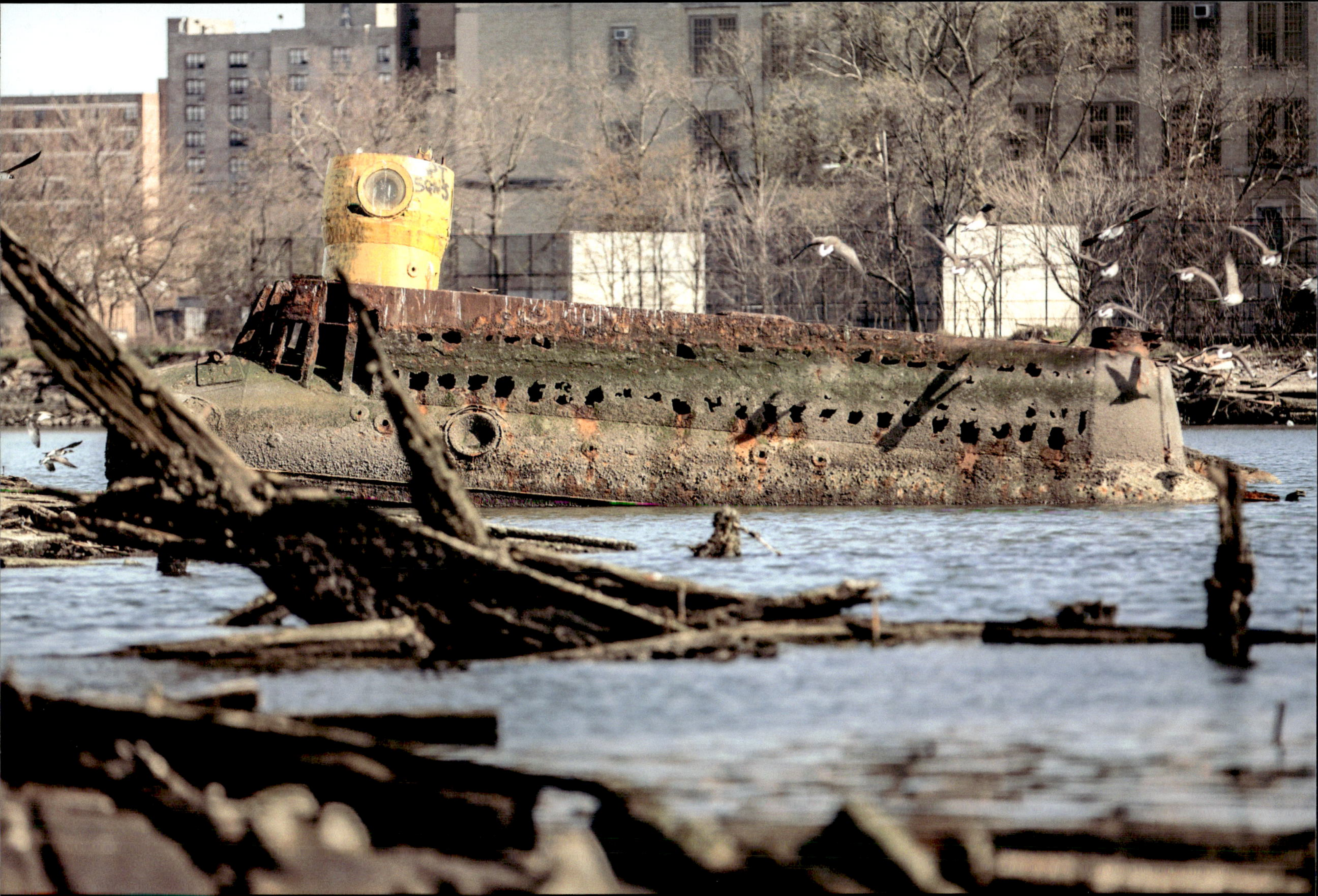

above The sunken remains of a homemade submarine linger as a monument to one man's broken dream.

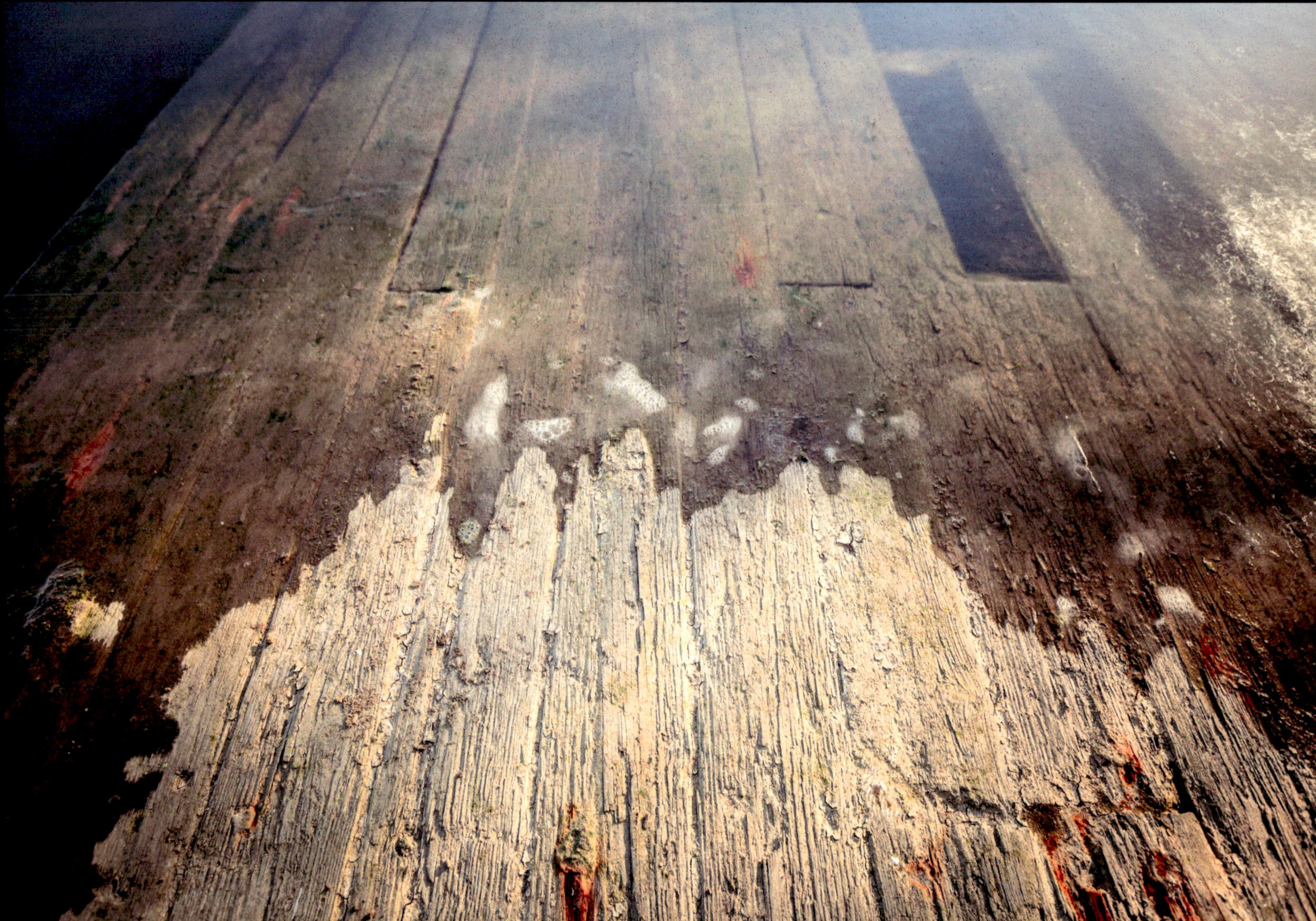

above There's a good chance the creek's nautical curiosities will be around for many years to come.

opposite Parks officials say that dislodging the vessels could release ancient toxins trapped in the muck.

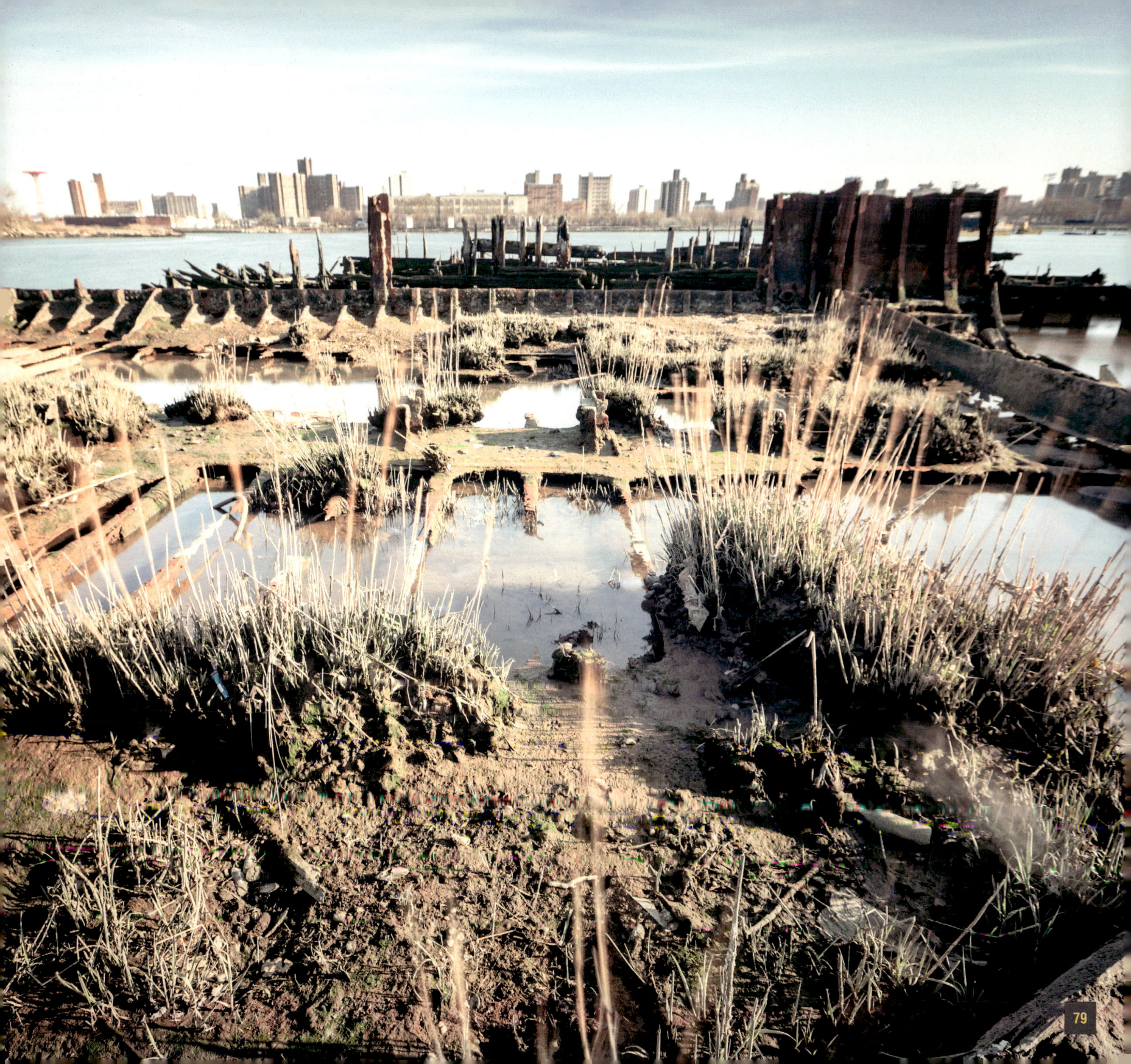

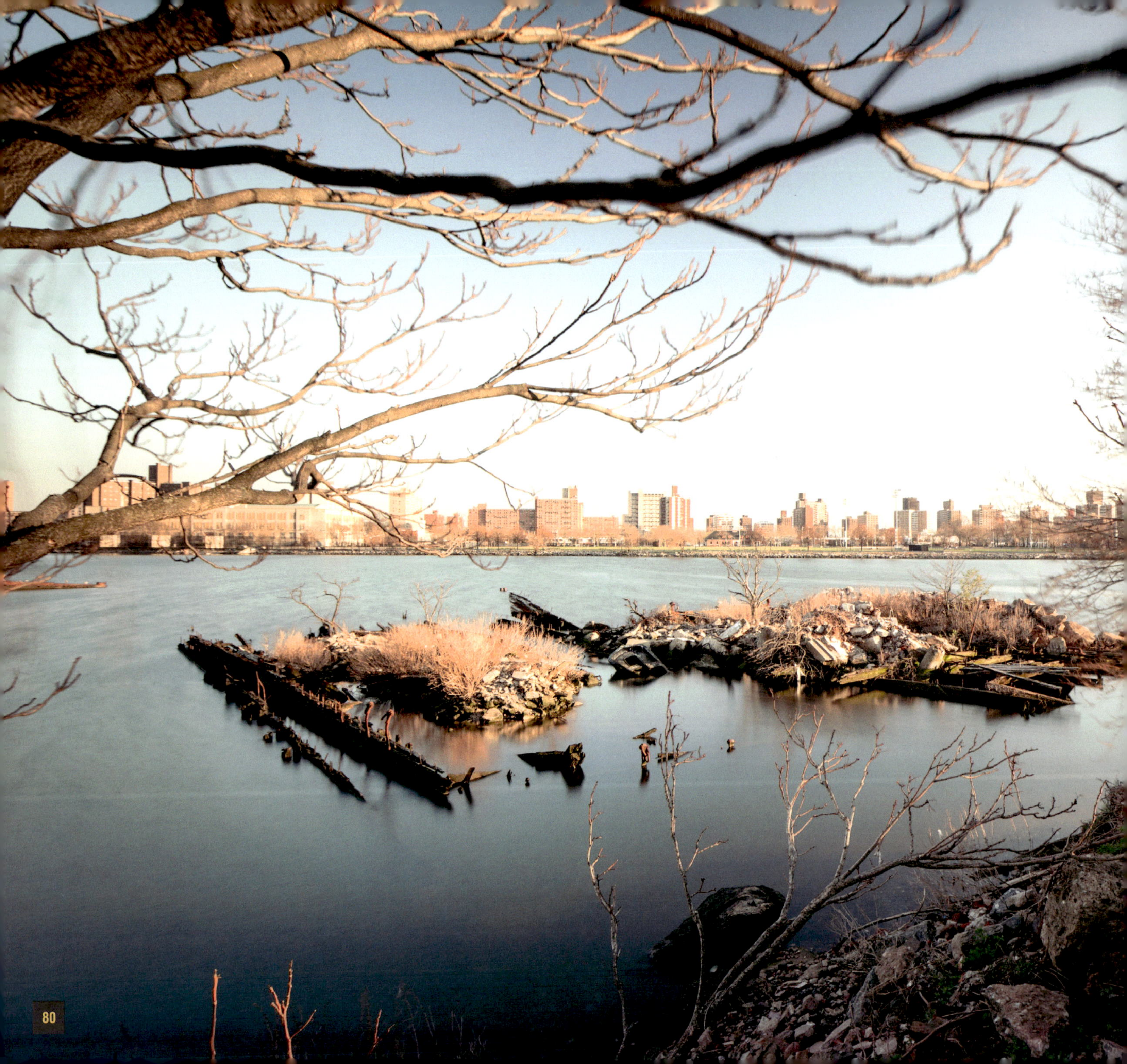

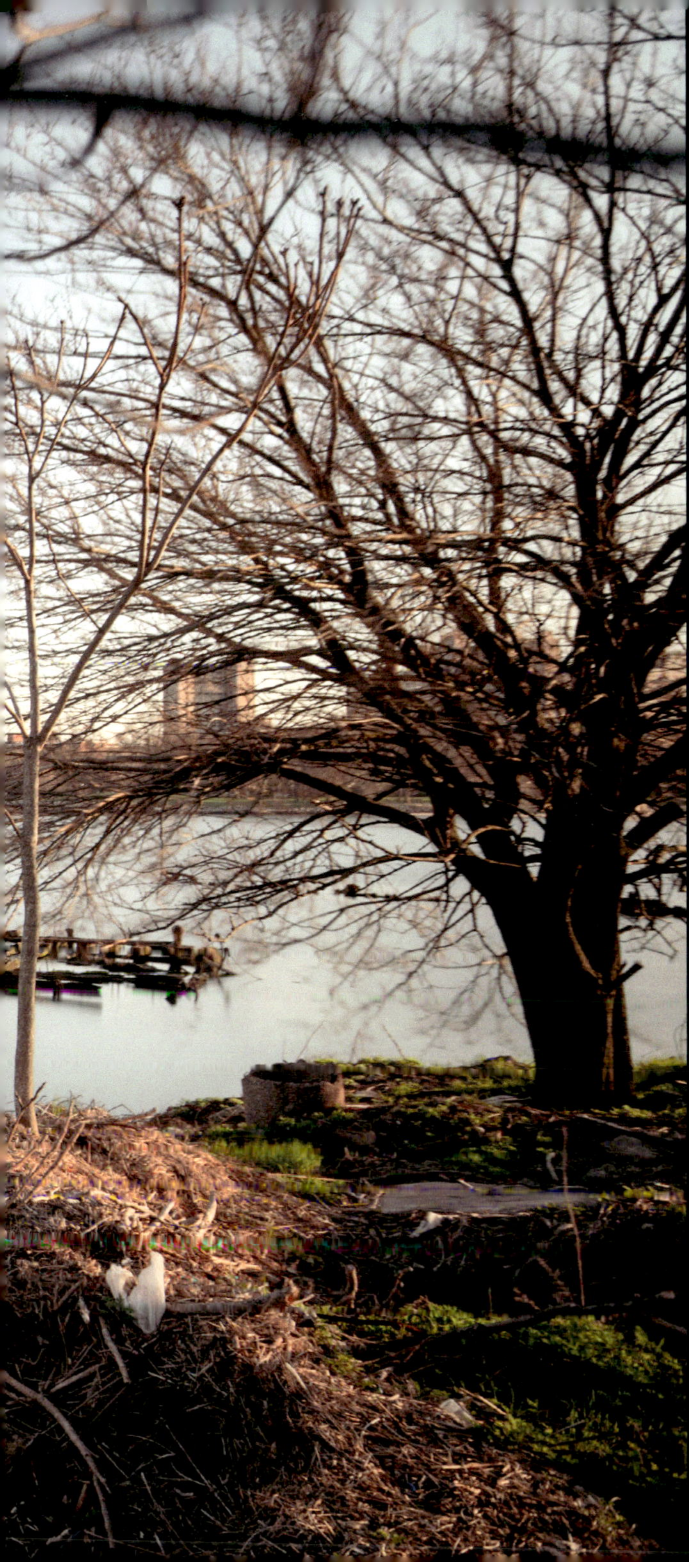

A trio of skeleton barges has become miniature islands at Coney Island Creek, teeming with birds and plant life.

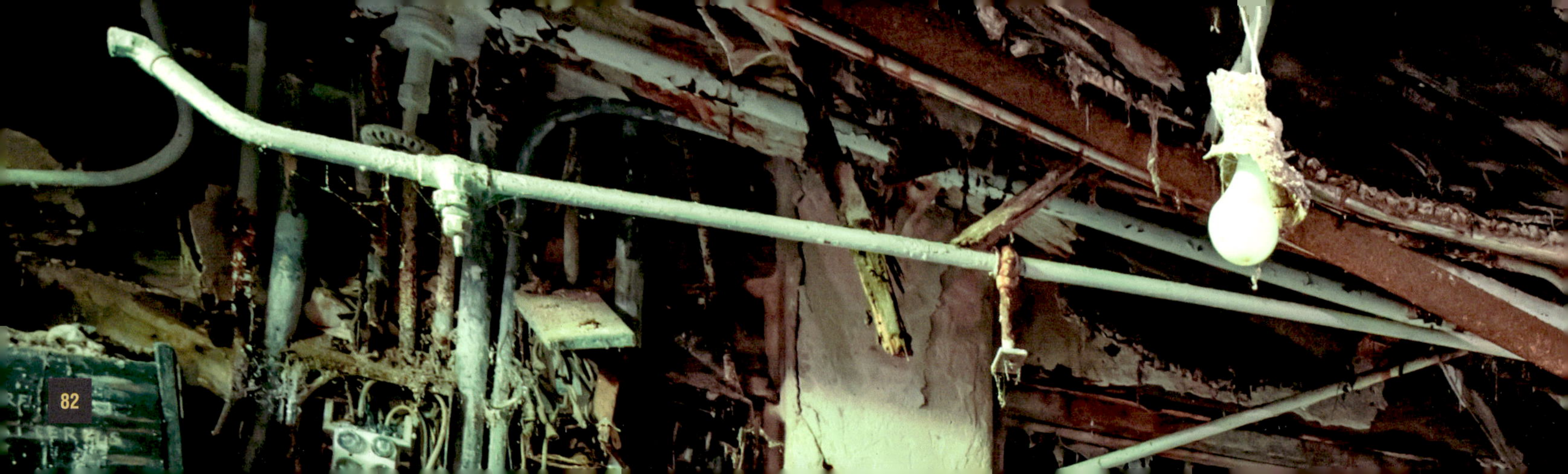

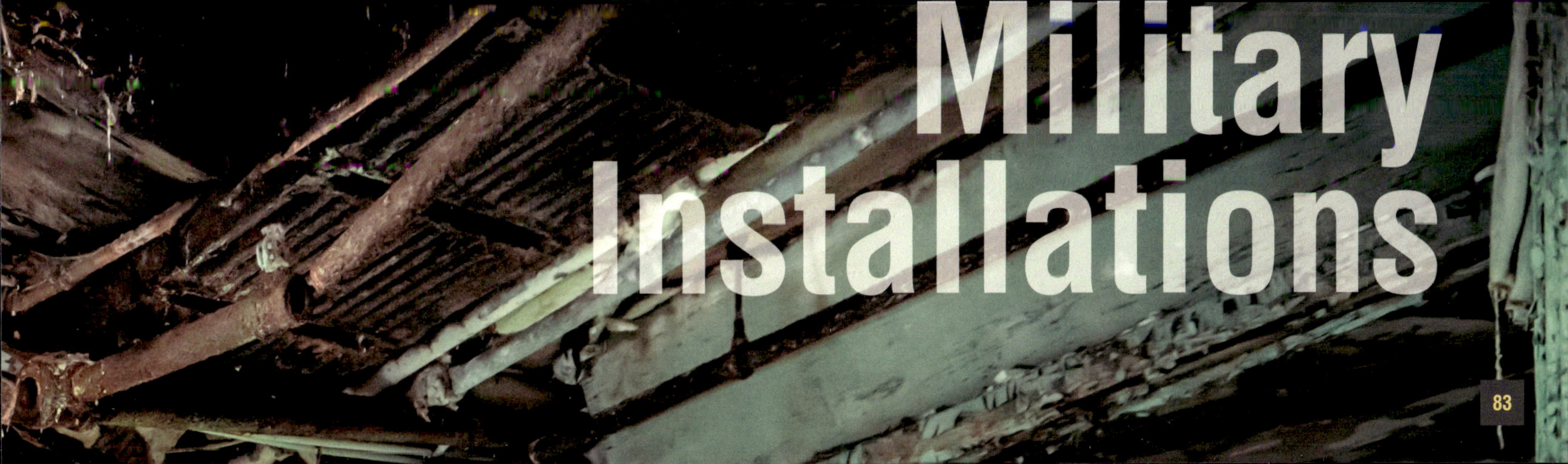

Military Installations

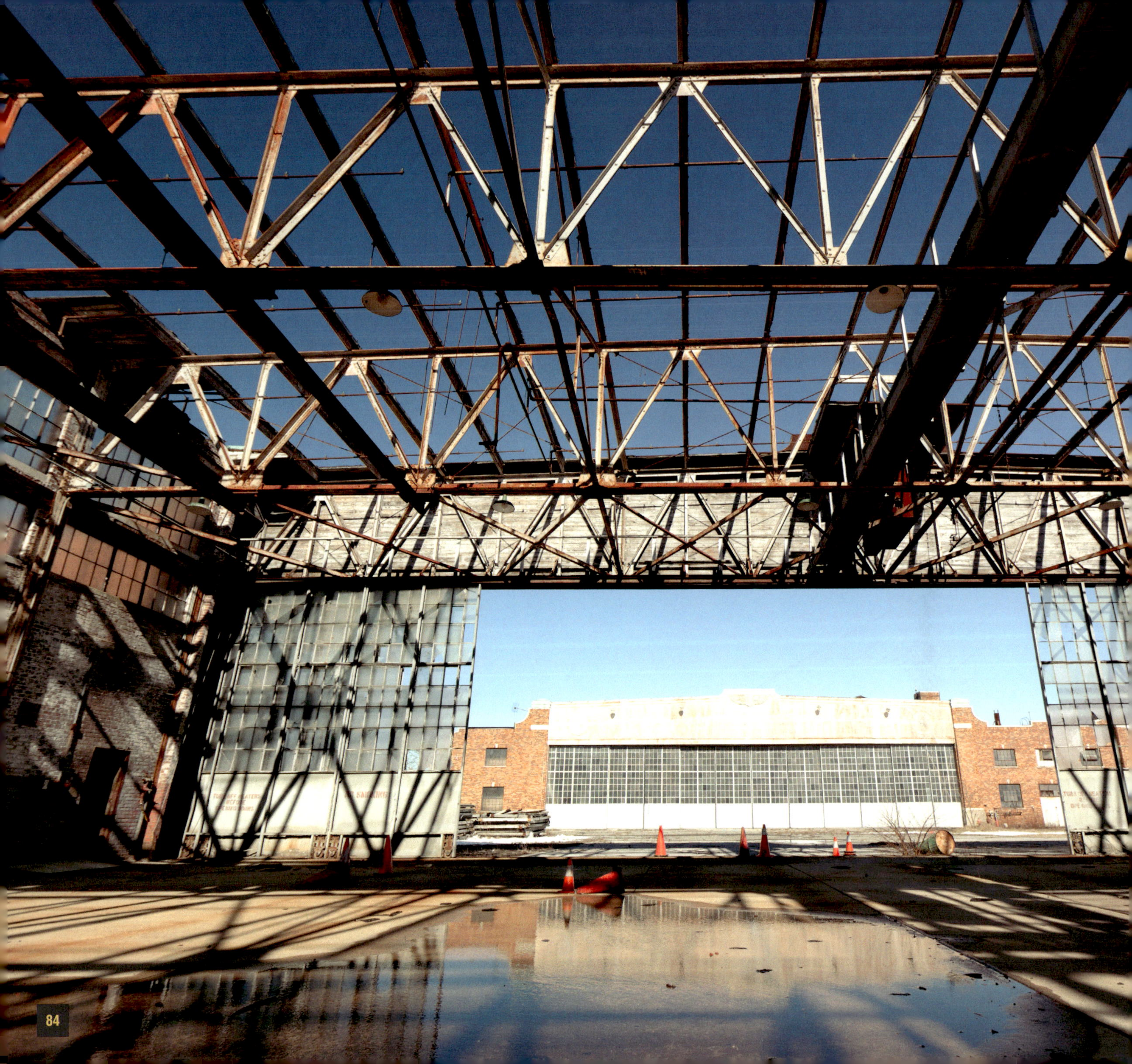

Floyd Bennett Field

Southeast Brooklyn

Having spent more than half a century as an industrial dumping ground, Barren Island was an unlikely choice to usher in the age of aviation as New York City's first municipal airport. An hour's drive from city hall, with no access to major highways or train routes, the site was heavily criticized by the local aviation community. But financial concerns ultimately outweighed their objections. Barren Island had one major advantage over the other proposed sites—the city already owned it.

The airfield was named for aviator Floyd Bennett, the Brooklyn native who broke barriers as the first to fly over the North Pole. Though he earned a Medal of Honor for his performance, historians have determined that the feat was a fraud. Perhaps he sold his soul for a ticker-tape parade; the remaining years of his life were fraught with failure. An attempt at a record-breaking trip to Paris ended in disaster shortly after takeoff, and he died from pneumonia the following year while attempting to rescue a shipwrecked crew off a deserted island in Canada. Two months later, a deserted island in the Jamaica Bay was named in his honor. Perhaps it too was doomed to fail.

The airfield was dedicated in 1931 with a spectacular air show and a crowd of 25,000 spectators. By all accounts, the airport was a fine one, with eight hangars capable of accommodating 50 planes, a state-of-the-art lighting system, and innovative accommodations for amphibious aircraft. But when the fanfares subsided, the airfield struggled to attract commercial carriers to its runways. At the time, airlines depended on airmail contracts to ensure profits on under-booked flights, and the Postal Service never agreed to transfer its operations from Newark Airport to Floyd Bennett Field. Only American Airlines® relented, beginning in 1937. As predicted, passengers complained of long transit times into the city.

In 1941, with the Second World War raging overseas, the Navy purchased the underused airstrip from the city and established a Naval Air Station at the site. Aircraft Delivery Units at Floyd Bennett Field were responsible for the commission, testing, and delivery of aircraft to combat zones throughout Europe and the Pacific. The field served the Navy as an Air Reserve Training Station until the 1970s, when most of its military functions were phased out and the vast majority of the property was abandoned.

opposite During World War II, Floyd Bennett Field was the busiest Naval Air Station in the United States.

Three conflicting plans emerged from the local, state, and federal governments on how to repurpose the newly available lands, but the winning bid came from the Nixon administration, which proposed including the site in the nation's first attempt at an urban national park. Largely composed of defunct military posts, the Gateway National Recreation Area included 1,300 acres of waterfront parkland scattered through broad areas of the Rockaways, south Brooklyn, Staten Island, and New Jersey.

At the time, housing officials accused the Gateway plan of creating a vast wasteland, and to some extent, their words proved prophetic. The Gateway area is currently the largest contiguous open space in New York City, but relatively few New Yorkers have heard of it. The property was allowed to languish during the Reagan years, when the National Parks Service was set back by a series of budget cuts. Meanwhile, many of the area's military structures—there are more than 400 scattered throughout the Gateway—have fallen into a state of disrepair.

The recent restoration of the airfield's administration building into a visitors' center is a significant sign of progress, but there's much work to be done. Parks officials have solicited the private sector for proposals to reuse the remaining buildings, which may offer the best hope for the future of park improvements. A $38 million sports and entertainment center salvaged four of the historic hangars, and several others are being repurposed as a natural gas metering station for a new pipeline, which has some locals up in arms.

The rest of the sparsely populated acreage of Floyd Bennett Field can feel deserted at times, but pockets of civilian activity are scattered throughout the park, including Brooklyn's largest community garden. In Hangar B, a group of enthusiastic craftsmen are preserving the airfield's legacy by restoring and displaying historic aircraft. Notably, it's the only legal campground within city limits. Offering some of the darkest skies in the five boroughs, the park is a meeting place for amateur astronomers on summer nights. It's the antidote to the manic pace of city life, just waiting to be discovered.

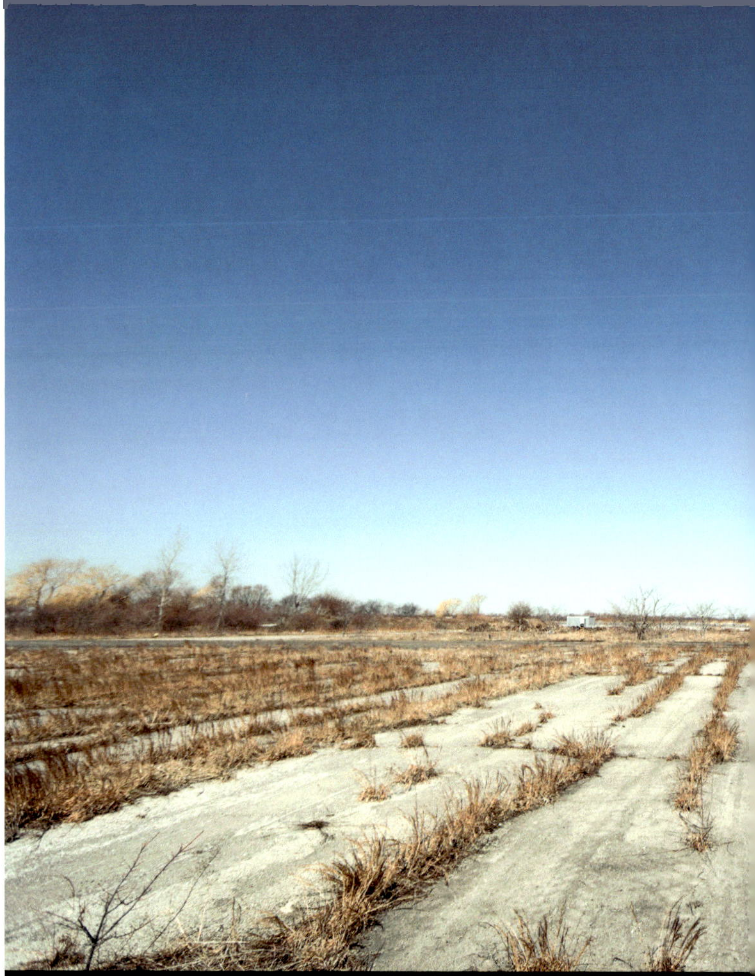

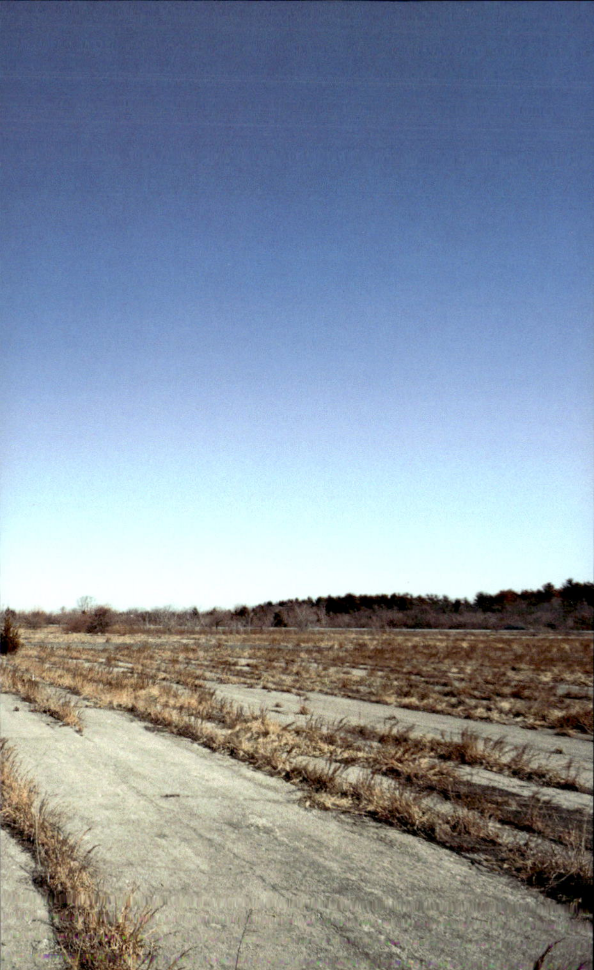

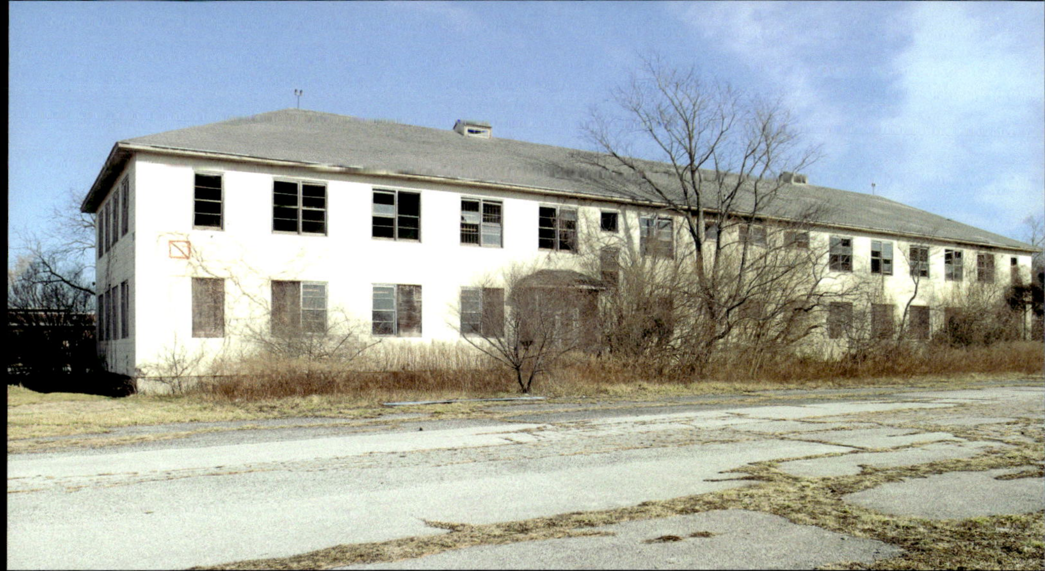

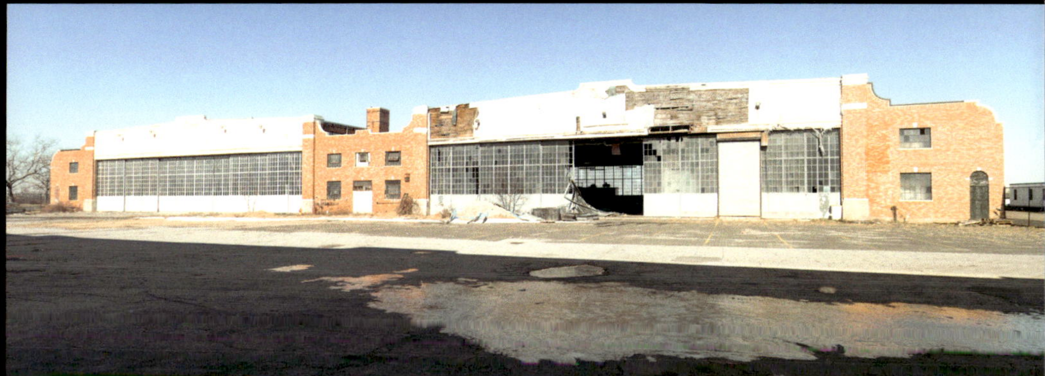

left Some of the old runways have begun to revert back to a natural state.

top The later buildings typify the blandly pragmatic architecture of military installations of the period.

bottom These historic hangars were the sites of dozens of notable achievements during the golden age of aviation, despite the airfield's failings in the realm of commercial flight.

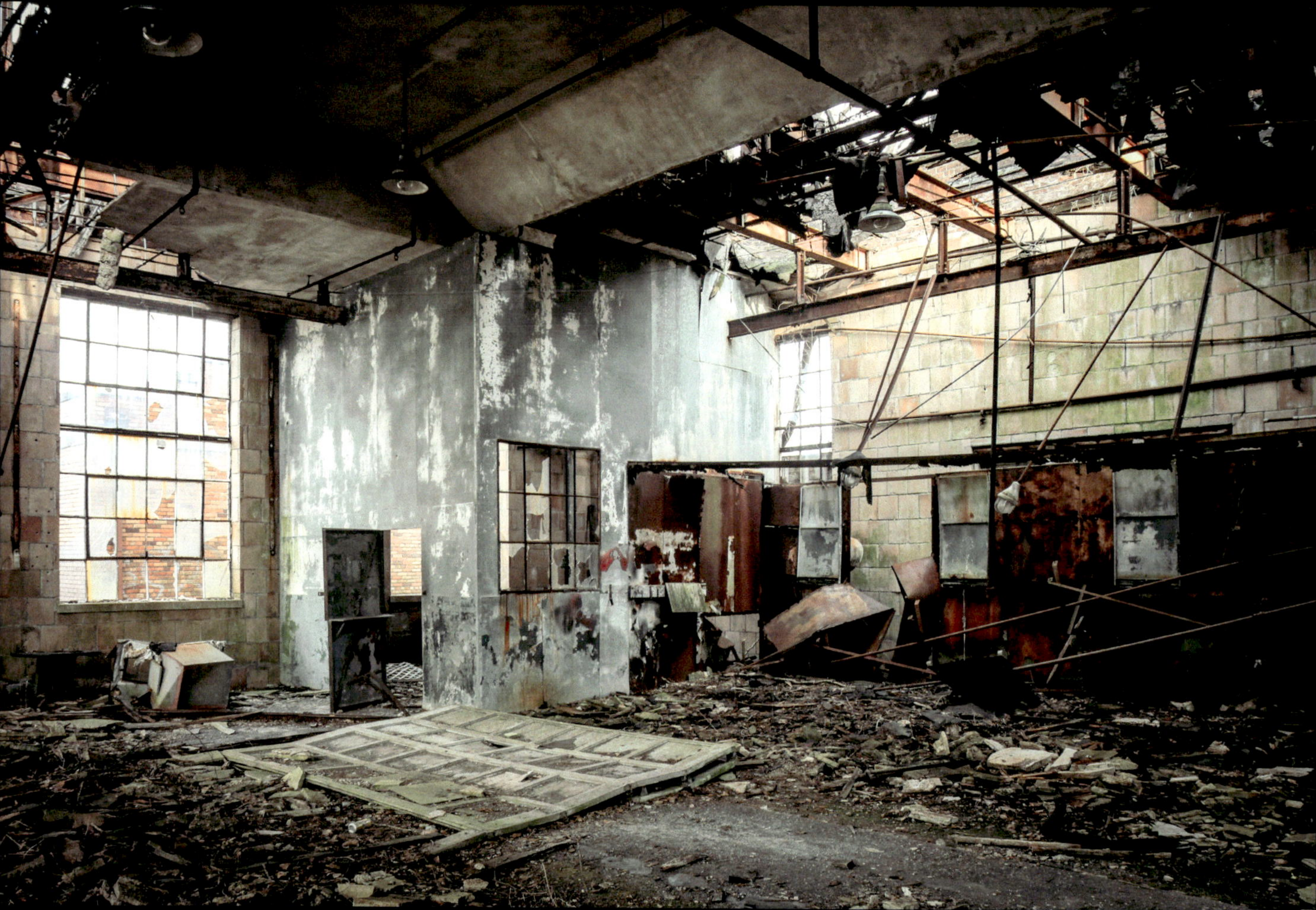

above A dilapidated maintenance building at the back of the hangars hints at what the interiors looked like before the cleanup.

opposite Feral cats abound at Floyd Bennett Field, choosing the loneliest places to die.

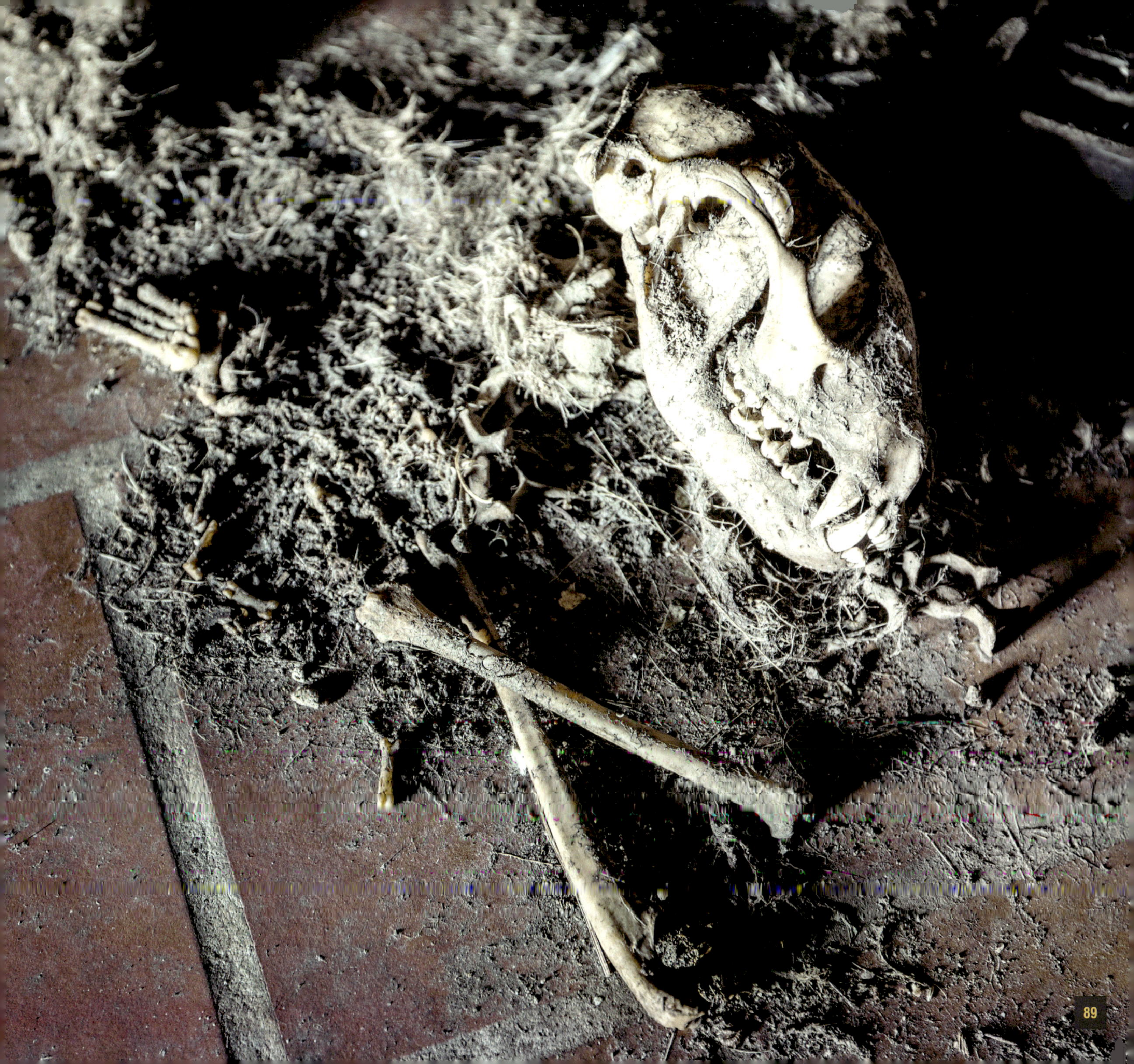

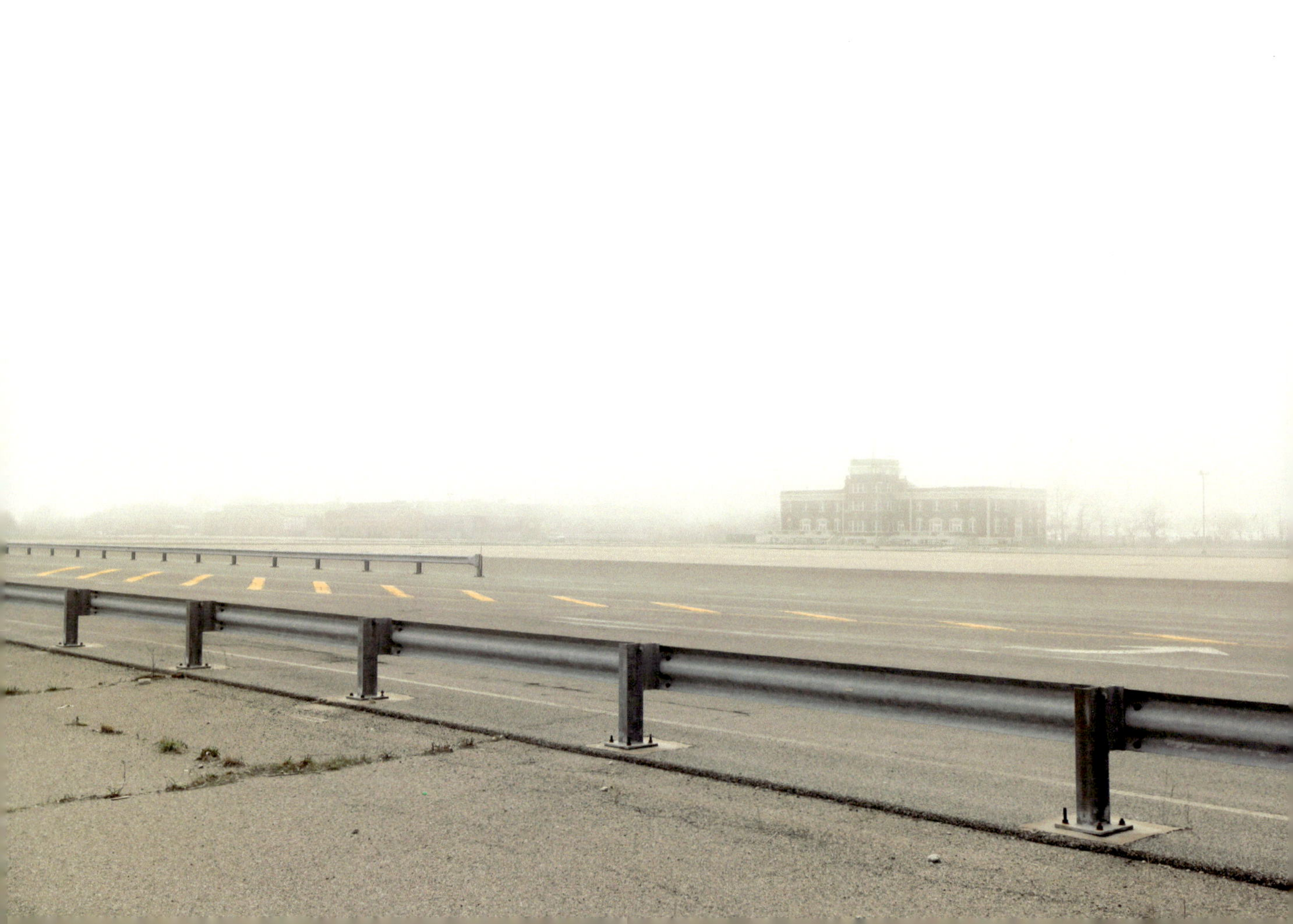

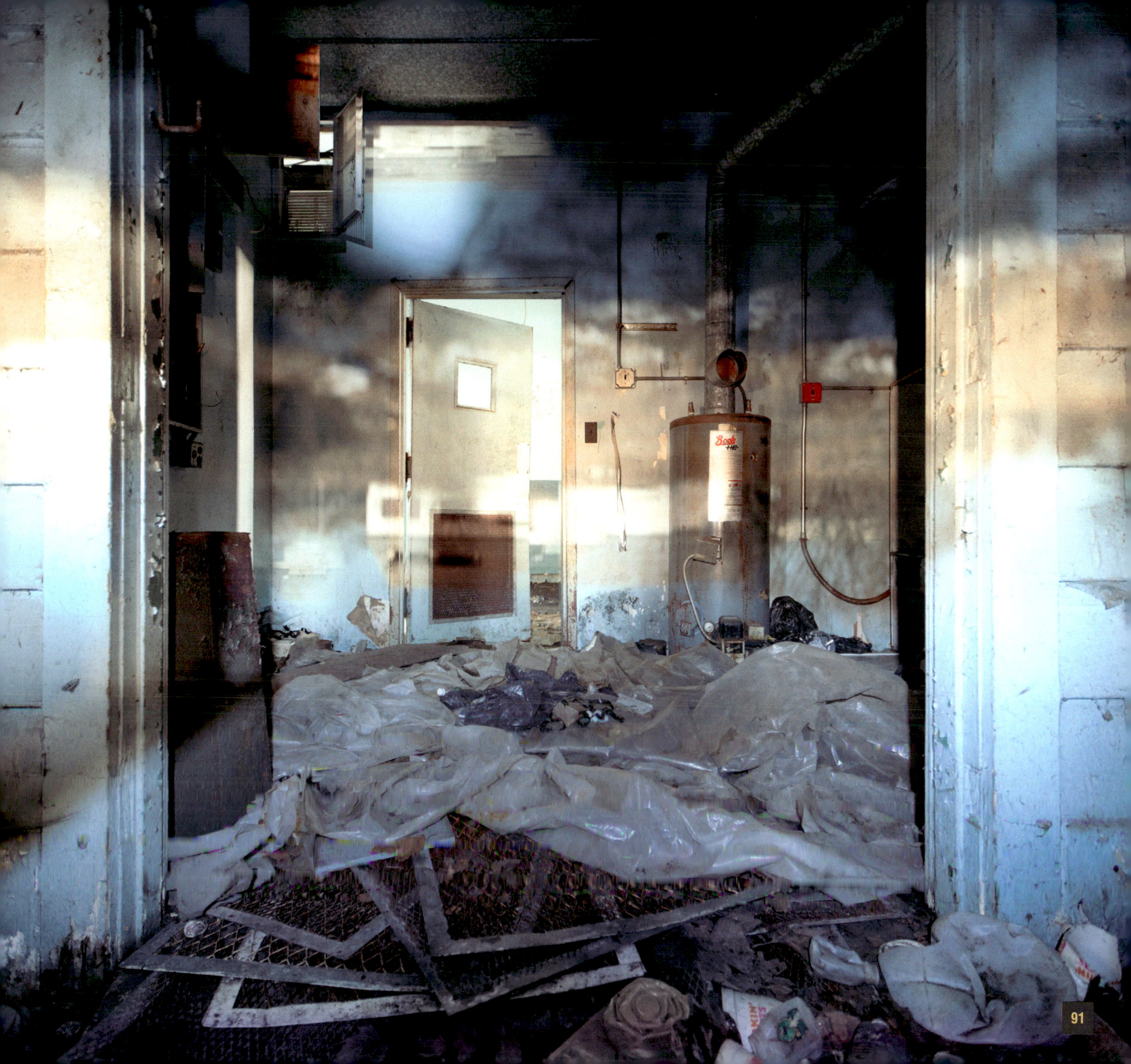

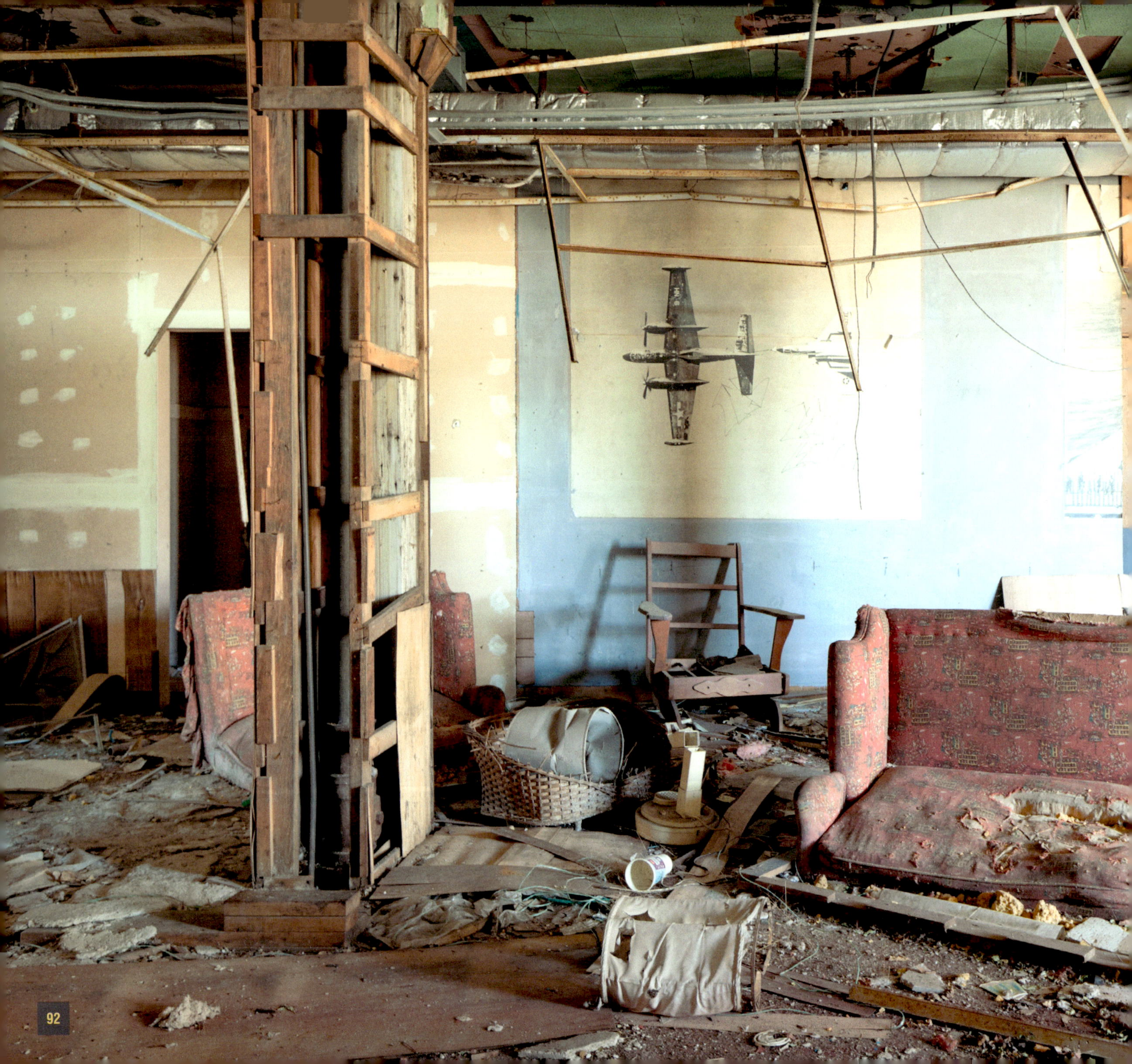

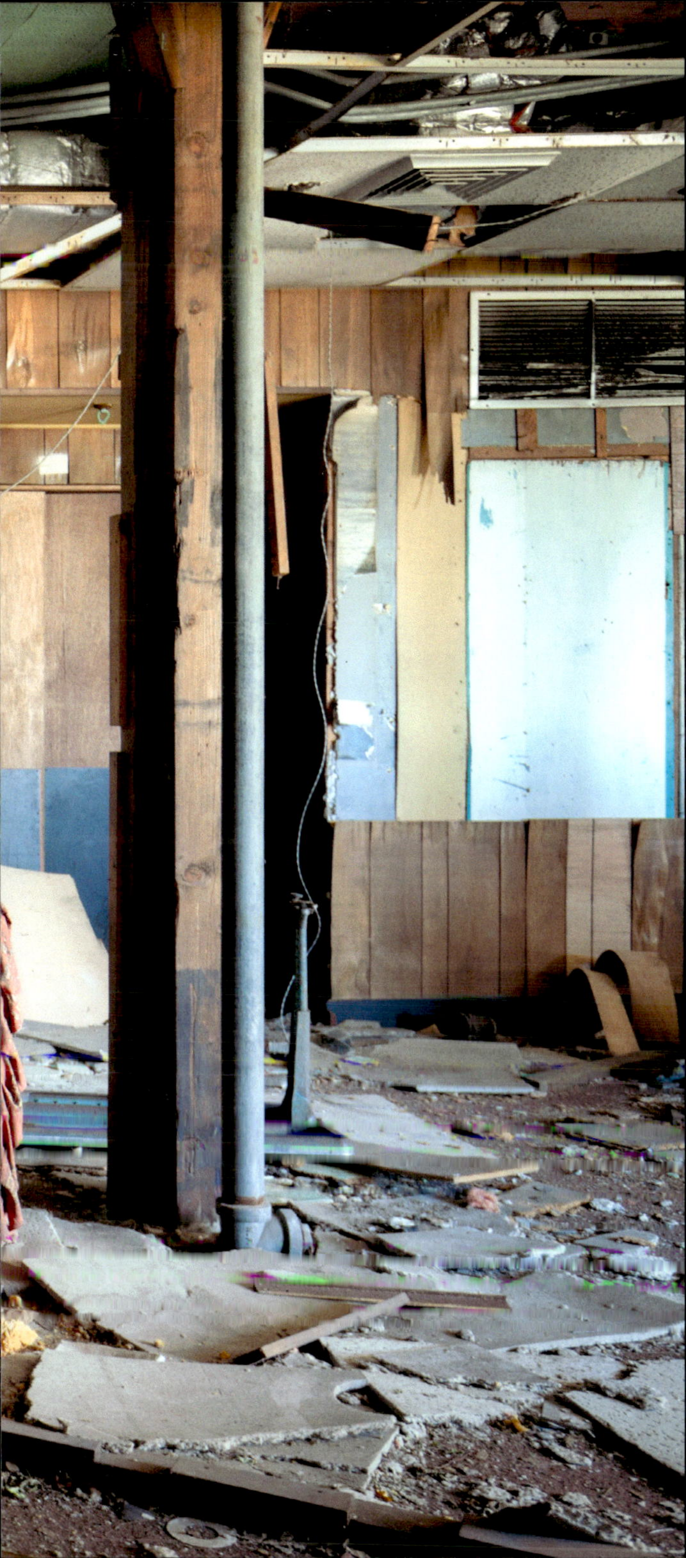

A peeling poster in an abandoned barracks offers a glimpse into the airfield's past. Seventies ephemera litters the floor—odd memos and catalogs from an age before e-mail are left behind with laconic diaries and paper valentines.

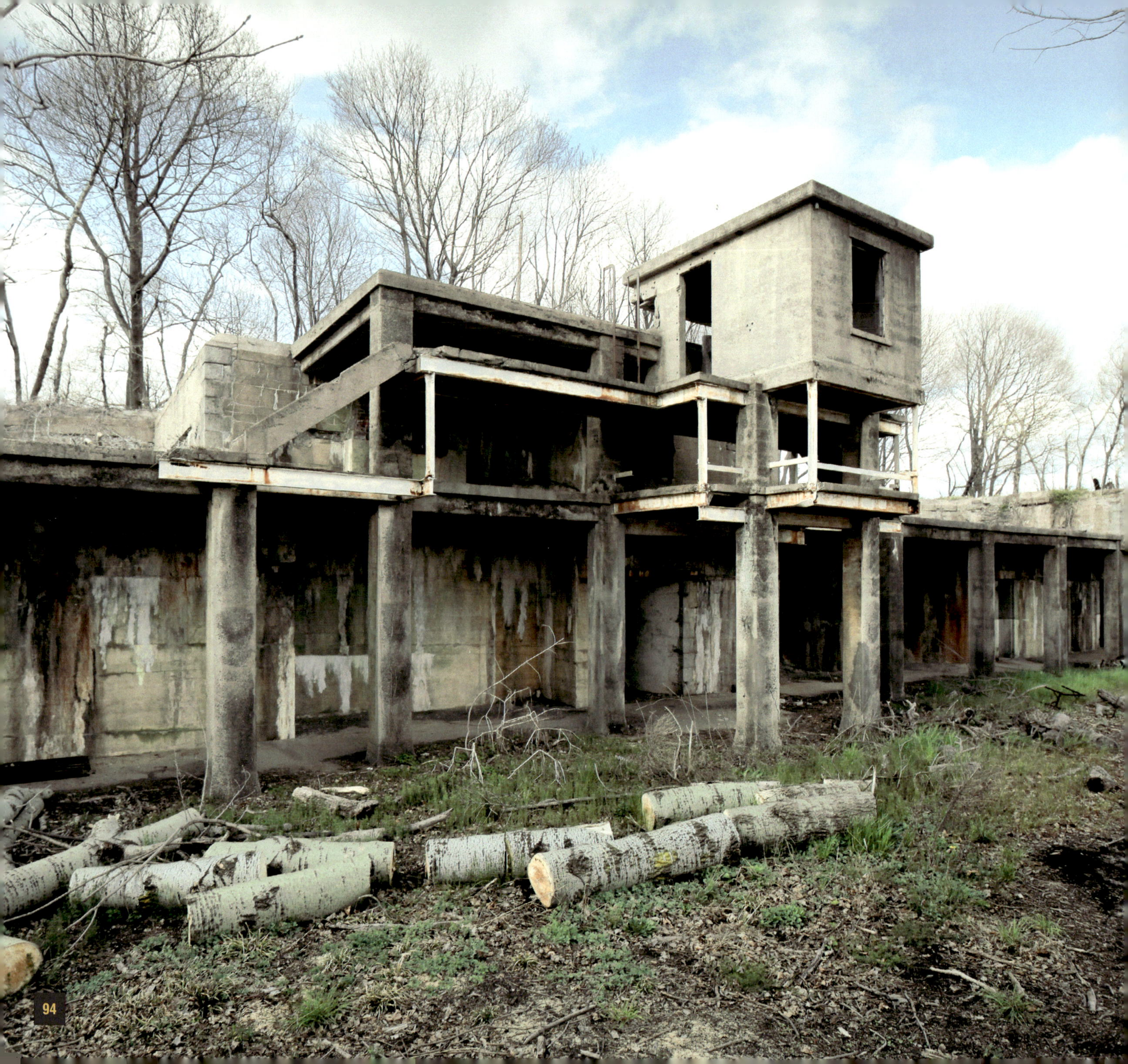

Fort Totten

Bayside, Queens

opposite At the northern tip of Fort Totten, a group of batteries constructed at the turn of the 20th century sits half-submerged in plant life behind a rusty fence.

The story of Fort Totten begins with a false start. In 1864, work stopped on the fortification at Willets Point just two years into construction, when advances in weaponry rendered the battery obsolete before it was even completed. What's left behind is essentially an abandoned construction site where massive granite blocks pile up in truncated columns, as if the workers had just left on a lunch break.

The historic battery forms the northern tip of Willets Point, a 136-acre peninsula on the northeast corner of Queens. Designed as the strategic counterpoint to Fort Schuyler in the Bronx, Fort Totten joined the ranks of a vast system of defense structures flanking the New York harbor. The area never saw combat, but the base proved valuable as an Army training ground from the 1860s well into the 20th century, later becoming an anti-aircraft defense site and hosting advanced research in military technology and medicine. Remnants of a rich military legacy overspread the grounds, including over 100 historic buildings, but many are crumbling to ruin today.

The decay started in the second half of the 20th century, when the advent of modern warfare and the rising unlikelihood of an attack on the New York harbor made the city's defenses unnecessary. The army declared the land surplus in 1967 and began phasing out its operations, officially decommissioning the base in 1995. With the property up for grabs, developers eyed the land for amusement parks, shopping districts, and housing developments, while locals lobbied for more parkland. The most unusual claim emerged from the Matinecock Tribe, a Native American group that had long been considered extinct by anthropologists. As the descendants of the peninsula's original inhabitants, the group insisted that they had a right to the land, citing the existence of an ancestral burial ground. But Fort Totten was ultimately ceded to the city for use as a public park.

When Fort Totten Park officially opened in 2005, Mayor Bloomberg predicted that the area was "certain to become one of New York's most popular parks." Some community members feared that the estimated 450,000 yearly visitors would disrupt parking, increase crime, and change the face of the neighborhood, but nearly 10 years later, tourism has yet to pose a problem.

The transition to civilian use has been understandably slow, but encouraging. Several nonprofit groups have occupied and renovated the remaining buildings, including the landmarked Officers' Club, which now serves the Bayside Historical Society as an educational facility and event space. Fort Totten now offers regular events and educational programs to draw visitors. On a sunny Sunday, the sidewalks are peopled with local families, and soccer games on the former parade grounds typically draw a crowd. Fort Totten may not be living up to its potential just yet, but word on this urban oasis is spreading.

Meanwhile, dozens of dilapidated officers' quarters, hospitals, bakeries, movie theatres, and laboratories vie for restoration, but so far sufficient funding has failed to materialize. The Parks Department and the Fire Department have found themselves charged with the difficult task of adequately caring for these buildings with extremely limited resources. Many of the structures were abandoned long before the military left Fort Totten, and for some, it's far too late to save them. Things couldn't get much worse at the ruinous Post Hospital, constructed in 1906, which could be called a preservationist's worst nightmare.

A short walk from the hospital will take you back another 80 years. Layers of history peel back like an onion on Willets Point, which was named for the family that once owned the peninsula. Constructed in 1829, the original Willets farmhouse is Fort Totten's oldest structure, though it's partially collapsed, brimming with holes, and completely overgrown. A sign placed in front of the wreck makes a humble plea, encapsulating the current state of affairs in the Fort Totten Historic District: "Please excuse my appearance, I am a candidate for historical preservation."

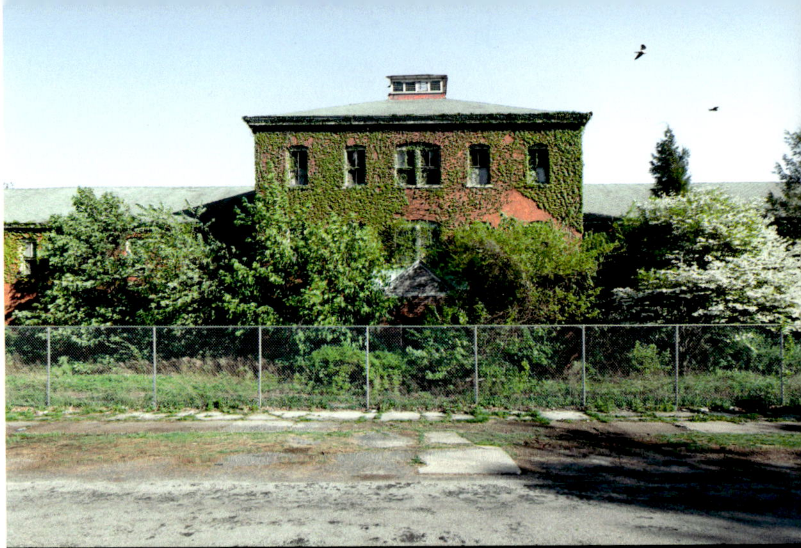

top A vine-covered barracks rests on the edge of the parade grounds.

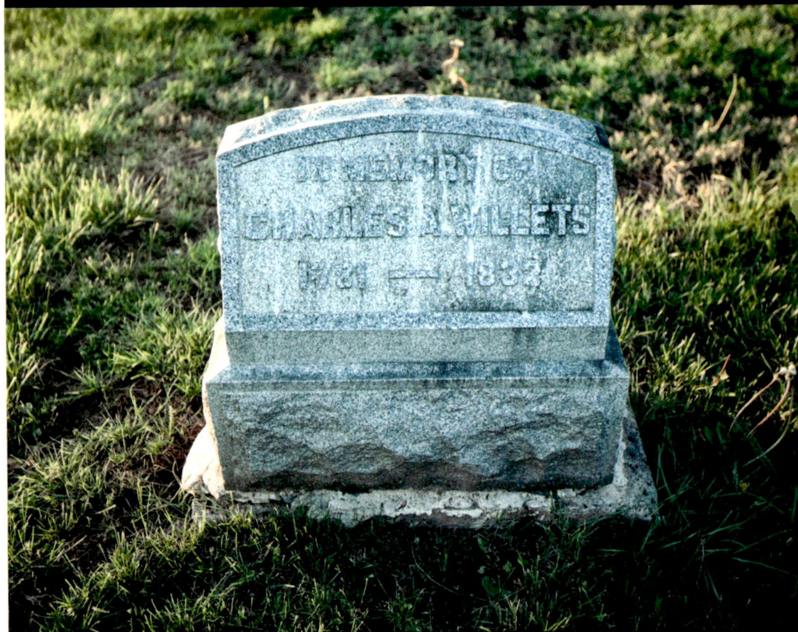

bottom The grave of Charles Willets serves as a reminder of the site's pre-military history.

opposite Hoary calcite formations suspend from vaulted casemates on the lower level of Fort Totten's Civil War battery, where granite walls grow green with age.

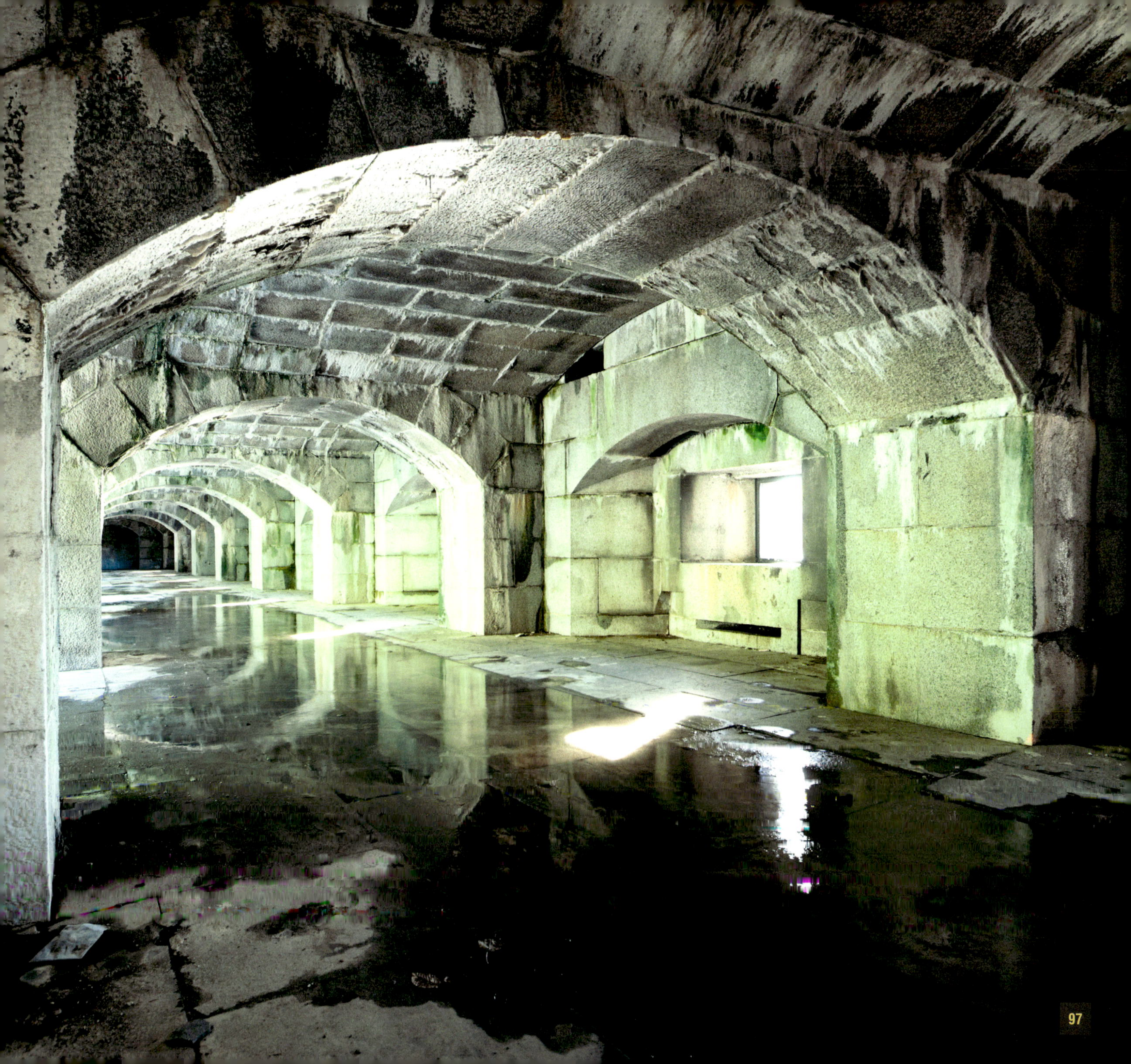

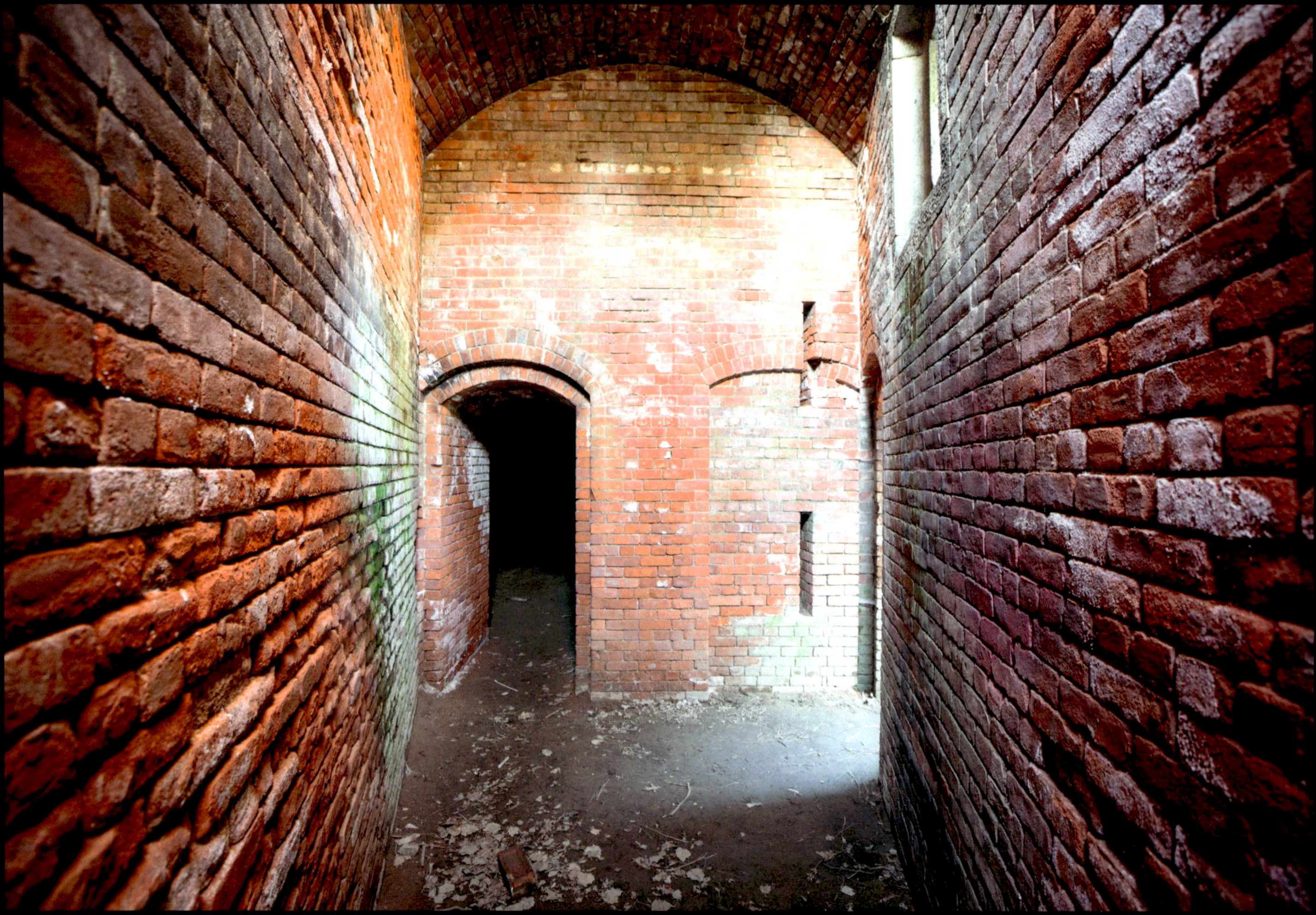

above A brick vault on the second level was once used to store gunpowder.

opposite Inside a second group of batteries, pencil-thin stalactites ornament a network of subterranean pits and passages, containing one piece of machinery that could date back over 100 years.

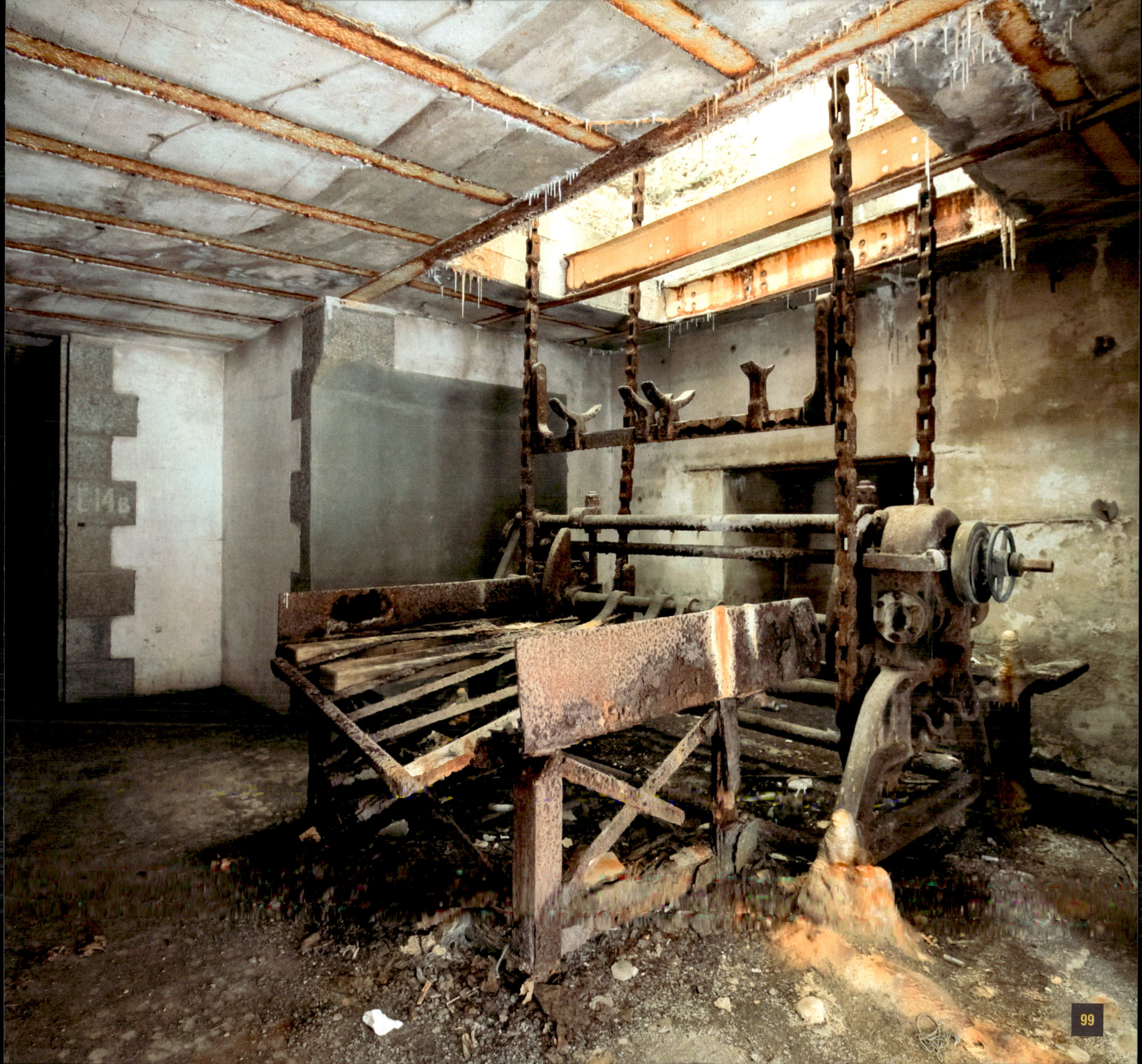

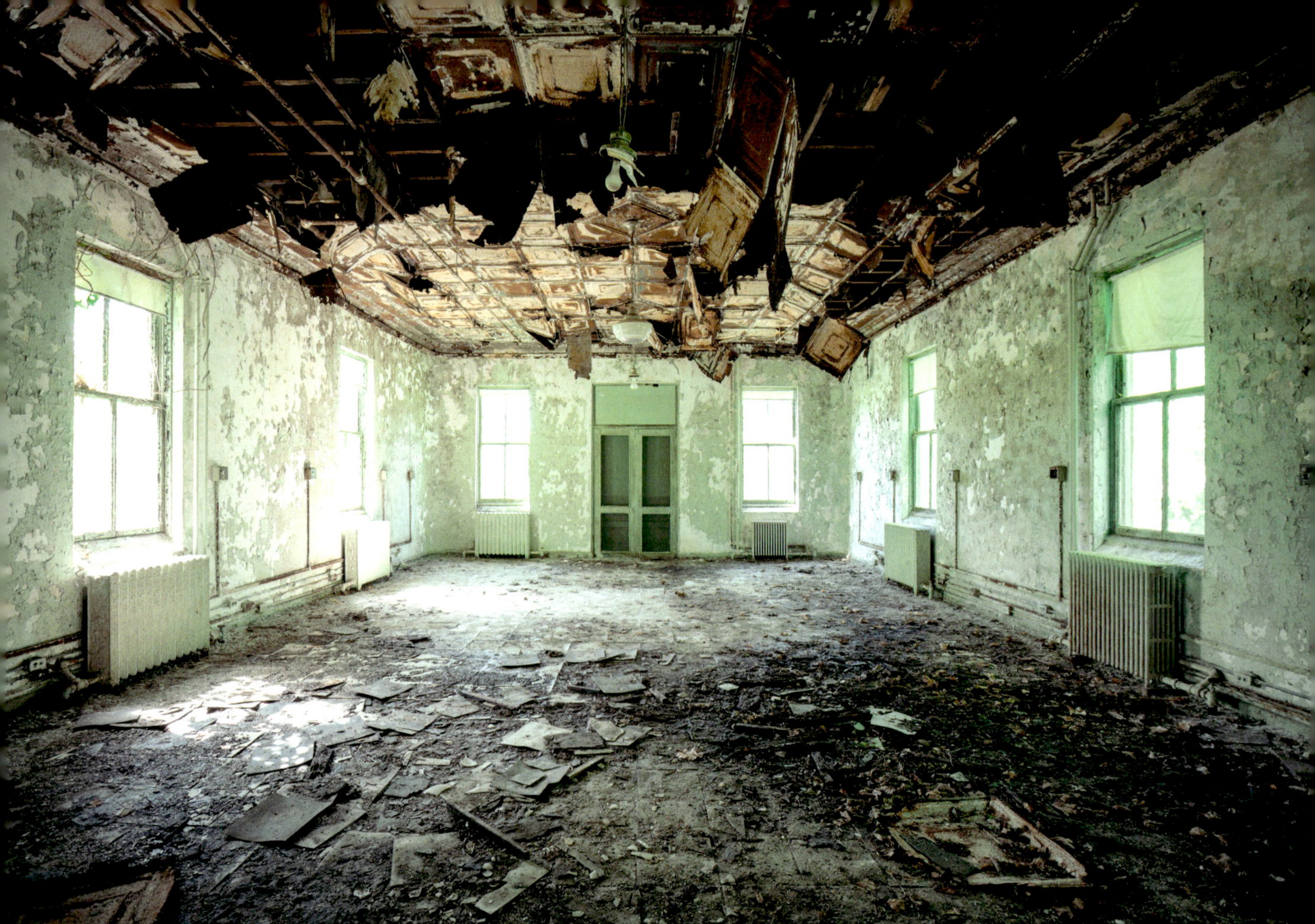

above On the eastern edge of the peninsula, the Fort Totten Post Hospital self-destructs in slow motion. The once-thriving infirmary with a 68-bed capacity exhibits a harrowing level of decay.

opposite A raccoon was unfazed by the devastation, but seemed as confounded by my presence as I was by his.

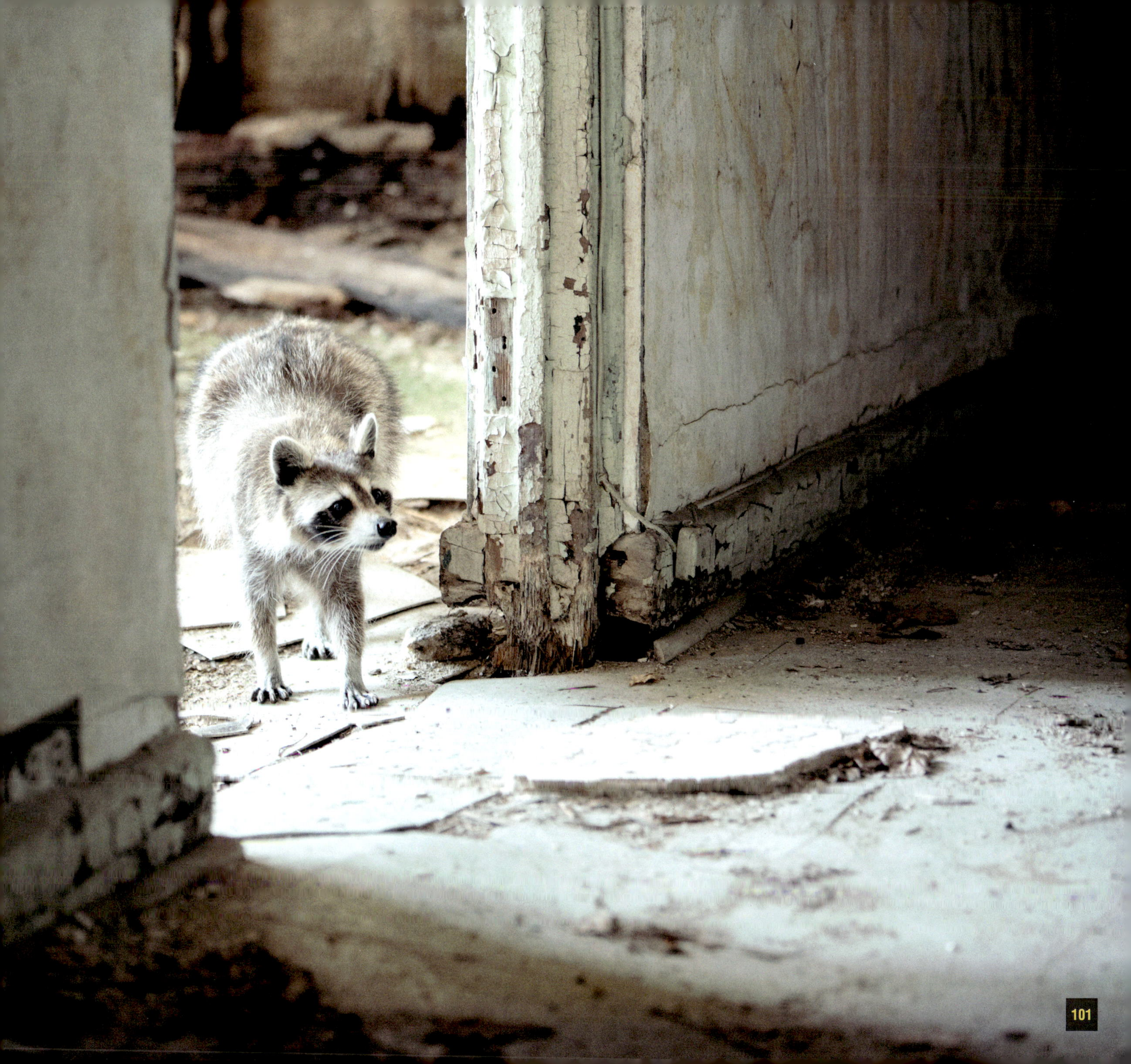

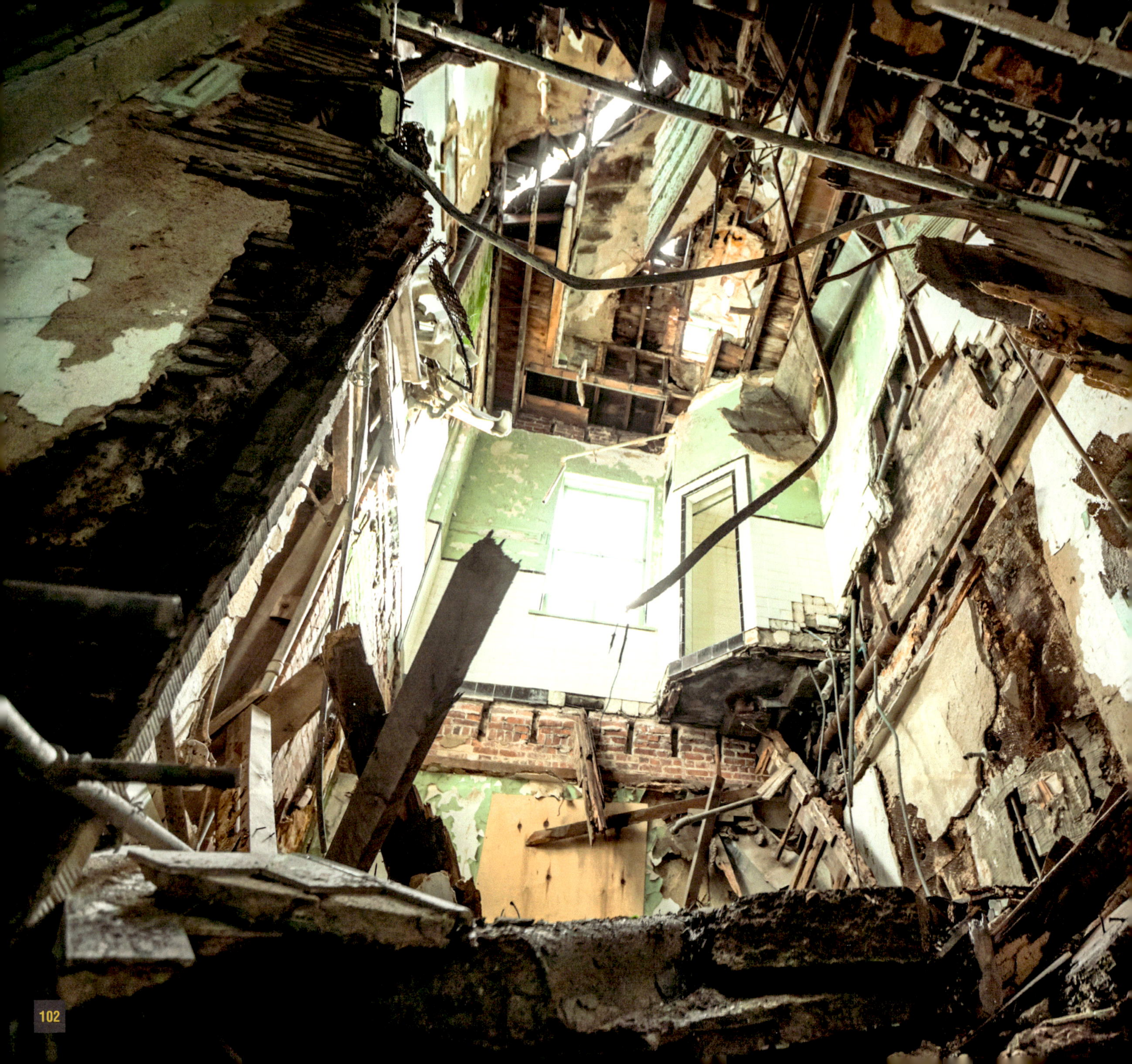

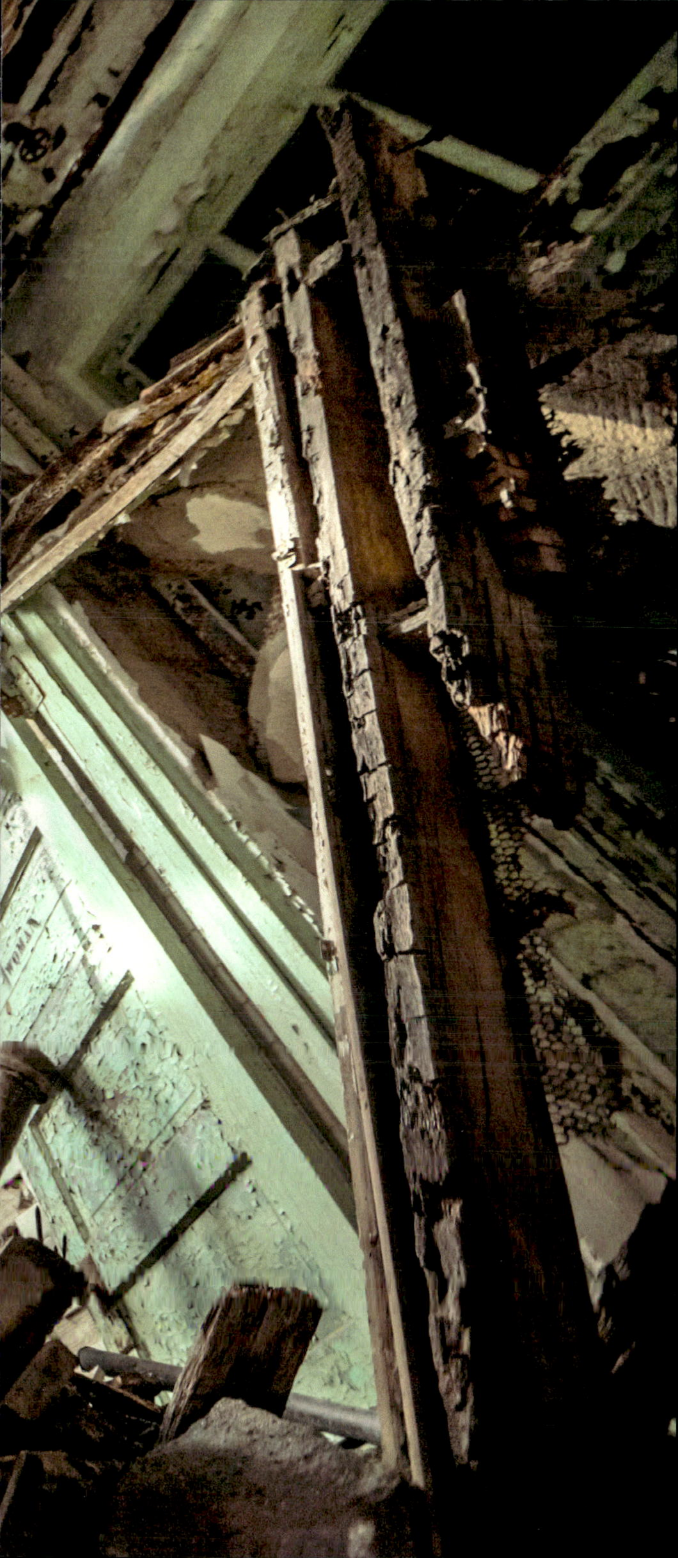

Some doorways give way to a four-story chasm. Buckling walls, bulging floors, and collapsed light fixtures mingle in the wretched sea-foam green interior.

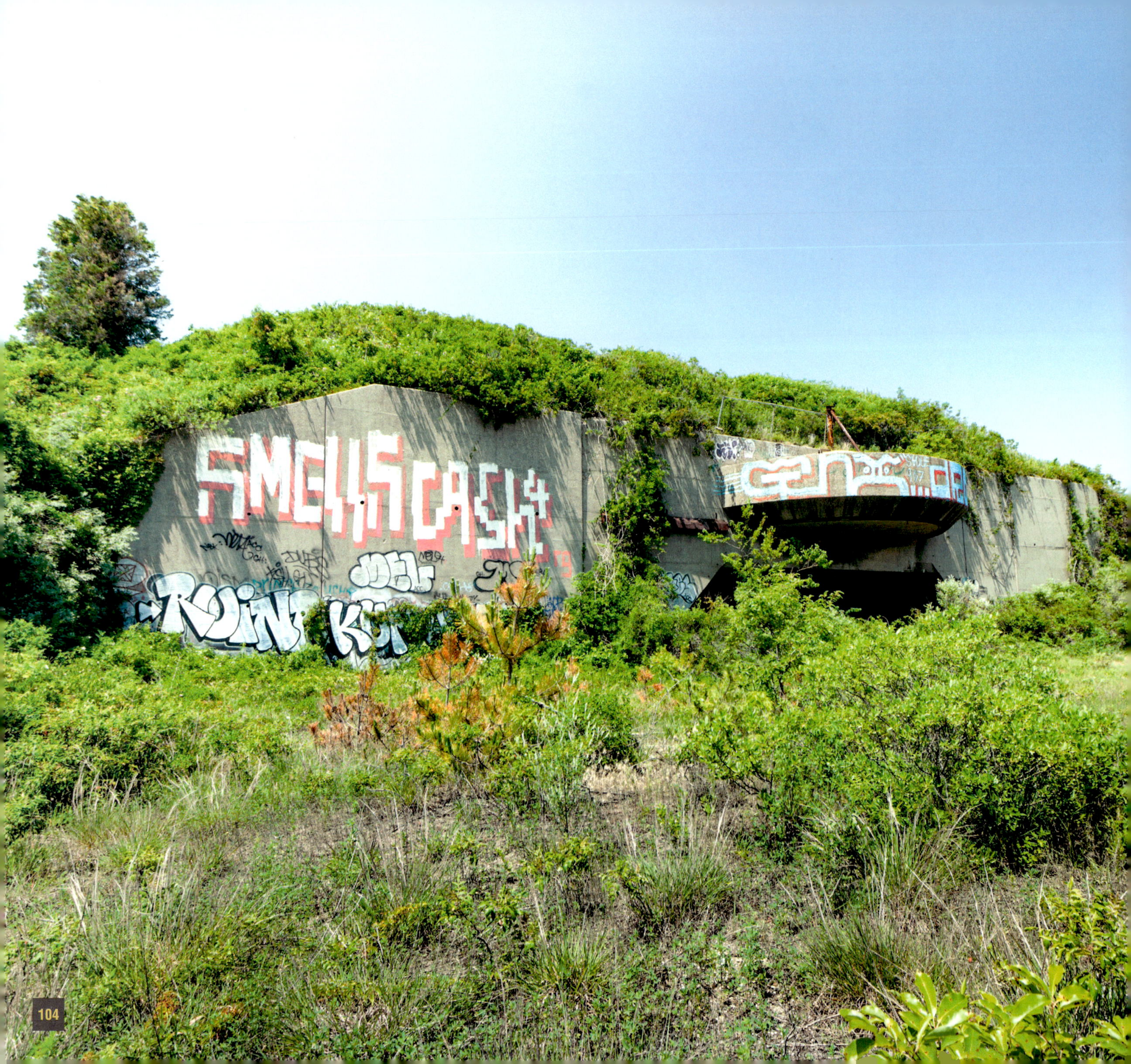

Fort Tilden

Rockaway, Queens

You wouldn't expect to find solitude by the sea in the United States' most populous city, but even in the height of summer, Fort Tilden can feel like your own private beach. Without lifeguards, snow cones, or a nearby bathroom, you're left with nothing but sandy stretches of unspoiled dunes, rotting bulkheads, and a familiar expanse of blue. It's an all-important escape for New Yorkers in the know, many of whom were greatly disappointed to learn that the beach was closed for the summer after Hurricane Sandy.

Fort Tilden is situated just inside the western tip of the Rockaway Peninsula, which is no longer reeling, but still recovering from the hurricane that ravaged the area in October 2012. In Breezy Point, just west of the base, over 100 ruined foundations stand as solemn reminders of the power of the storm.

With Fort Tilden beach closed, the base is all the more empty, silent, and serene, but tranquility is nothing new at Fort Tilden. Like so many of New York City's ex-military installations, the strategic post was never brought to bear against an enemy combatant, but stood at the ready for half a century to defend the city from those who would do us harm, outfitted with the latest military weaponry.

The area's first military endeavor came during the War of 1812, but Fort Tilden wasn't commissioned until 1917, when emergency fortifications were constructed in preparation for World War I. In the 1920s, the installation expanded its role as an anti-aircraft defense site, hosting a number of "war games" in which battles on land and sea were simulated for training and testing purposes. Only a small caretaker detachment was stationed at the post prior to the onset of the Second World War, when 1,000 men moved in to form a Coast Artillery Corps.

opposite Battery Harris remains the most striking remnant of Fort Tilden's military legacy.

In 1946, the base entered another period of diminished activity, during which its barracks were converted to provide public housing for 350 civilian families. The structures were reclaimed during the Cold War, when the 69th Anti-Aircraft Artillery Battalion was established at the site. Later, the base was the first to receive a Nike Hercules and its successor, the Ajax, which, as the largest supersonic surface-to-air missiles of their time, were capable of launching a nuclear warhead.

The missiles were patrolled by armed guards and German shepherds 24 hours a day until they were removed as part of a treaty between the United States and the Soviet Union in 1974. At this point, only 123 servicemen were stationed at Fort Tilden, and the Department of Defense announced plans to deactivate the post. With beach access and a pleasant natural setting, the base made an excellent addition to the Gateway National Recreation Area.

Unlike Fort Totten and Floyd Bennett Field, the majority of Fort Tilden's ex-military structures have been demolished, leaving most of the property to return to a natural state. Past the playing fields, the park gives way to wooded dunes and a circuitous network of walking and biking trails, where a half-dozen dilapidated structures lie half-concealed in a lush landscape of gnarled pines and shrubbery.

Just when you think you're walking in circles, the peculiar contours of Battery Harris appear from an earthen mound, skirted with sun-bleached planks leading up to the top of the casemate. From the summit, sea breezes ripple through maritime forests and the gray Atlantic suspends from a blue horizon. At your back, a hazy Manhattan skyline grows taller and shinier, but at Fort Tilden, it couldn't feel further away.

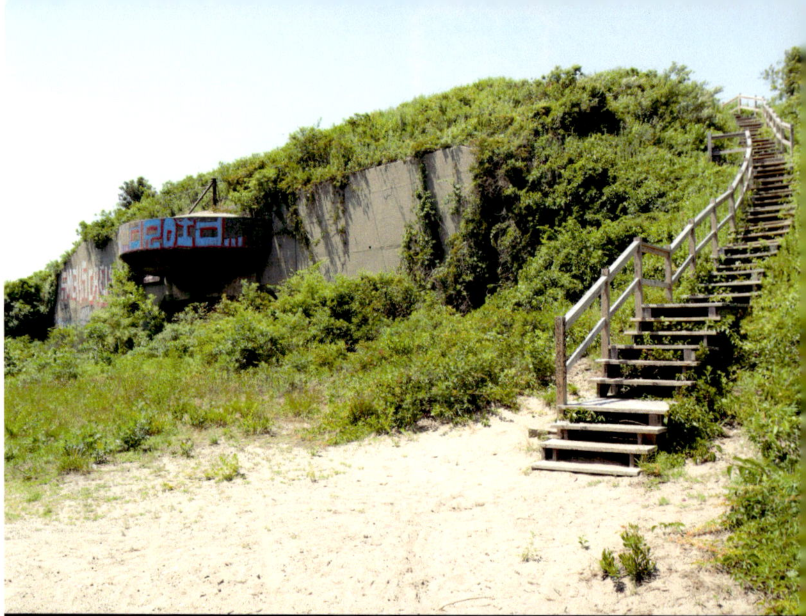

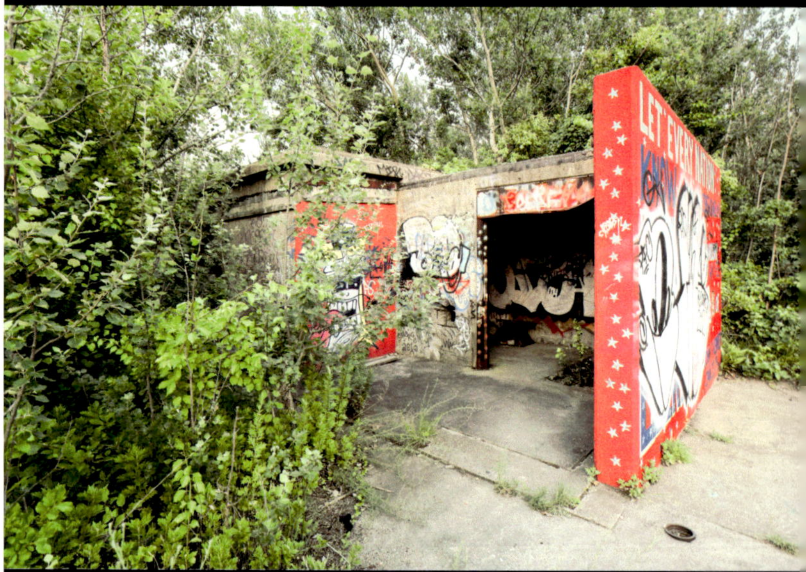

top A rickety stairway leads to impressive views of the New York harbor.

bottom A concrete shell marks the site of an old power generating station.

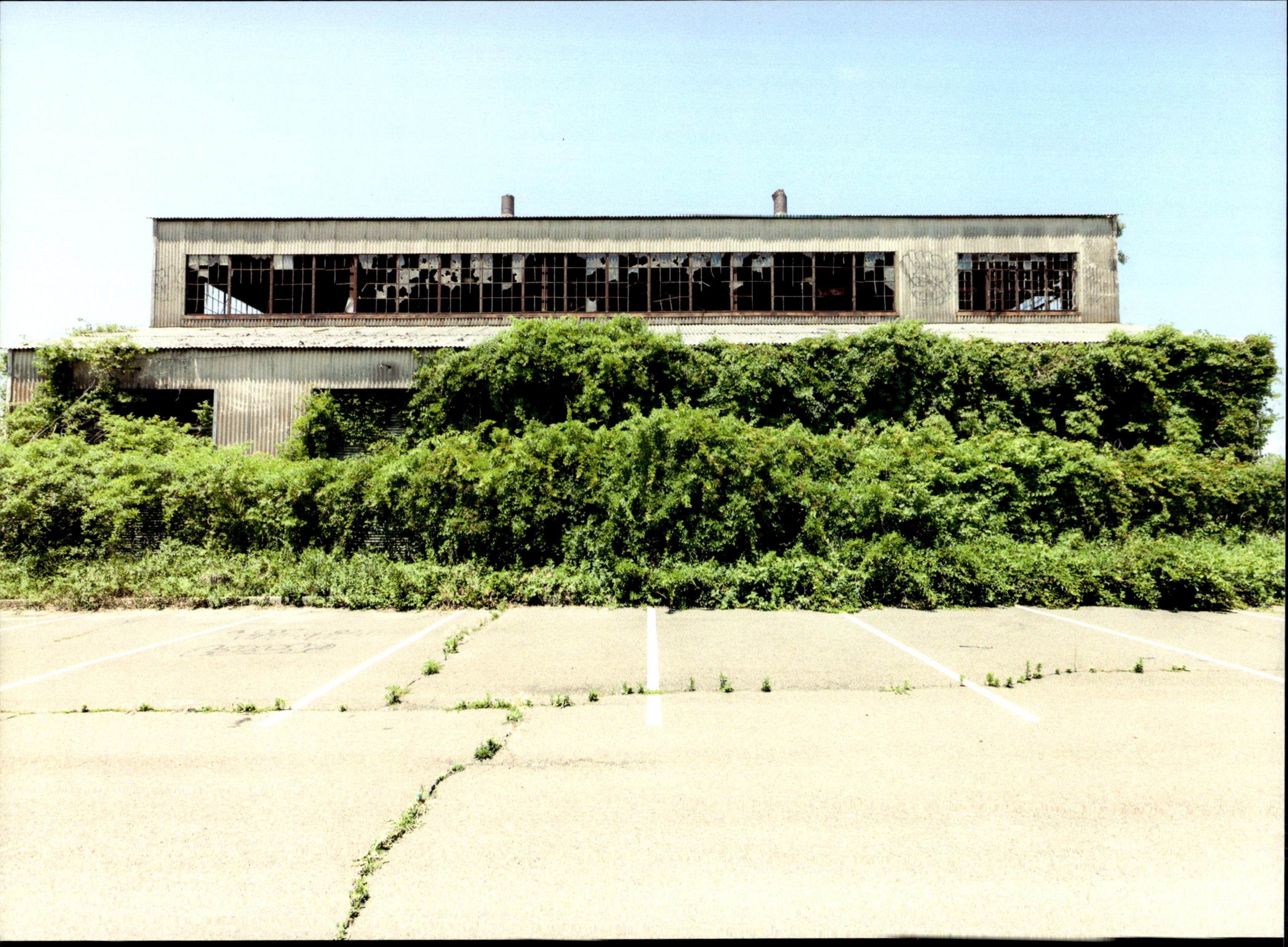

above This abandoned warehouse is the largest of Fort Tilden's few remaining structures.

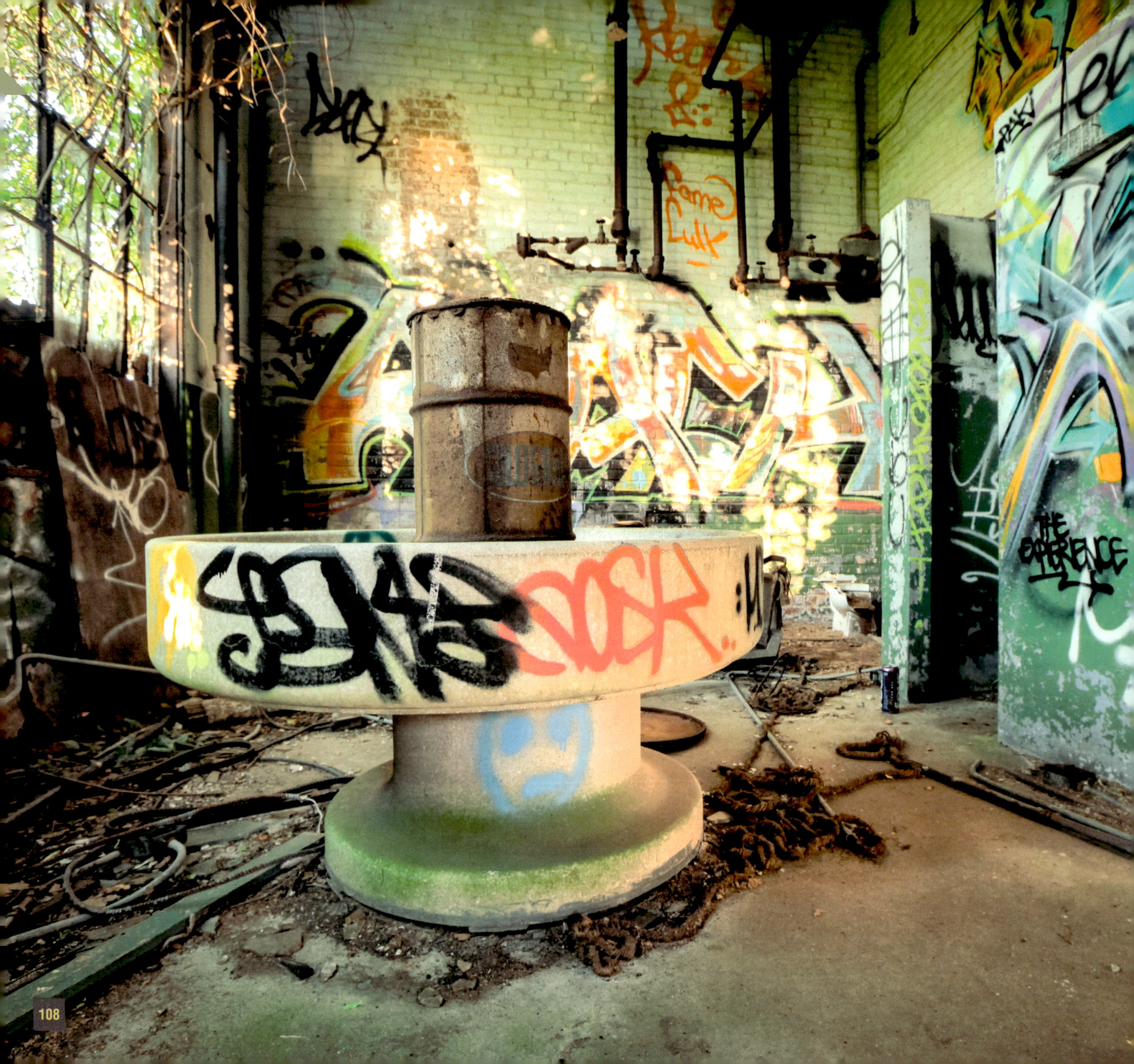
THE EXPERIENCE

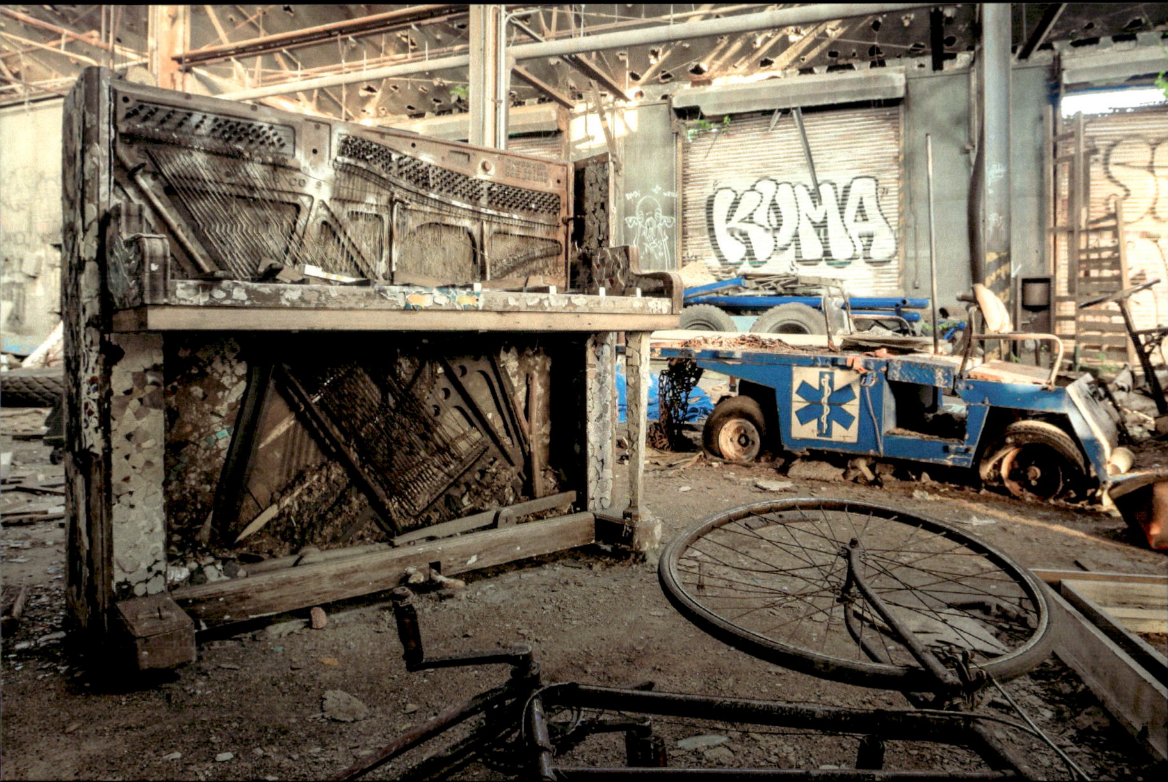

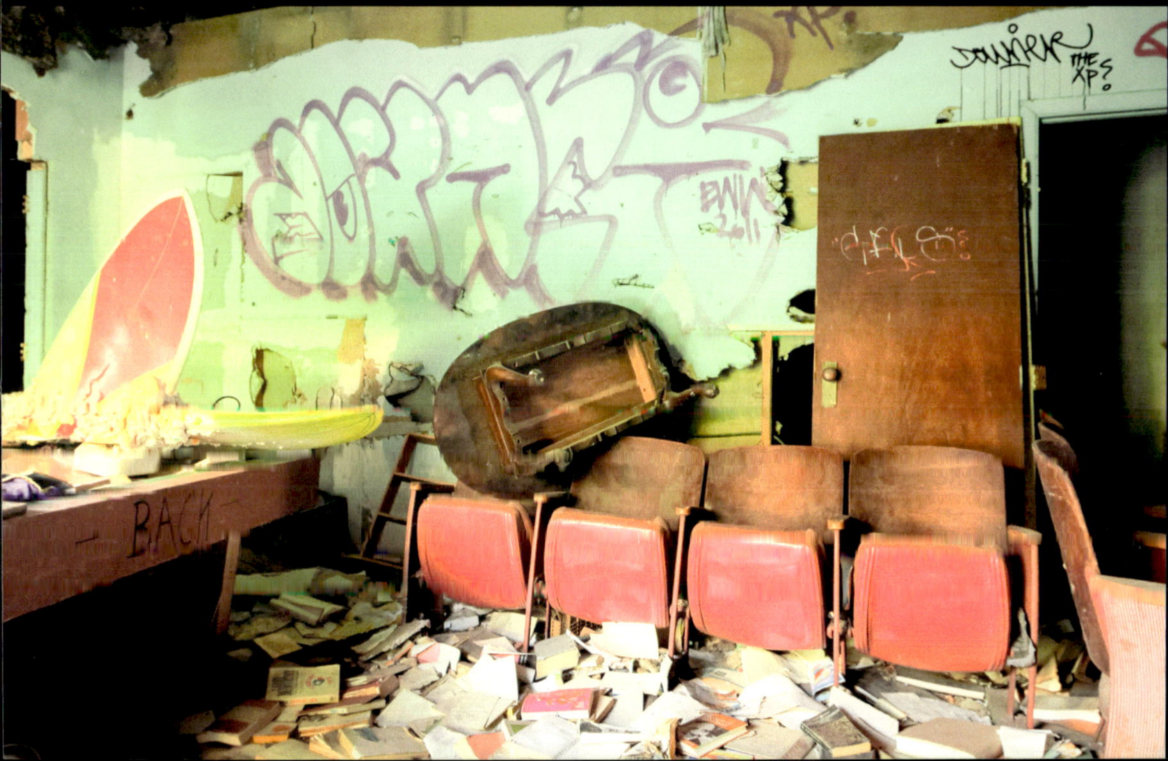

opposite Inside, a washroom has been covered with graffiti.

top Objects accrue from decades of park activity; the building had apparently been used to store theatrical props from a nearby stage.

bottom The tumbledown shed next door is filled with old books, a pool table, and discarded furniture.

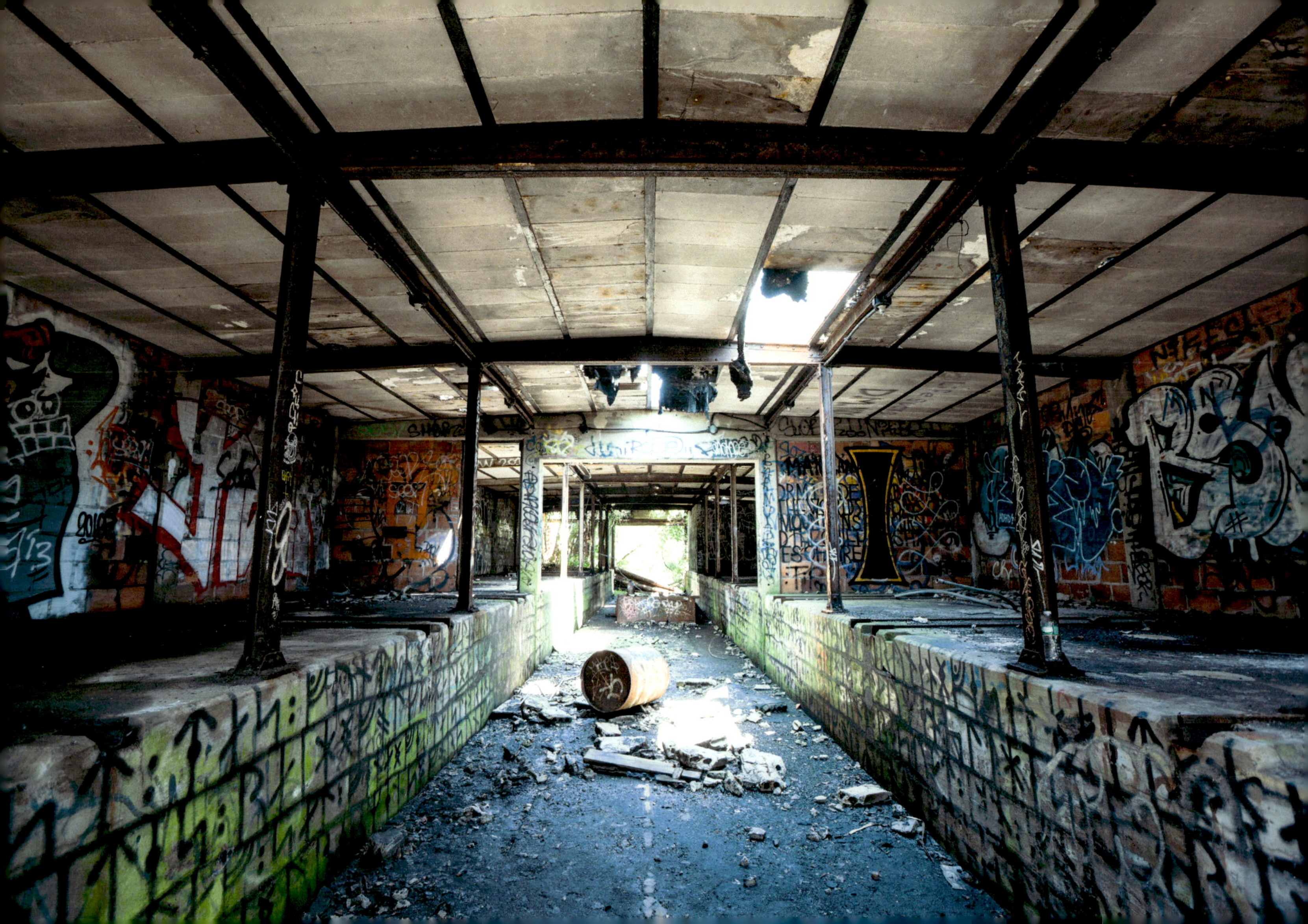

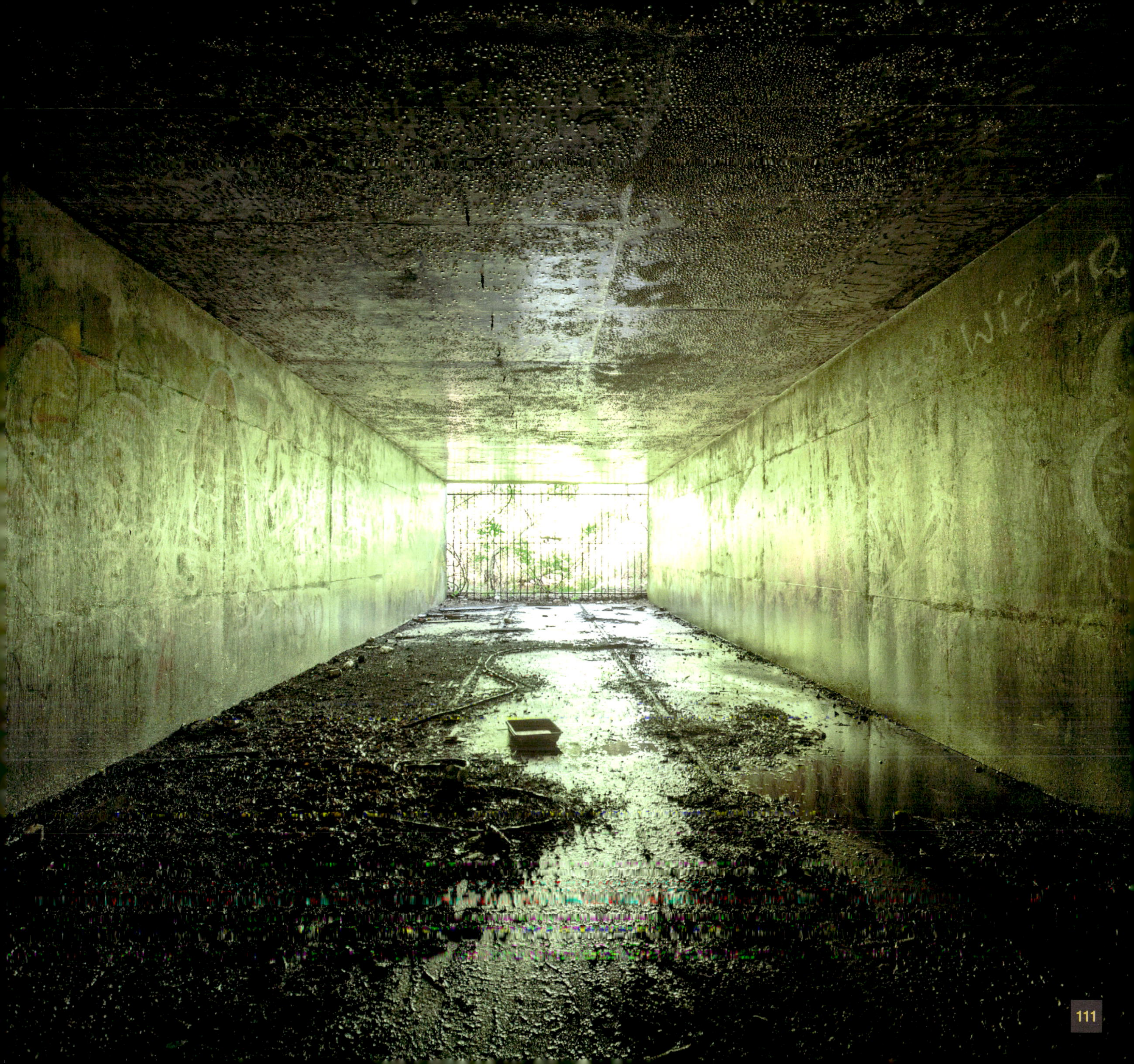

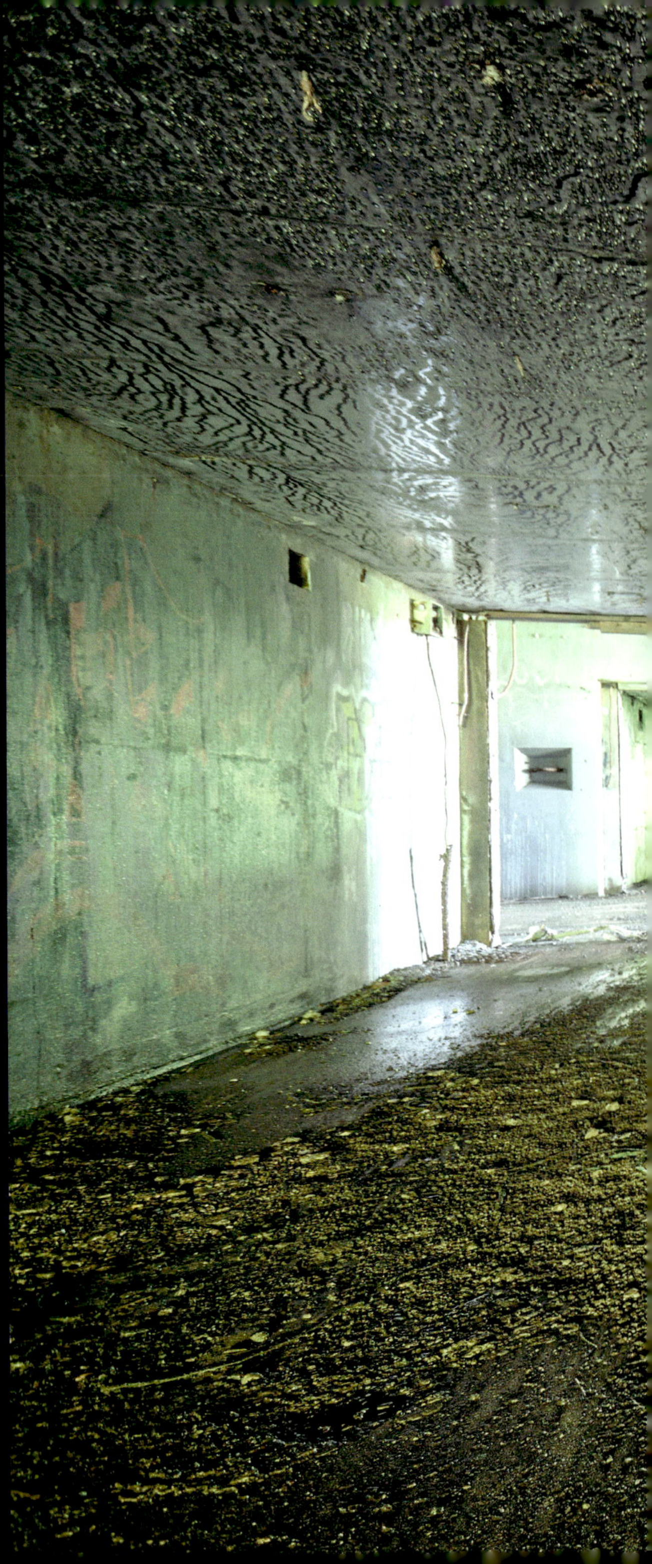

Inside Battery Harris East, corroded doorways lead to pitch-black powder rooms and magazines.

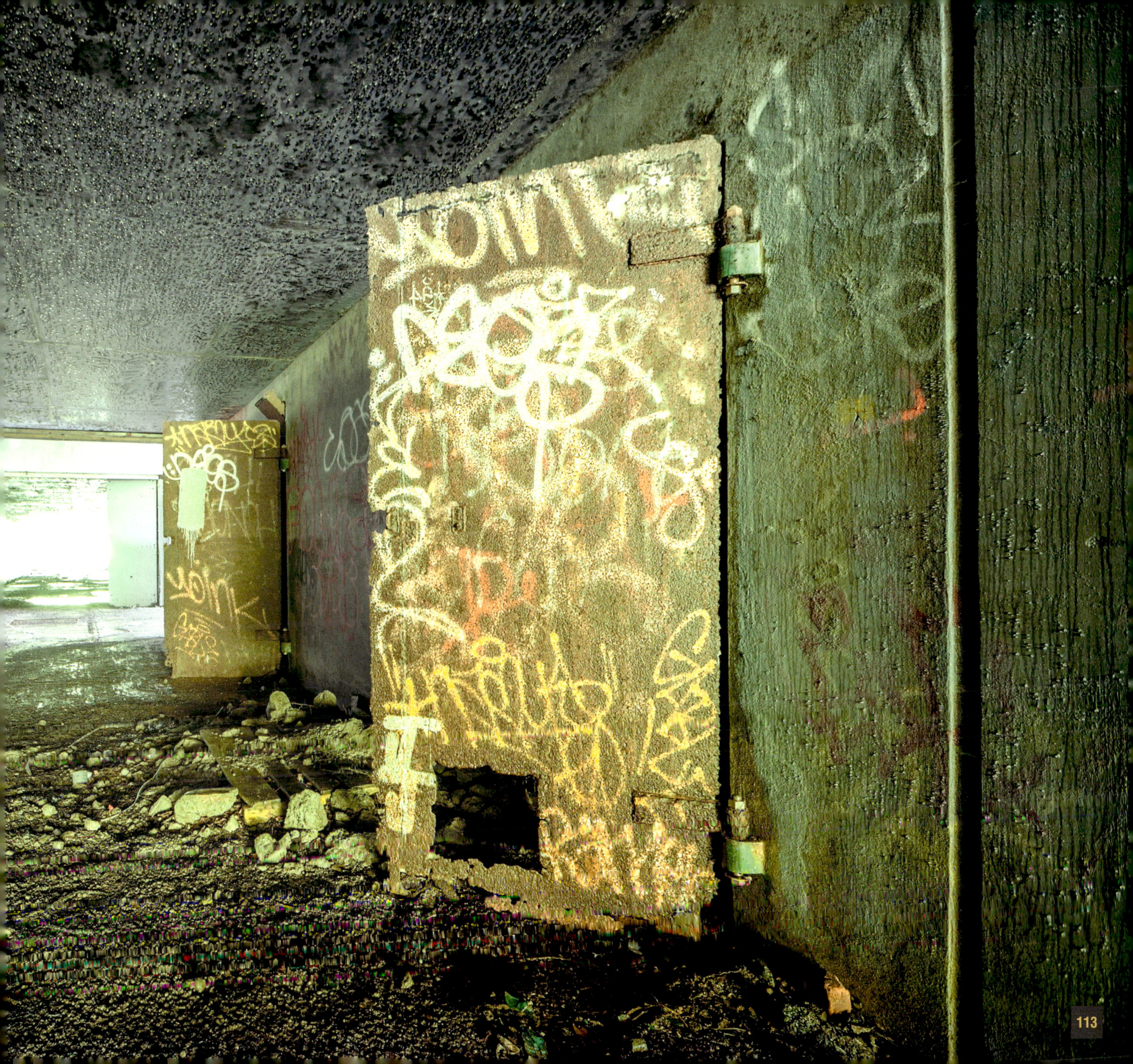

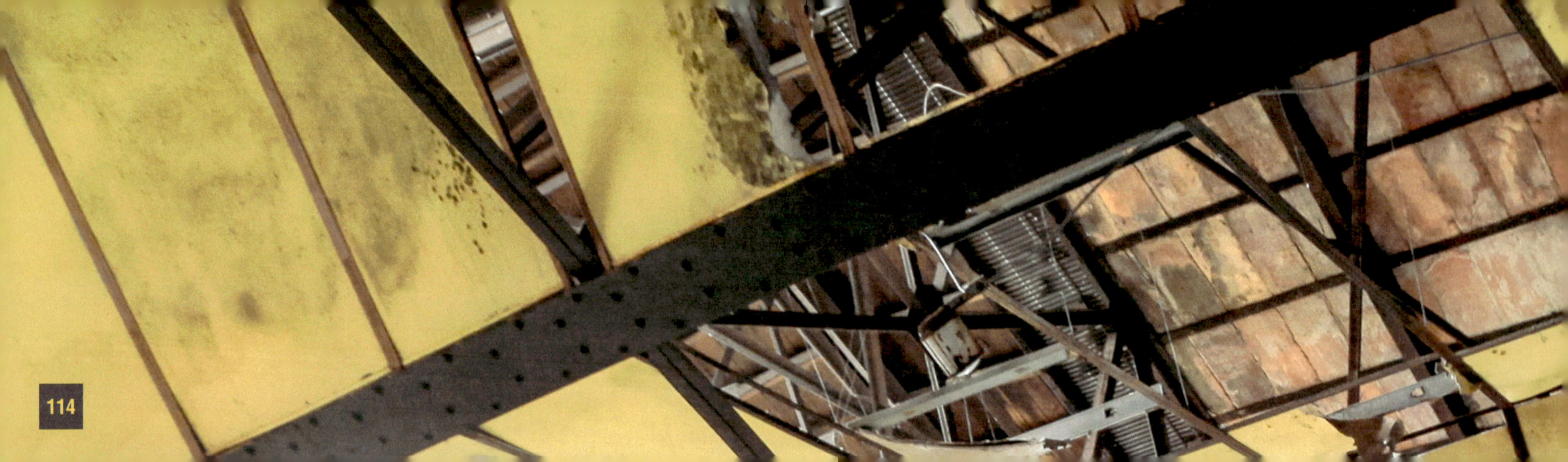

The Gowanus Batcave

Bush Terminal

The Domino Sugar® Refinery

Industrial Sites

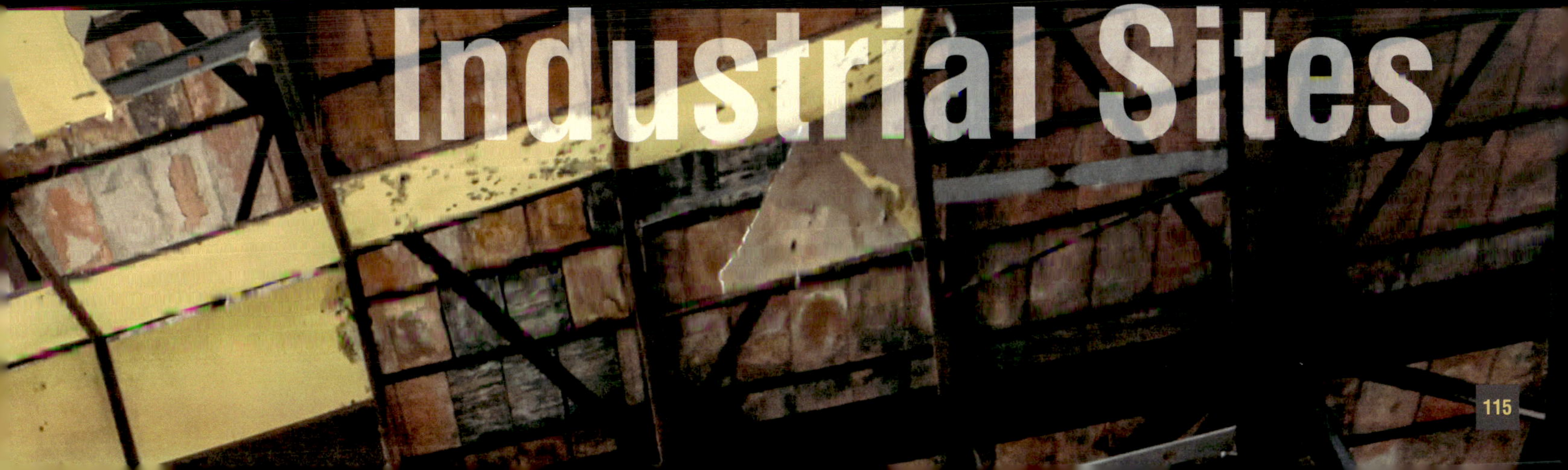

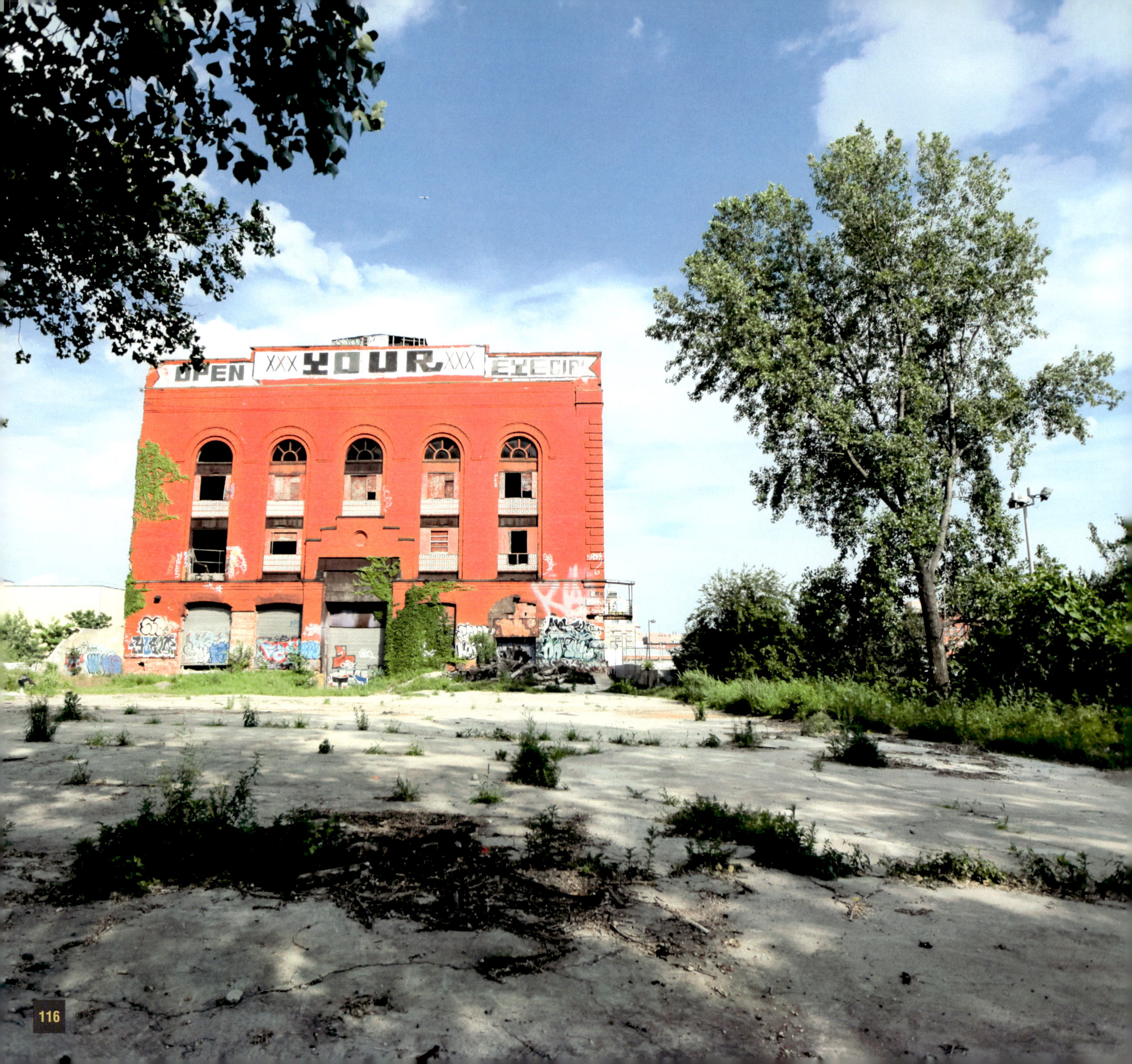
OPEN
XXX YOUR XXX

The Gowanus Batcave

Gowanus, Brooklyn

Not long ago, a pack of teenage runaways lived the dream in Gowanus's infamous Batcave, shacking up rent-free in an abandoned MTA powerhouse on the shore of the notoriously toxic Gowanus Canal. Out of the grime, in back rooms and crooked halls, the artifacts of this sizable squatter settlement remained to enlighten, amuse, and unnerve the intrepid few who entered the structure, until it was cleaned up in preparation for a new development.

The plant was constructed in 1896 to serve a rapidly expanding subway system in the outer boroughs. Originally known as the Central Power Station of the Brooklyn Rapid Transit Company, the powerhouse was positioned near the Gowanus Canal to facilitate an efficient intake of coal to power an arsenal of steam-driven generators. The plant's technology couldn't keep up with the times, and after a brief second life as a paper recycling plant (and later a klezmer dance hall), the structure was abandoned. Today, it's commonly known as the "Batcave," allegedly named for the creatures that once lived in its broken-down ceiling.

In the early 2000s, a colony of homeless young people settled inside the building, establishing a thriving, peaceable community. At onset, the squat was kept under the watchful eye of a few individuals who ensured hard drugs and detrimental criminal activities were kept at bay. But before long, authorities made their first attempt to evict the punk-rock squatters, leaving the colony without its guardians.

Over the next two years, heroin use grew rampant, and a wave of brutality overwhelmed the structure. Drug-induced violence culminated in a series of nightmarish events; one resident was thrown from a window, another overdosed and was left on the street for law enforcement to find. Frightened community members saw to it that the Batcave colony was ousted indefinitely in 2006.

opposite On the bank of the toxic Gowanus Canal, the Batcave's dilapidated façade conceals a sordid wonderland within.

The residents are long gone, but most of their humble furnishings remained when I visited in 2012. Fashioned in old corner offices of the power plant, some living quarters were generously sized and complete with beds, bookshelves, and lounge chairs. Others were no larger than a closet. Album covers, skulls and superheroes, and a general state of chaos were prominent features of these impromptu bedrooms. While large-scale pieces by notable graffiti artists dominated the Batcave's main hall, the most intriguing artworks could be found on the bedroom walls. Always obscene, typically humorous, and occasionally clever, these amateur scrawls portrayed a community of fun-loving, hard-living, creative youth, though some inscriptions tended toward the dark and morbid, pointing to a deep resentment for society and obsessions with death and suicide.

It's no wonder so many lost souls found solace here—the Batcave's eye-popping top floor certainly felt like a sanctuary. Light rain filtered down from a collapsed ceiling in a sweeping mist. In a permanent puddle, arched reflections of the clerestory windows trembled. Interweaving supports shimmered like the facets of a diamond as you moved throughout the space—it was a crust punk kaleidoscope that constituted one of the most spectacular abandoned sights in New York City.

In 2012, news broke that the Batcave had been purchased by a developer with plans to convert the power station into artists' studios and an exhibition space, marking a significant step in Gowanus's contentious transition from industrial wasteland to trendy residential neighborhood. Fortunately, the structure itself will be saved, and with it, a piece of Brooklyn's industrial legacy. The days are numbered on the Batcave's exquisite decay, but its iconic edifice will remain, marking the spot where a youthful dream lived and died.

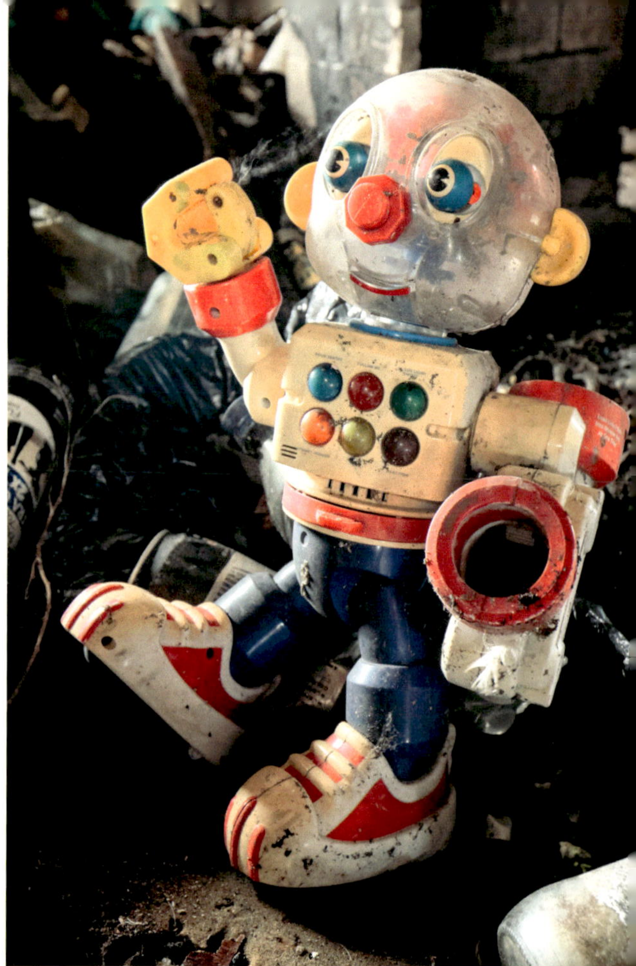

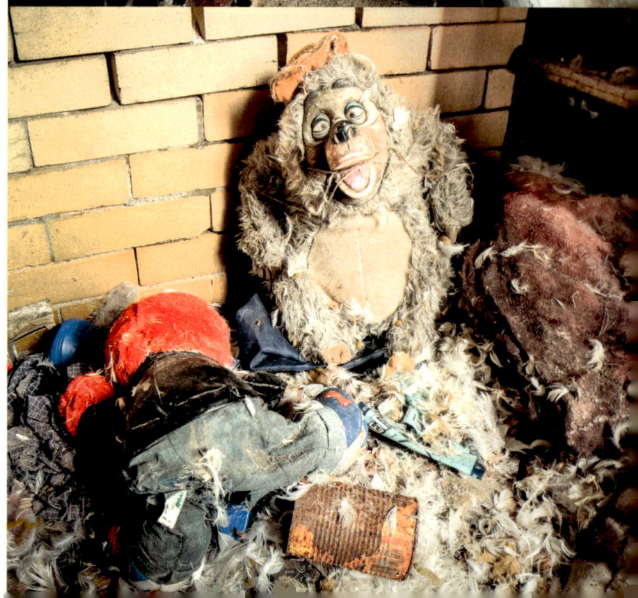

top A freaky Fisher-Price® robot lies mired in filth.

bottom Stuffed animals are the most abundant artifacts.

opposite Pleated ceiling panels on the top floor once muffled the hum and hiss of a mammoth industrial undertaking, but their effect is more visual now.

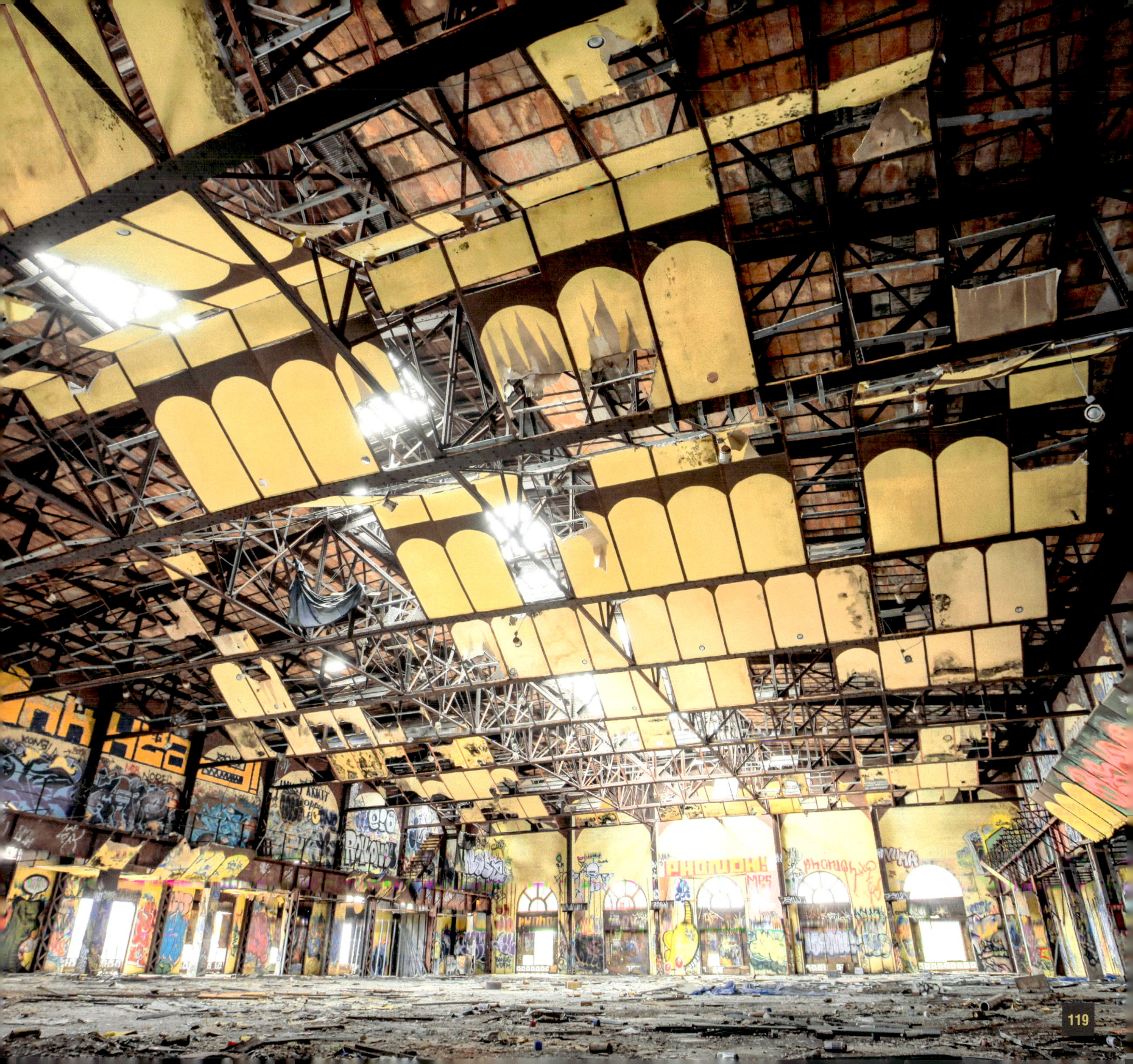

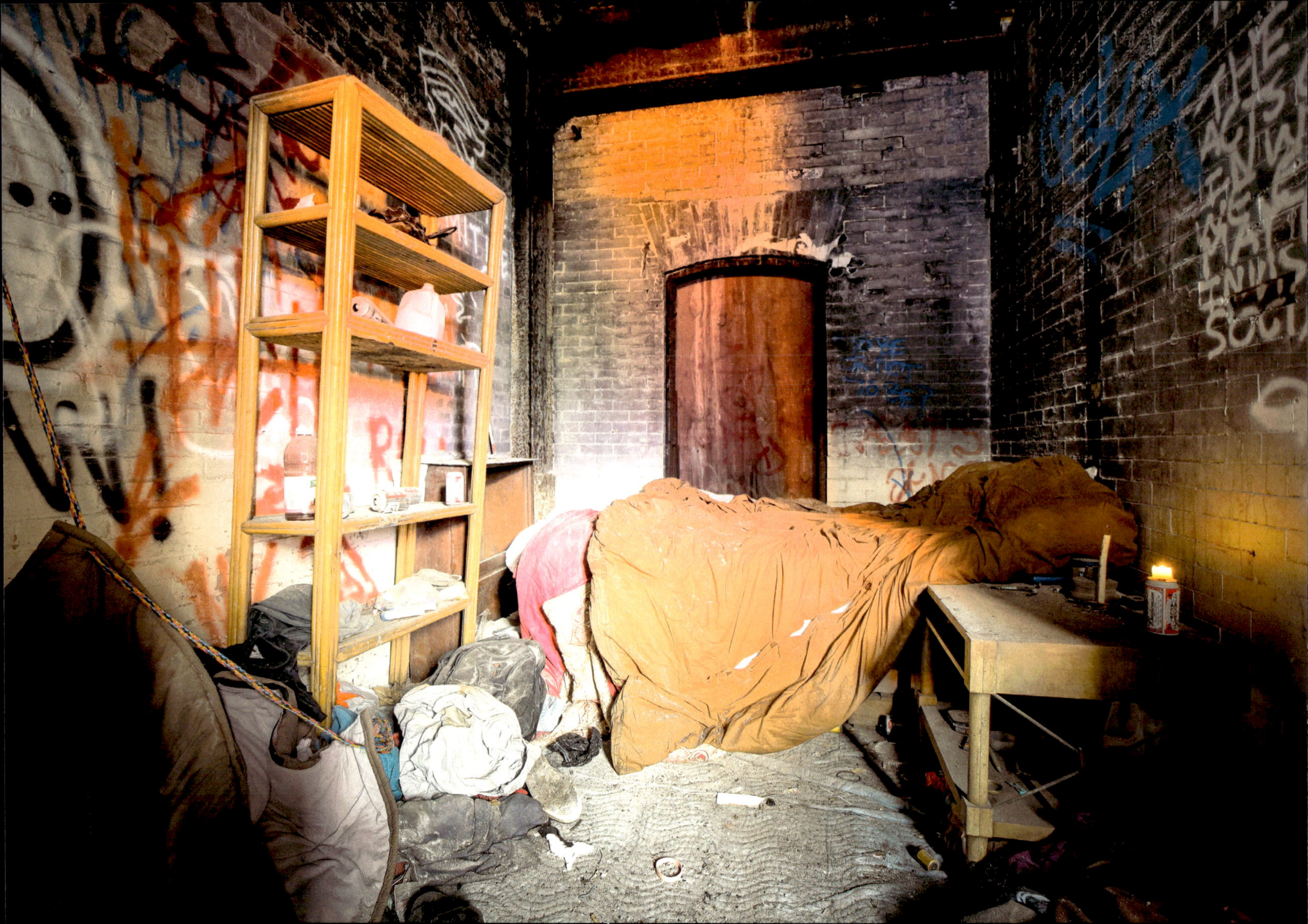

There was an aspect of inhabitance in some of the rooms that often had me looking over my shoulder, half expecting to come face to face with a young man or woman who lived there.

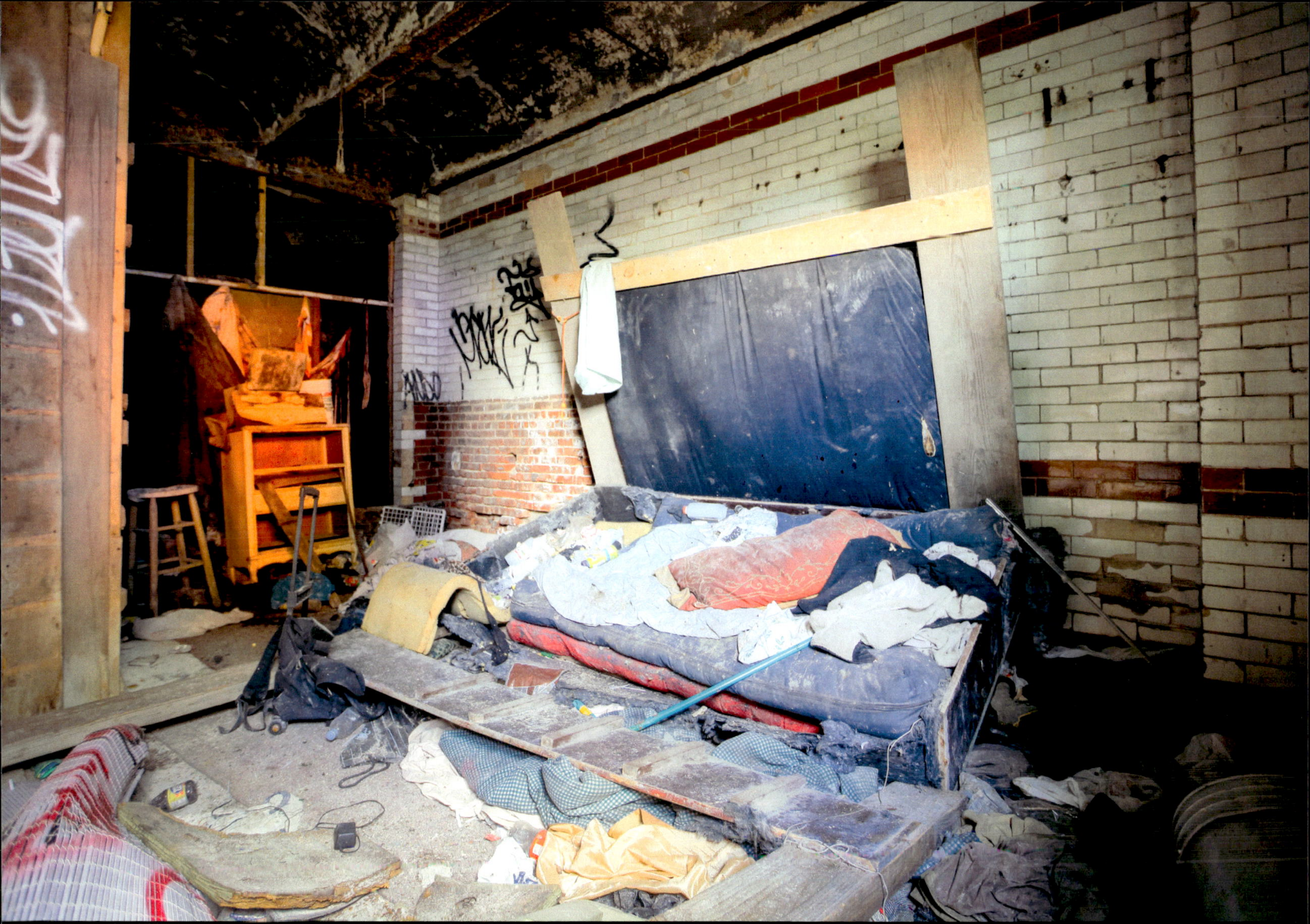

But only their objects remained to tell their stories—seasons squandered in cheap beer and rolled cigarettes, late nights

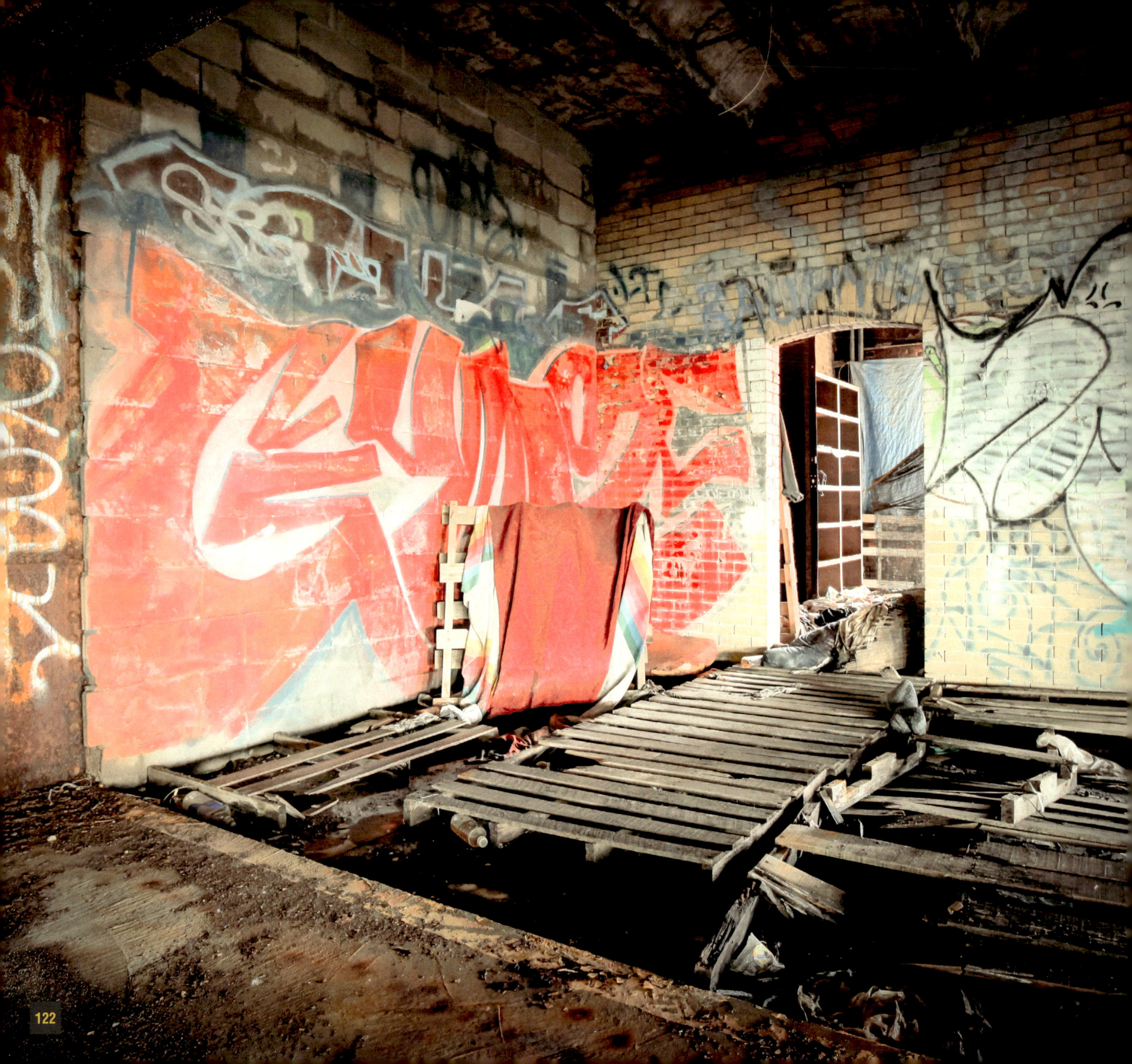

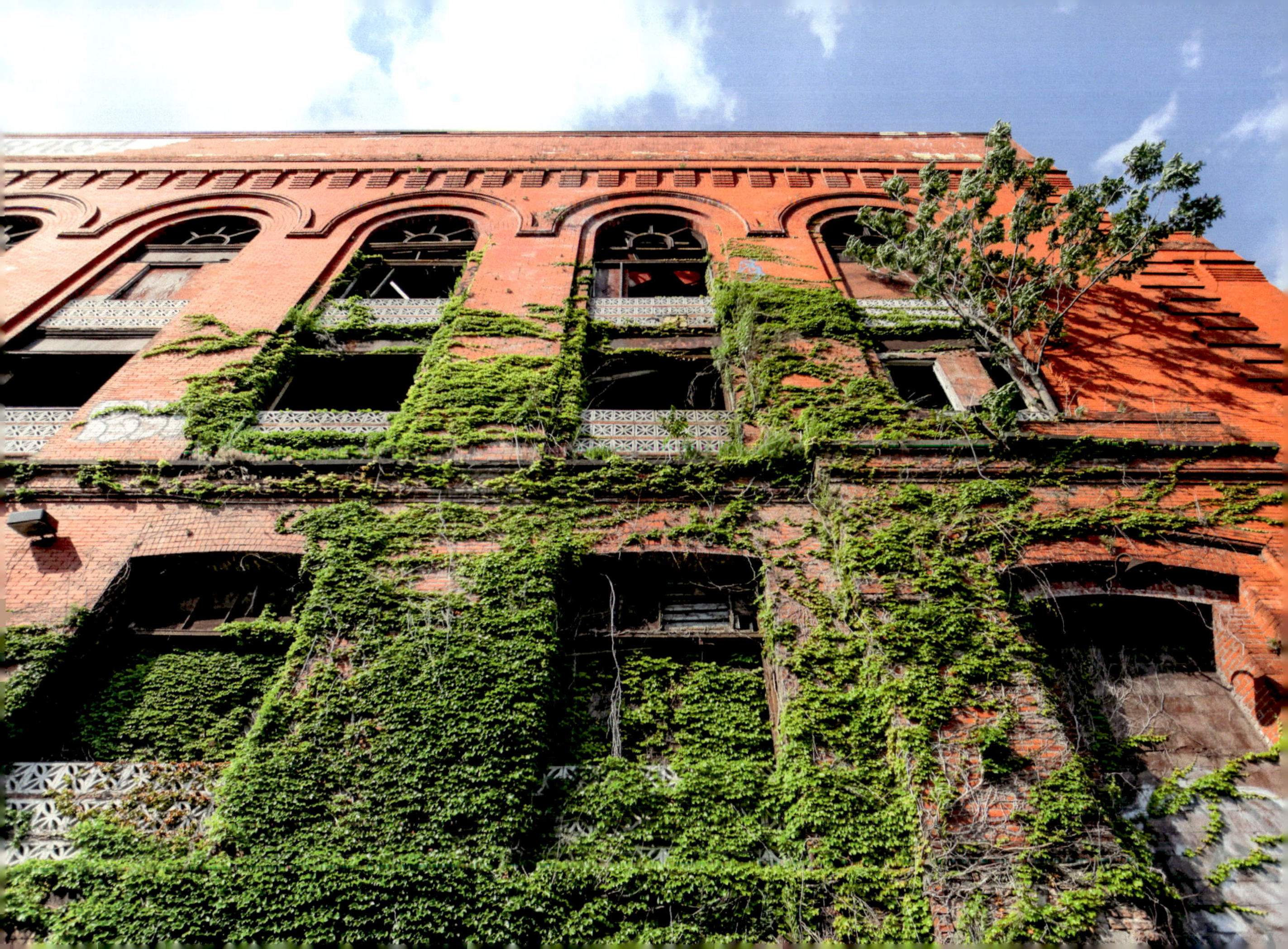

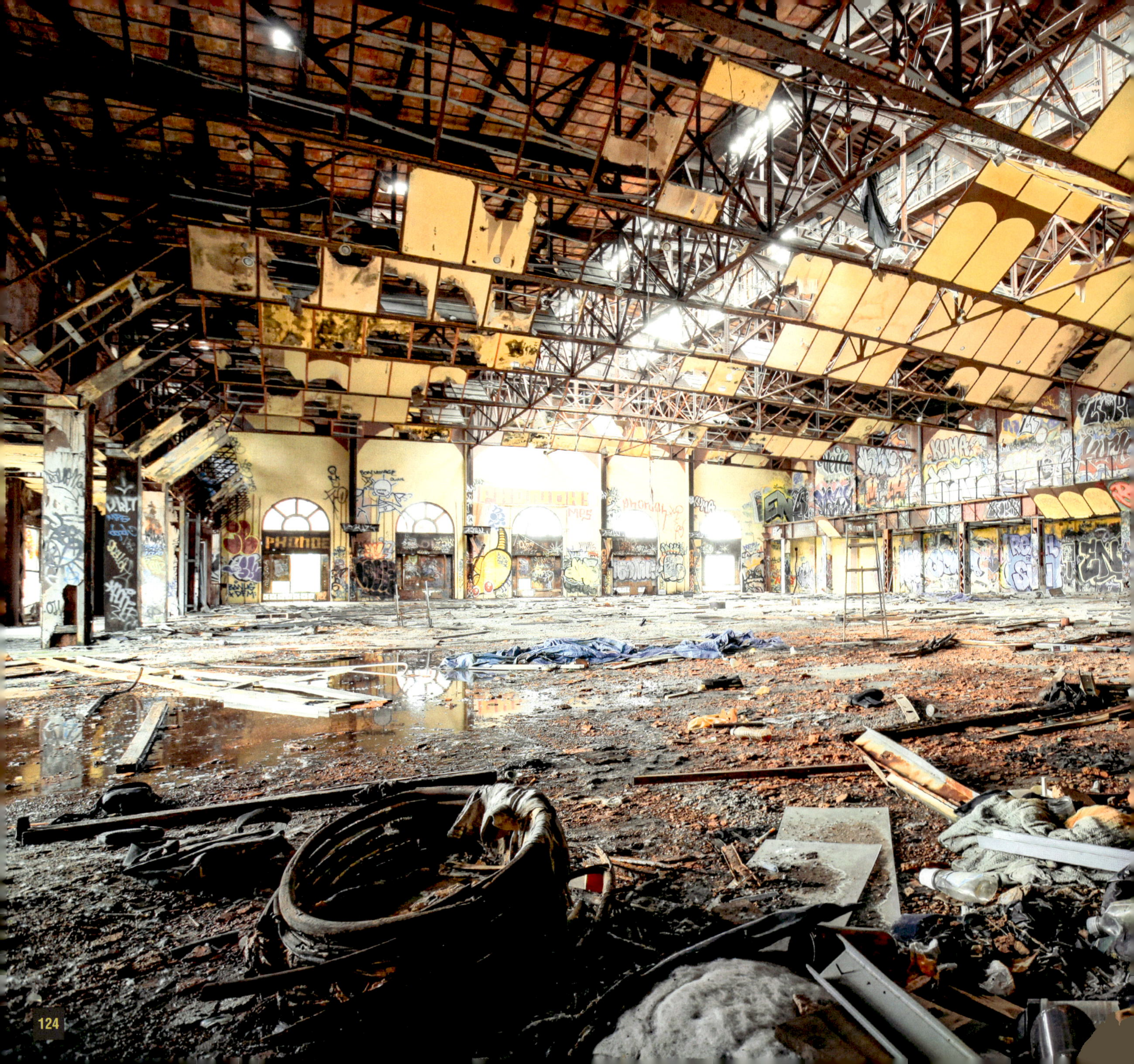

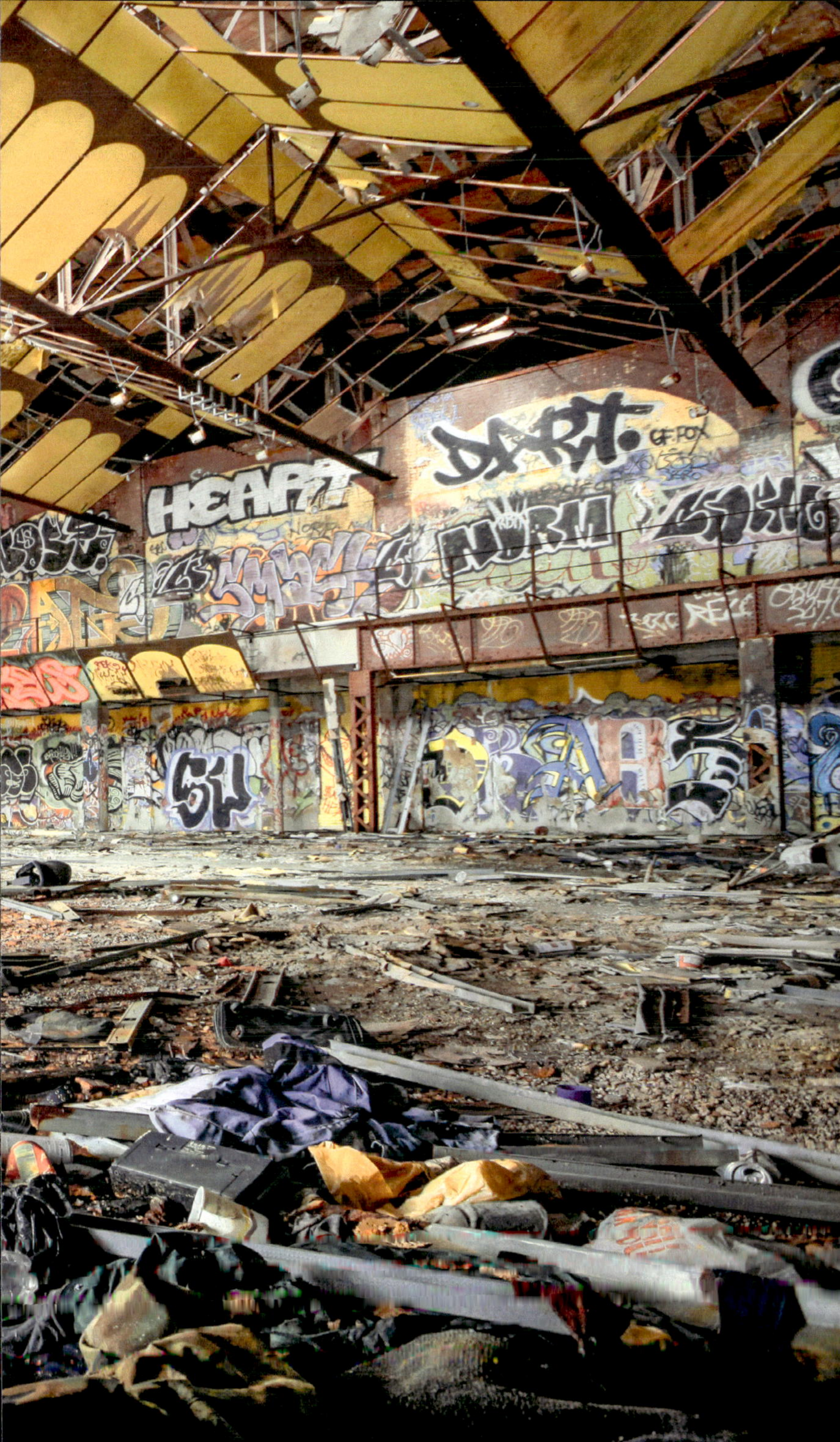

The stunning top floor of the Batcave hosted numerous illicit parties in recent years, until a new owner sealed off the structure. The Brooklyn underground has lost one of its most beloved spaces.

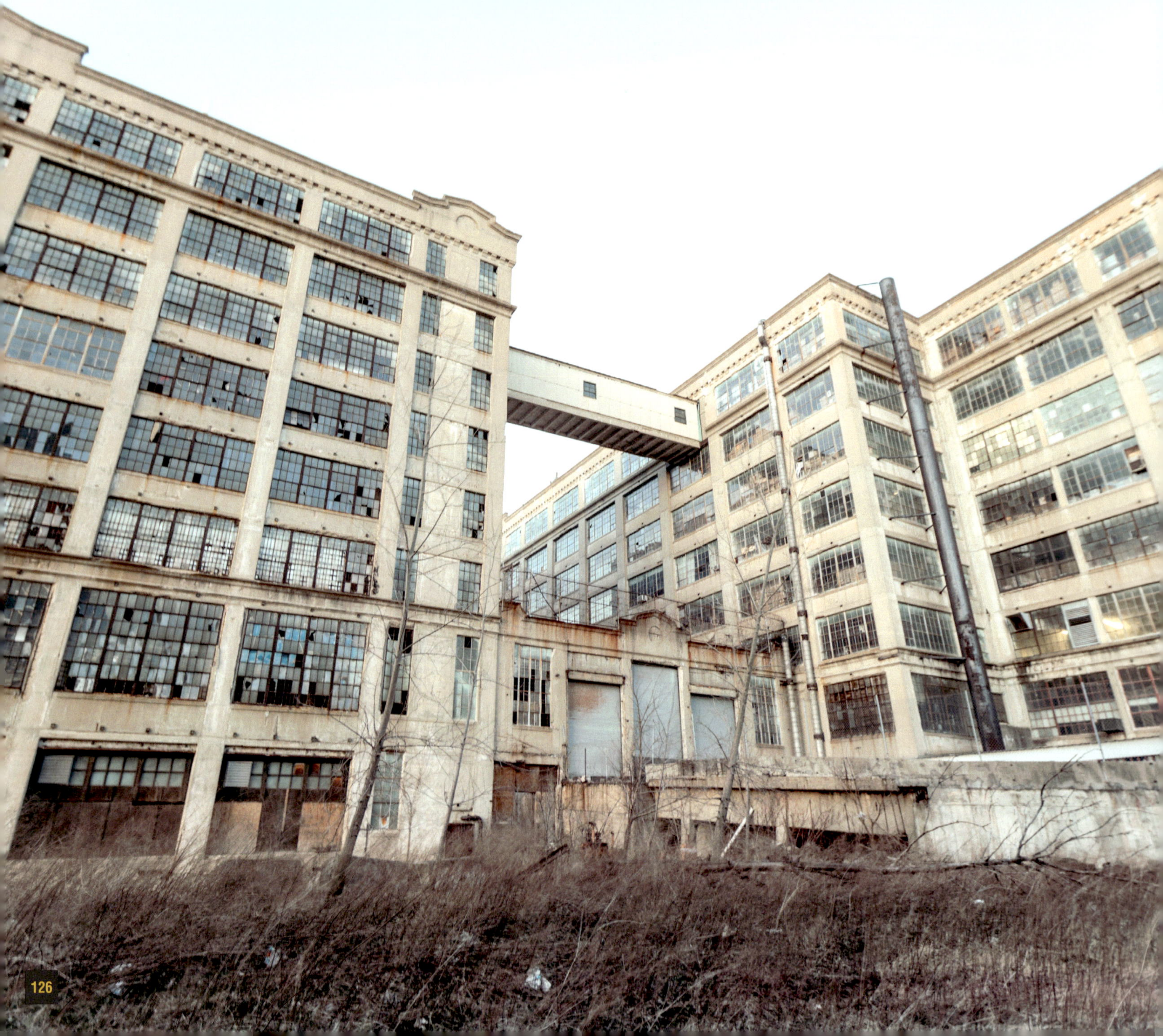

The Bush Terminal

Sunset Park, Brooklyn

Past the Gowanus Expressway, pedestrians drop out of sight and a hush descends over Sunset Park, Brooklyn. Buildings stretch westward toward the harbor, growing longer, grittier, and decidedly industrial. Dilapidated warehouses flank the streets, but this isn't a ghost town. At the water's edge, machinery hums, workmen joke, a 16-wheeler rumbles by—it's the sound of industry surviving on the Brooklyn waterfront.

This land was home to little more than a deserted fisherman's shack until the ambitious son of an oil tycoon realized its potential, transforming the dumping ground for his father's refinery into one of the most enduring manufacturing hubs in Brooklyn. The man was Irving T. Bush and he called his masterpiece the Bush Terminal.

His design allowed for fully-integrated receiving, manufacturing, and distribution, saving companies a fortune in trucking costs, and offering small concerns the resources that were traditionally only available to major corporations. Conceived as a "city within a city," the Bush Terminal was equipped with seven piers capable of accommodating 35 ships, an arsenal of tugboats, trucks, and barges, 19 buildings for warehousing and manufacturing, and 36 miles of exclusive railroad track with connections to every major line. Covering 200 acres, the Bush Terminal was the world's largest multi-tenant industrial facility, employing over 30,000 workers at its peak.

The terminal was so efficient that the U.S. Navy chose to commandeer four of its warehouses during World War I. In a letter to Franklin D. Roosevelt (Assistant Secretary to the Navy at the time), Bush intimated, "it's almost as though I am paying the penalty of having created the best facilities of their kind." Later, Bush would cooperate with the military again by spearheading the design of the Brooklyn Army Terminal, located just to the south.

Occupancy at the Bush Terminal has dipped from time to time, but it's largely been spared from the neglect and abandonment so rampant across other areas of the Brooklyn waterfront. In the 1980s, residential conversions in Manhattan forced many manufacturers into the outer boroughs, concentrating industrial operations in affordable Sunset Park. As shipping practices evolved, so did the function of the Bush Terminal—by the 1970s, its seven original piers were rarely used, but most of its buildings still function today for storage, distribution, and light manufacturing.

opposite As of 2006, the vacancy rate for industrial buildings in Sunset Park was less than 1%, but a few pockets of the sprawling Bush Terminal remain underused.

Despite its resilience, the Bush Terminal can't help showing its age; much of its infrastructure dates back to the early 20th century. In 2007, the New York City Economic Development Corporation (NYCEDC) introduced an investment plan to revitalize the Sunset Park industrial district, updating antiquated facilities to create a "21st-century model for diverse, dense, and environmentally-sustainable industry." The long-term plan includes the adaptive reuse of the terminal's industrial spaces, reactivation of rails and rail floats, and the construction of a public waterfront park on the site of the Bush Terminal Piers.

Construction is progressing on the park, which will open this part of the waterfront to the public for the first time. The city took over the site in the 1970s with plans to convert four of the piers into a containerized shipping terminal, but construction hit a roadblock when authorities discovered that the contractor was using questionable materials as landfill. Polluted with arsenic, lead, oil sludge, and industrial waste, the site was labeled a brownfield and forgotten until 2006, when the city was awarded $17.8 million from the state (the largest grant ever given for a brownfield remediation) to clean up the site.

Long-term renovations are planned for the three remaining piers as part of the NYCEDC's vision for the waterfront, but until these investments are made, the derelict quays provide a vital habitat for waterfowl. Behind a chain-link fence, the area is left largely undisturbed, and the beach is riddled with ancient odds and ends from another age of industry—hooks, nails, and sunken ships clink like latchkeys against the brimming tide.

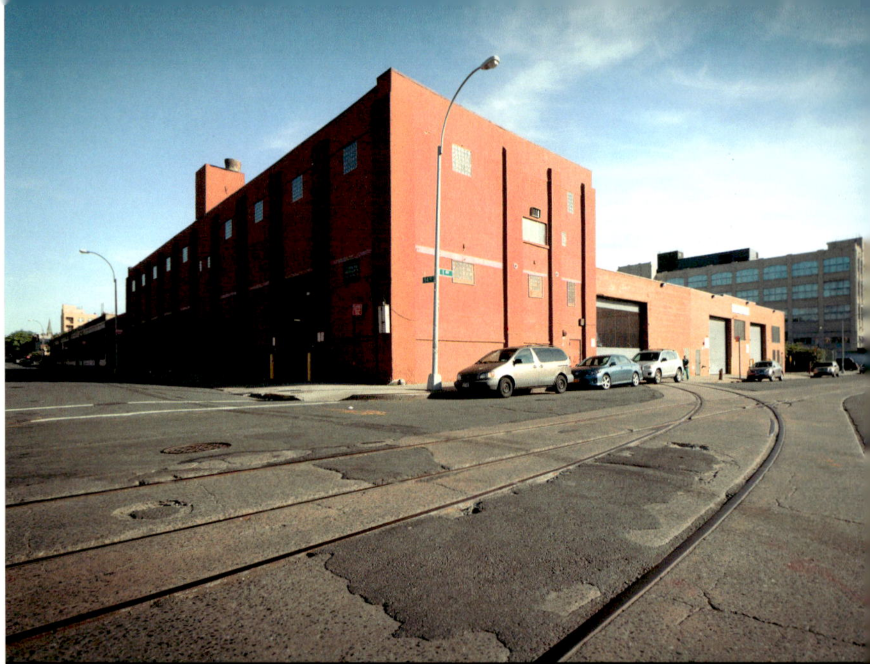

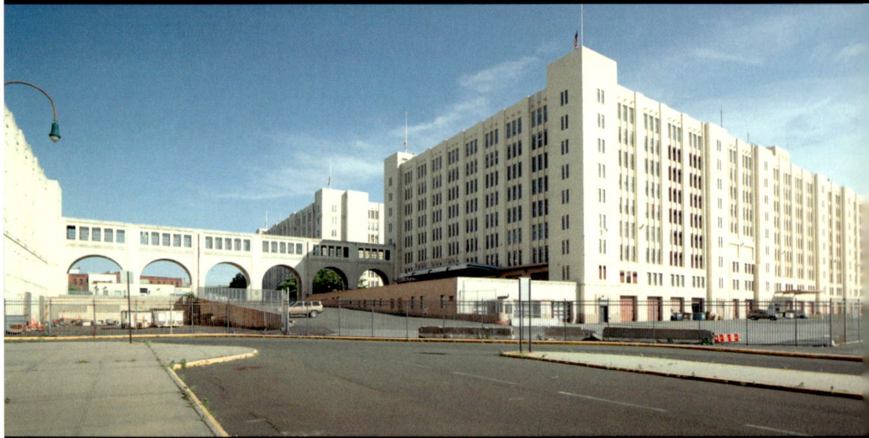

top The Bush Terminal's network of rails is still visible on 1st Avenue.

bottom The neighboring Brooklyn Army Terminal was designed with the help of Irving Bush.

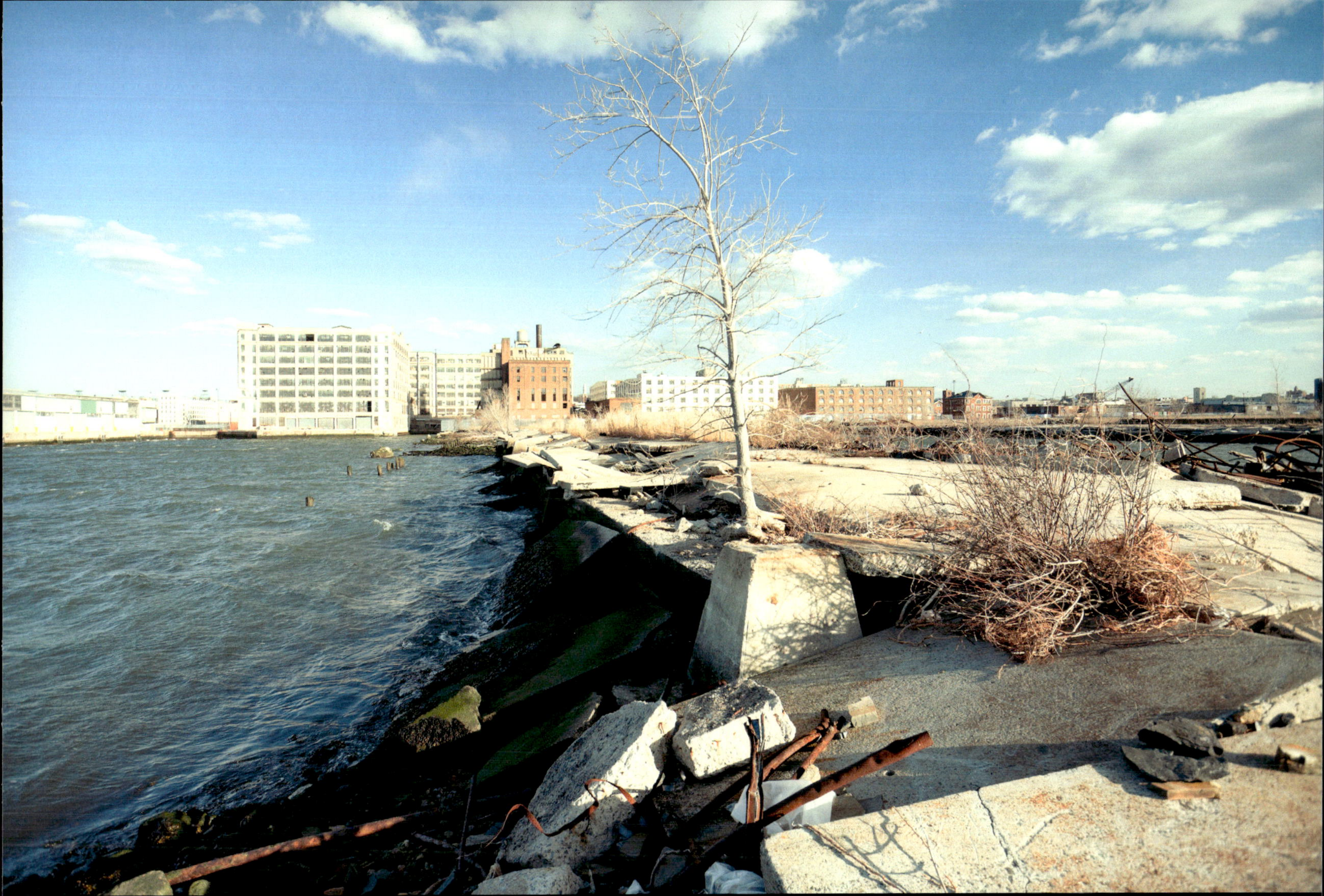

above Long-abandoned piers at the north end of the terminal collapse into the harbor.

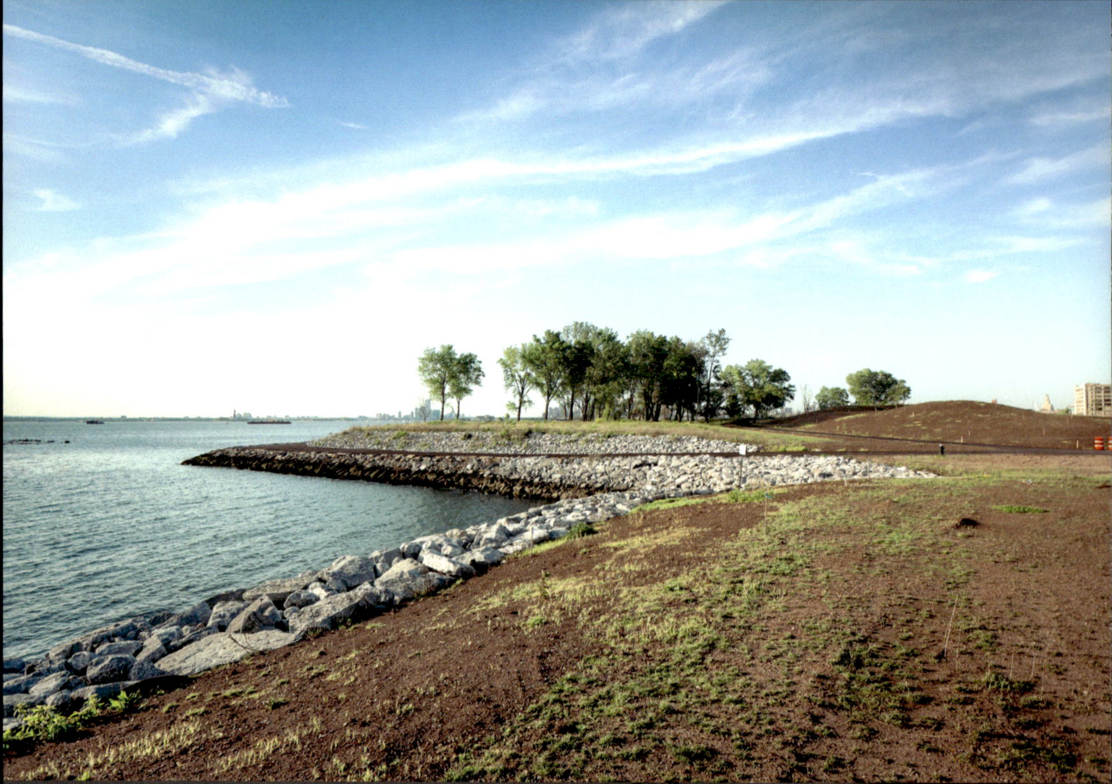

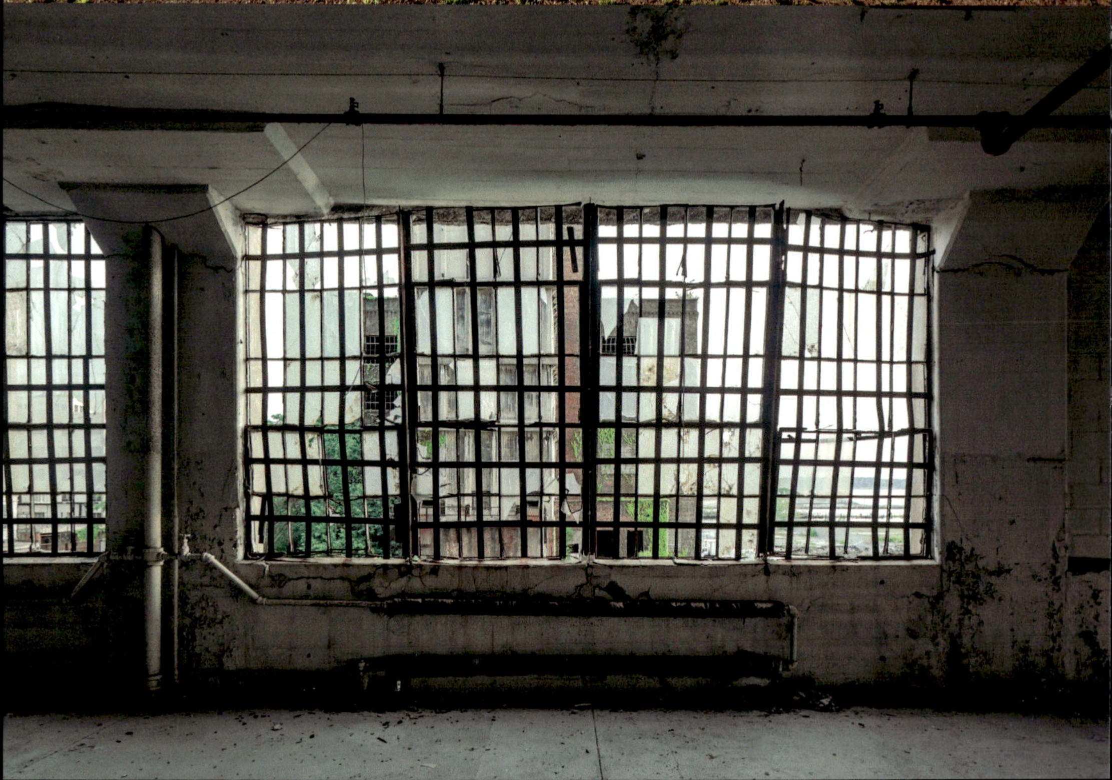

top Construction progresses on Bush Terminal Piers Park, which will soon include ball fields, picnic and fishing areas, and an education center.

bottom The walls of the Bush Terminal's manufacturing spaces were 80% glass with a total of 263,740 windowpanes, though many have fallen out over the years.

opposite Warehouse interiors have been adapted by a diverse group of modern tenants, including garment factories, toymakers, furniture builders, cosmetics companies, and artisanal chocolatiers.

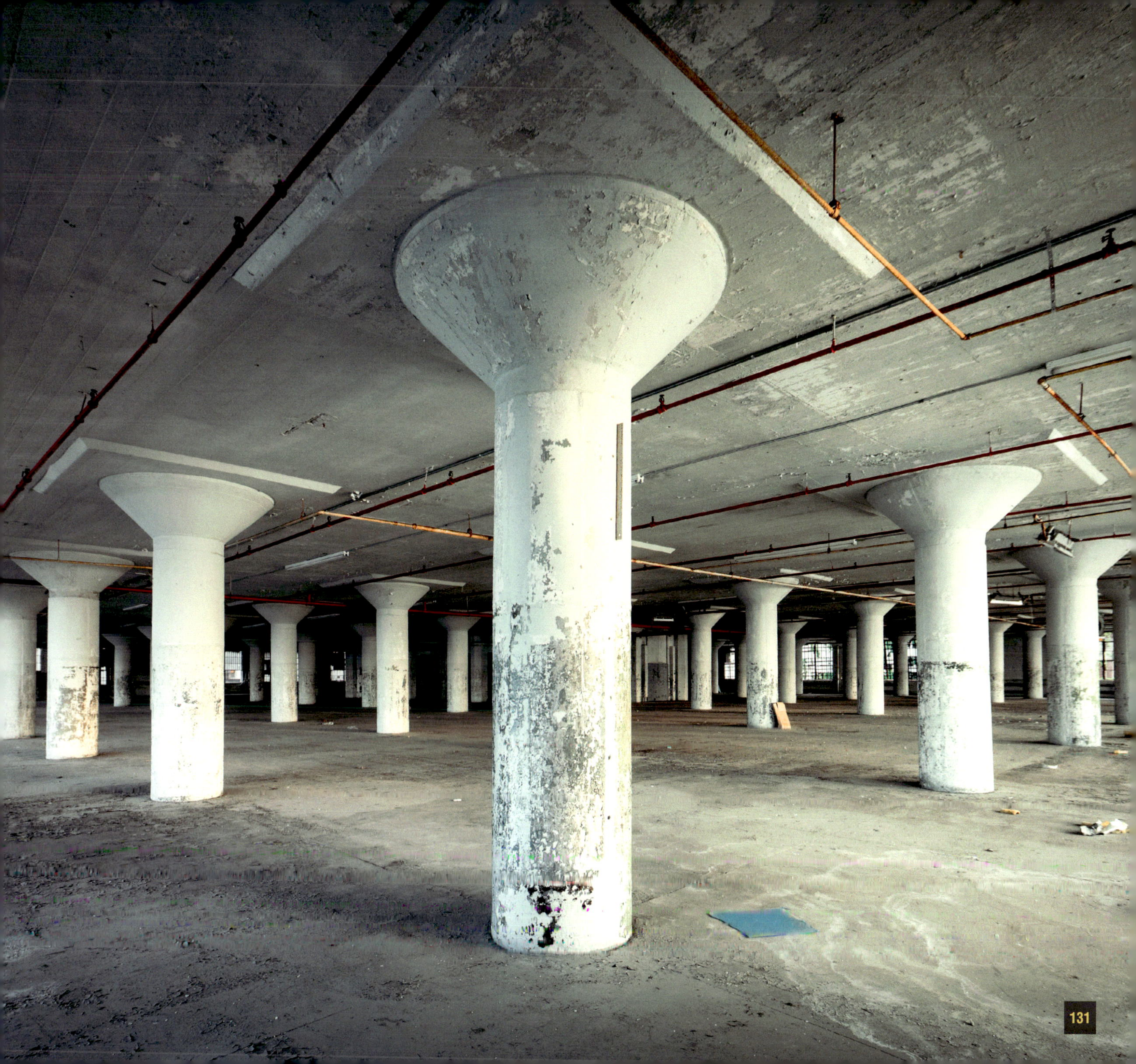

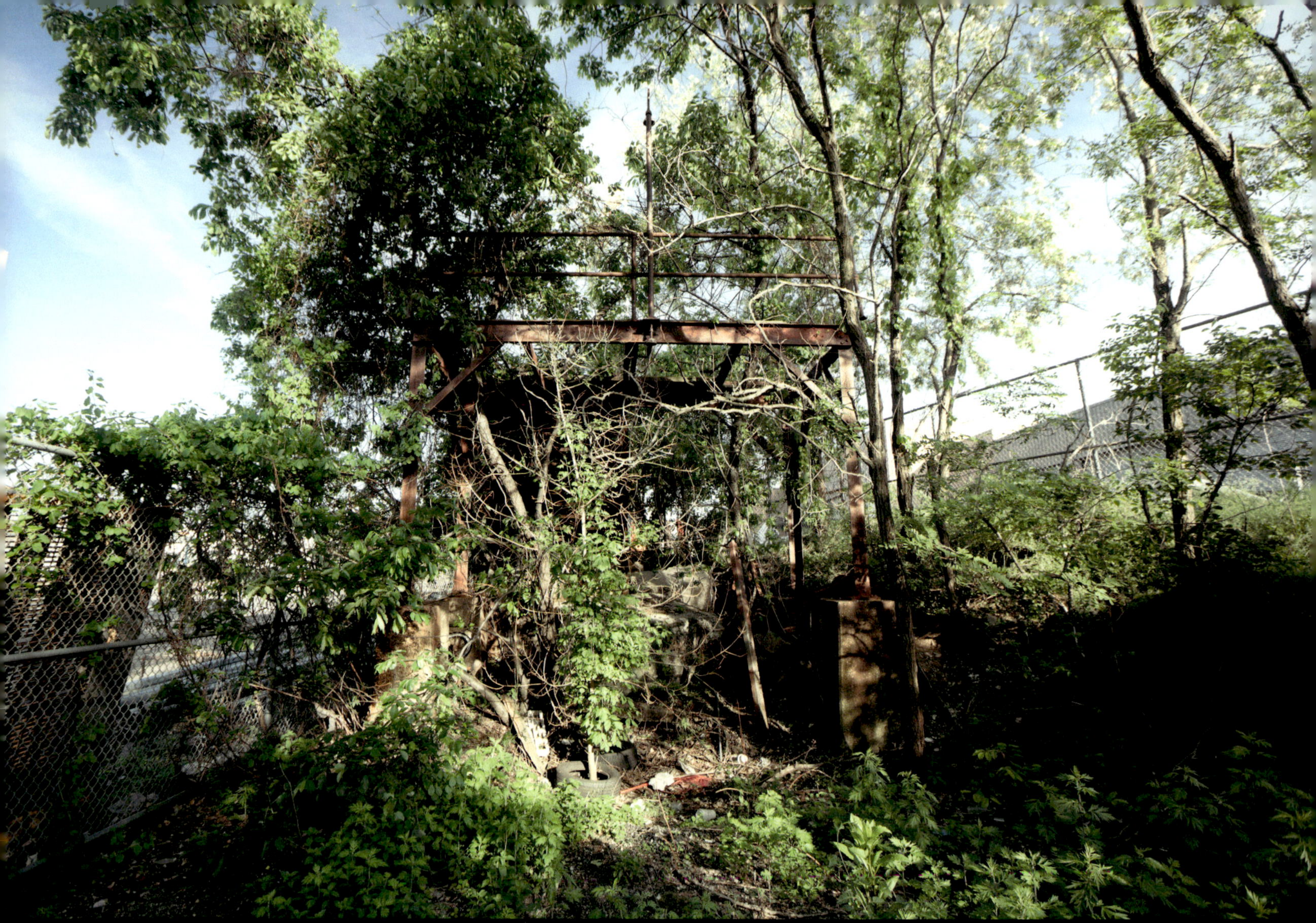

above Old relics remain in wild pockets of the waterfront. A rusty lookout is difficult to discern through a copse of trees, tucked away between fenced-off industrial back lots.

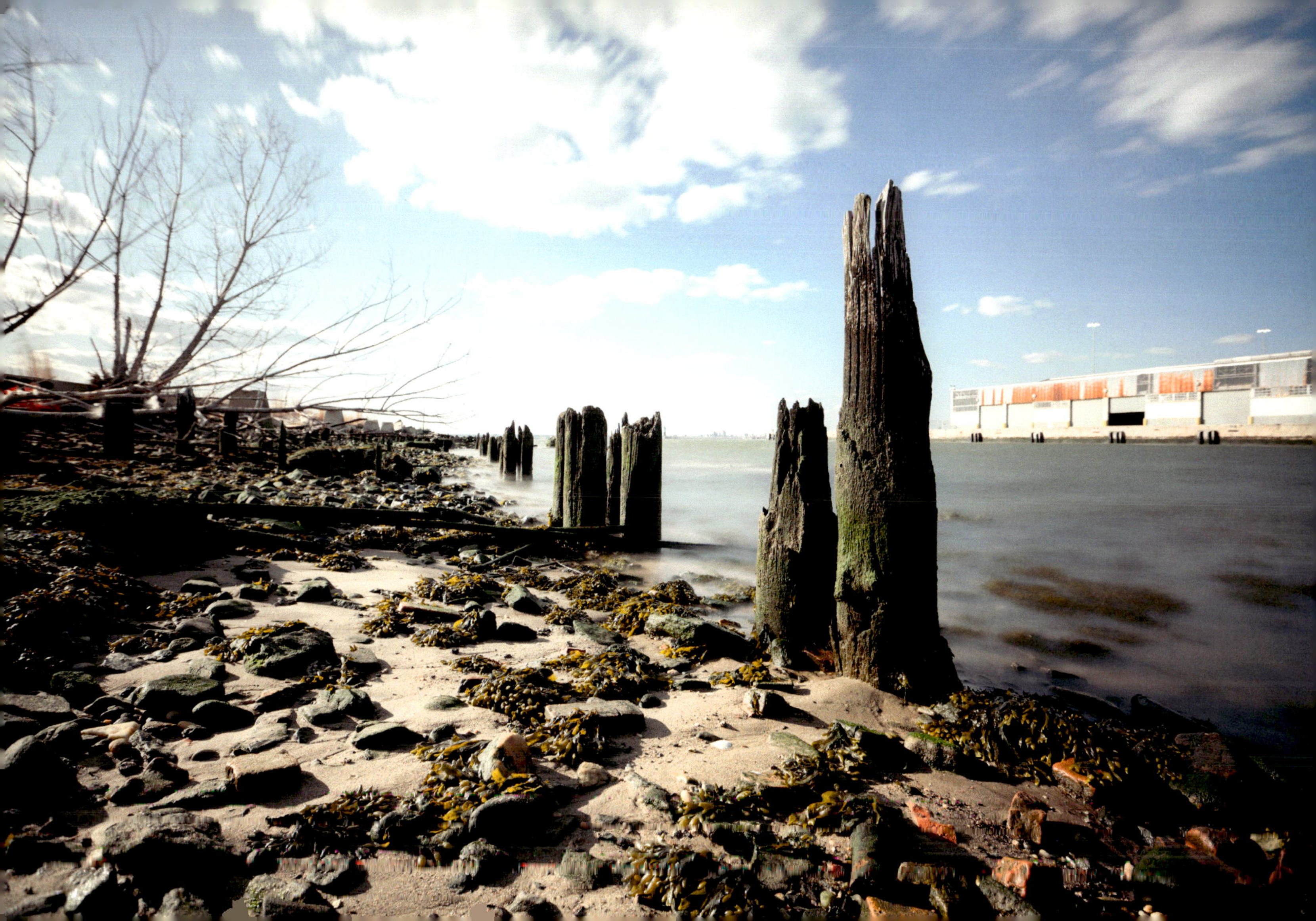

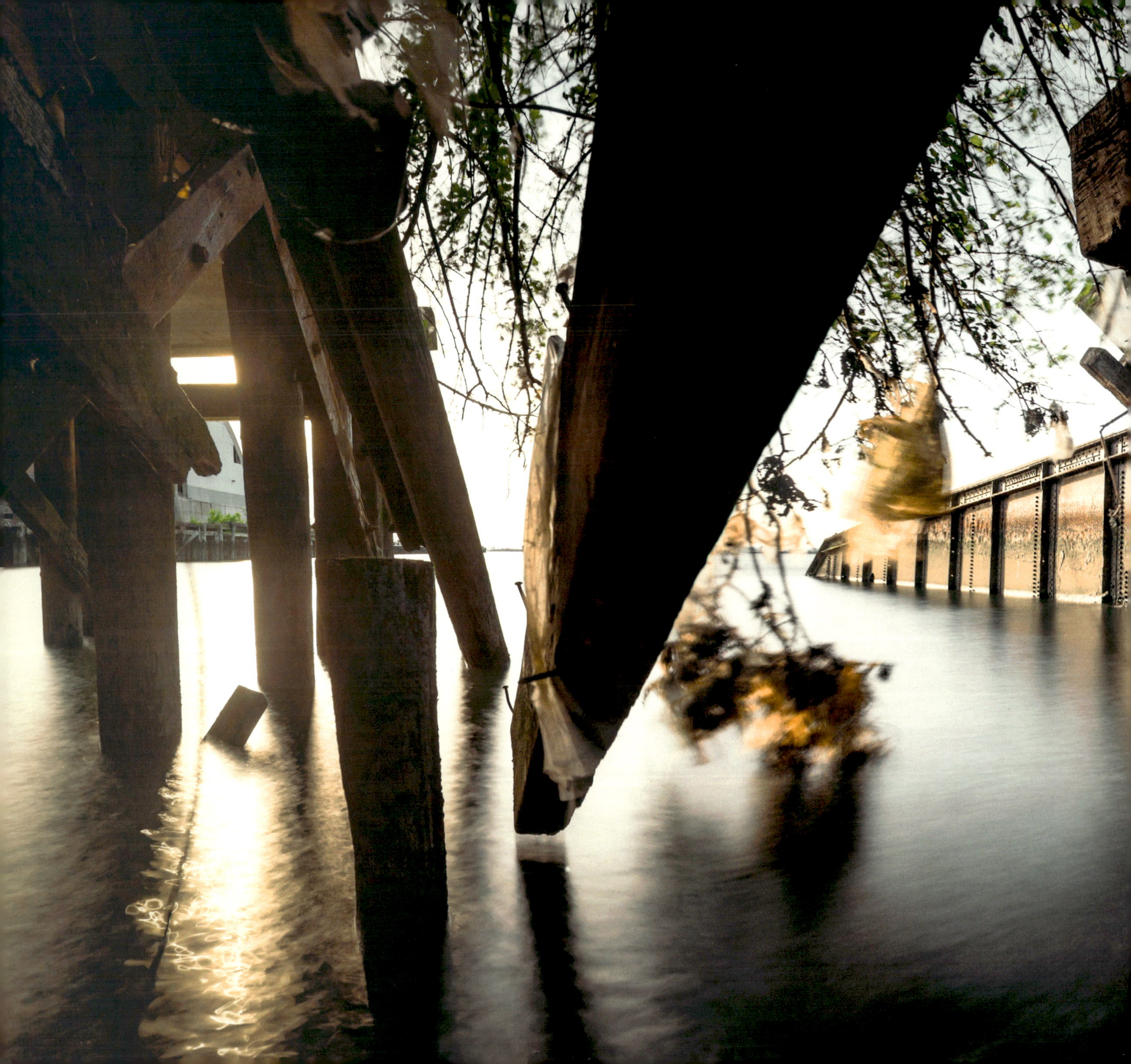

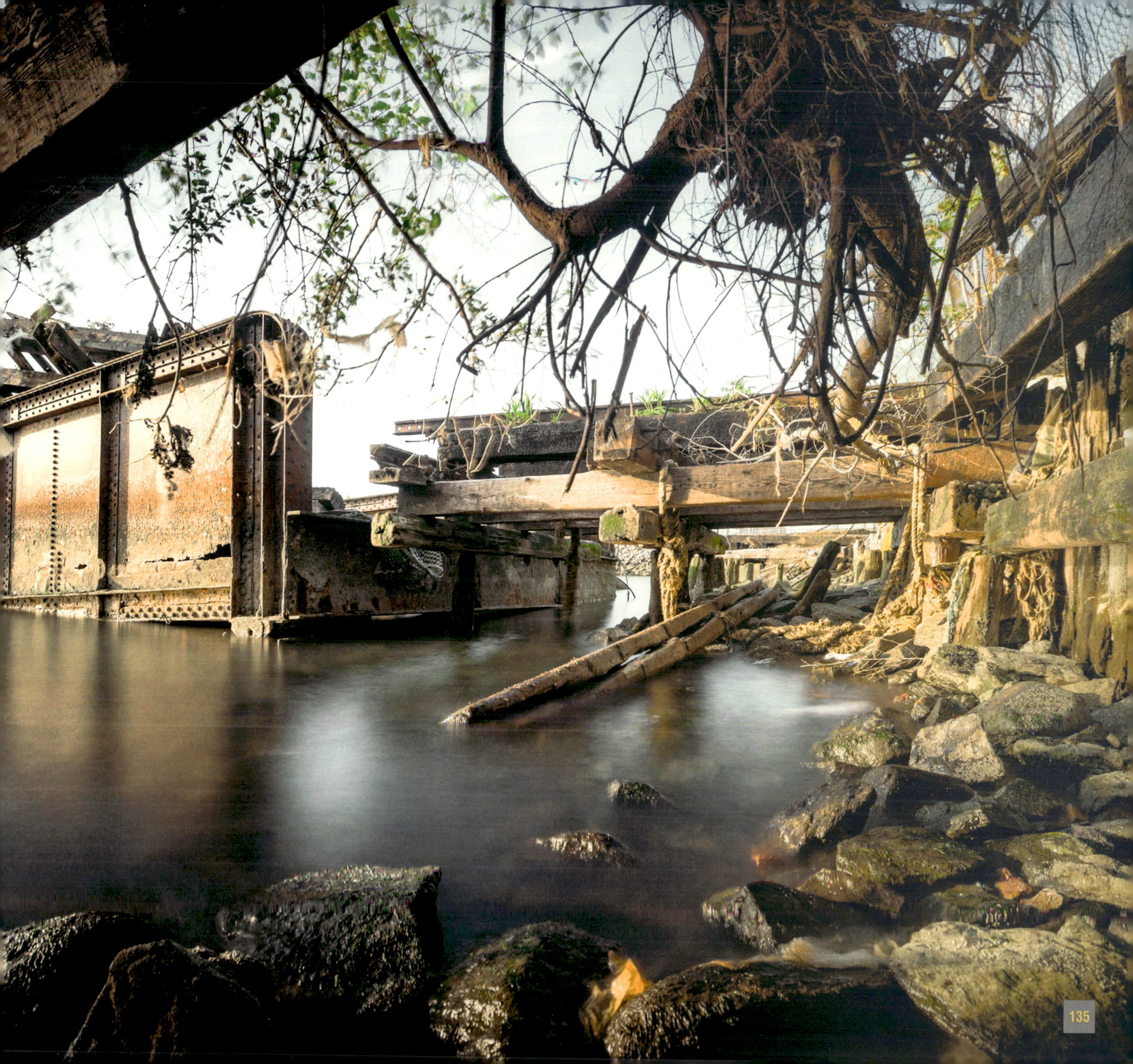

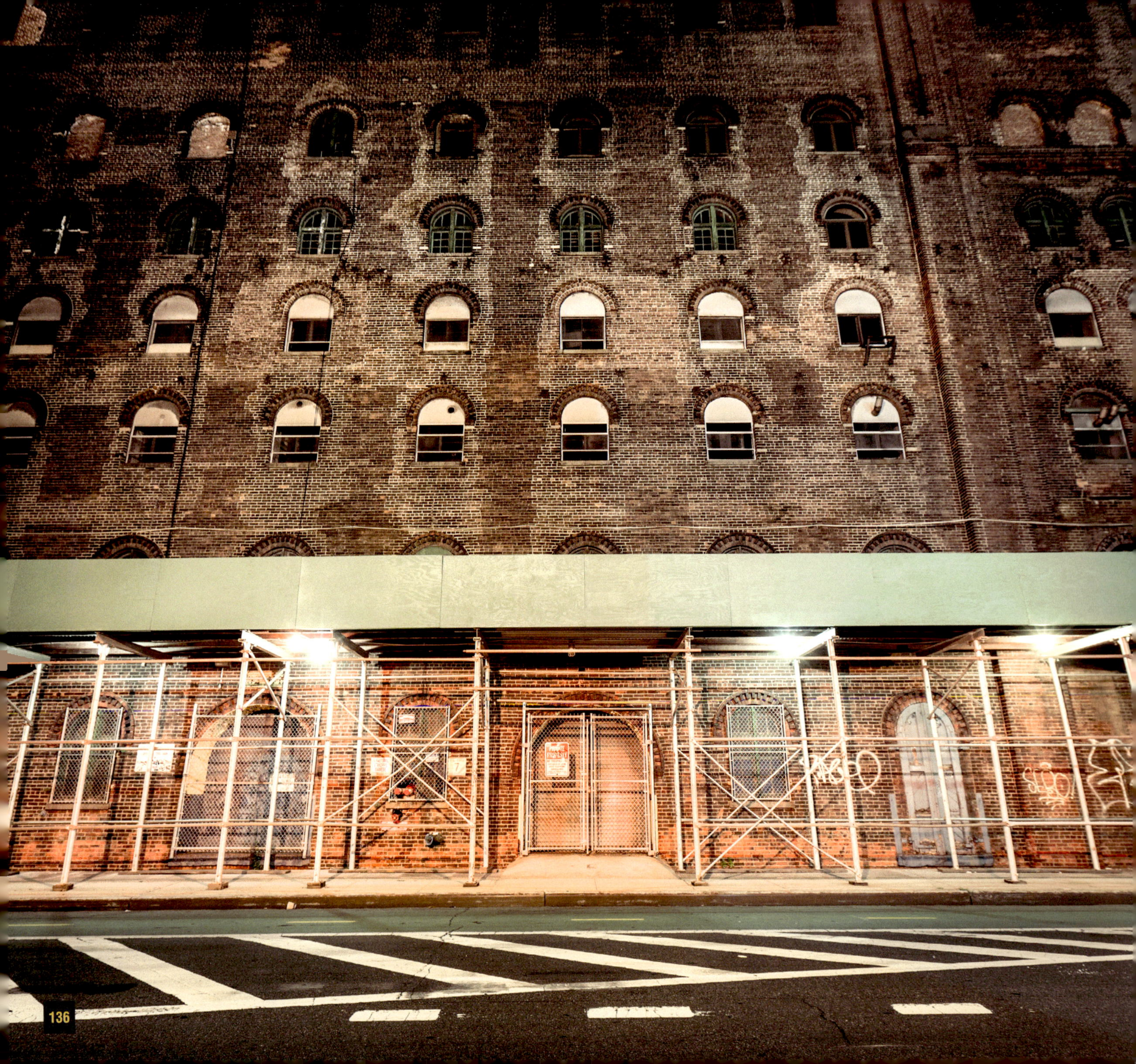

The Domino Sugar® Refinery

Williamsburg, Brooklyn

Situated on an 11-acre parcel of waterfront in the shadow of the Williamsburg Bridge, the derelict Domino Sugar® Refinery remains one of the most recognized remnants of Brooklyn's rapidly disappearing industrial past. But plans for a modern, mixed-use megacomplex are putting an end to the decaying colossus that was once the largest refinery in the world.

In the late 19th century, Brooklyn was responsible for over half of the country's sugar production, with Havemeyers & Elder's Sugar Company leading the pack of more than 20 major refineries that called the borough home. The factory's signature building—a monolithic red brick structure that still stands today—was constructed in 1884 to replace an older sugarhouse that had been destroyed in a catastrophic fire.

Three years later, 17 of the largest sugar refiners in the United States merged to form the Sugar Refineries Company Trust, which was reorganized as the American Sugar Refining Company® and branded as Domino Sugar in 1902. Domino and its predecessors operated on the waterfront for a total of 148 years, employing over 5,000 workers capable of producing over three million pounds of processed sugar a day. Over the course of the 20th century, the growing use of high-fructose corn syrup and artificial sweeteners led to a steady decline in demand for old-fashioned cane sugar, and production at the Williamsburg plant ended in 2004.

The same year, the nonprofit Community Preservation Corporation (CPC) purchased the site for $58 million. Their plan would preserve and renovate the central refinery building—landmarked in 2007—and raise a battalion of architecturally offensive residential high-rises in the footprint of the surrounding industrial complex, razing the raw sugar warehouse (constructed in 1927) and the packaging house (a 1962 addition) in the process. After years of planning and a hard-fought rezoning battle, the CPC ran into dire financial straits, and the project fell through. The site found a new buyer in noted New York City development firm Two Trees, the group largely responsible for the reinvention—and gentrification—of Dumbo, a nearby waterfront neighborhood with a comparable industrial past.

opposite The Domino Sugar® Refinery's signature building awaits its transformation to modern office space.

The plan is similar in scope to the vision of the CPC, with several key changes. The buildings rise higher—up to 60 stories—to allow for more park space, including a one-acre "Domino Square," where builders envision film screenings and outdoor concerts. Some of the structures include open spaces and sky bridges as innovative solutions to preserve harbor views for the inland community. The landmarked refinery building will be preserved and converted to office space, and several pieces of machinery will be salvaged for inclusion in a public "artifact walk."

In the face of such monumental changes, this may be of some consolation to those nostalgic for the waterfront's blue-collar legacy. As the industrial titan is preened and polished into the marketably modern New Domino, another of the city's rough edges will be smoothed over in favor of gleaming glass. Not surprisingly, the project has been met with contempt by some locals. After dark, a nearby apartment building cries foul to the night sky. "Save Domino" shines like a beacon over a Williamsburg waterfront in transition.

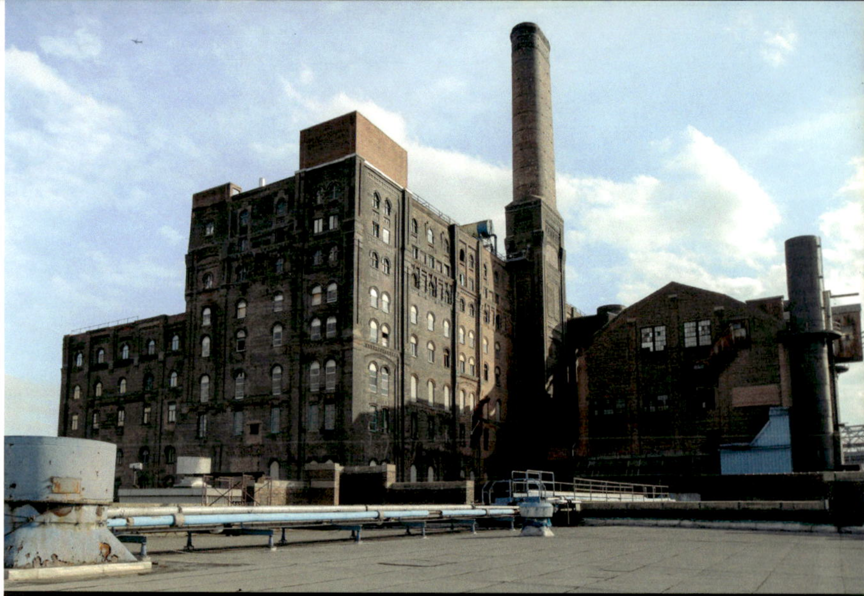

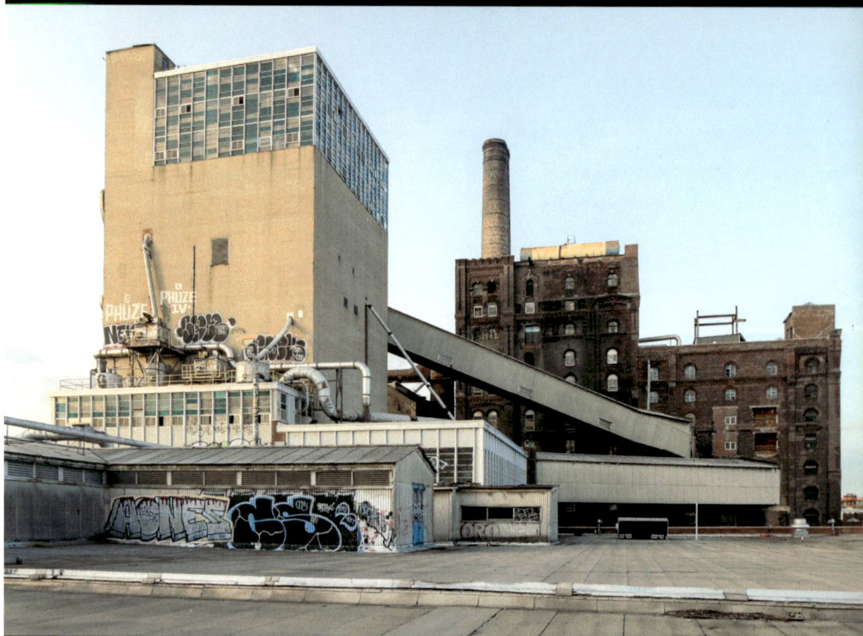

top The landmarked structure will undergo a gut renovation as part of a massive development on the site of the former factory.

bottom A partial view of the complex from the roof of the packaging plant, which is slated for demolition.

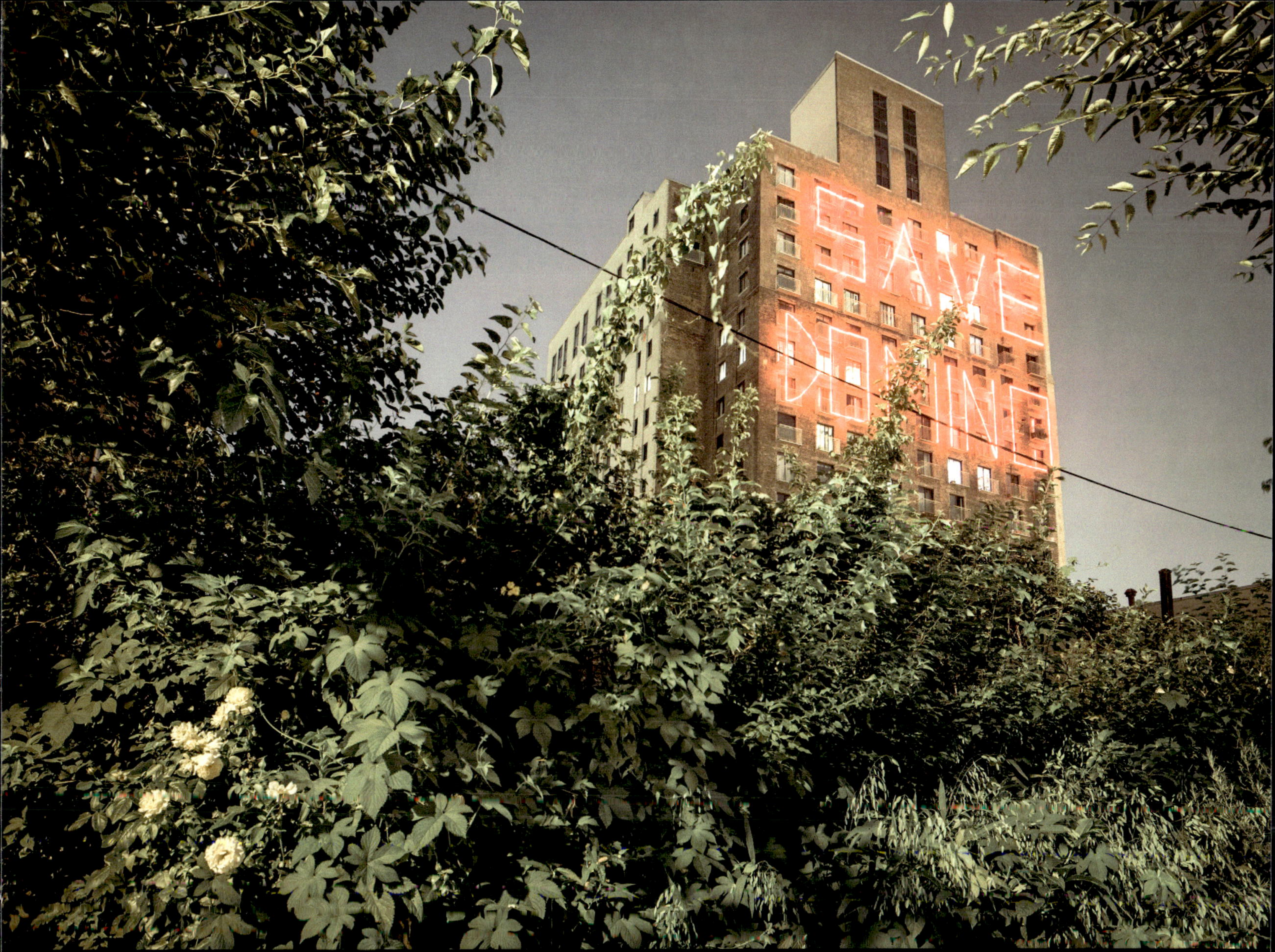

above A building owner installed this

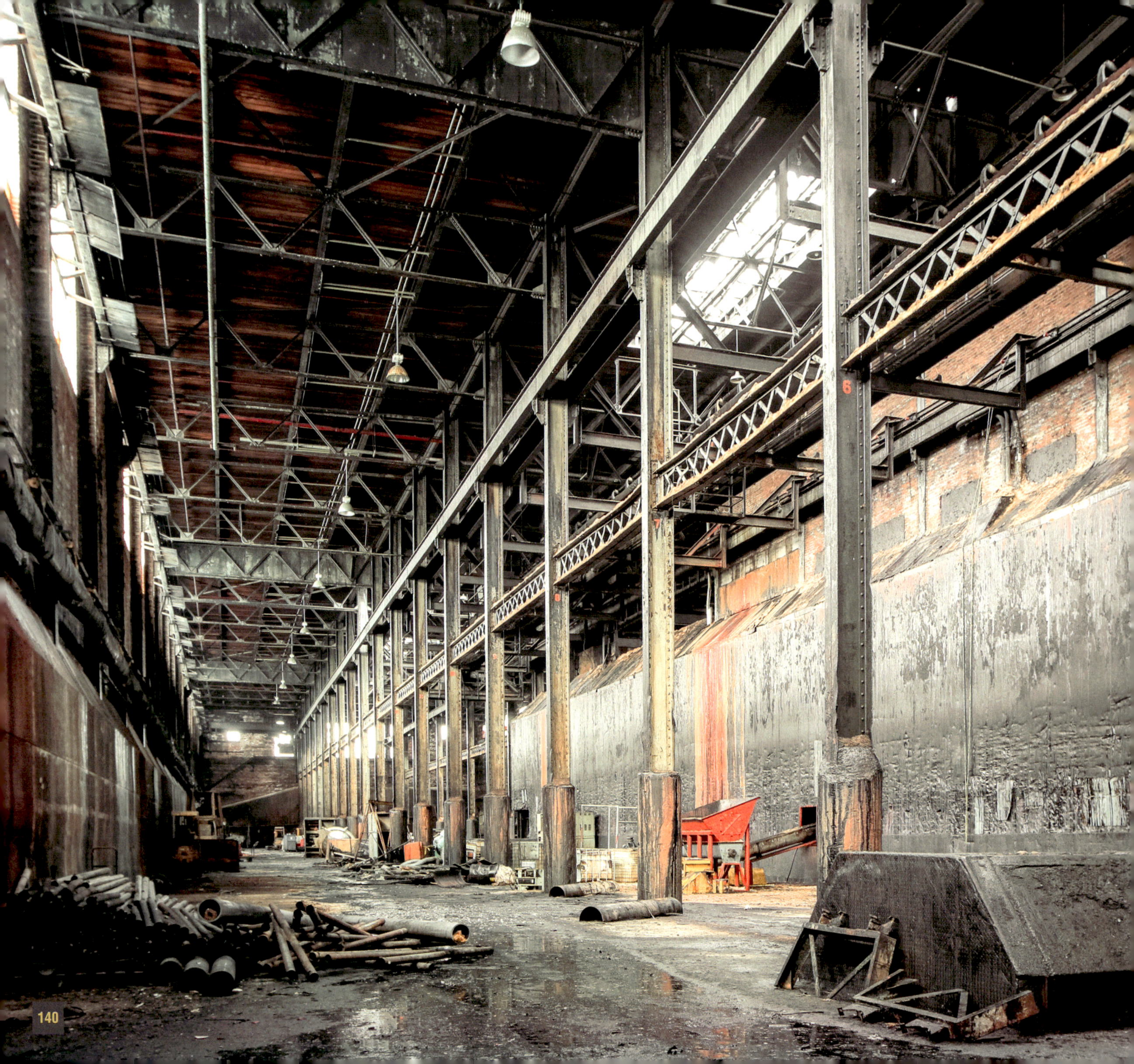

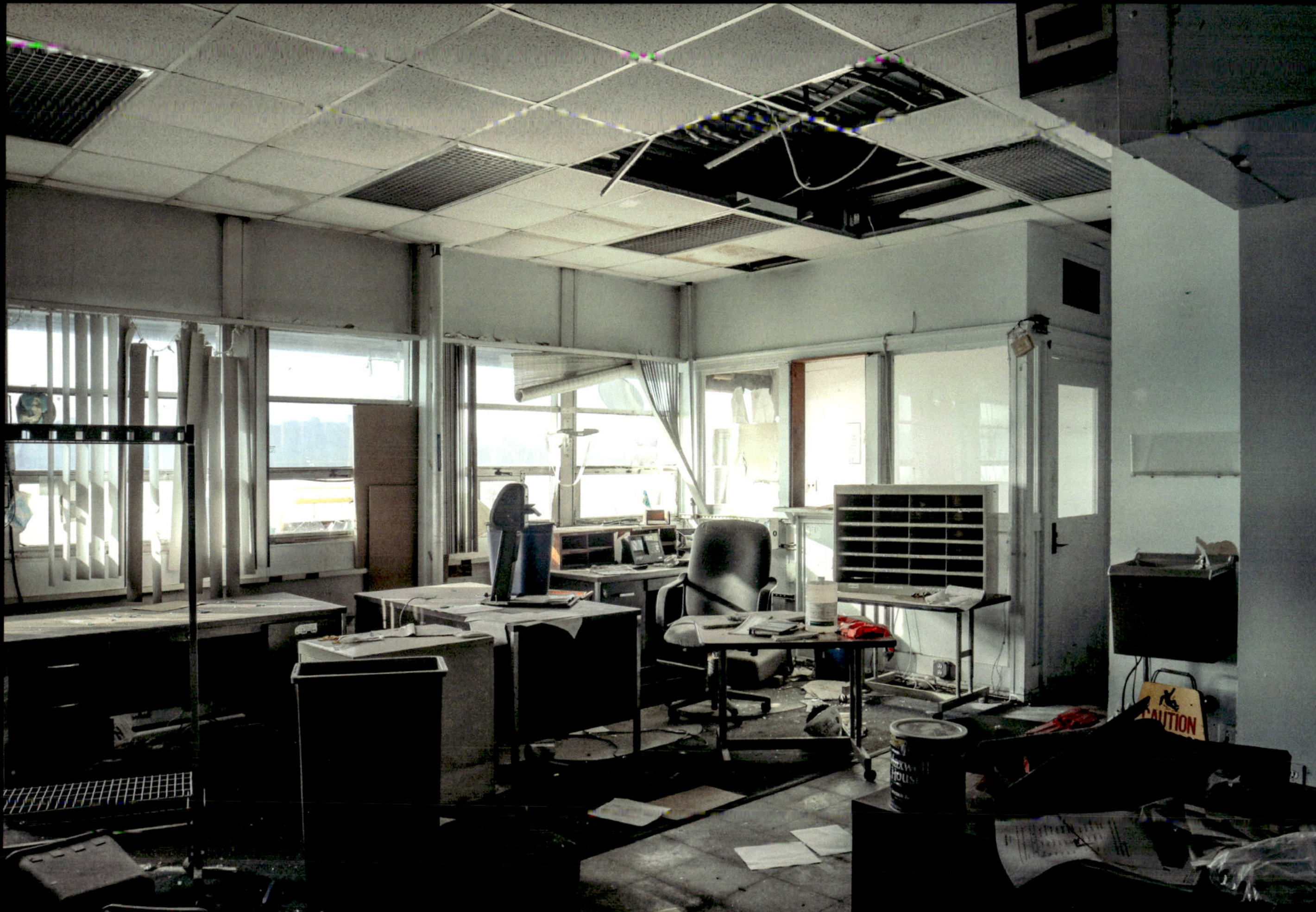

opposite Until recently, the cavernous raw sugar warehouse was coated with shallow puddles of tar and gluey byproducts. Prior to demolition, it was used for high-profile events and site-specific art installations.

above An emptied office overlooks the East River, with a calendar dated to 2004.

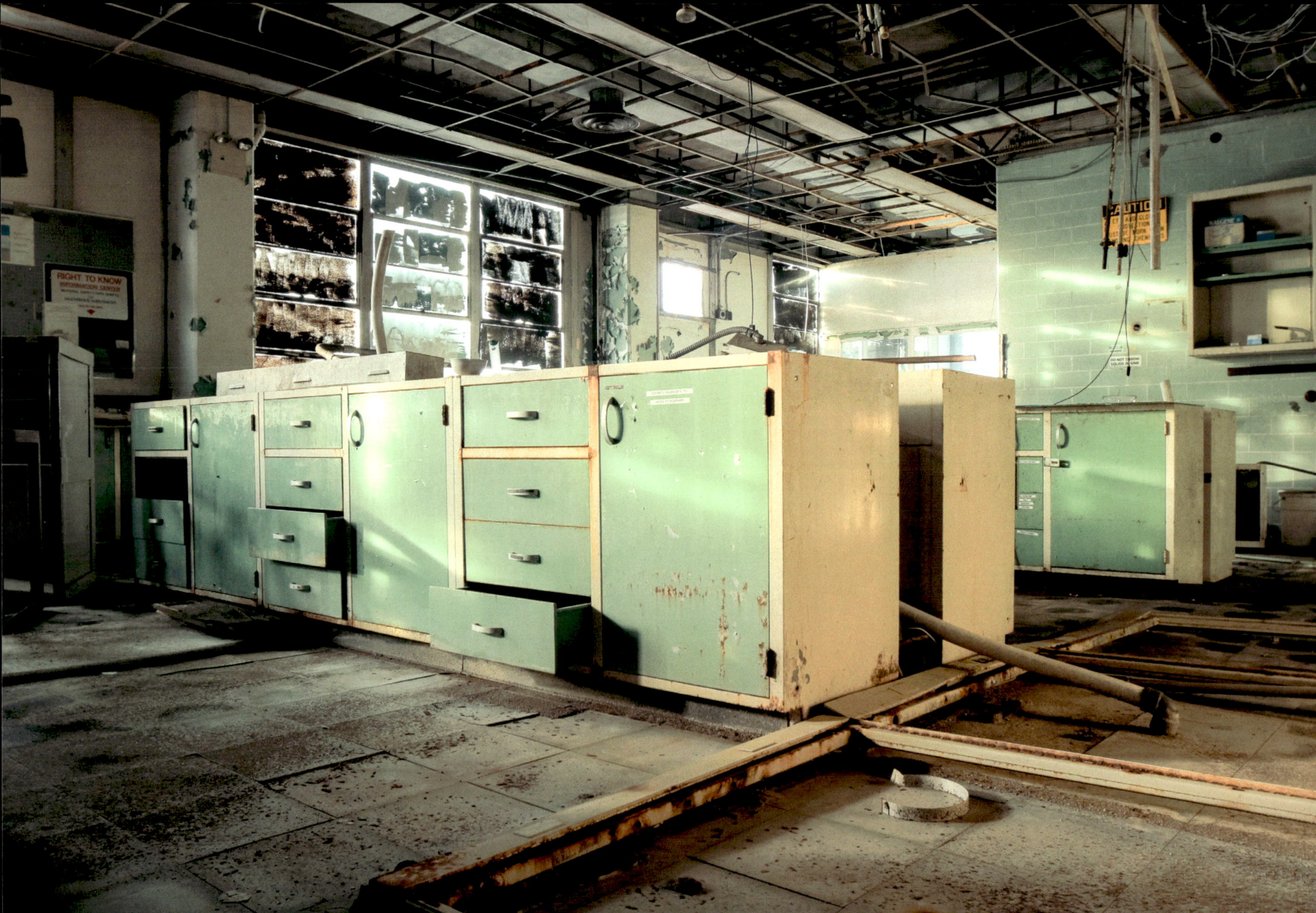

Evening light leaks through a storage room in the packaging plant.

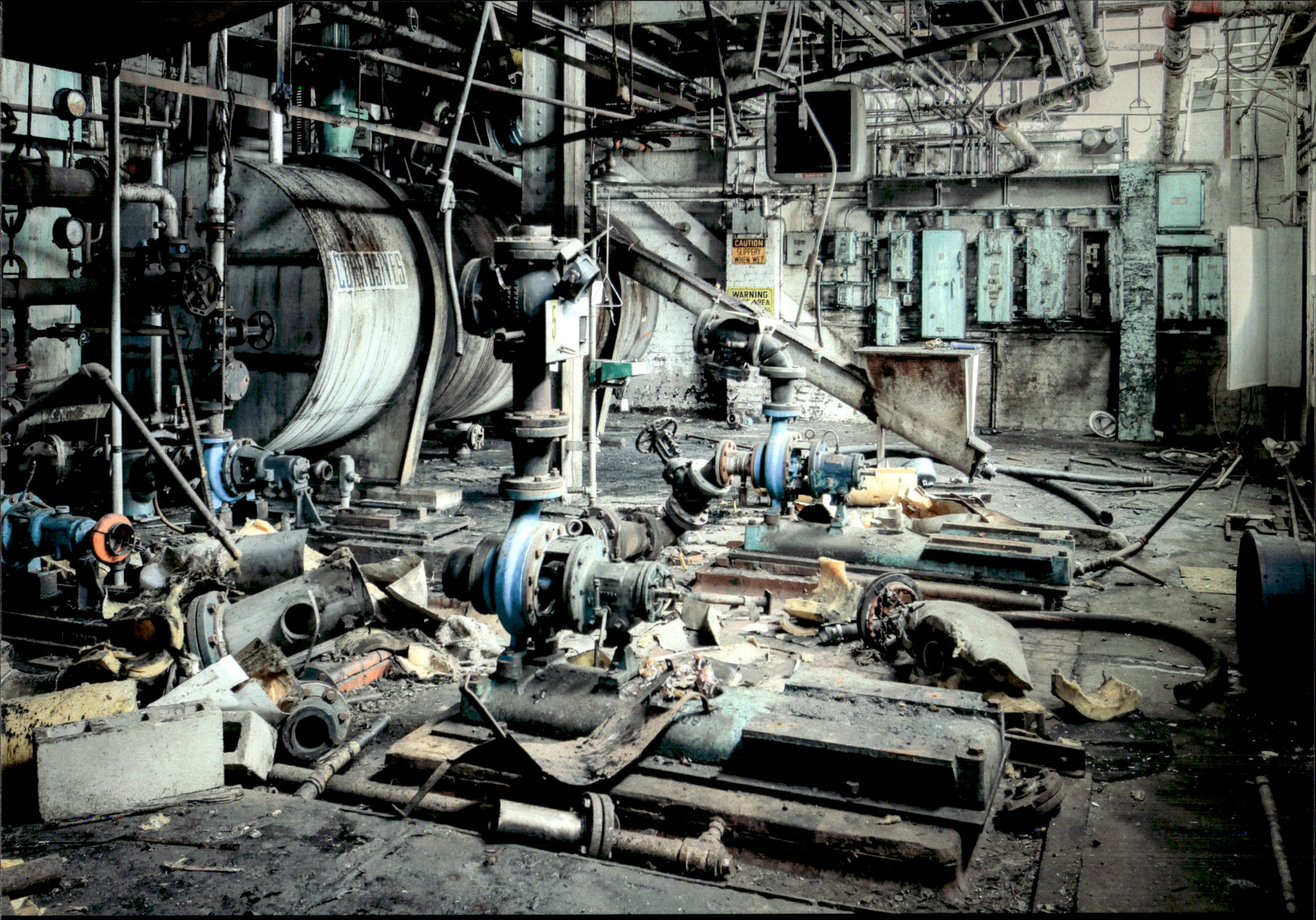
CORROSIVES
CAUTION
SLIPPERY
WHEN WET
WARNING

In its final moments, the Domino Sugar® Refinery slips further into a speedy decay, introducing an element of the exotic to an already unfamiliar environment.

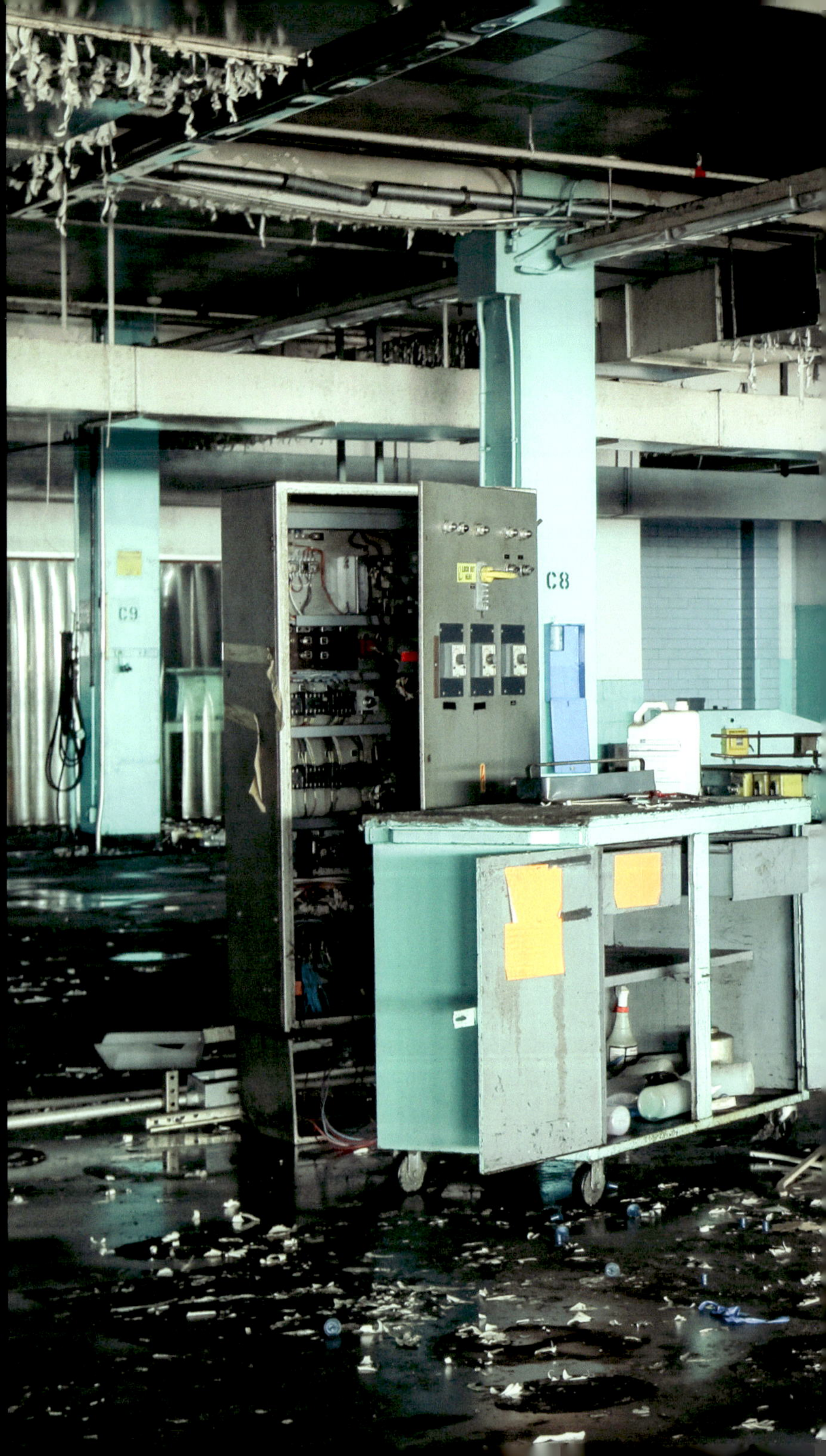

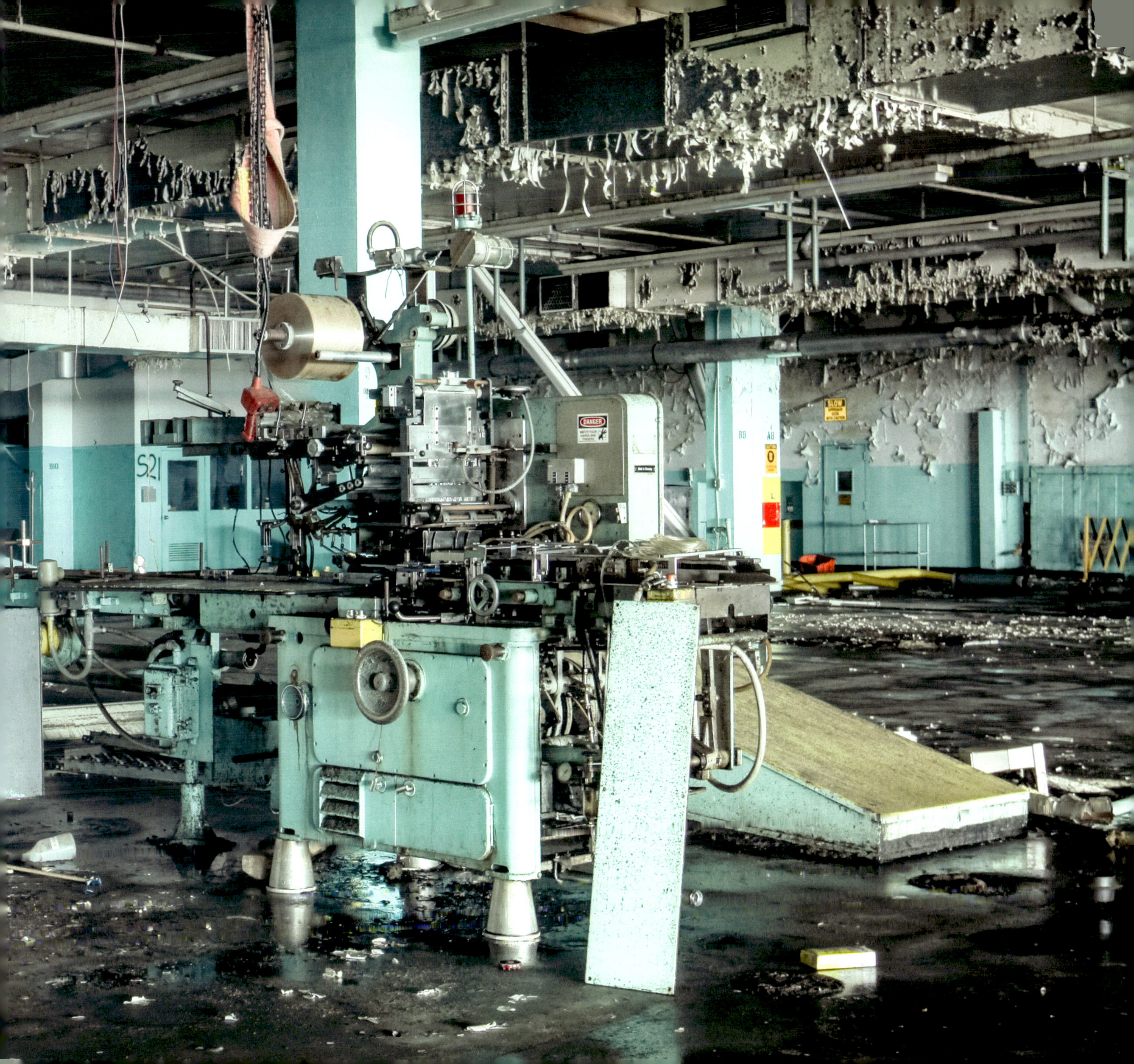
DANGER
S21
SLOW

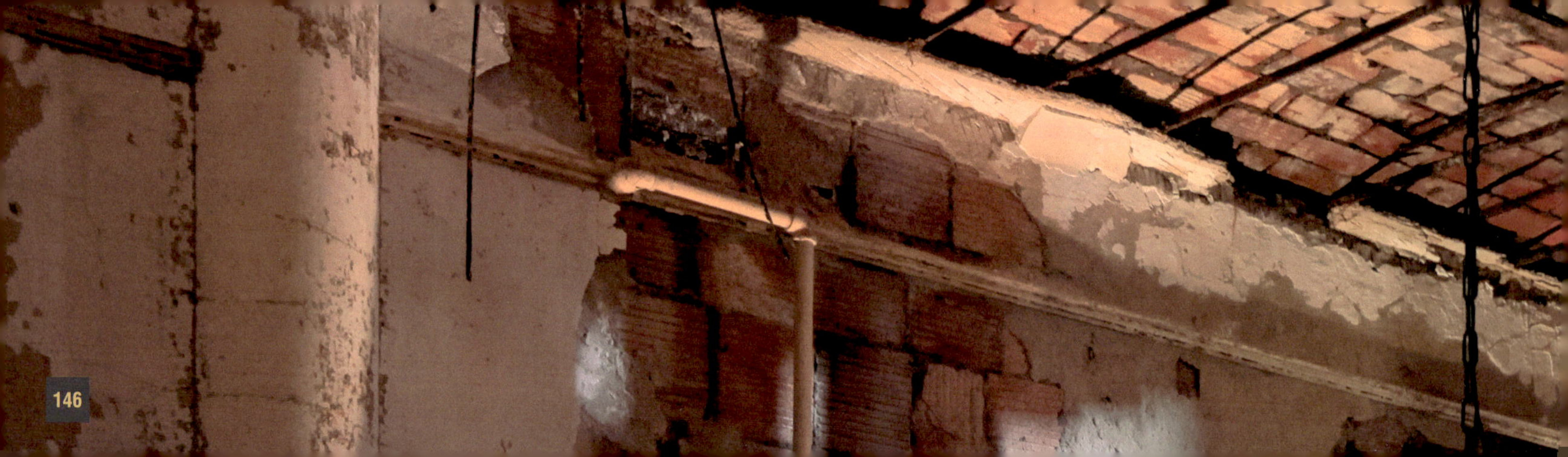

Forgotten Places

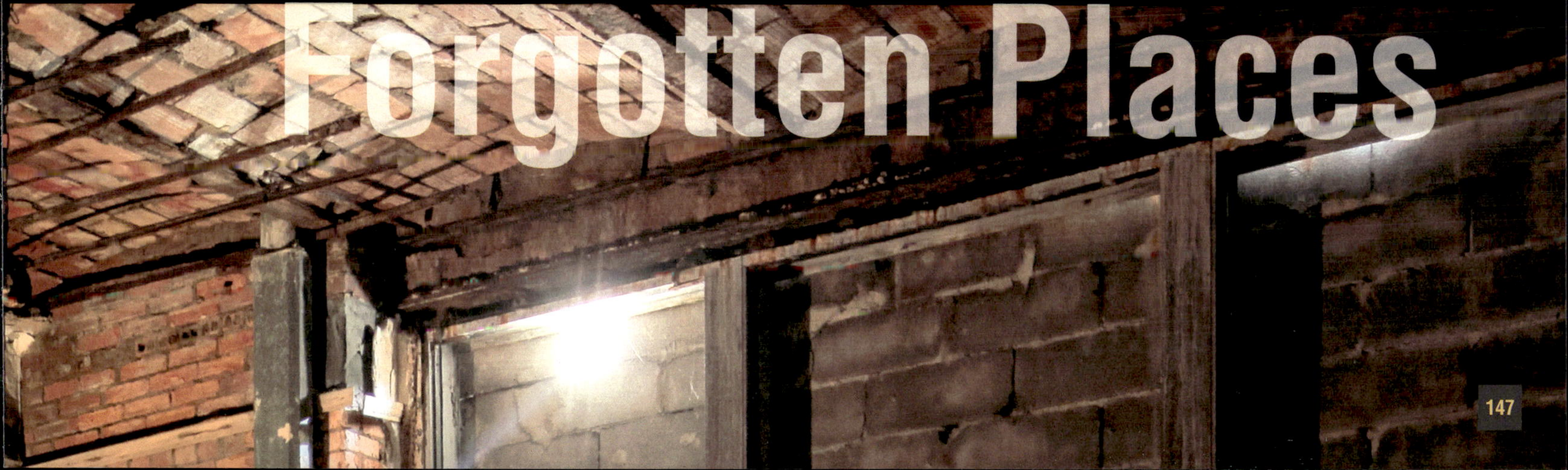

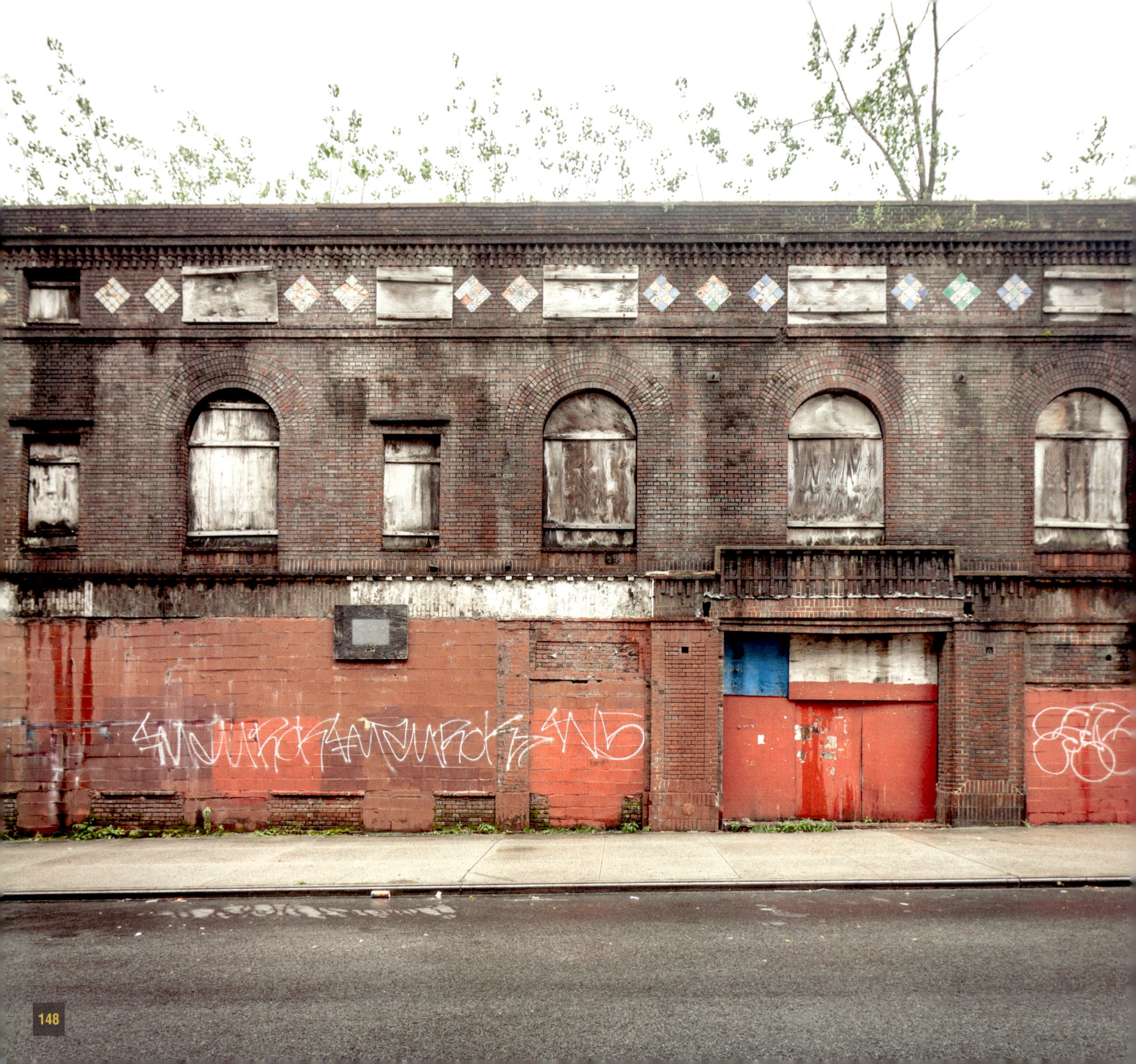

The Harlem Renaissance Ballroom

Harlem, NY

Langston Hughes had the Renaissance Ballroom in mind when he described a "Golden girl / in a golden gown / in a melody night / in Harlem town." But the "mellow magic of dancing sound" hasn't filled the Rennie in decades, and its devastated interiors do little to dignify its history. The dance floor sprouts mushrooms today, but 80 years ago, it quaked with the frenzied rhythms of the Lindy Hop.

Harlem was constructed at the turn of the 20th century with upper-class whites in mind, but a lag in public transit made it difficult for developers to attract their ideal tenants. Landlords turned to African Americans, and by the 1920s, the area had become a flourishing center of Black culture. The Harlem Renaissance was born, and with it, the Harlem Renaissance Ballroom.

The Ballroom was completed in 1924 as part of a larger entertainment hub that included a bustling casino and 900-seat theatre. Notable for being built and operated by black businessmen, the Rennie was the only upscale reception hall available to African Americans at the time. Prize fights, concerts, dance marathons, film screenings, and stage acts were held at the Renaissance, along with elegant parties and meetings of the most influential social clubs and political organizations in Harlem. The community's elite gathered to dance the Charleston and the Black Bottom to live entertainment by the most renowned jazz musicians of the age.

The nightspot also played host to the nation's first all-black professional basketball team. The New York Renaissance, a.k.a. the Renaissance Big Five, were considered by many to be the best team in the world in their day. On game nights, portable hoops were erected on the dance floor, converting the ballroom into a stadium. Following each game—almost invariably a victory for the Rens—a dance was held where players would mingle and jive with the choicest ladies of Harlem. The team barnstormed in towns across the country, playing exhibition games in which coveted matches with white teams drew the largest crowds. In their best season, the Rens set a record with 88 consecutive wins that has yet to be broken by any professional basketball team.

opposite Subtle architectural details on the ballroom's facade exhibit a North African influence.

White businessmen took over the Harlem Renaissance Ballroom during the Great Depression, but the site remained a center of the community until it closed down in 1979, unable to compete with newer social clubs. In 1991, the property was purchased by the Abyssinian Baptist Church, located next door to the casino, which was once the largest Protestant congregation in the country, and continues to prosper today as a driving force of change in the neighborhood with deep ties to Harlem politics. Established in 1989, its nonprofit arm, the Abyssinian Development Corporation (ADC), had invested over $500 million in community development as of 2008, becoming the most influential social service and housing provider in Harlem.

The ADC originally planned to renovate the site back to its historical role as a social hall and community space, projecting to complete the project by 1995. But in the intervening years, they introduced a new plan that diverged sharply from their traditional housing ventures. While a portion of the property would be utilized as retail and community space, only 20% of the residential units would qualify as affordable. The rest of the 19-story construction would be set aside for market-rate condominiums.

The site of the former theatre is now an empty lot, but contrary to some reports, the Renaissance Ballroom still stands. Plans call for the preservation of the ballroom's facade, but the interior is coming down as soon as Abyssinian can secure funding—a bleak economic climate has forced the ADC to postpone the development once again.

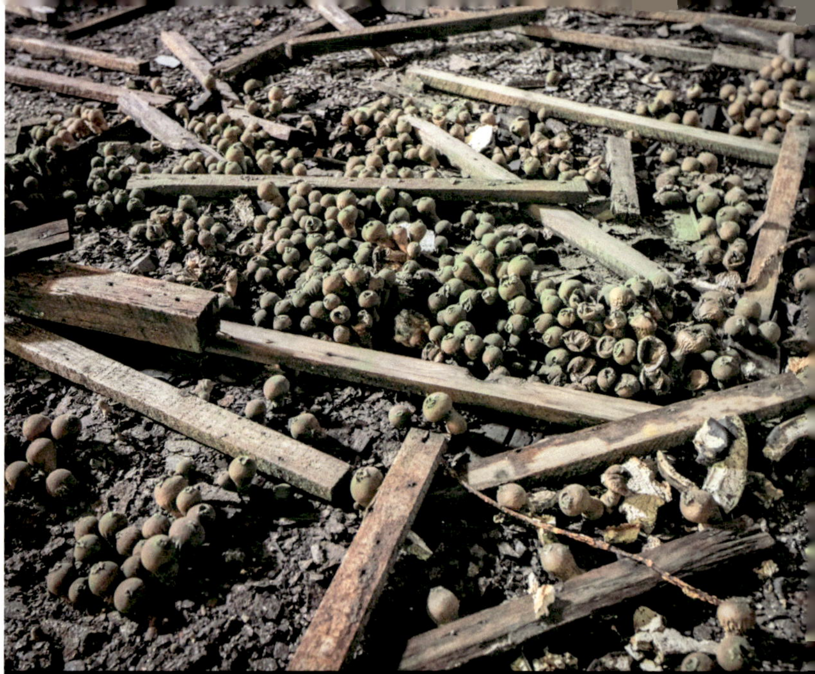

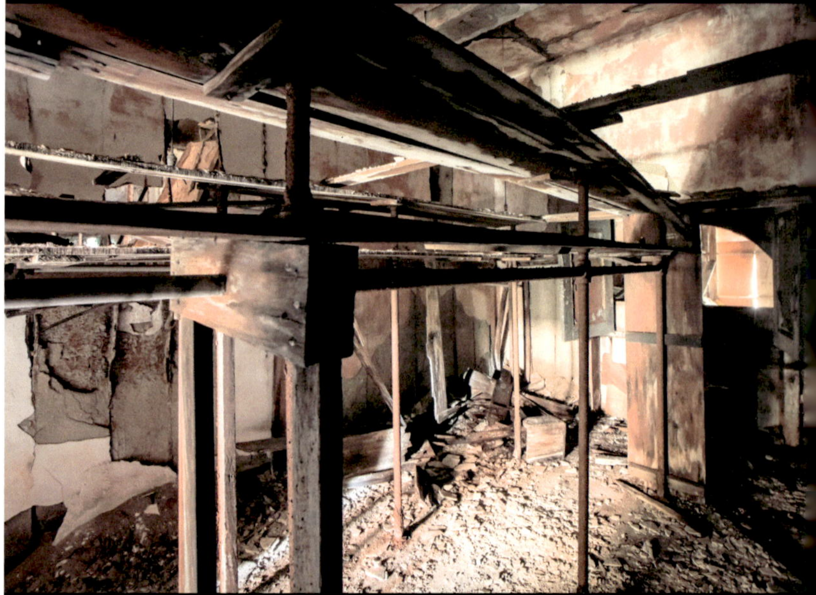

top Reduced to mulch in places, the dance floor supports a thriving fungal colony.

bottom The men's coatroom remains largely intact.

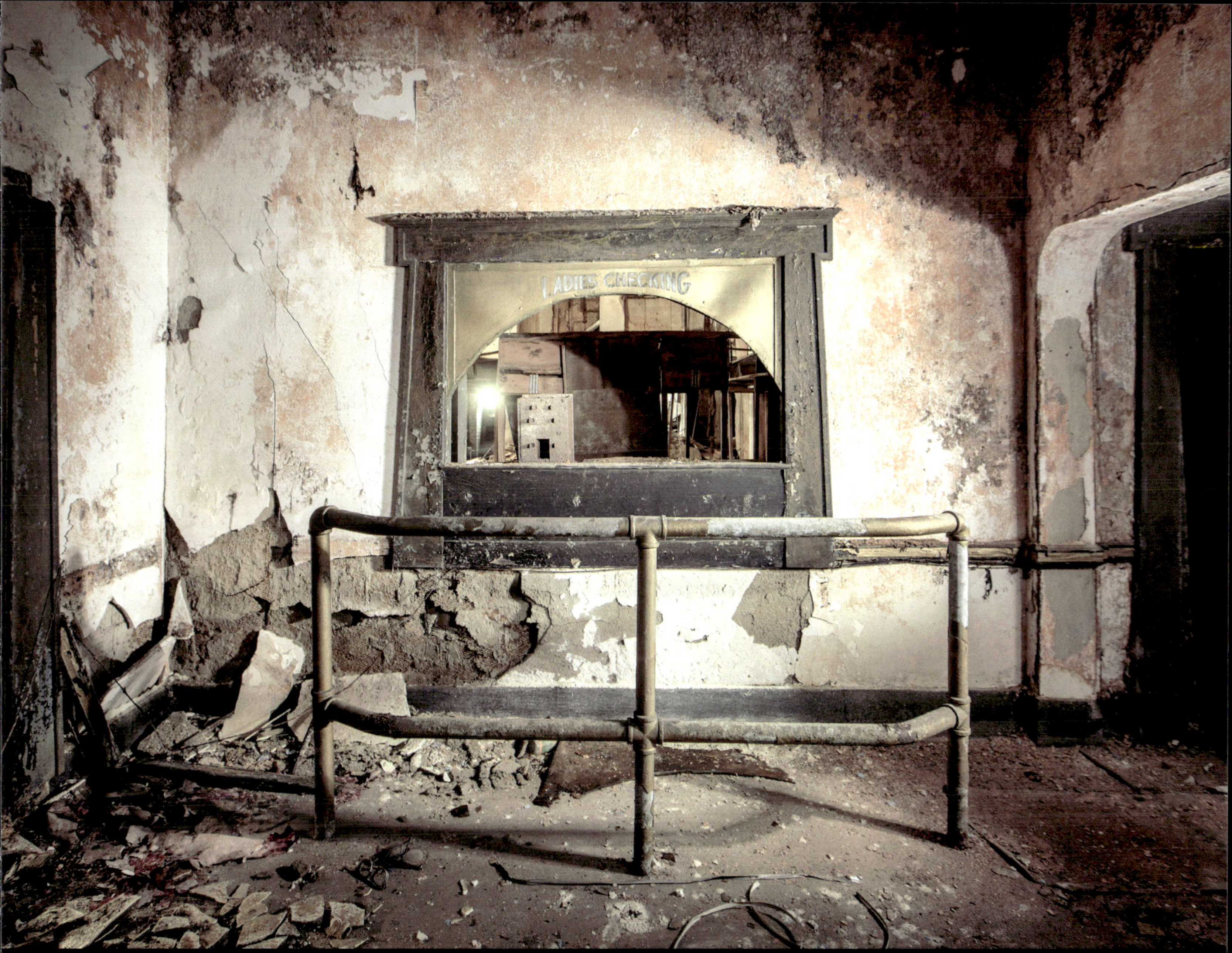
LADIES CHECKING

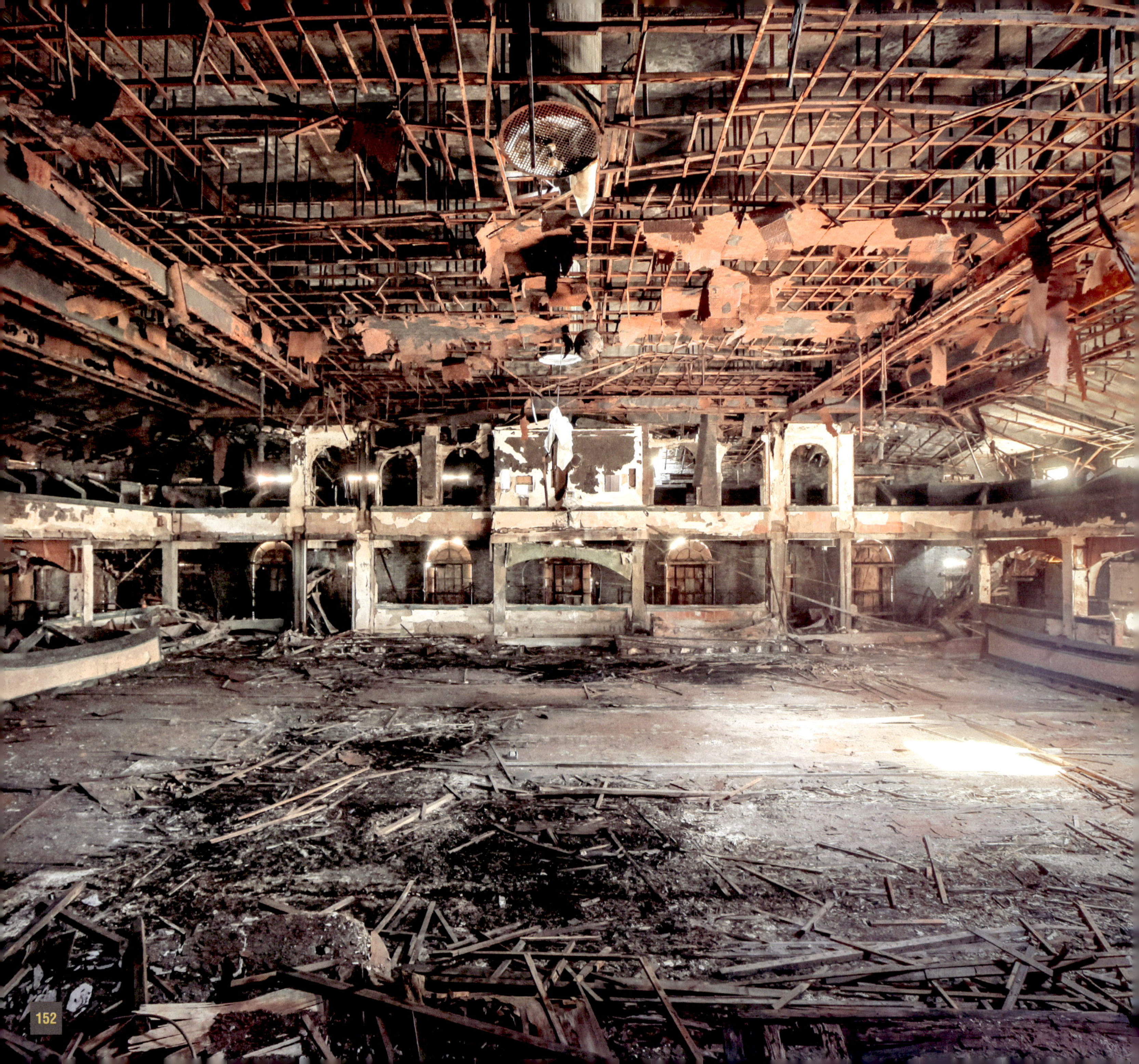

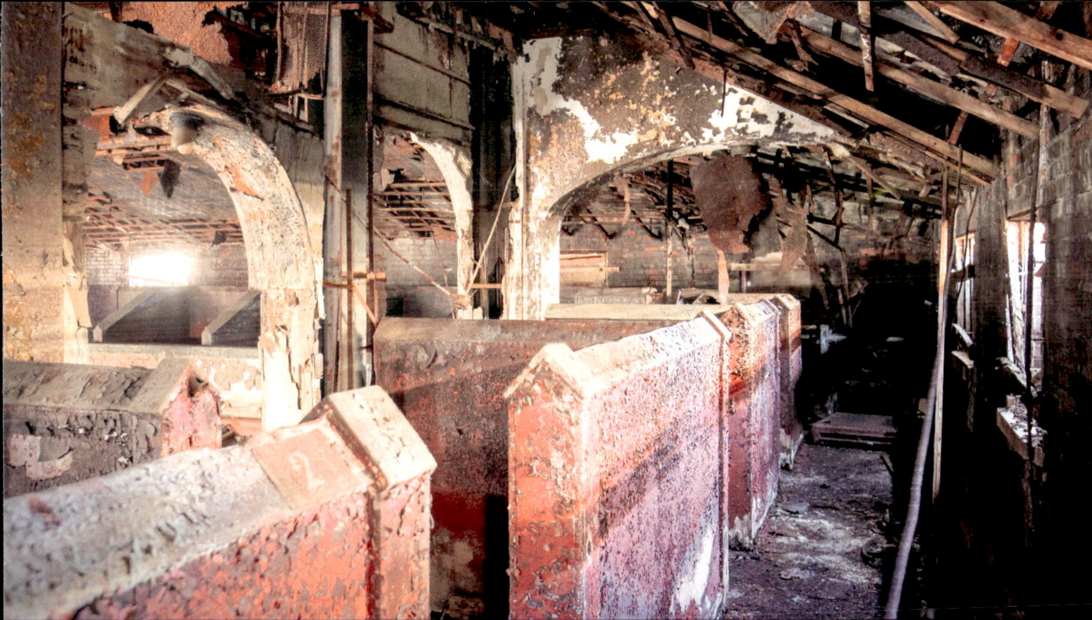

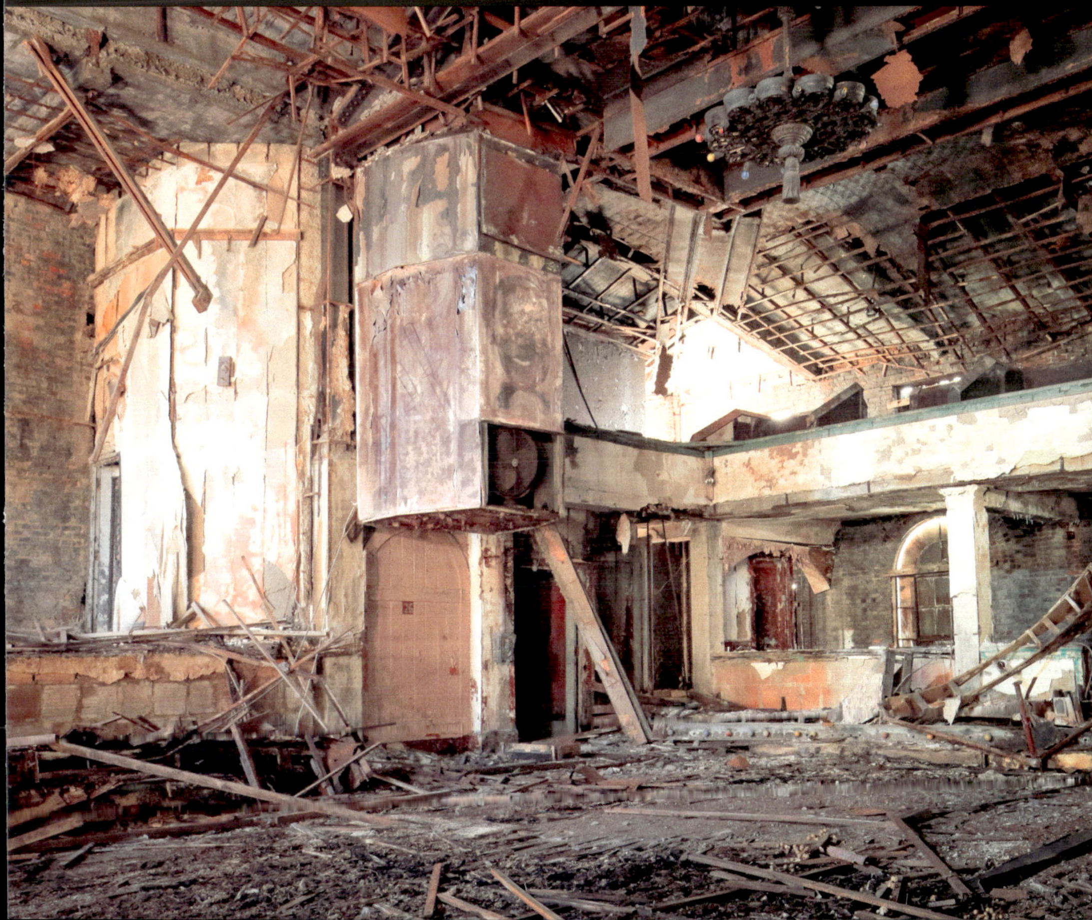

opposite The sense of history here is palpable, and the deterioration absolute. It's no wonder Spike Lee used this location as a nightmare crack den in *Jungle Fever*.

top Box seats offered the best views of the dance floor. Seat numbers are still pinned in the balcony.

bottom Ghostly images of jazz singers and blasting trombones barely cling to the proscenium of the ballroom's weathered stage, once graced by Duke Ellington, Count Basie, and Ella Fitzgerald.

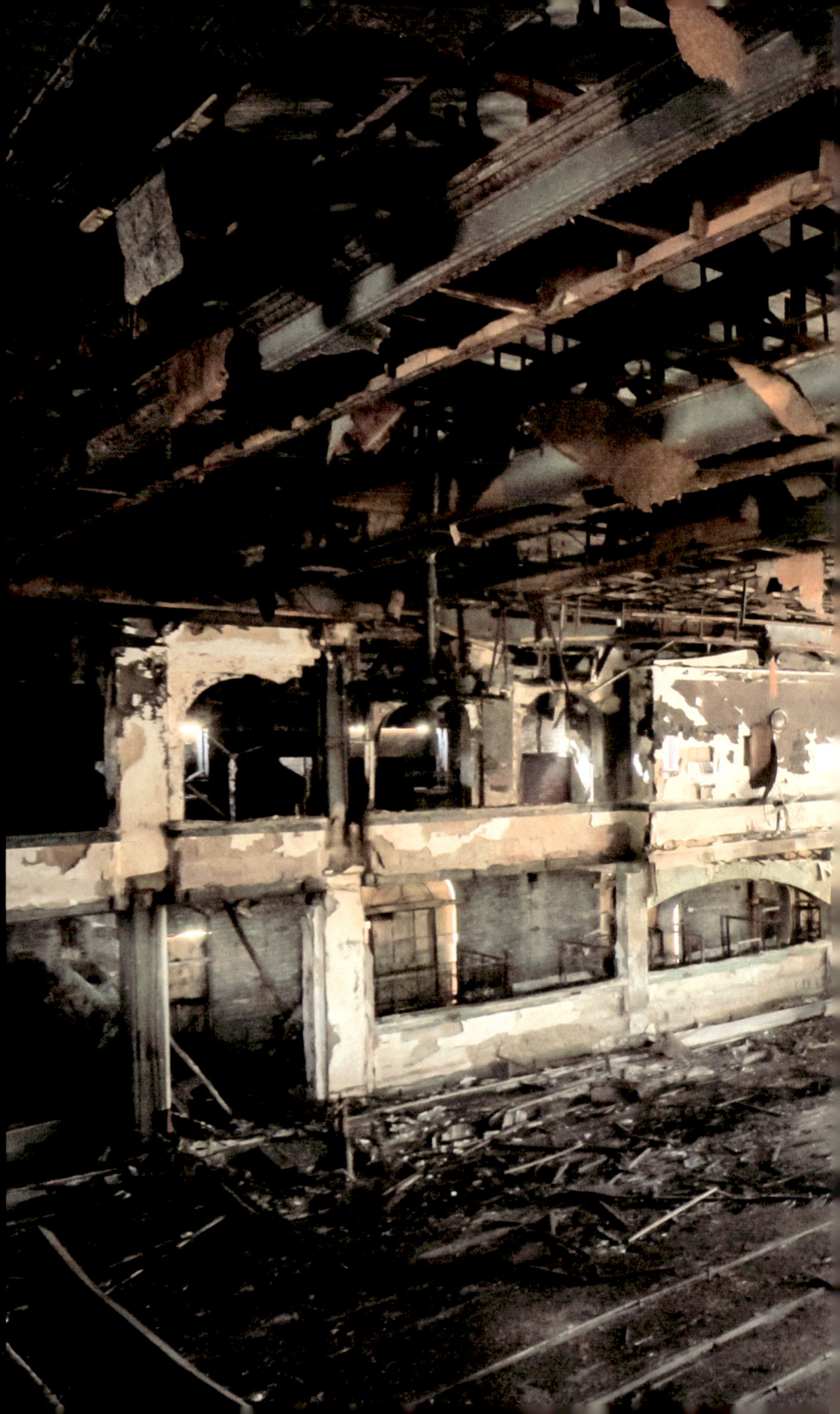

Light leaks through a caved-in ceiling, exposing the diaphanous remnants of a golden age.

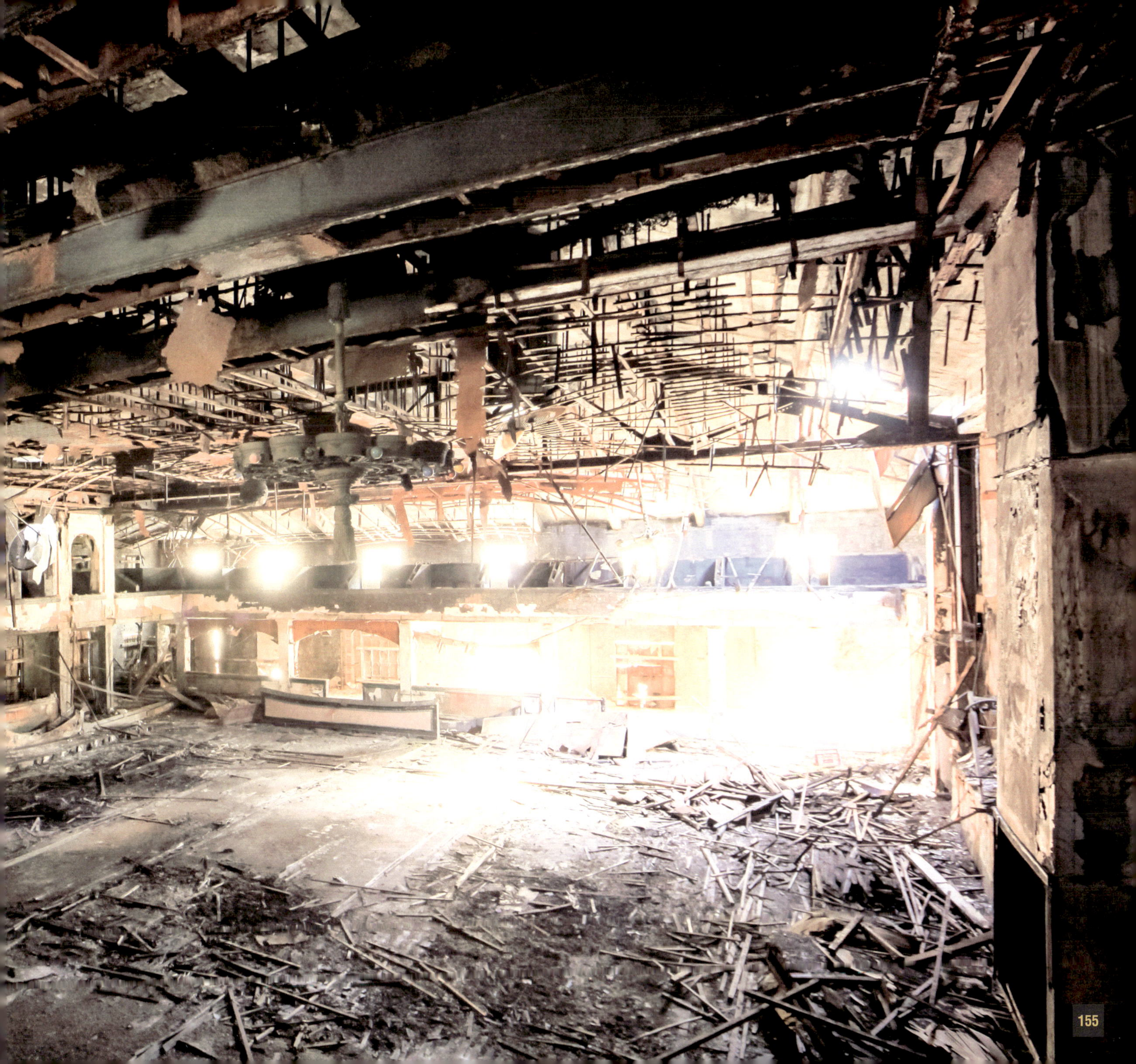

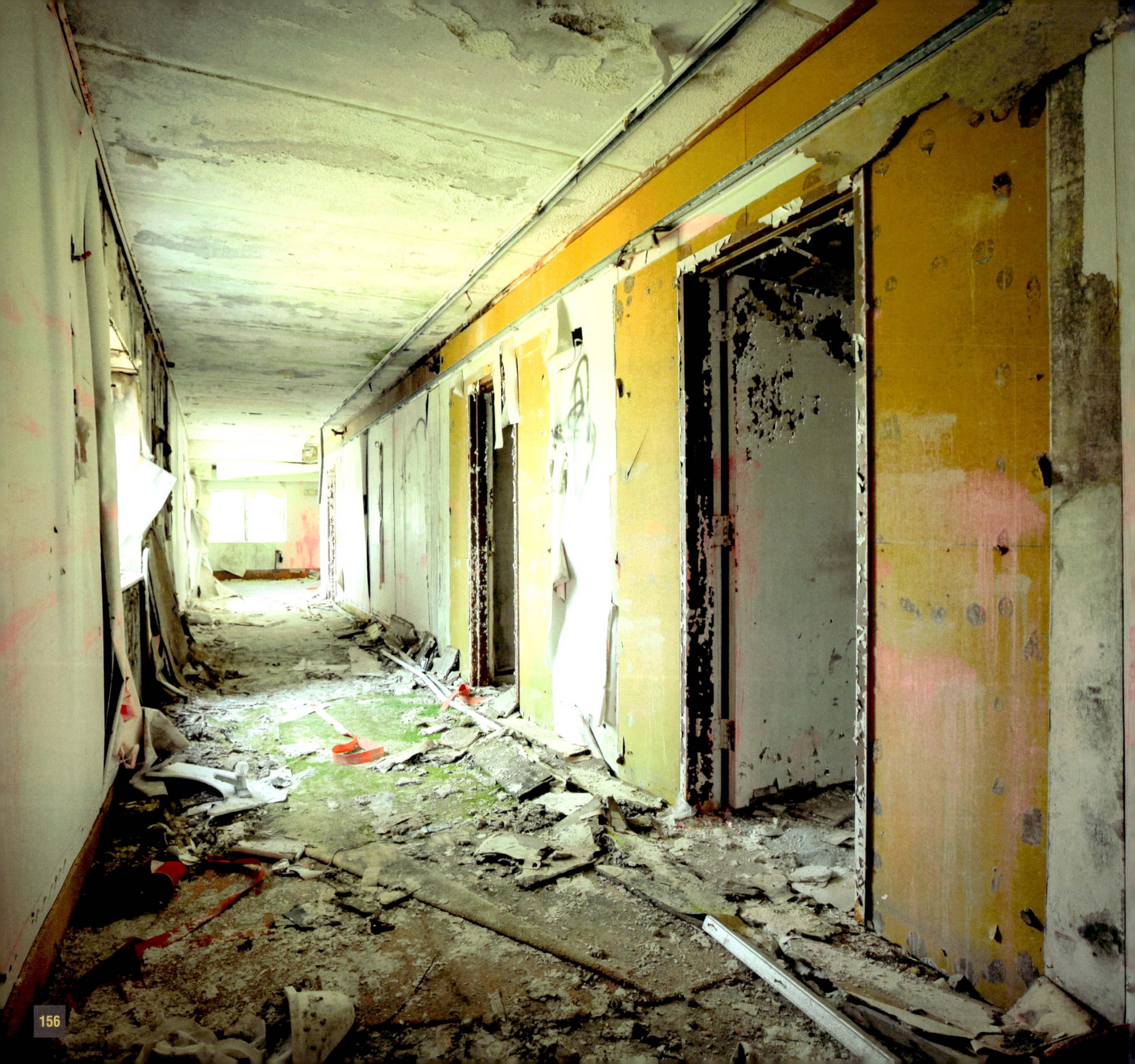

Grossinger's Catskills Resort

Liberty, NY

Past a deserted security desk, waist-high grasses choke back the yawning entrance to the Jennie G. Hotel, whose toppled fence serves more as an invitation than a barrier. In the sleepy town of Liberty, New York, this derelict hilltop lodge is not only a popular destination for urban explorers, it's a daily reminder of the town's old eminence, visible from miles around.

In its time, Grossinger's Catskills Resort was a fantasy realized, where wealthy businessmen, celebrity entertainers, and star athletes gathered to mingle with those whom they liked and were like, to see and be seen, and to enjoy, rightly so, the things they enjoyed. As the slogan went, "Grossinger's has everything for the kind of person who likes to come to Grossinger's."

A generation ago, this region of the Catskills was known as the Borscht Belt, a tongue-in-cheek designation for a string of hotels and resorts that catered to a predominantly Jewish customer base in a time when discrimination against Jews at mainstream resorts was widespread. In popular culture, the most notable representation of this time and place is *Dirty Dancing,* which was supposedly inspired by a summer at Grossinger's. The unexpected success of the movie had little effect on the long-struggling resort—in 1986, a year before the film was released, Grossinger's ended its 70-year legacy.

The Grossingers were Austrian immigrants who opened a small farmhouse to boarders in 1914 after years of struggle in New York City and a failed farming venture. They quickly gained a reputation for their exceptional hospitality and incredible kosher cooking and outgrew their ramshackle farmhouse, purchasing the property that the resort still occupies today.

The resort's rise to prominence is largely attributed to the Grossingers' daughter Jennie, who worked as a hostess in its early years. Later, Jennie's legendary leadership would transform the resort from its humble beginnings to a massive 35-building complex—with its own zip code and airstrip—attracting over 150,000 guests a year and establishing a new type of travel destination that renounced the quiet charms of country living for a fast-paced, action-packed social experience that met the expectations of a sophisticated New York City clientele.

Every sport of leisure had its own arena, with state-of-the-art facilities for handball, tennis, skiing, ice-skating, barrel jumping, and tobogganing, along with a championship golf course. In 1952, the resort earned a place in history by being the first to use artificial snow. Its famous training establishment for boxers hosted seven world champions, and its stages launched the careers of countless well-known singers and comedians. In its day spas, beauty salons, ballrooms, and auditoriums, guests were offered a level of luxury that even the wealthiest individuals couldn't enjoy at home, earning Grossinger's the nickname, "Waldorf in the Catskills."

opposite The ransacked Paul G. hotel shows the hallmarks of a recent paintball game.

By the late '60s, the Grossinger's model had started to fall out of favor as cheap air travel to tourist destinations around the world became readily available to a new generation. After the property was abandoned, several renovation attempts were aborted by a string of investors. Widespread demolition greatly diminished the sprawl of the original resort, but several buildings remain. Most have been stripped of any vestige of opulence, and some structures are barely standing, no more so than the former Joy Cottage, whose floors might not withstand the footfalls of a field mouse.

Areas across the region that once relied on a thriving tourism industry have fallen into depression or emptied out. Now, the Catskills region is attempting to rebrand and update its image, having held an online contest to determine a new slogan. The winner? "The Catskills, Always in Season."

Though it remains to be seen whether the coming seasons will bring new visitors to the struggling region, there's no doubt they'll serve to erase its outmoded reputation. With each passing year, in ruined hotels across the Catskills, the physical remnants of lost vacations dwindle. Scattered in photo albums, hidden in bottom drawers, excerpted from yellowing newsprint, the memories will follow, clearing the way for new journeys. Before it's forgotten, here's another look inside the celebrated resort.

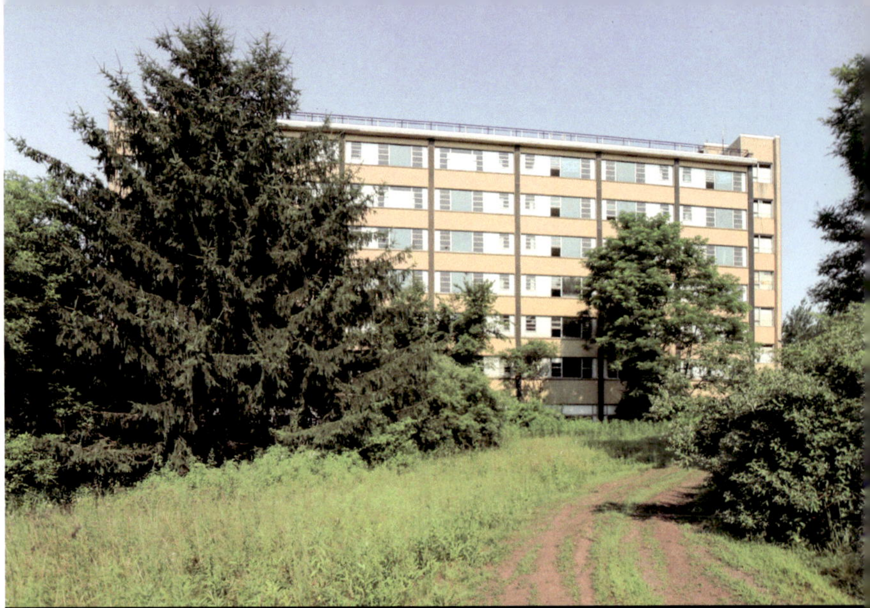

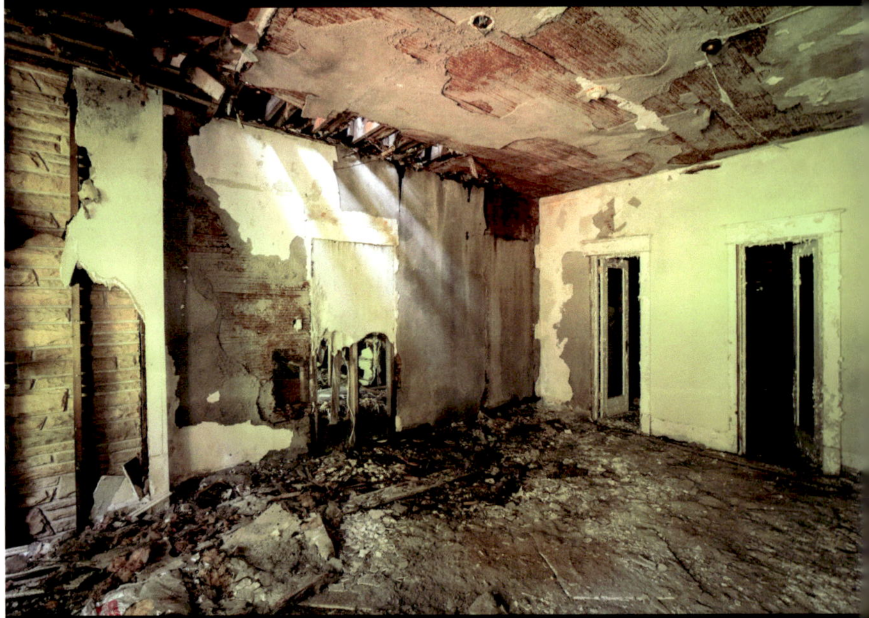

top The Jennie G. Hotel.

bottom Just as quickly as the resort prospered into a world-class destination, it's descended into decay.

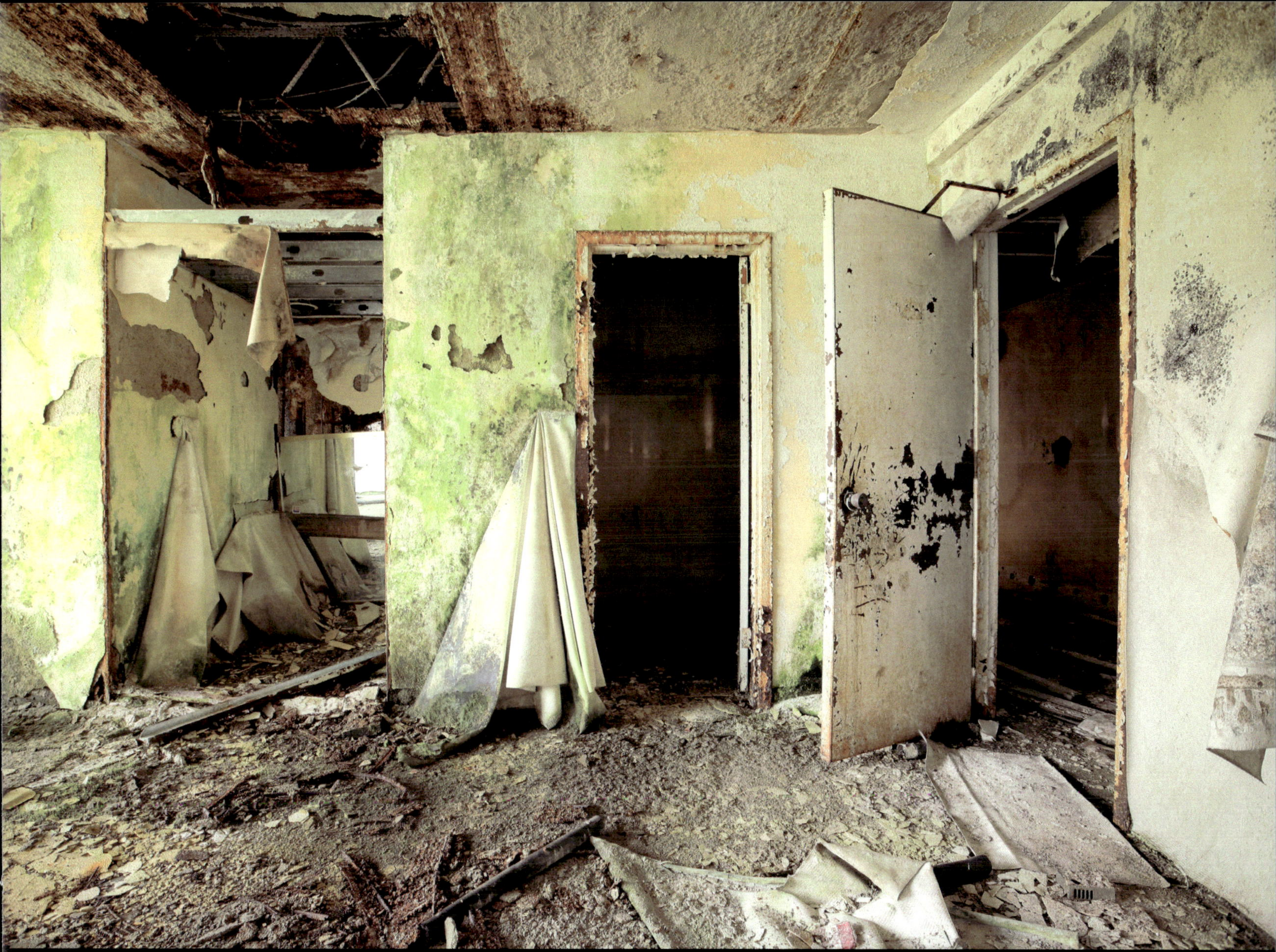

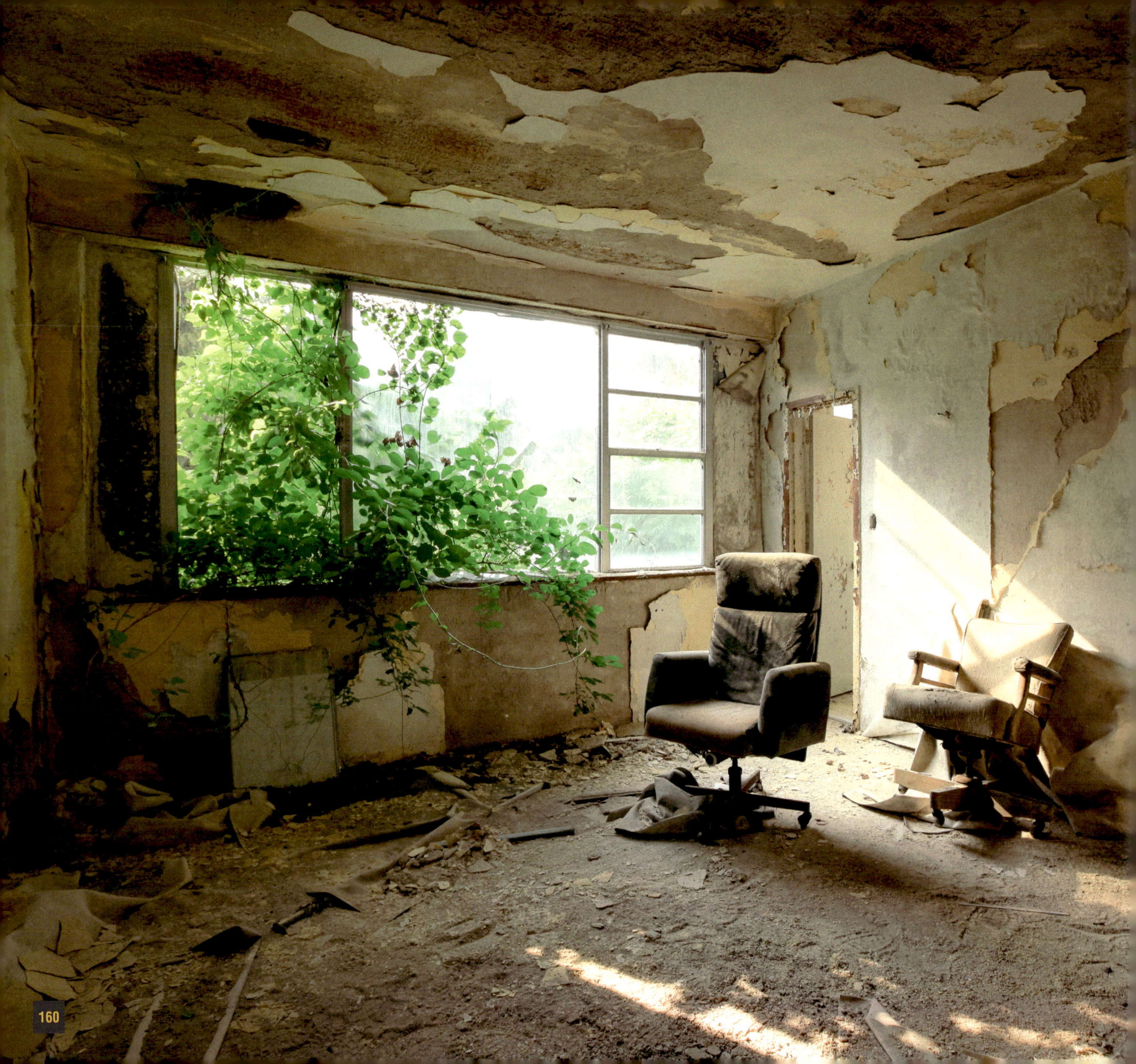

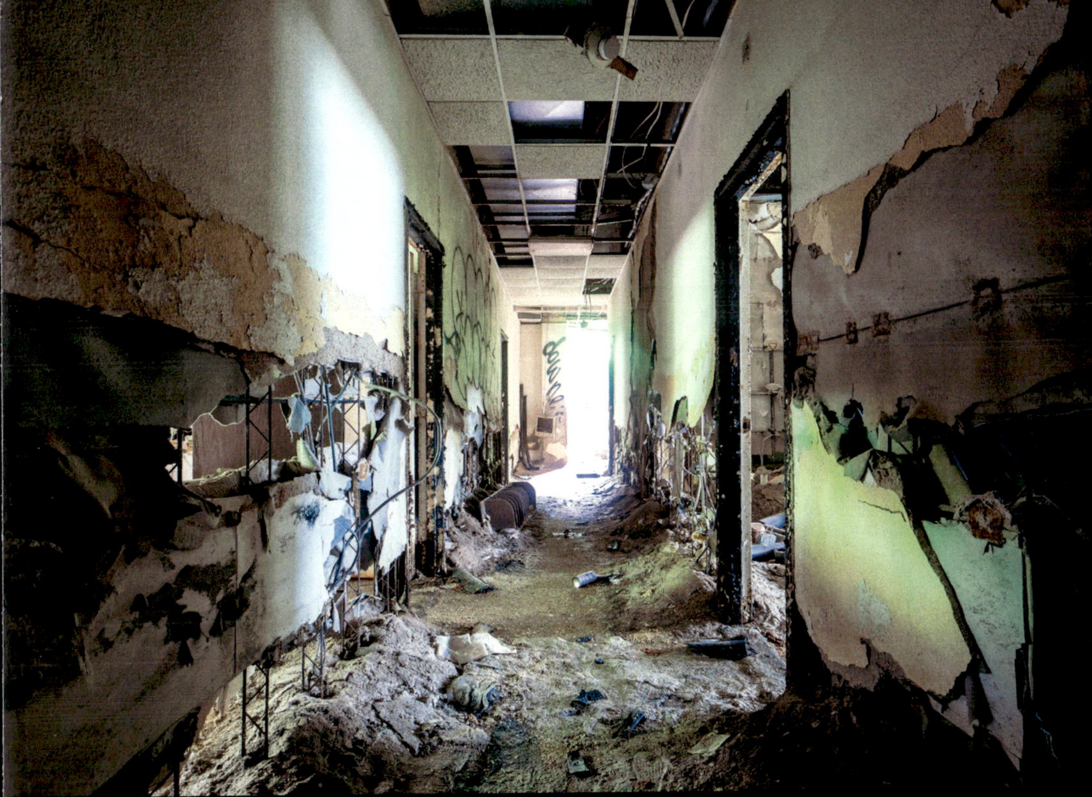

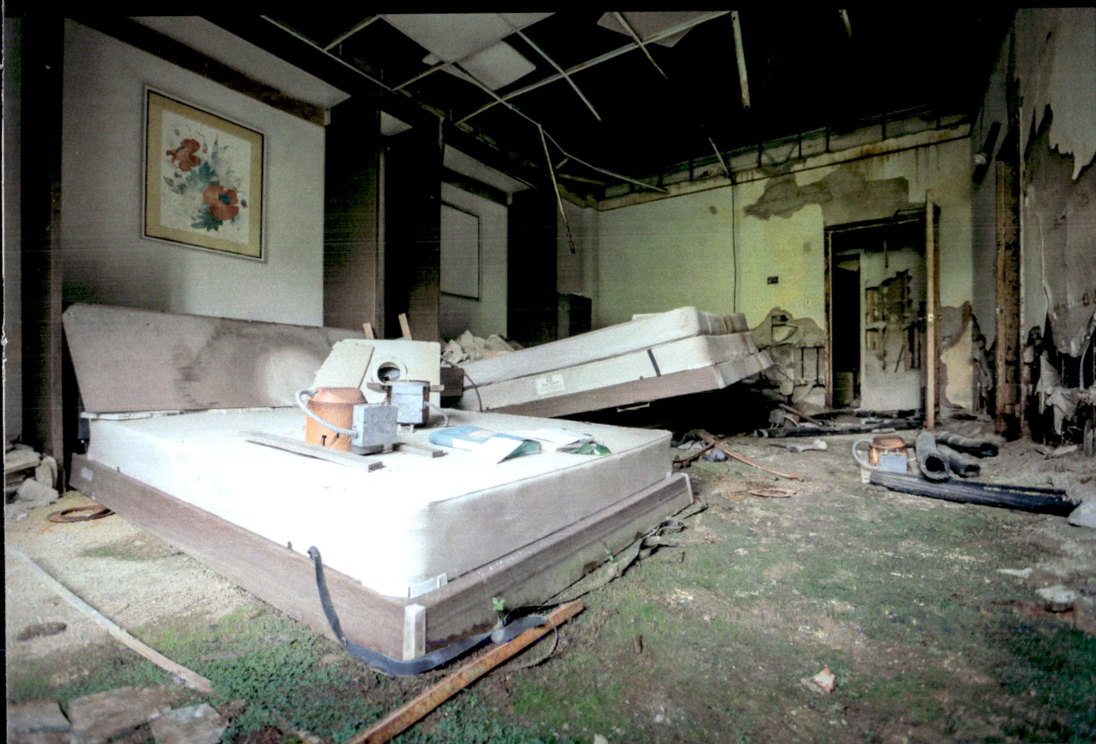

opposite The verdant Catskills encroach on a second floor suite.

top The soggy ground floor is in worse shape, though it contains the most artifacts.

bottom One room holds two murphy beds and a carpet of moss.

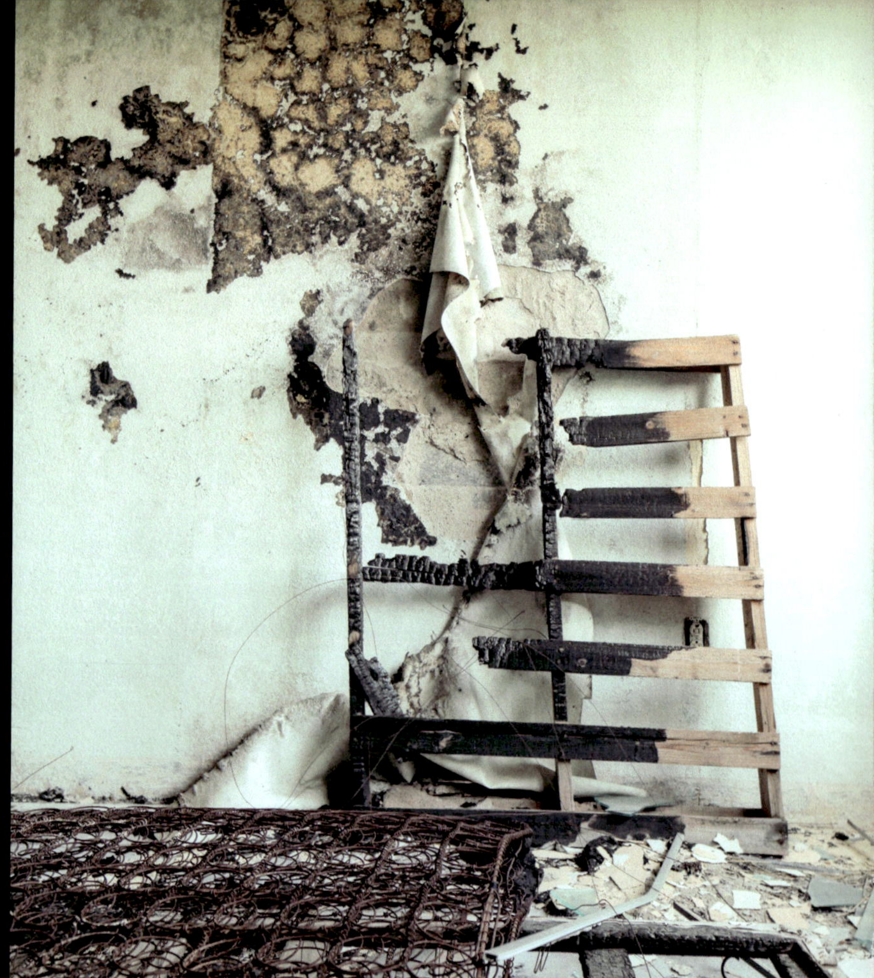

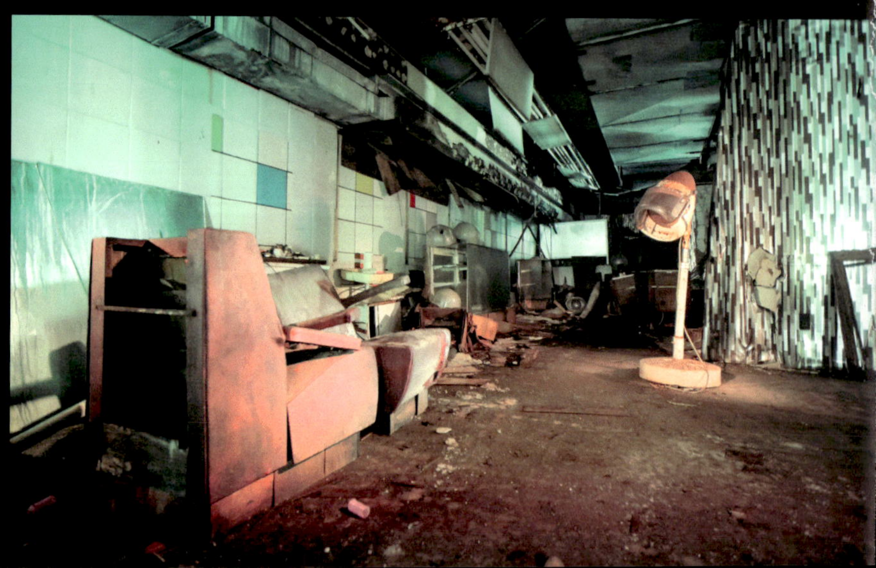

top A botched attempt to burn down the hotel left these remnants.

bottom The former beauty salon offers a glimpse into the level of luxury the resort aspired to in its day. Creams, ointments, and make-up remain on the shelves of the spa.

opposite A cheerful striped motif in a collapsing ice skating facility hints at happier times.

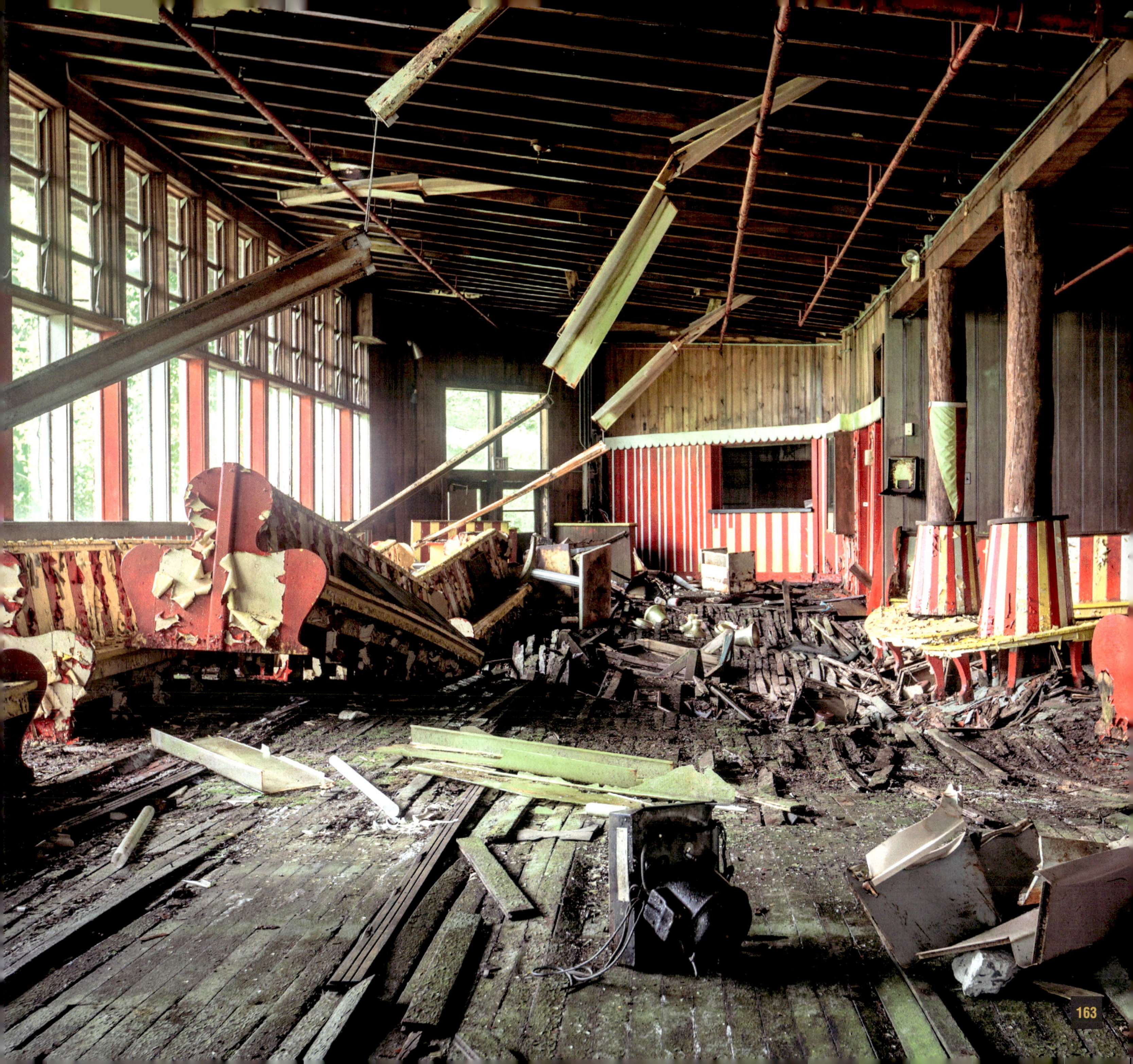

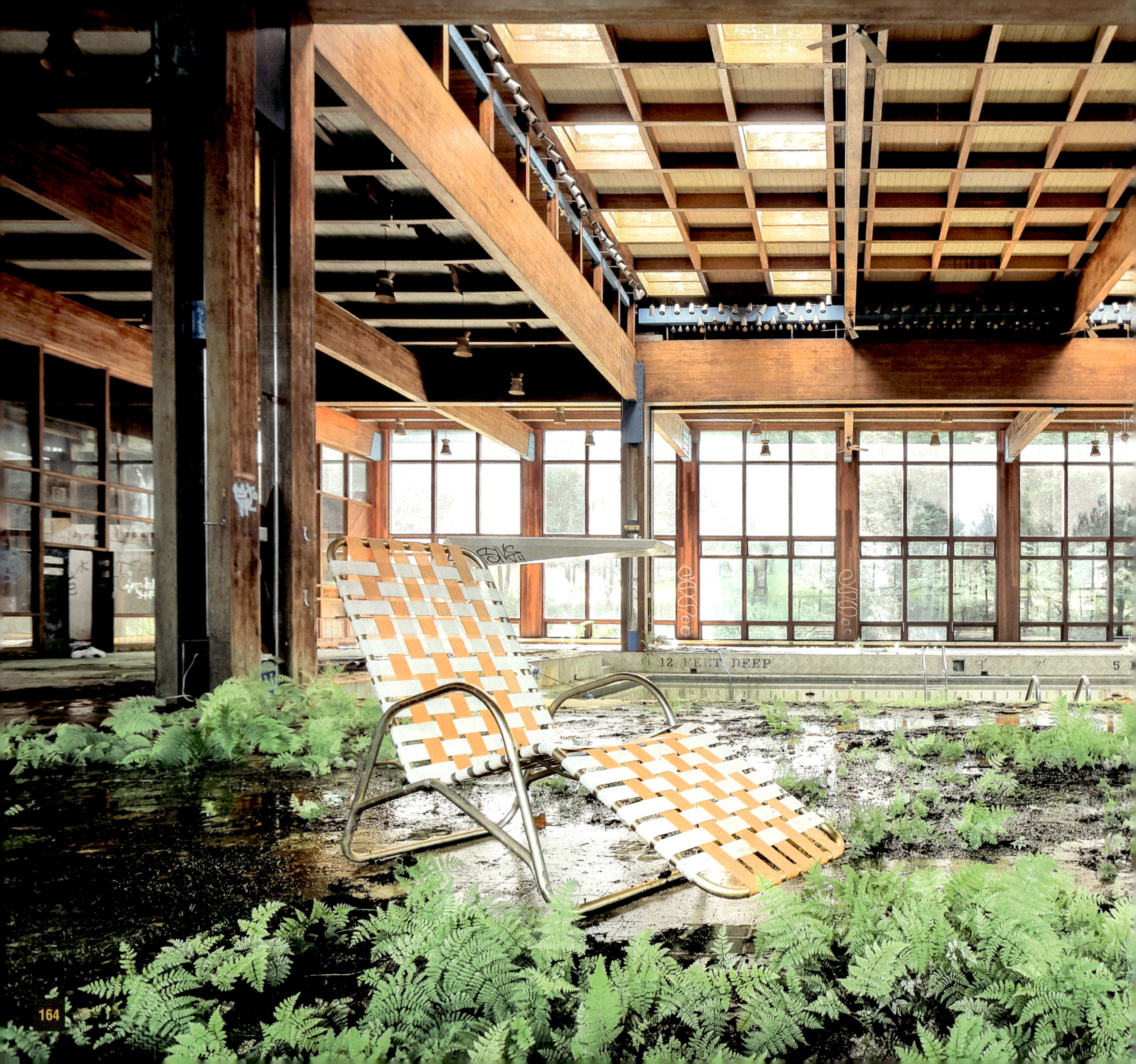
12 FEET DEEP
5

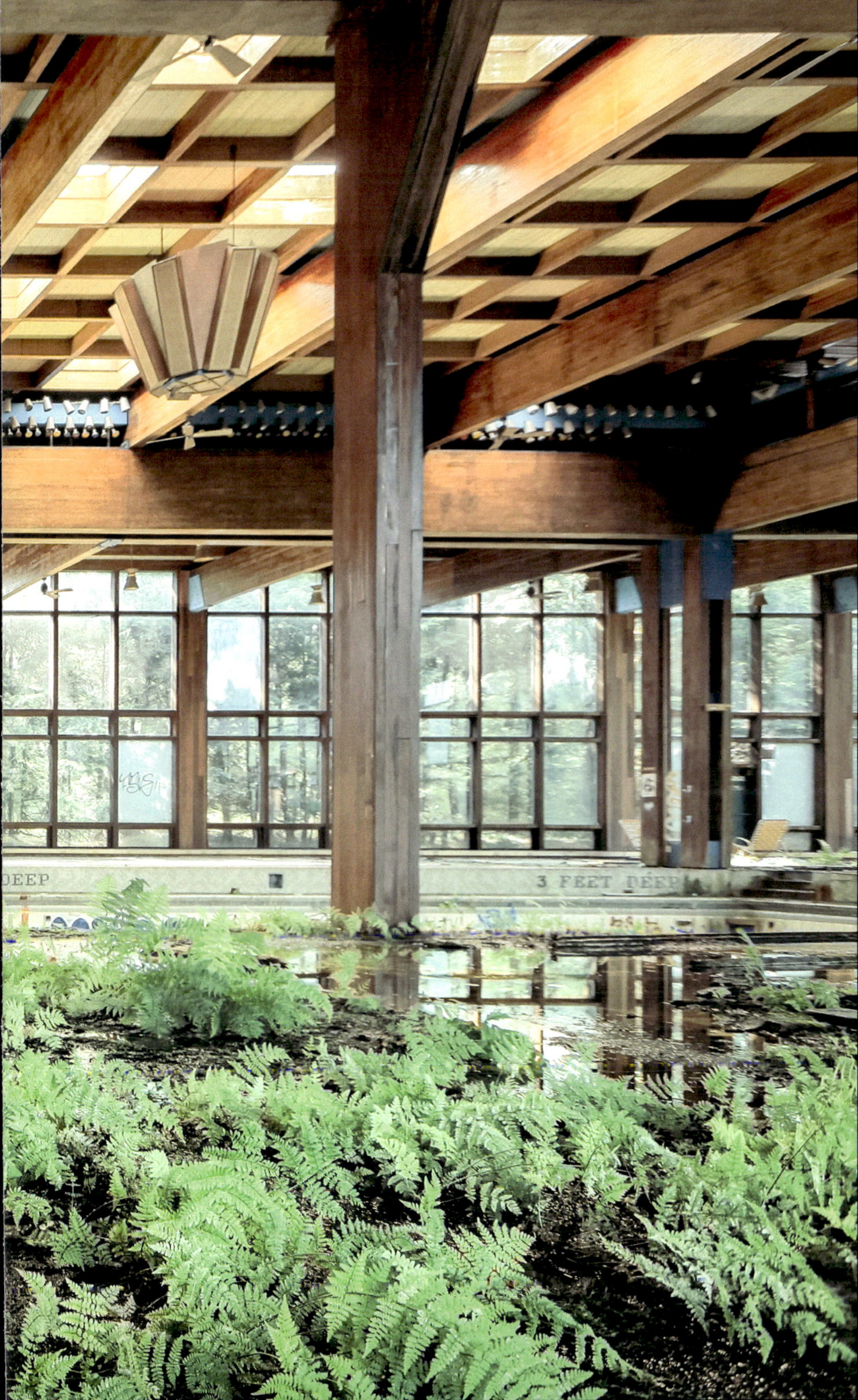

The years have transformed this neglected natatorium into a flourishing greenhouse. Ferns prosper from a moss-caked poolside, unhindered by the tread of carefree vacationers.

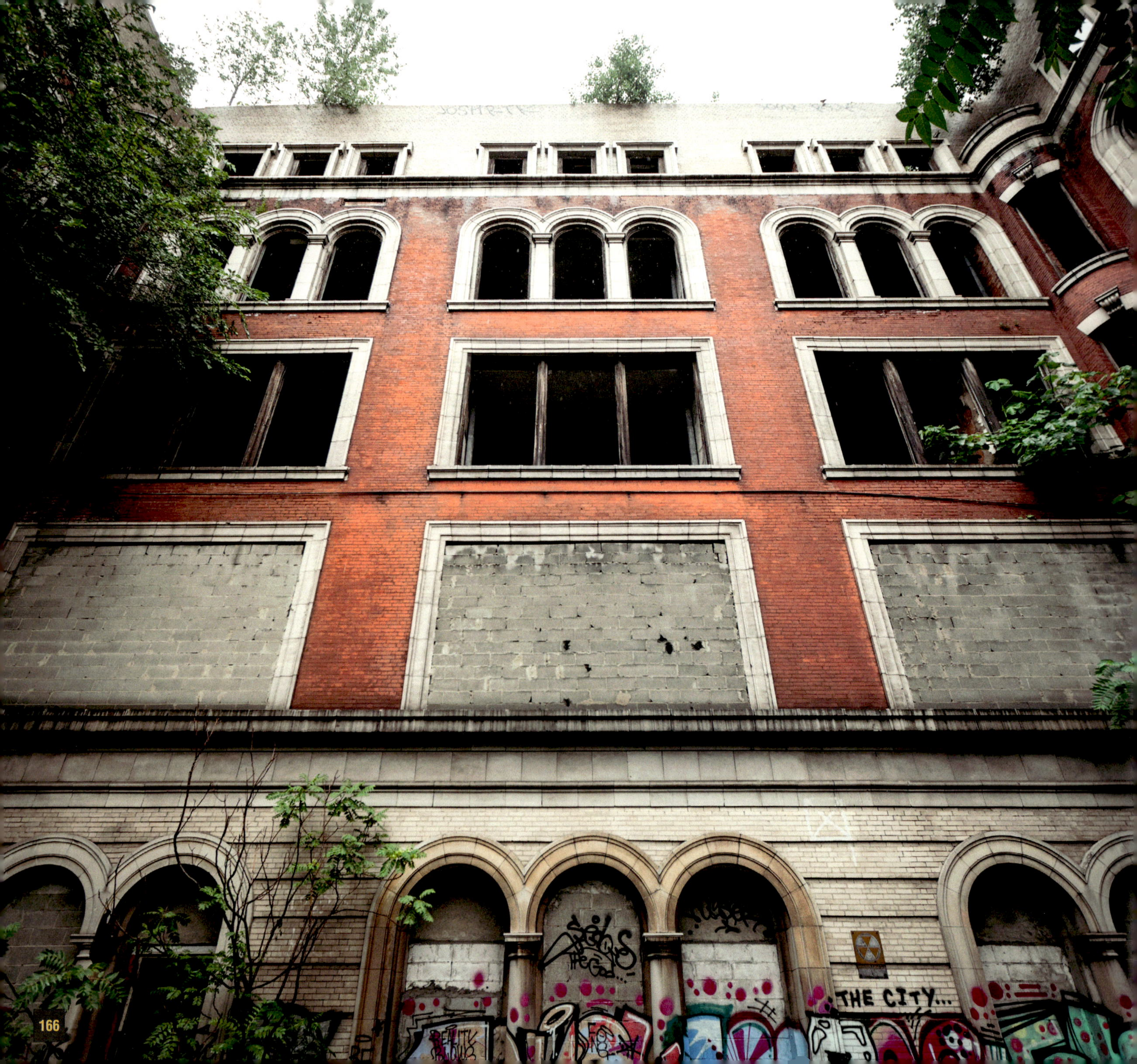
THE CITY...

P.S. 186

Harlem, NY

School's out forever at P.S. 186. The aging Italian Renaissance structure has loomed over West Harlem's 145th Street for 111 years, but it's been vacant a third of that time. The school was considered dilapidated when it shuttered 37 years ago, but today its interiors feel more sepulchral than scholastic.

The Boys and Girls Club of Harlem (BGCH) purchased the site in 1986 for $215,000 under the condition that new development would be completed within three years. As a nonprofit, the BGCH was exempt from property tax, and therefore had little incentive to do something with the property as the structure deteriorated and the costs of renovation mounted. After several decades of inactivity, the group introduced a redevelopment plan that called for the demolition of P.S. 186 and the construction of a 200,000–square foot mixed-use facility with affordable housing, commercial and community space, and a new public school.

News of the school's demolition mobilized area residents to save the structure. A series of local petitions and letter-writing campaigns championed the preservation of P.S. 186 and gained the support of the New York Landmarks Conservancy, though a landmark bid was blocked at a 2010 community board meeting. At the time, owners insisted that rehabilitating the decrepit building was a financial impossibility, but in a surprising turn of events, the BGCH recently downsized the plan in favor of preservation, taking advantage of tax credits to renovate the historic structure.

It's a rare victory for preservationists, and an unlikely one given the school's history—when the building was last in use, community members wanted nothing more than to see the place razed.

In addition to generally run-down conditions, safety was a major concern at P.S. 186 in its final years. The design allegedly had the potential to trap "hundreds of children and teachers" in the event of a fire. Doors on the bottom floor had to remain open at all times to keep the outdated floor plan up to code, leaving the building completely vulnerable to neighborhood crime. Quoted in a *New York Times* article, the school's principal at the time claimed that, "parents have been robbed in here at knife point, and people…use this building as a through-way." In a 1972 incident, two youths, including the 17-year-old brother of a P.S. 186 student, broke into room 407 and raped a teacher's aide at gunpoint.

opposite Abandoned for close to four decades, the imposing façade of P.S. 186 has become a subject of fascination for residents of 145th St.

Increasing community concern reached a boiling point earlier that year when 60 members of the African American empowerment group NEGRO (National Economic Growth and Reconstruction Organization) moved into the school to call for an evacuation of 600 students on the top three floors. The stunt caught the attention of the Fire Department, which toured the school later that week. A deputy chief couldn't identify a serious problem, but was forced to evacuate the remaining 900 students when he was unable to activate the fire alarm. Inspectors discovered that wires leading out of the alarm system had been cut, although a school custodian claimed that the alarm system had worked during a routine test that morning.

By 1975, funding was at last approved for a replacement school, and much to the relief of parents, plans were put in place for the immediate demolition of the aging firetrap. No one could have predicted that 37 years later, P.S. 186 would be getting a second chance. With $50 million secured for the redevelopment of the building, it looks like the weird and wonderful interiors of this long-abandoned school may be budding for the final time.

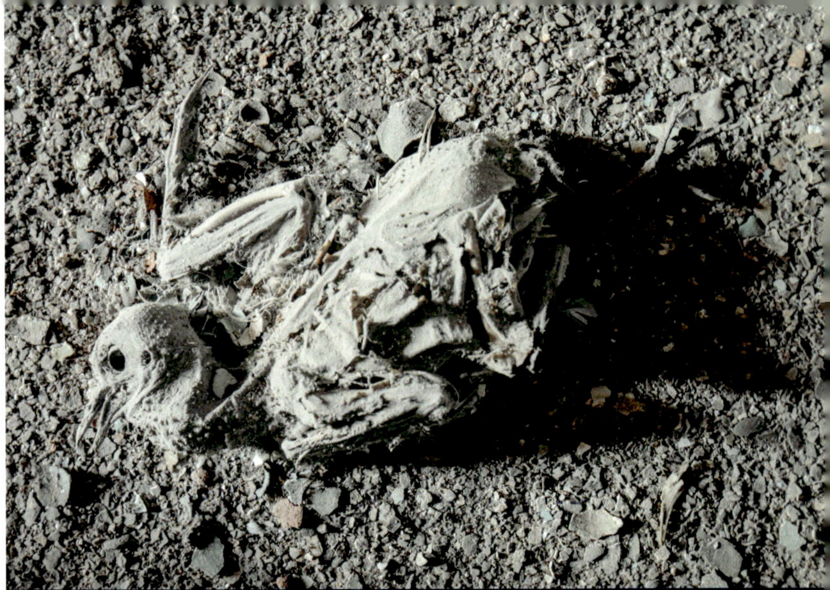

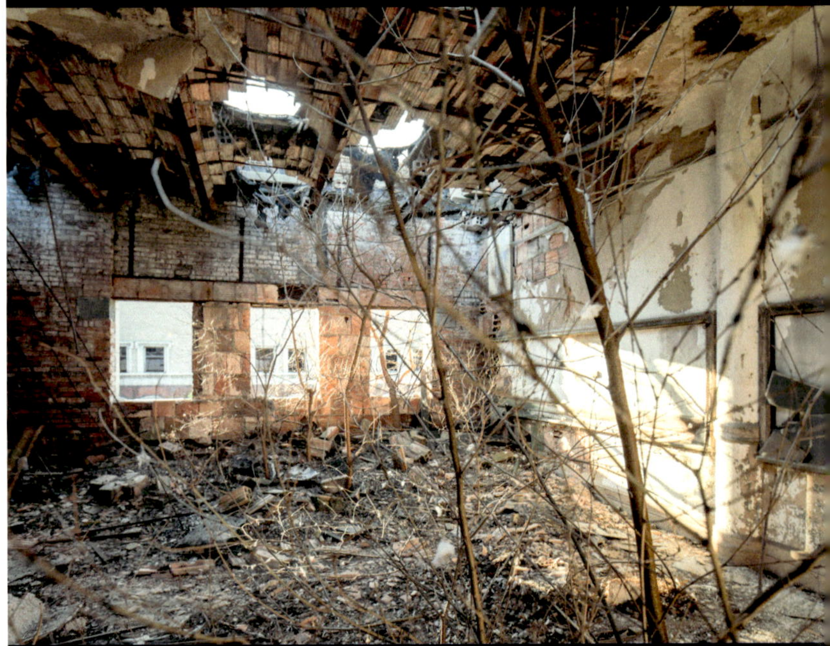

top The upper floors of the school harbor a population of dozens of mummified pigeons.

bottom During the winter months, barren saplings lend an air of melancholy to the wrecked interior.

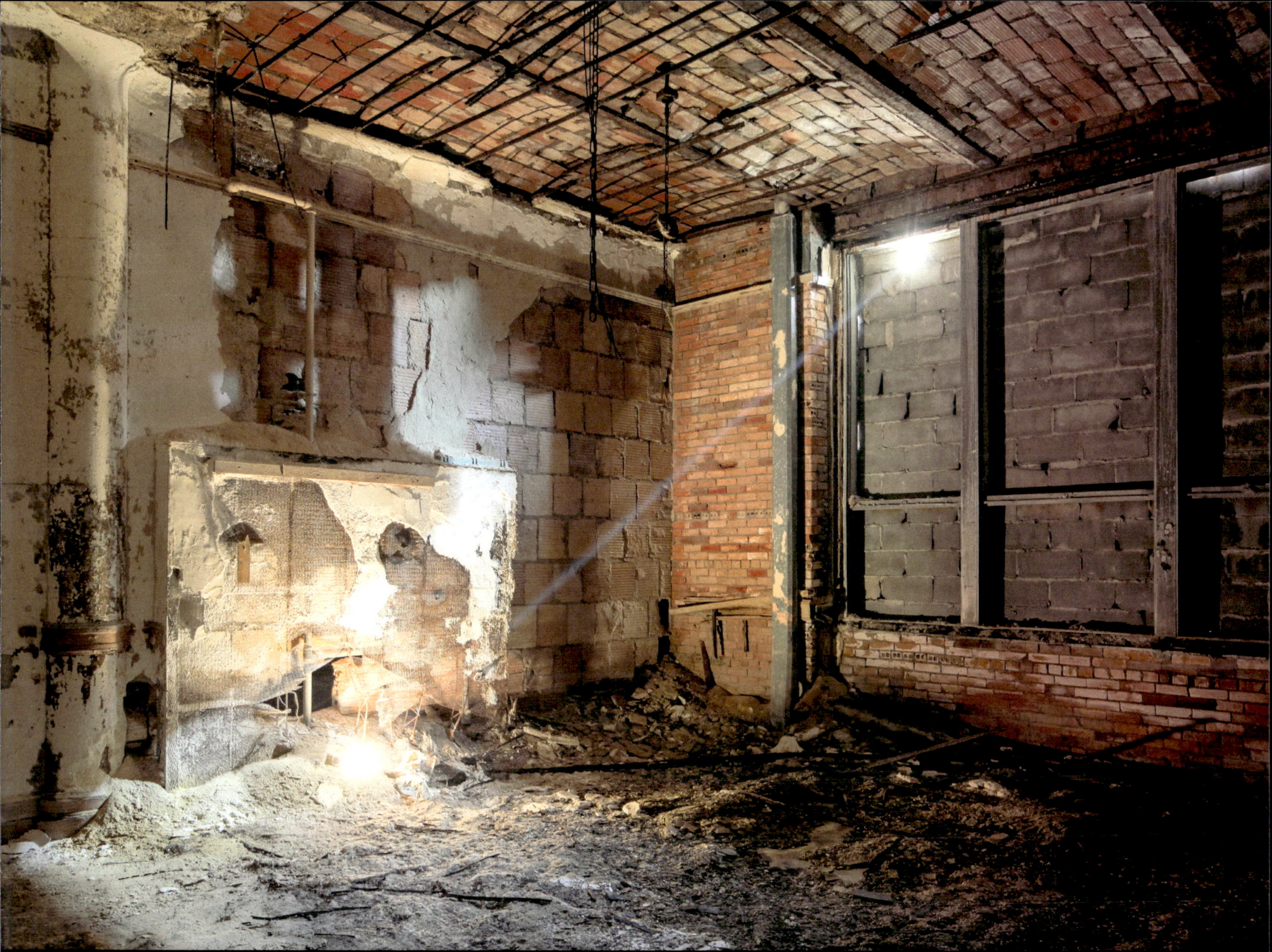

above Cinder blocks had been installed on windows of the bottom two floors to discourage vandals.

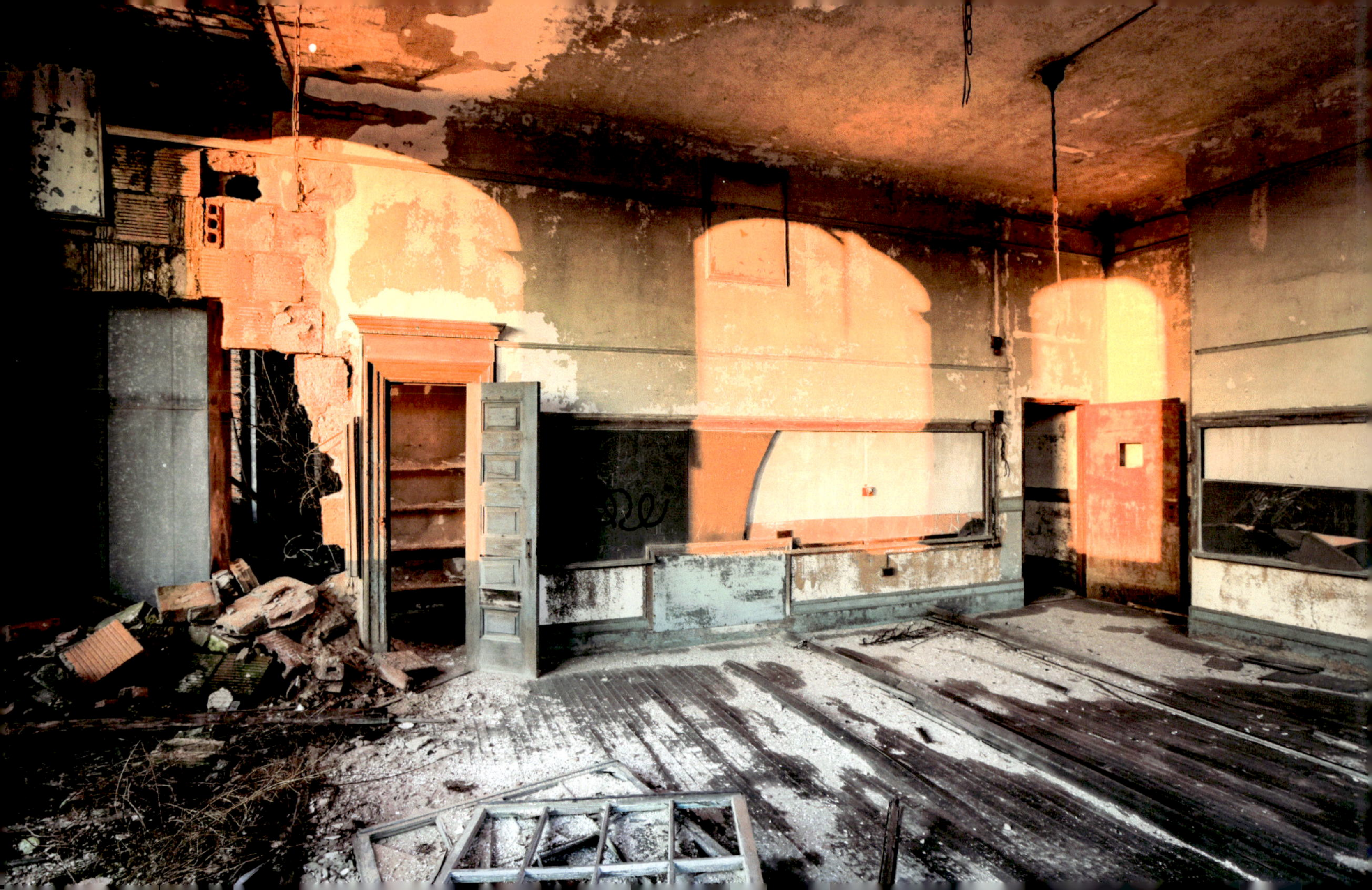

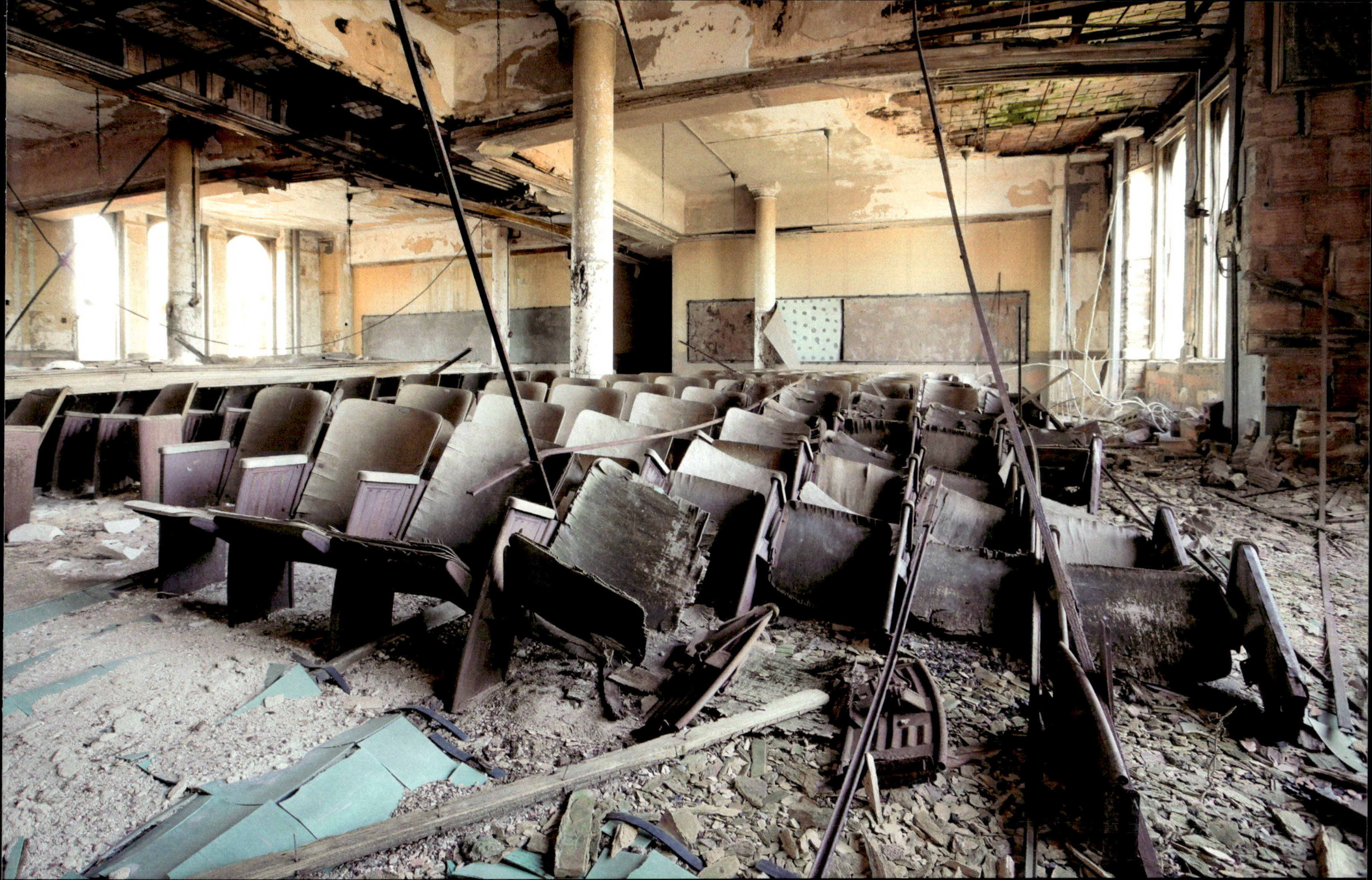

Seating rots into the floor of the school auditorium. Windows gape on three out of five floors of the building, leaving interiors completely exposed to the elements.

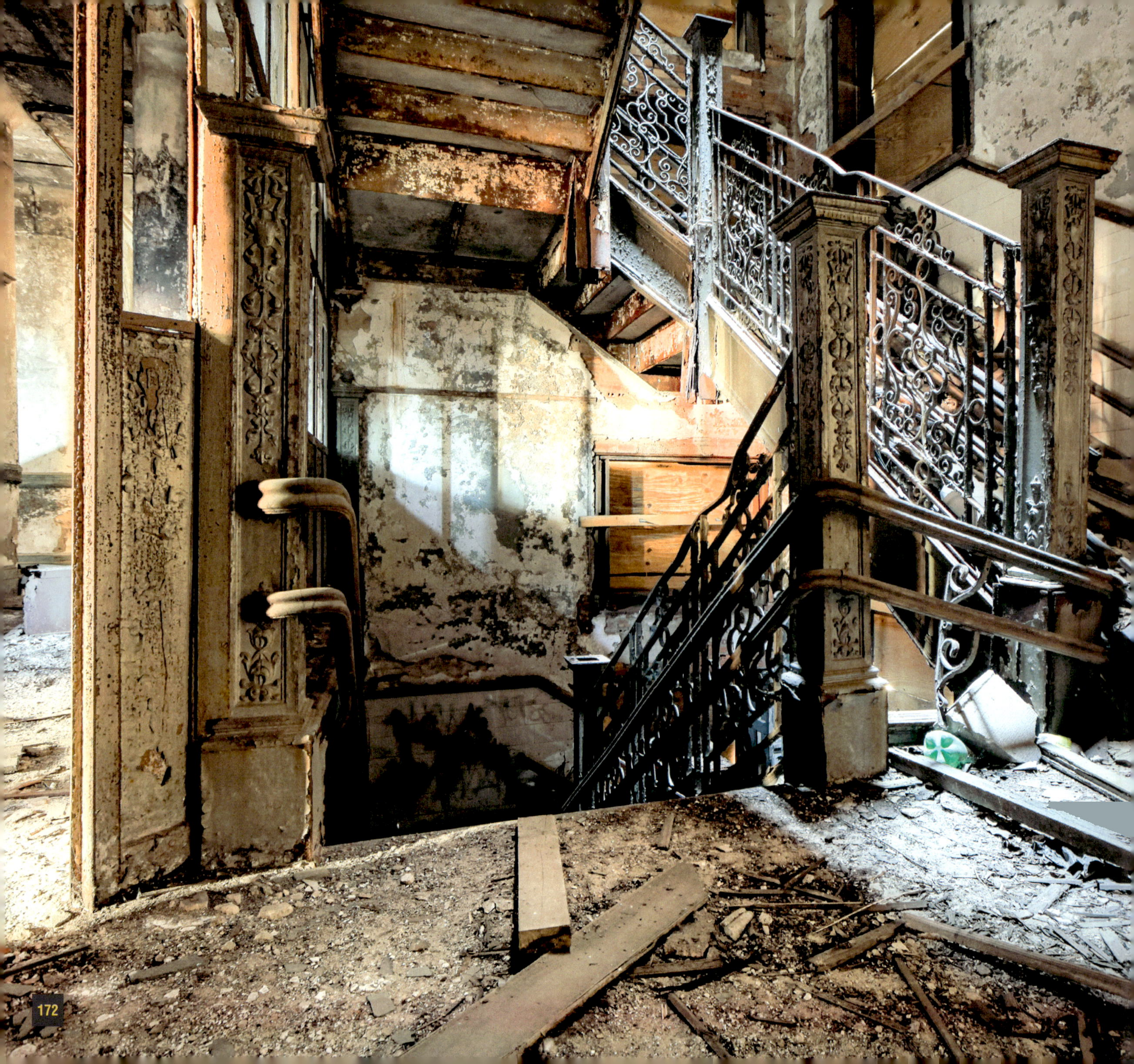

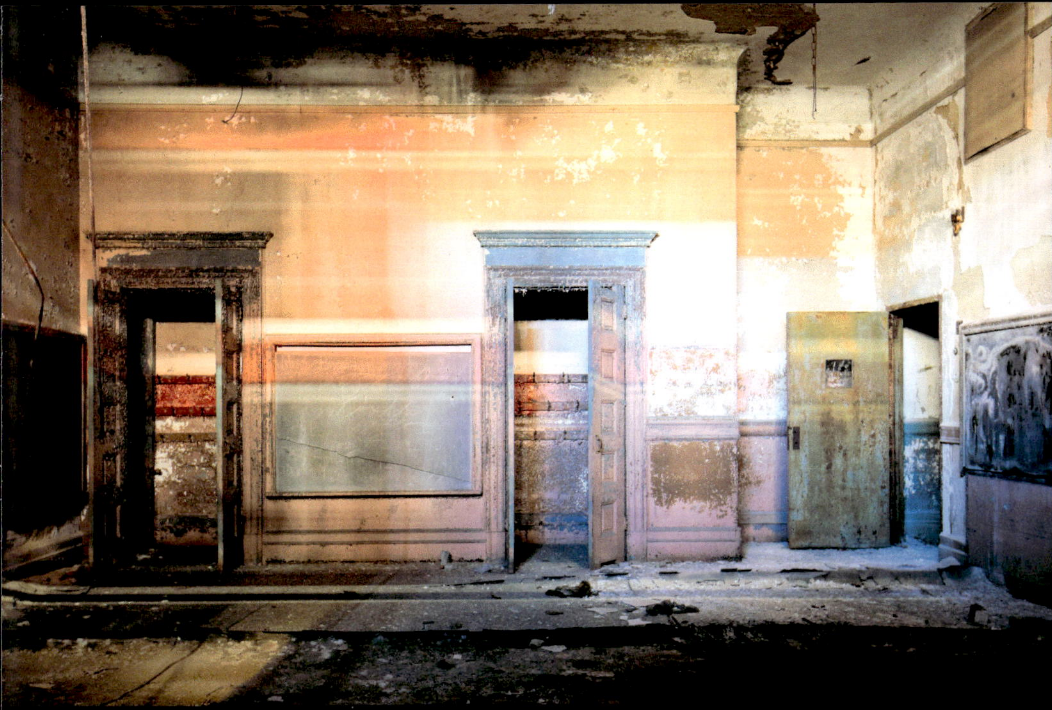

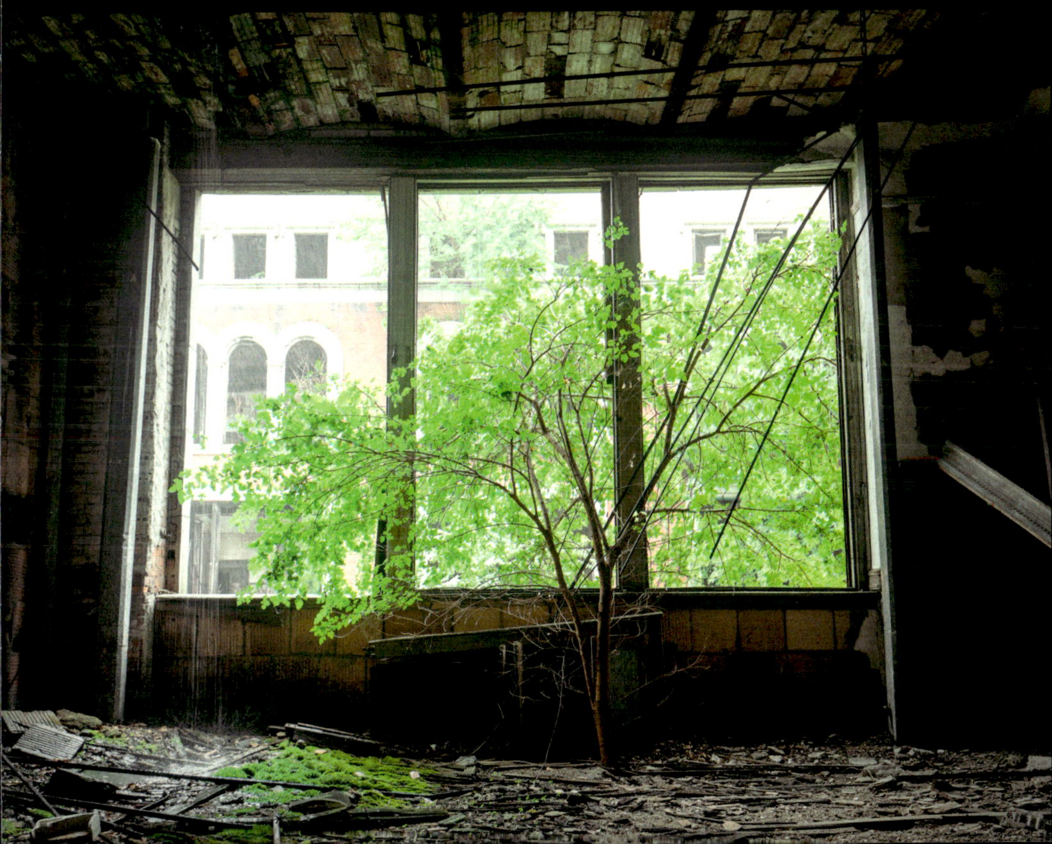

opposite A staircase is filled with debris, but retains some elegant wrought iron details.

top A long exposure reveals bands of color projected onto this classroom, a vibrant variation on a camera obscura.

bottom Rainwater cascades from a collapsed ceiling during a midsummer downpour.

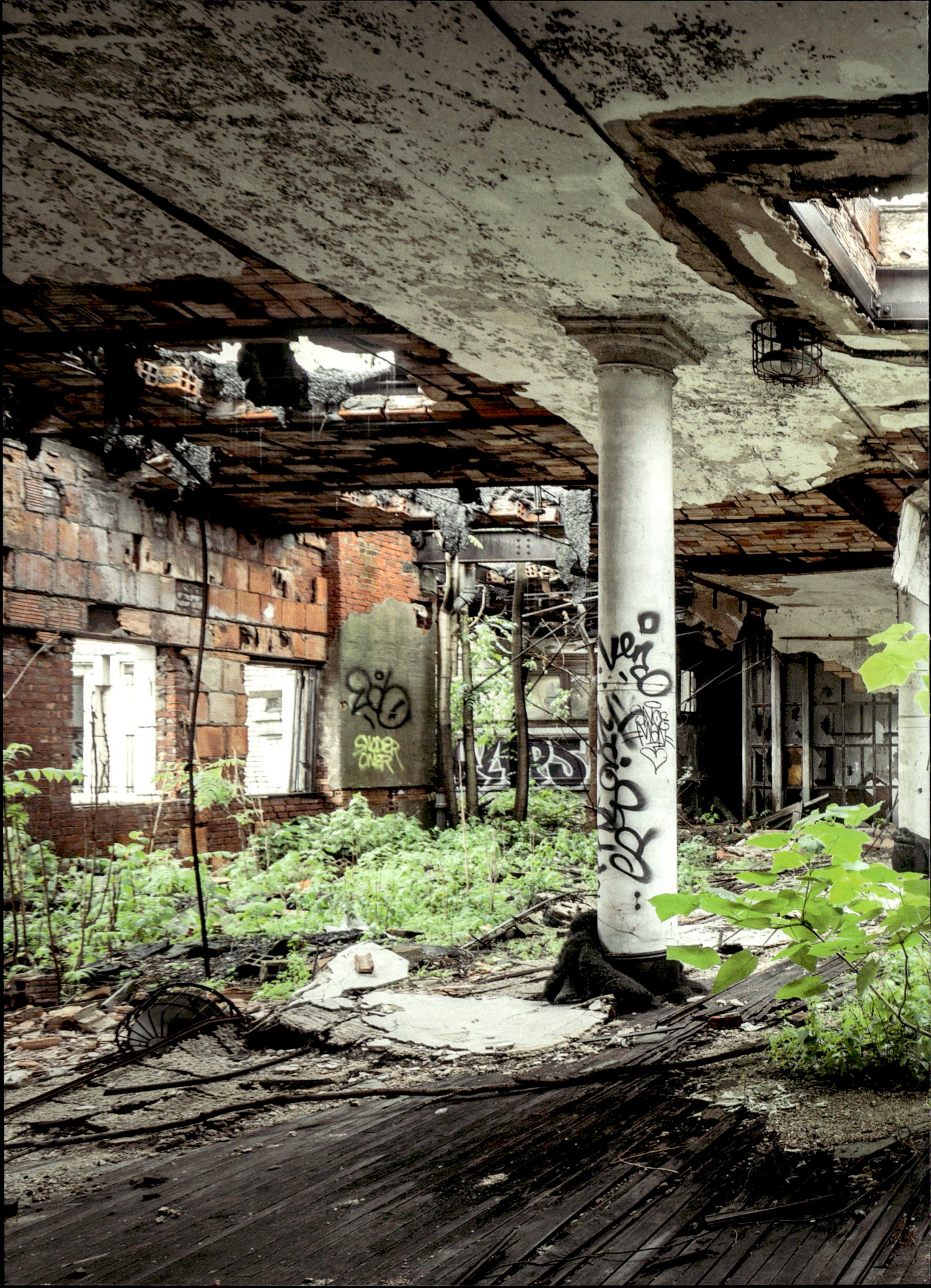

The school is transformed by the seasons. In early July, lush vegetation lends a renewed vitality to the gloomy interiors of P.S. 186.

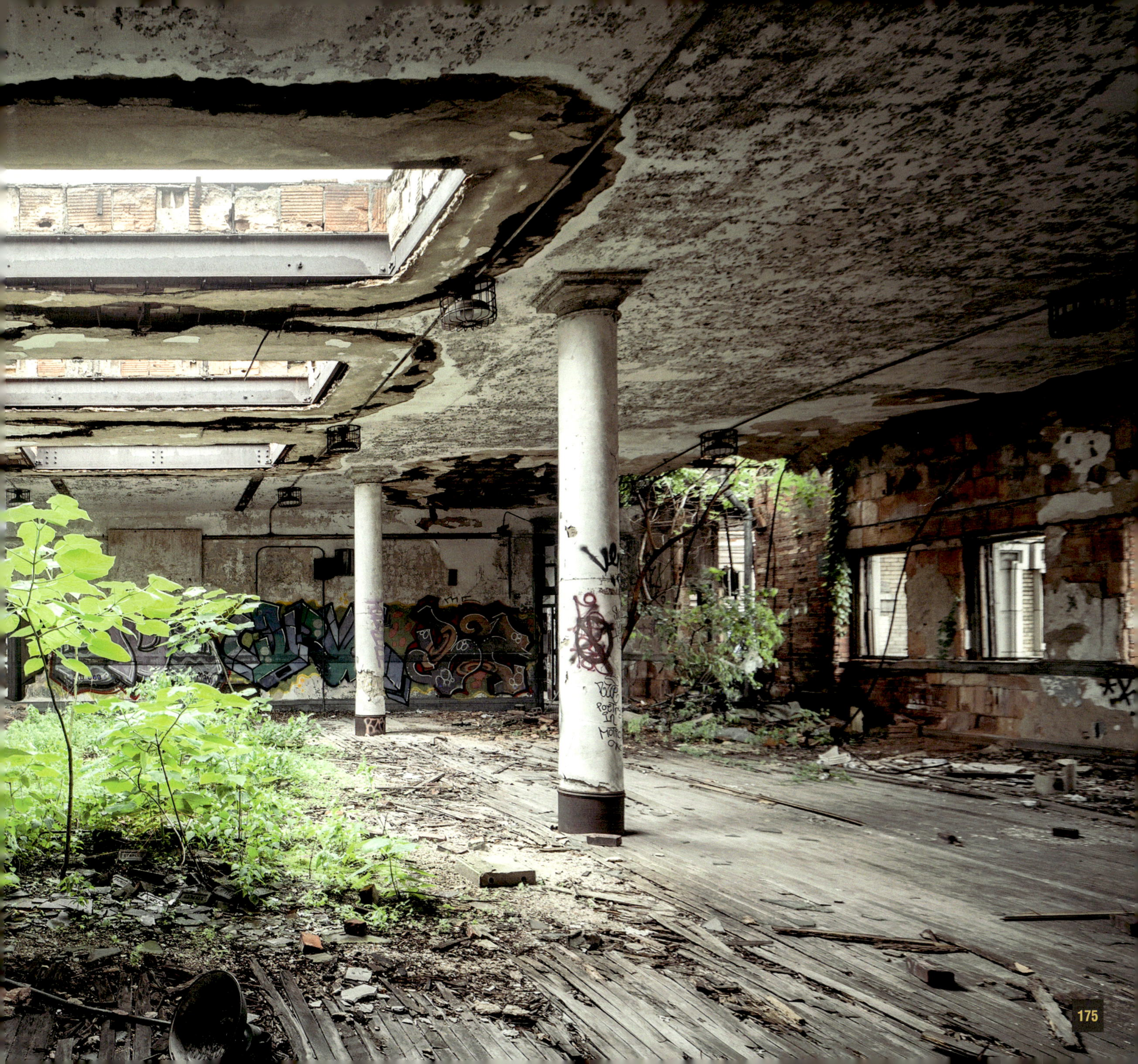

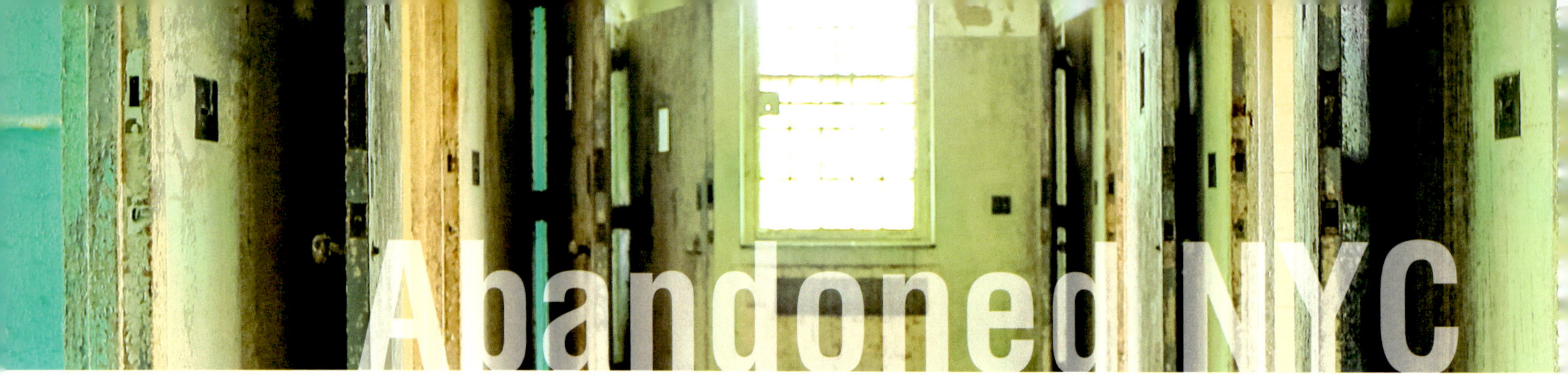

Will Ellis is a Brooklyn-based writer and photographer. Since 2012, he's documented the beauty and history of dozens of New York's abandoned spaces, which he posts regularly on his blog, AbandonedNYC.com.

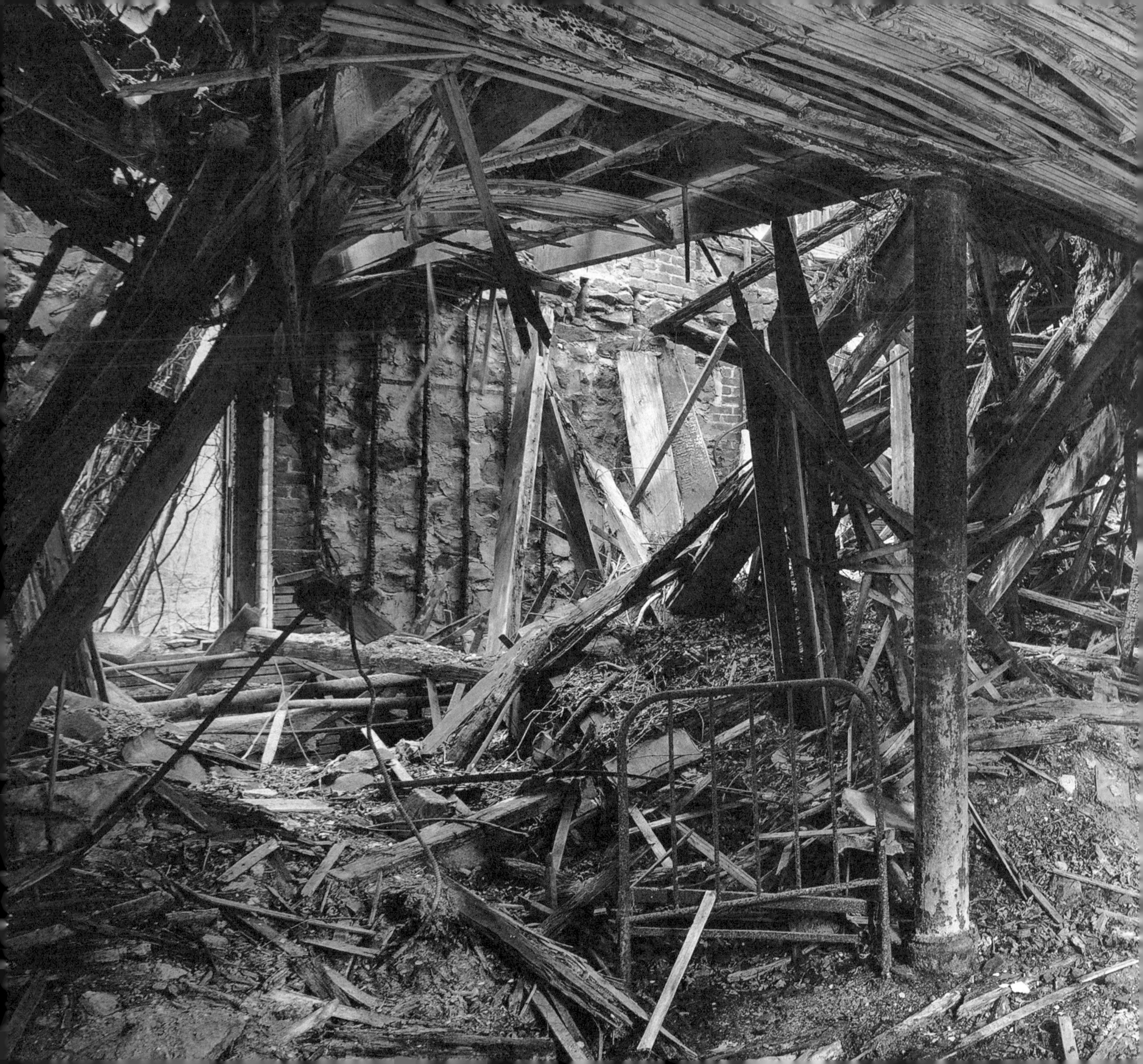